Beware of the Actor!

The Rise and Fall of
Nicol Williamson

MARTIN DOWSING

Copyright © 2017 Martin Dowsing

All rights reserved.

ISBN: 1978036256
ISBN-13: 978-1978036253

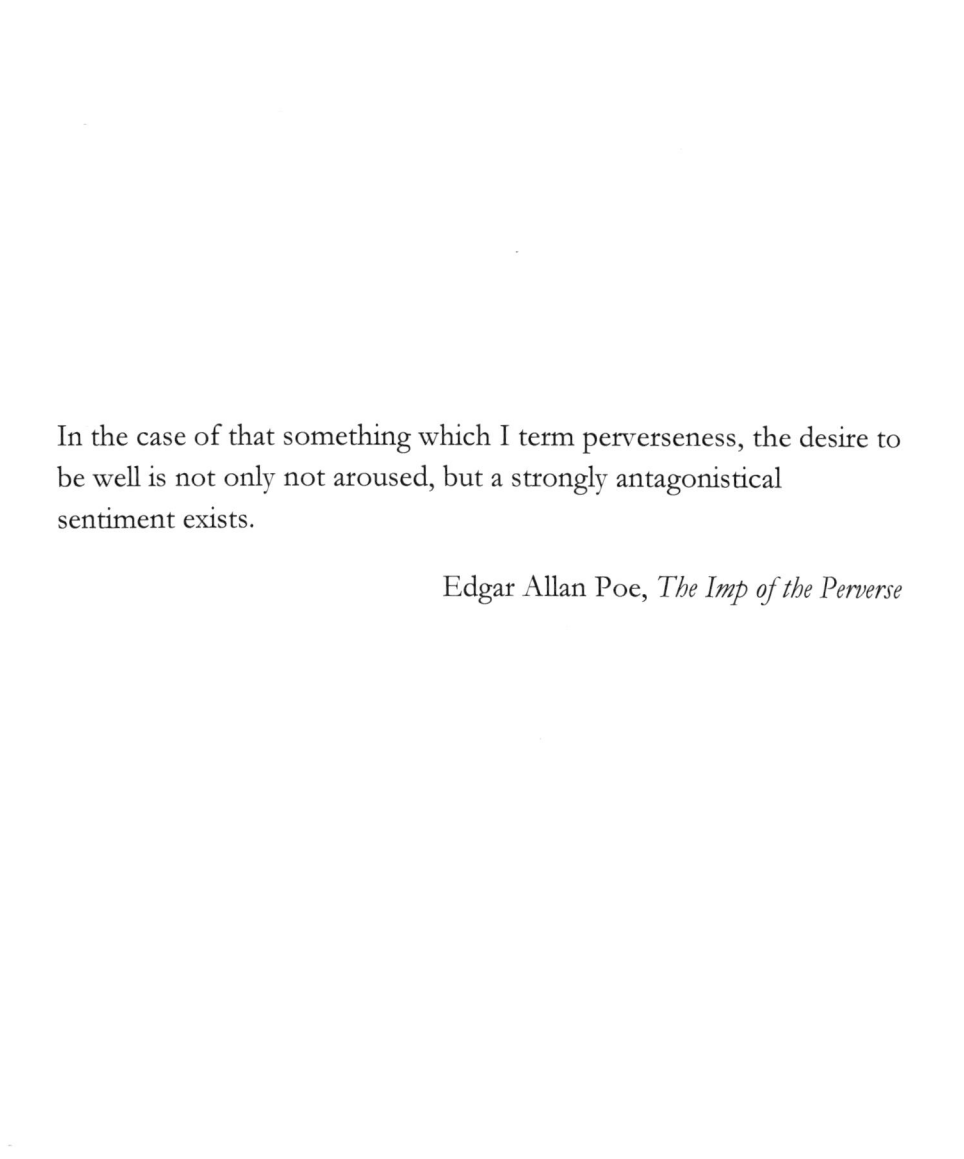

In the case of that something which I term perverseness, the desire to be well is not only not aroused, but a strongly antagonistical sentiment exists.

> Edgar Allan Poe, *The Imp of the Perverse*

CONTENTS

Introduction	7
1. A Tape Recorder Between Two Ears	11
2. Pretending to Corpse	23
3. As Hungry and as Generous as a Lion	40
4. Not the Most Disciplined of Young Actors	50
5. *Inadmissible Evidence*	61
6. The Nothingness in the Little Eden Afternoon	70
7. Broadway Bound	82
8. The Sign of the Cross	94
9. *Hamlet*	110
10. Corridors of Power	122
11. Domestic Bliss	133
12. A Coiled Cobra	152
13. Company Man	162
14. Little John and Sherlock	178
15. Nic Wrecks Rick's *Rex*	189
16. A Series of Unfortunate Events	197
17. Letting the Buggers Suffer	208
18. 'A dream to some, a nightmare to others…'	221

19. The Curse of Mac B	232
20. Normal and Quite Happy	243
21. Odd Choices	252
22. Things Fall Apart	270
23. Last of the Controlled Madmen	280
24. Too Little, Too Late	293
25. Almost Done	304
26. The Swirling Purple Mantled Elbow	320
27. Retreat to Lindos	329
28. Seamus the Squamous	340
29. Nicol Remembered	350
Afterword by Luke Williamson	359
Bibliography	361
Acknowledgements	363
Notes	365

Introduction

By 1969, Nicol Williamson seemed to have the world in the palm of his hand. Five years earlier, he had literally become famous overnight – on the 9th of September, 1964, to be precise. His leading role as burnt-out solicitor Bill Maitland in John Osborne's play *Inadmissible Evidence* at the Royal Court theatre is still acknowledged to be one of the longest and most difficult ever written. A number of more famous actors had declined the part, perhaps because its difficulty made failure seem a far more likely prospect than success. Nicol had held the audience spellbound for three hours, immediately attracting a surge of press interest as a result and becoming an instant celebrity. His performance would be one of the most talked about in the history of 20th century theatre.

Perhaps even more impressive than the reviews he received and the awards he won throughout the '60s were the plaudits from theatrical heavyweights; Osborne proclaimed him 'the best actor since Marlon Brando', Samuel Beckett credited him with 'a touch of genius', and Laurence Olivier was reported to have considered Nicol his only serious rival. He astonished his contemporaries in the film world by turning down many lucrative offers, choosing instead to take *Inadmissible Evidence* to America. He finally began accepting leading roles in films at the end of the decade, making a number of intelligent, challenging pictures that made little impact at the box office. Still, it didn't seem to matter – in 1969, he stormed the Roundhouse like a Shakespearean rock star playing a new kind of Hamlet, vital, alive and decisive, in an interpretation which remains influential to this day. The following year he became the first actor invited to perform at the White House. By this point, it was not unusual for him to be labelled 'the world's greatest actor'.

Even greater things were expected of Nicol in the years to come, and he was closely followed by the press. Being not averse to a pint, a punch-up, a backstage tryst or a provocative remark, Nicol made good copy. Indeed, stories about him are still numerous, many of which have passed into theatrical lore. He famously walked off in the middle of a performance on more than one occasion and was equally notorious for having struck his fellow actors on stage – once with a hefty slap in the face, another time with the flat of a sword. He had even punched a powerful Broadway producer early in his career but still somehow managed to go on to play more leading roles on Broadway than any other English actor. Less of a womanizer than many of his contemporaries, he could nevertheless count Marianne Faithfull and Sarah Miles among his conquests. It is scarcely surprising, then, that Nicol has often been painted as a heavy-drinking hell-raiser but, although he certainly had that side to him, he was a far more complex man than this suggests. Some found him to be morose and misanthropic by nature, but his mood could change suddenly and with little warning. Displays of belligerence or generosity were equally likely. He was also a talented singer and pianist, a writer of poetry, autobiographical prose pieces, screenplays, songs and one published novel.

Most of all, he was an actor of unique and mysterious power – as the playwright and theatre director Peter Gill said, '... he was enormously gifted – the most unusual actor I've ever seen in my life... There he was – lanky, ranging, awful sort of yellow hair, not a pleasant voice, Birmingham-Scottish, and yet he was a riveting actor, very funny, he spoke marvellously. *Nobody* was as good as Nicol Williamson in the right part...'

Few could have foreseen that Nicol's career had already reached its peak as the '70s dawned. His stage appearances would become increasingly sporadic and his film work seemed to gradually dwindle away, although there would still be the occasional triumph on the way down. On stage in the mid-'70s he played Coriolanus, Macbeth and Malvolio, as well as Chekhov's Uncle Vanya – performances which remain vivid memories to those lucky enough to have seen them. He was marvellous on film as a twitchy, neurotic Sherlock Holmes in *The Seven-Per-Cent Solution*, as a funny and moving sidekick to Sean

Connery's Robin Hood in *Robin and Marian* and, of course, in his most eccentric performance as Merlin in John Boorman's *Excalibur*. However, compared to many of his contemporaries, he was far from prolific. As an admirer who had first seen Nicol in his late '60s films *The Bofors Gun* and *The Reckoning* on television during the late '80s, I found it difficult to understand why he was by that time only being glimpsed occasionally in throwaway roles in Hollywood movies like *Black Widow* and *Exorcist III*. Something had clearly gone wrong, but what?

When Nicol died at the end of 2011, he had not made a film for fourteen years or acted on a stage for ten. Meanwhile, fellow actors of his generation like John Hurt, Anthony Hopkins and Ian McKellen had gone on to hugely successful careers despite having taken considerably longer to make a name for themselves. Nicol Williamson, on the other hand, had faded away until he had disappeared altogether, god knew where.

When the press got wind of Nicol's death five weeks after the event, the majority of the obituary writers had to rely chiefly on a piece written about Nicol by Kenneth Tynan for *The New Yorker* some forty years previously (a piece which itself contained certain inaccuracies). There seemed to be a remarkable lack of information about his more recent activities. According to the obituarists, the actor had been living in Amsterdam, but he had in fact sold his house there several years earlier and settled in the village of Lindos on the Greek island of Rhodes. There was also division on Nicol's age at the time of his death, some saying he had been 73, and others 75. The reasons for his absence from the world of acting for so many years remained a mystery, although rumours suggested a number of possibilities: the booze had got the better of him; he was so difficult that he was considered unemployable; he had developed severe stage fright; he had become disillusioned with acting and simply retired.

It seemed to me that Nicol's journey might very well be a story worth telling, and certainly no-one had done so before. Like so many other admirers of his talents, I wondered what were the true reasons for the decline of his career and his subsequent disappearance and particularly whether his fearsome reputation was the result of a few minor incidents blown up out of proportion or was genuinely deserved.

In researching this biography, I visited numerous archives and interviewed or corresponded with over 50 people who had been friends or colleagues of Nicol's to try to discover what proportion of what I had heard and read could possibly be true. I made some surprising discoveries, such as the fact that Nicol had been married not once but twice, although very few people knew about his second wife. Despite the fact that in his lifetime Nicol seemed to have inspired almost as much enmity as affection, it was clear that most people who had known him had something they urgently wanted to say on the subject of Nicol Williamson, perhaps because they too were trying to resolve something in their own minds, in many cases about their own relationships with him. Even those who did not much care for him personally greatly admired his talent and were keen to be heard. In the four years it has taken to write this book, I have been on a fascinating, moving, bemusing and always thought-provoking mission.

Nicol Williamson led what is usually referred to as a 'colourful life'. By the time I sat down to write these chapters, I knew this was a wholly inadequate description for his skills and passions, triumphs and flaws, humour, enthusiasms and dark days; in short, for the intermittent but unforgettable genius of this extraordinary man.

Chapter 1 – A Tape Recorder Between Two Ears

Nicol Williamson's parents were married on the 25th of March 1936. His father, Hugh, was a burly, 6 foot 3 inch, 18 stone Scotsman then incongruously employed as a hairdresser's assistant, but he was a handsome man and Nicol later said that he bore a resemblance to Ronald Colman, the dapper Hollywood star of the '30s and '40s. Hugh was hastily marrying Mary Brown Hill Storrie, three months pregnant at the time. Mary was of a more artistic disposition and good at painting and dancing. Both were 22 and, although the pregnancy was the catalyst for the marriage, it was a love match rather than a shotgun wedding.

Hugh, who had also dabbled in fairground boxing, was the son of Thomas Williamson, a wagon wheel presser, and lived in Wishaw, a small town 15 miles southeast of Glasgow. Thomas, or 'Tom' as he was generally known, did not approve of the wedding because, after Hugh and Mary had become engaged, it had emerged that Hugh's former girlfriend was pregnant by Hugh. Tom felt strongly that Hugh should have done 'the right thing', broken the engagement and married her instead. Hugh, however, viewed this as the unfortunate result of a casual fling and, despite the fact that it meant a son, Ian, being born out of wedlock, would not allow himself to be trapped for life in a loveless marriage. In the face of strong pressure from his father and others, he had willingly agreed to provide support for the boy but remained steadfast in his determination to wed Mary, whom he considered his true love.

Mary lived in the larger town of Hamilton three miles from Wishaw and was the daughter of Murdoch Storrie, a coal miner who had been a Lance Corporal in the Argyll and Sutherland Highlanders and was killed in the First World War. In those days, Scottish regiments fought in kilts and were known by the Germans as the 'women from hell.' Murdoch Storrie lost his life retrieving bodies from no-man's-land towards the end of 1917. Aged just 26, he left behind a widow, Agnes, who scraped a living as a china painter, and three children – Mary, Archie and Flora, the last of whom would be dead from pneumonia before her second birthday.

Not only was a honeymoon completely out of the question on such a low income, but Hugh could not even afford to take the whole day off and returned to work at the hairdresser's after the wedding. He moved in with Mary's family at 192 Quarry Street, Hamilton. In August, the couple had a scare when Mary suffered a haemorrhage and nearly lost the baby. A month later, Thomas Nicol Williamson was born at 4.45 a.m. on September 14, 1936 at Beckford Lodge Maternity Hospital. Named 'Thomas' perhaps in a misjudged attempt to pacify Hugh's father by naming the child after him, this was soon dropped in favour of the more distinctive 'Nicol'. However, 'Thomas' would remain Nicol's legal first name for the remainder of his life.

As the nation geared up for war over the next couple of years, this presented new opportunities for unskilled workers like Hugh Williamson. In 1938, he moved with his new family to 89 Hanson's Bridge Road in the Pype Hays area of Erdington, a suburb of Birmingham, and took a job in a foundry. Mary contributed to the household income by painting flowers and other designs onto porcelain, a skill learned from her mother. She became pregnant again and gave birth to a girl. The child was named Agnes after Mary's mother, but was called Senga (Agnes backwards). When the Second World War began, the family were living very close to Castle Bromwich Aerodrome, which began to be used as a fighter base by the Royal Air Force. A new aeroplane factory was also built nearby, and Hugh and his brother Jack soon found employment there helping to produce Spitfires. This occupation saved them from being conscripted but was not without danger as the factory soon became a target for the Luftwaffe. Air raids began in August 1940 and Heinkel He 111s would fly so low over the house on their way to bomb the aerodrome that it was possible to see the faces of the pilots. Hugh would stand in the garden and throw half-bricks at them. Understandably, the now four-year-old Nicol was soon evacuated back to Scotland to live with his paternal grandparents. It seems likely that he did not fully understand why he was being sent away, and certain that he would have much rather remained with his mother and father. Senga was considered too young to go and this caused Nicol to believe that she was loved more than he. While he would always maintain a good relationship with both his parents, he would later say in reference to his enforced exile that, 'the trauma stays with you forever.'[1]

Nicol's formative years would be further tainted by the fact that his grandfather, despite sharing the name of Thomas, was very hard on him. Although he does not seem to have been physically abused, Nicol was treated very coldly and became a target for the resentment which Thomas felt when Hugh had ignored his wishes and married Mary. The result was that Nicol soon came to detest his grandfather and developed a deep-seated sense of insecurity which he would learn to hide but would never lose. Whilst in Scotland, he also frequently played with his half-brother Ian without having any idea that they were related.

Nicol was surrounded by music throughout his childhood – both his mother and grandmother were fine singers – and he used to enjoy the company of a piano player named Jimmy Duncan, whom he would pester to play 'In the Mood' over and over again. However, a new interest would soon come to dominate his attention. In the '40s, the primary source of home entertainment was the radio, or 'wireless', and, like many other children of this era, Nicol would listen with rapt attention not just to music but to a diverse range of radio plays. In April 1943, *Saturday Night Theatre* debuted with the Dorothy L. Sayers murder mystery *The Man with No Face*. Nicol was hooked. Tuning in every week, he became familiar with a wide number of popular plays and it is this Saturday night ritual which seems to have been the origin of his desire to be an actor. Nicol's fascination with the voices issuing from the big box in the living room led him to imitate the voices he liked and, to the great amusement of the adults, act out scenes from the plays he had enjoyed. He was so good at this that, when he was ten years old, he even persuaded a BBC producer to give him his own radio programme. The programme itself has since been lost in the mists of time and all that is really known about it now is that it was entitled *Highland Blathering* and that Nicol did all the patter.

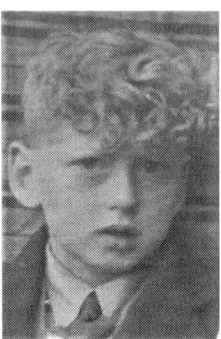

Nicol at the age of 8
(courtesy of Luke Williamson)

As the war drew to a close he returned to live with his parents in Birmingham and attended Gunter Road Primary School. By his own admission, he quickly forgot about Scotland and enthusiastically embraced his new life as a 'Brummie', enjoying excursions into the Warwickshire countryside. He also lost his Scottish accent, although he would have no trouble resurrecting it flawlessly for a number of future acting parts.

It had been obvious from an early age that Nicol was an unusually intelligent child and so it was no surprise when, in 1947, he achieved a good result in his eleven-plus exam and was able to attend the Central Grammar School for Boys. Admission to a grammar school rather than a secondary school was a considerable advantage in those days.

A fellow pupil at the school was Tony Garnett, who would later have a highly successful career as a film and television producer, notably in collaboration with Ken Loach on *Cathy Come Home* and *Kes*. Garnett remembered,

> I lived on the next street. They were 1930s – both streets – they were very small, semi-detached houses with a garden, which at that time would have been a very aspirational house for skilled workers. We were exactly the same age and in the same year, so we would go up Eachelhurst Road and get a bus there to school. We were divided into three classes – I was in 1A, Nicol was in 1C, so it wasn't as though we were in the same class, but we knew each other like you know schoolmates, although we weren't intimates. The school was next to a paint factory and it was not salubrious, and pretty rough in those days, although Nicol's height and manner would have got him out of most trouble. Most people would have been too scared to want to take him on, so I don't think he got into a lot of danger or problems, but the older boys would say, 'Come and see the black hole of Calcutta!' to a little boy who'd just started school, and then they'd push his head down the loo and pull the chain, the usual stuff. There were two storeys, so on the second one, what they did to me was – we had short trousers with braces in those days – and they'd hold you by your braces and hang you out the window. So it wasn't a school for young gentlemen!
>
> One of the things that I remember about Nicol at school was that, even as a young teenager, his mimicry was incredible. He had like a tape recorder between two ears. The only person as good as that I ever met was Peter Sellers. They both had that sort of knack of imitation, and I vividly recall one afternoon after school, everyone was playing chess and Nicol was playing with his back to the door. But of course, it was never enough for Nicol just to play chess, he was imitating the headmaster, who gloried in the name of Sir Rodney M.S. Paisley-Bart, MA. He was a baronet – and this was a really rough Birmingham Grammar School, I mean one of the rougher ones, so god knows how Paisley got to be head there, but anyway he did. Nicol was impersonating him brilliantly and the whole class were falling about laughing and not playing chess at all, they were just absolutely in tucks! So was I. And then Sir Rodney appeared at the open door and gradually one or two noticed that he was there listening to Nicol impersonating him and they stopped and froze… and more boys stopped and froze, and the laughter died. And it was only when the laughter had completely diminished that Nicol

noticed he'd lost his audience – because he was completely in the performance – and he looked around and all the boys were looking at the door, so Nicol turned round and there was the boss. And there was this long silence, which Paisley was very good at keeping, and then he said, 'Enjoy your chess, boys,' and went off home. It was a sort of theatrical moment which Nicol was very good at, even though he did it involuntarily.

He was also a bit naughty. They had a bell outside that they pressed in the head's office to call everybody in. It was an electric thing, one of those bells with a hammer. So Nicol got up on somebody's shoulders one day and stuck a piece of wood between the hammer and the bell, so that when they pressed the button to bring everybody in, nothing happened, and that caused considerable confusion amongst the staff. So that's the sort of boy he was.

He was very tall, very thin... his manner would change a dozen times a day. His favourite one was a sort of supercilious superiority, and a very posh voice that he'd put on. But his normal accent was Birmingham like mine. So he was the great school entertainer even then, without any question. I'm not saying he was popular. You didn't know who you were talking to in a way.

As we went through the school we both got involved in school plays. I remember I played Wackford Squires once, so that must have been a Dickens adaptation, and we also did *Julius Caesar*. I think I was Brutus and Nicol might have been Anthony, so we did a lot of that. He was always acting at school – in the school plays, but also every day, impersonating people, putting on funny voices, making people laugh. He always had an audience. His mock innocence was brilliant. Sometimes the teachers would have to smile, but with a lot of those teachers, it was difficult to make them smile. I think they hated being teachers, really. But we were a pretty rough, unruly pile of boys, I think, looking back.

One teacher at Central Grammar would have a huge influence on Nicol and become a mentor to him – a relationship which continued long after Nicol left the school. His name was Tom Reader and his subject, appropriately enough, was English. He encouraged Nicol in his first forays into acting more than anybody else. Tony Garnett:

Tom Reader was very influential on me too. A lot of the teachers were crap, they'd just tell you to do some work while they sat at their desk marking the homework from the night school they'd done the night before. But Tom Reader was a very good English teacher, a kind man, and he really took care over his work, and it doesn't surprise me at all that Nicol was influenced by him. And of course, English literature would have been one of the few things that would have interested Nicol, so he'd gravitate towards Tom Reader, and I'm sure he appreciated Tom as much as I did. He was for us the best teacher.

Nicol's first performance on a stage was as a tiger in a school play, but it remains unclear at exactly what age he made this debut. Towards the end of his time at Central Grammar, Nicol played Marlowe's *Doctor Faustus* in a school production which Garnett remembered as 'very assured and watchable, far better than the usual schoolboy stuff'. The opening night was sparsely attended but Nicol's performance was apparently so spellbinding that word of mouth alone caused the following three shows to be full to capacity. He was rewarded with a small cash grant to attend an interview at a drama school in London, possibly RADA, but he spent the money on a trip to Stratford-upon-Avon instead. However, the success of *Doctor Faustus* helped him to win a scholarship to the local drama school. In a less serious vein, Nicol also teamed up with a fellow schoolmate, David Parry, on a camping trip to Wales one Easter, during which they created an unusual act in which Parry was a ventriloquist and Nicol the dummy, but with Parry sitting on Nicol's knee.

Nicol contributed to the family income at this time by delivering groceries on his bicycle for Ehrets Store and Post Office, but acting remained at the forefront of his mind and he also joined an amateur theatrical group called The Varley Players, who put on plays in the church hall of St Mary's Church in Pype Hays. Another member was Topsy Jane, who would go on to marry Tony Garnett and star opposite Tom Courtenay in *The Loneliness of the Long Distance Runner* before disappearing into a tragic obscurity.[2] Nicol was also a member of the local Boys' Brigade, a Christian institution similar to the

Scouts. In 1951 he won the junior prize for Scripture Knowledge and was awarded a copy of *The Coral Island* by R.M. Ballantine which he kept for the rest of his life.

Around the time that Nicol left Central Grammar, the family moved to another house on the same street, 119 Hanson's Bridge Road, along with his maternal grandmother, Agnes, while his Aunt Margaret – a widow now that Nicol's Uncle Archie had died in 1952 – remained at number 89. He then began his three-year scholarship at the Birmingham School of Speech Training and Dramatic Art, where he became friendly with an aspiring young actress, Mary MacLeod, who shared his Scots-Birmingham background. She later became known as the first actress to appear in a full-frontal nude scene on screen in Lindsay Anderson's film *If...* Another fellow student was Anita Brown, who remembered,

> He was my first boyfriend, slightly edgy which I liked, and we both were against the 'Establishment'. Luckily, we were nearly always paired together for scenes at drama school because we were better than all the rich kids there. The school, we both agreed, was more like a finishing school. I left after the first year and I didn't see him again until years later in London after a performance. I went to the stage door thinking he might not remember me, but he came bounding down the stairs saying, 'Anita! Oh, how lovely!' and we spent hours in a pub until his evening show.

Nicol did not regard his years at the school as being very productive as he had become frustrated at finding much of his time taken up by essays and literature classes rather than by learning the craft of acting. He would later say that the only things he had learned there were movement and breath control and that otherwise he had felt his time to be better spent going to the cinema. However, he was given the chance whilst at the school to gain some real experience – an opportunity offered only to a select few stand-out students.

Bernard Hepton, later a well-known actor in British television drama of the 1970s in shows such as *Colditz* and *Secret Army*, was at this point a 30-year-old actor who had been at Birmingham Repertory Theatre since 1953 and was directing his second production, a version of *Anatol* by Arthur Schnitzler, starring the now-forgotten Robert Chetwyn. In a letter to the author, Hepton explained,

> The Rep and the Theatre School had an arrangement whereby students could be given the opportunity to be in a performance on stage when the need arose, usually to play small parts, walk-ons or in crowd scenes. Choosing such a student was the school's prerogative, agreed with the director.

Birmingham Repertory Theatre was the most prestigious rep theatre in the country at the time and therefore, as Hepton went on to say, 'the one every young actor wanted to join.' The Rep had the luxury of four-week runs as opposed to the one- or two-week runs of most other rep theatres, and it had provided early work for such luminaries as Laurence Olivier, Ralph Richardson and Paul Scofield. In 1956, the twenty-year-old Albert Finney was attracting attention there.

Anatol opened on the 20th of March 1956 and Nicol, who had been cast as a waiter through the arrangement with the school, was billed for the first and last time as 'Nick Williamson'. Unfortunately, what could have been the beginning of a career went awry when Nicol failed to appear for a performance, apparently because he had thought there were no shows on Easter Monday (or so he claimed) and he had gone to see a film. He was promptly fired by the company director, John Henderson. It was not to be the last time that Nicol was found to be somewhere other than where he was supposed to be. Sixty years later, Bernard Hepton's only recollection of Nicol was as 'a student who was of the opinion that a non-speaking waiter was not worth his time nor attention.' Taking into account both his already well-formed character and his teenage triumph with *Doctor Faustus*, it is unsurprising that Nicol was already sure of his talent and had little patience for such baby steps. This attitude was bound to be viewed as arrogance by his elders, and he never would be able to adopt a humble demeanour no matter how much it may have been in his best interests to do so. Those at the drama school who had arranged the opportunity for Nicol were aghast. He was threatened with expulsion and it was suggested that he should repay his scholarship money. Neither of these came to pass but he left without finishing the course. However, as Nicol well knew, any plans that he might have made at this time would soon have been frustrated anyway by compulsory National Service.

In early 1957, Nicol was assigned to the 33rd Parachute Light Regiment, Royal Artillery, which had been deployed in Cyprus to provide support in the Suez crisis just a couple of months previously. They were now reassembled at Lille Barracks, Aldershot, where new conscripts joined the ranks. Nicol was given the job of dispensing the rations in HQ Company. He became known as 'Big Nick' and was fortunate in having to share a room with only one other person – the company butcher – as many others had to sleep in dormitories which were inspected constantly.

Nicol's assignation to a parachute regiment was at his own request. Others often saw him as impressively fearless, but one thing that scared him was heights, so by joining the paras he was forcing himself to confront this fear head-on. He did fourteen jumps in two years, but otherwise considered this period of his life to be an even greater waste of time than drama school had been, although the experience would later come in somewhat useful on two occasions when he played characters undergoing their National Service. Nicol won prizes for running and high jumping whilst in the army, but later said that the only thing he really learned was how to avoid the unpleasant jobs. However, it was also during this time that he made his film debut, albeit a not particularly auspicious one.

The Square Peg was a vehicle for the popular comic actor Norman Wisdom and involved a scene about halfway through the film in which Wisdom boards the wrong plane and finds himself mixed up with a squad of paratroopers. As he comes to the realisation that he too will be expected to jump, he runs into the cockpit in a panic only to be met by the baleful glare of Nicol Williamson as the pilot. Nicol was on screen for only a couple of seconds, had no dialogue, received no credit and seems never to have mentioned his appearance in the film to anyone.

Around the time that Nicol was demobbed, Hugh Williamson left his job in Birmingham and returned to Scotland to start his own business in Glasgow. He set up a small factory and began producing ashtrays and aluminium sticks for deoxydising steel. Upon leaving the army, Nicol joined him and they worked together for nearly a year. Unsurprisingly, however, Nicol had no intention of making a career out of it and, although disappointed, his father did not stand in his way when Nicol decided it was time to leave.

Nicol at the age of 22
(courtesy of Luke Williamson)

Michael Culver (far left) and Nicol Williamson (far right) in
Sinbad the Sailor at Dundee Repertory Theatre.
(Napier Studios Ltd / courtesy of Michael Culver)

Chapter 2 – Pretending to Corpse

Towards the end of 1959, Nicol landed his first paid professional acting job playing Jonas, a belligerent pirate, in a version of *Sinbad the Sailor* at Dundee Repertory Theatre. Established in 1939, the theatre had a capacity of 420 and was located at number 6 Nicoll Street – possibly one reason why he would choose to be billed as 'Nicol' rather than 'Nick' from this point on. *Sinbad* opened on the 23rd of December as the company's traditional end-of-year pantomime. Nicol had been given the part by Raymond Westwell, a 40-year-old actor and director who was running the Rep at the time and directing most of the plays. Westwell – a former member of the Royal Shakespeare Company – was, according to Dundee Rep actor Michael Culver, 'a very nice man, and a good spotter of talent.'

Nicol's part of Jonas was the sidekick to Culver's in *Sinbad*, and the two would subsequently appear in around twenty plays together at the Rep. Culver, son of the famous actor Roland Culver, recalled Nicol arriving at the theatre for his first day at work:

> This extraordinary figure came in with this terrible old pair of jeans on and a sweater down about three inches below his knees in a singularly hideous green and yellow mix – a sort of Fair Isle bizarreness – and with this curly, funny hair. I thought, 'Oh well, we're doing a pantomime so it doesn't really matter – but what's he going to do for anything else?' I suppose I was a bit of a snob, or certainly I had very pre-conceived ideas in those days about what everything should be like.

The Courier and Advertiser, one of Dundee's two local newspapers, noted that Nicol played one of 'the roughest sailors ever afloat' but as it was hardly serious drama it is not surprising if his colleagues failed to quite realise the extent of the talent hidden away in this tall, thin, odd-looking 23-year-old. When the play closed on the 13th of January, Nicol became unemployed, although Westwell promised to keep him in mind if any suitable opportunities arose. He returned to

Glasgow where, some weeks later, he managed to find a job singing with a local dance band.

In March, Westwell began making plans to stage Shakespeare's *Henry IV Part 1*, an ambitious production by rep standards, and one which would require a larger cast than usual. He proved true to his word and asked Nicol to return. Nicol accepted immediately and quit the band. Westwell cast him as Sir Walter Blunt – already a step up from *Sinbad*. However, Nicol was first to play the small part of a police sergeant in *Any Other Business*, a boardroom thriller. It was the first production at the Rep to be directed by Anthony Page, a 24-year-old assistant stage manager from London's Royal Court Theatre who had been born the son of a Brigadier General in India during the days of the British Raj. Page was there as a guest to stage this one production before handing the reigns back to Westwell and returning south to direct a play at the Richmond Theatre. Given the routine nature of this first collaboration between Page and Nicol, they must have had little inkling of quite how important to each other they were to become.

Life at the Rep was extremely demanding for both cast and crew, but provided an invaluable training ground. Each play ran for two weeks, with rehearsals of the following production taking place in the afternoons. Many other local rep theatres performed a new play every single week, so a fortnight was something of a luxury in comparison and allowed for a higher standard of work. At Dundee, the actors would begin rehearsals at 10 a.m. every weekday, have an hour off for lunch, continue until 5.30, and then have a break before the evening performance began at 7.30. This would finish between 9.30 and 10.15, after which the actors would go back to their 'digs' for a late supper – but still have to find time to learn their lines for the following day's rehearsals. Their digs were usually little more than a room to sleep in someone else's house, with breakfast served and supper left in the kitchen. Matinee performances took place on alternate Saturdays, with the evening performance following soon after, so the actors worked very long hours and had only Sunday off, much of which was also frequently taken up by learning lines and so on.

Nicol appeared in unremarkable roles in three more plays and was then absent from the following three productions, a period beginning in late June and finishing in late July. It is not known how he spent this time, but at some point during the year he narrated a short film entitled *Over the Capel to Birkhall*, which documented a march by the Battalion of the Black Watch, a regiment of the Royal Highlanders.

Nicol's future at the Rep must have looked decidedly uncertain as the theatre was in financial crisis at this point – five consecutive plays had lost an average of over £400[3] each, including prestigious productions such as *Henry IV* and Arthur Miller's *A View from the Bridge*. Westwell's decision to build up the company in preparation for *Henry IV* had certainly not helped. Given the situation, the theatre had little choice but to let some of the less experienced actors go, but fortunately Nicol had by this time proved himself useful and versatile enough not to be among them.

He returned to play his first lead as McCrimmon in *Mr Bolfry* by James Bridie, with Westwell again the director. The play had originally been staged in 1943 with Alistair Sim as McCrimmon, a minister in the highlands of Scotland during the Second World War. Two soldiers have been billeted with McCrimmon, a man so pious he objects to the drinking of tea on the Sabbath. With nothing better to occupy their time, the soldiers discover an ancient book on witchcraft in the study and inadvertently conjure up the Devil (the 'Mr Bolfry' of the title) who then engages in a battle of wits with McCrimmon. Michael Culver recalled that 'It was only when Nicol walked into rehearsals and started playing McCrimmon that I thought, "This bloke is seriously good!" I mean, he just had a natural authority and an ability to lift the piece off the page and make it real.'

Indeed, it was not only Culver who began to take notice of Nicol – he was also singled out for praise in the local press for the first time and, according to Dundee's *Evening Telegraph*, his performance 'contained all the smouldering fire that by right should rest in a scholarly highlander cradled in the Kirk.'

At the beginning of October, Raymond Westwell left to become Artistic Director of the National Theatre in Perth, Australia. Meanwhile, Anthony Page had been touring as director with the *The Long and the Short and the Tall*, a play about British soldiers in Malaya which had originally been a hit at the Royal Court. As the tour finished its run, Page was invited back to Dundee to helm the next three productions, the first of which would be a much-needed success. *Roar Like a Dove* was a Highland-set comedy in which Nicol played a supporting role as a bagpiper. It proved to be so popular that some performances were sold out and it was actually held over for an extra week. Page followed this with the comic murder mystery *An Air for Murder*, in which Nicol played an Irish ex-soldier, a part which gained him more praise in the local press – the *Evening Telegraph* said that he was 'getting better with each part' and complimented his 'sleight with words.'

Five Finger Exercise with Michael Culver
(Napier Studios Ltd / courtesy of Michael Culver)

Page then gave Nicol a chance to get his teeth into something more substantial in Peter Shaffer's *Five Finger Exercise*, in which the *Evening Telegraph* said that he had 'brilliantly played the focal figure of the son'. Donald Howarth, a playwright whose work had been produced at the Royal Court, stepped in to direct the next production, an Agatha Christie whodunit called *The Unexpected Guest*, but by this point it had been decided that Page was the man to replace Westwell on a more permanent basis. He would direct almost all of the plays in which Nicol acted at the Rep during his remaining year. It had also been decided that the theatre needed a separate business director, so John Henderson was recruited for the position – the same John Henderson who had fired Nicol from Birmingham Rep in 1956. Henderson was not initially pleased to find him employed at Dundee, but nevertheless accepted the situation.

Nicol was clearly straining at the leash by this time and, learning that Page was planning to do *Death of a Salesman*, he attempted to persuade the director to cast him in the lead. However, this was not to be, perhaps because even Page felt that casting such a young and relatively inexperienced Birmingham-Scottish actor as a 63-year-old American was pushing it a bit, or perhaps Henderson vetoed the idea. Whatever the reason, the part of Willy Loman went instead to an outsider, Bruce Boa, a Canadian actor who – being only 30 years old – was still surprisingly young for the role. Two other actors who were not part of the company were also brought in to play Loman's sons. Edward Fox, a then unknown 23-year-old, appeared as Biff, and his brother, 'Happy', was played by 25-year-old Scottish actor David Andrews (later a successful television director). Andrews had previously worked under Page's direction in *Live Like Pigs* at the Royal Court, where he had also attended Page's Stanislavsky-based acting classes:

> I think Tony [Page] was in many ways gifted and really had a grip on how to get actors to deliver wonderful performances. I didn't care for him too much – he could be very insensitive and he could tread on people quite easily – but I owe him a great deal because of what I

learned from him in his improvisation classes. He idolized Nicol and I think he was a bit in love with him, actually.

Nicol, bitterly disappointed, had to make do with a supporting role as Uncle Ben, but still managed to deliver a striking performance which remained a vivid memory for Andrews 55 years later:

> Eddie [Fox] and I had to do a scene where we're sitting right down in the front of the stage, almost into the audience, and Uncle Ben approaches us from the back of the stage (the stage being raked[4]), quite a good position to make an entrance from, and he came bearing down on us, a gigantic figure in a black astrakhan coat and a homburg hat with a walking stick. He just looked absolutely amazing, he really was an incredibly imposing figure. He would come down, rest on his stick, glower down at us and address us as the two boys that he was trying to encourage to do great things like *he* did. And he would corpse us! Nic would boss his eyes at us while he was playing the scene and put us in absolute hysterics. I hated him for it and I hated myself for being stupid enough to let it affect me. I would have been terrified of taking him to task about it because he was such a huge man and he was quite powerful. I was much worse than Eddie Fox – Eddie managed to control himself better than I did. I used to hate Nic every night for doing that, but it was an astonishing act, really. His whole performance as Uncle Ben was really extraordinary.

However, although Andrews greatly admired Nicol as an actor, his opinion of him as a fellow human being was less flattering:

> I found him thoroughly unpleasant and I didn't enjoy being in the same company with him – I thought he was overweening, he was terribly, *incredibly* self-centred and very ungenerous towards his colleagues, but he had this amazing presence and I don't think – except for Peter O'Toole – I certainly hadn't worked with somebody that had such a tremendous stage and screen presence as he did. You had to acknowledge this *incredible* talent – he *seethed* talent!
>
> I can remember sitting on a bus with him for some reason and he was holding forth about women and what kind of sex women liked. He

was very hot on that and he thought he knew everything about it and he was quite graphic, I have to say. He was a strange, strange man.

Despite a strong lead performance by Bruce Boa and an excellent response from those who attended, *Salesman* played to disappointing numbers. Anthony Page also came in for criticism regarding his decision to bring in outside actors, although Edward Fox would return in the spring.

The traditional end-of-year Christmas panto, *The Heartless Princess*, saw Nicol cast as 'Leonard, a very clever fox' and presented him with an opportunity to reveal his other talents. *The Courier* said that he 'excelled as a singer, pianist and dancer, and displayed a most refreshing wit. Most of the fun flowed from him.' The *Evening Telegraph* concurred, saying that, in his role as a 'much-harried fox with a luxurious brush and a gleam in his eye,' he had 'kept the fun at a high pitch with a flow of Doric.'[5]

Unfortunately, Nicol's individual success was not reflected in the theatre at large as they had been unable to duplicate the popularity of *Roar Like a Dove*, and the financial situation continued to be precarious. By the beginning of 1961, the Rep was in serious trouble again, largely due to the box-office failure of *The Heartless Princess*, which had been an expensive production to mount. The theatre had been surviving largely on a combination of various grants and subsidies and the generous contributions of a few wealthy patrons. Frantic appeals were made, with locals being encouraged to donate whatever they could afford, no matter how small. The theatre was again saved, but it was becoming obvious by now that its long-term survival was unlikely if such events continued.

John Henderson decided a change of strategy was required, and that all efforts should be geared towards filling seats. He cancelled a proposed production of Harold Pinter's *The Birthday Party* just before rehearsals were to begin, feeling that the chances of it being a box-office failure were too great.[6] He insisted that Anthony Page should instead stage *See How They Run*, a farce by Philip King, which had a good track record as a reliable popular success. Henderson may well have been correct in his judgment as the play turned a profit. In the meantime, Nicol had appeared in the American comedy *Born Yesterday* as a drunken lawyer. This was followed by co-starring opposite Lillias Walker in *Love from a Stranger* and his small part as an army sergeant in *See How They Run*. However, despite Henderson's new regime, the Rep continued to produce some more artistically ambitious work as the Arts Council's Approved Plays Scheme stated that at least one out of every three productions should be deemed 'worthwhile' by their committee in order for the theatre to receive a grant.

Nicol's next part was a major role in *The Critic and the Heart* by Robert Bolt, who had recently had a huge success with *A Man for All Seasons*. The author had refused every request to stage this earlier work since its original production three years earlier, so the fact that he had granted permission to Dundee Rep was seen as quite a compliment to the theatre. However, such an intellectual piece was a risky venture considering the circumstances, and *The Courier* expressed concern that the play failed to engage the audience. Nicol, on the other hand, was awarded with a large headline proclaiming 'Nicol Williamson takes Rep honours' accompanied by his picture and a review stating that his performance as a struggling young artist had been the 'bright spot' of the evening.

The Rep's subsequent production was an adaptation of *Great Expectations*, with Edward Fox returning to play Pip and Nicol as the blacksmith Joe Gargery. Estella was played by Kate Binchy, a young actress from Dublin who had made her Dundee debut playing opposite Nicol in *The Critic and the Heart*. She remembered Nicol as being 'very affecting' as Gargery and went on to say this:

> One night he never came on and I was left waiting for him on the stage. That's a terrible thing to happen because you don't know what to do. I probably ended up making some feeble excuse and simply leaving the stage. I remember finding him in the big wardrobe space at the back and he'd just completely missed it – I forget why, but I remember rushing at him and hitting him as hard as I could, which was futile if you knew

what size he was! But it relieved my feelings because I was so furious at him. Of course, he only laughed!

Although the amount of leading parts he was given increased during his time at the Rep as both his reputation and confidence grew, Nicol also continued to play small parts throughout his time there – a situation not unusual in a repertory company. Of the thirty-two plays in which he appeared, no more than a quarter could be said to have featured him in a leading role, and those leads he did play were never of the romantic hero sort – in fact, two were in I-married-a-psycho thrillers, Agatha Christie's *Love from a Stranger* and Patrick Hamilton's *Gaslight*, in both of which he was said to have been quite terrifying. Most of his time was spent playing a variety of police sergeants, blackmailing butlers and comic character parts such as an apparently deceased millionaire who returns briefly to life in *The Biggest Thief in Town*.

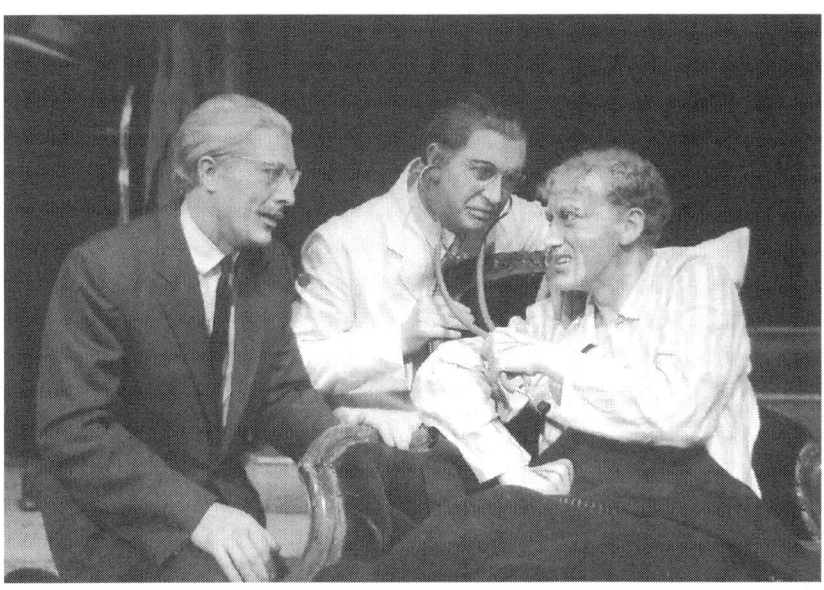

The Biggest Thief in Town with Michael Culver (left)
(Napier Studios Ltd / courtesy of Michael Culver)

In *The Cat and the Canary*, Nicol even doubled as Hendricks, a guard from the local asylum, and as the housekeeper, Mammy Pleasant, an 'old negress'! The actress who had originally been cast felt embarrassed at having to play such a part and had not been performing well in rehearsal. When Nicol tried to help by demonstrating how it should be done, he found Anthony Page eyeing him curiously. Page persuaded Nicol to play the role, which involved him blacking up, donning a wig and wearing an ankle-length dress. Nicol agreed on the condition that he would be billed in the programme as 'Magnolia Russell'. According to Michael Culver, however, 'it didn't matter what part he was given, he was good in every single part he did'.

Nicol was absent for the play which followed *The Cat and the Canary* but returned for *A Streetcar Named Desire*, in which he appeared as Harold Mitchell, the role played by Karl Malden in the Marlon Brando film. It was said to have been one of the Rep's best productions. By this point, the local press seldom failed to mention Nicol and he received his usual good notices. The production also featured, in a small role, a new addition to the company by the name of Glenda Jackson who, like Nicol, would benefit from a strong creative relationship with Anthony Page. Jackson later remembered,

> I got the job at Dundee through the good offices of Miriam Brickman, who was the casting director at the Royal Court. I think that someone had either fallen ill or dropped out of the company and they needed somebody quickly and so she recommended me to Tony Page and I went up there to play as cast in the Rep. It was quite a remarkable company, actually, looking back on it – Nicol was there, Edward Fox, Prunella Scales… I can't remember the whole gamut but it was a very interesting cast and, of course, it had a very, very interesting director in Tony Page.
>
> I sat on the fire escape in *A Streetcar Named Desire* – I can't even remember if my character had a name. But he [Nicol] was also doing a play – the name of which I don't remember – in which he played a sixty-year-old man. We were all in our early twenties. That was the thing that I

remember first and most about him, just what a remarkable actor he was because if you hadn't known he was 20, you would absolutely have believed he was 60.

Jackson was given the lead in the next play, *Fools Rush In*, a comedy in which she was a bride having last-minute doubts. Nicol was an uninvited guest at her wedding who turns out to be her estranged father and, according to *The Courier*, 'sails through the play delighting in the trouble he causes'. Peter Gill, then a promising young actor, arrived in Dundee at this point to appear in the Rep's next production. He remembered it this way:

> Anthony Page – who had been Lindsay Anderson's assistant director on *The Long and the Short and the Tall* at the Royal Court Theatre in which I had been an understudy – asked me to join the company for a production of a contemporary Russian play called *In Search of Happiness* by Victor Rozov.
>
> I travelled up to Scotland by train with Elizabeth McLennan, who had also been cast in the play, and we arrived in Dundee late in the evening just in time to catch some of *Fools Rush In*, the light comedy which was currently playing. On stage were the two juveniles, Edward Fox and Glenda Jackson, and sitting in the corner of the room , presumably playing the father, was one of the most unactorish and unusual-looking actors you have ever seen – long, thin, of indeterminate age and seemingly out of place, with crinkly yellowish hair, and utterly riveting. I don't remember more at this distance. I can only remember him as being out of the ordinary, and compelling without in any way being glamorous.
>
> Anthony had assembled as good a company of actors as could have been seen in a small regional theatre then. It included, as well as Nicol, Edward and Glenda, Lillias Walker, Gawn Grainger, Lucinda Curtis, Michael Culver, Terry Palmer, Kate Binchy and Jeffrey Wickham. It may be that the boys shared one dressing room. I was certainly in one with Nicol and Michael Culver. Nicol was not favourite with the company and my memory is of hypochondriacal attention-seeking and constant whining about the evils of the London theatre in which he hadn't yet worked.

The financial situation had finally improved somewhat throughout 1961, with the local press beginning to show greater support, and the receipt of a grant from Scottish TV. One result of this was that *In Search of Happiness* was filmed for television at the theatre (without audience). Nicol played Fyodor, a henpecked intellectual who is the eldest son of a fatherless family struggling to make ends meet in an overcrowded flat. He later said that he had suffered a crisis of self-doubt in his acting ability for the first two nights before finally regaining his confidence on the third. However, although he felt he had been giving a poor performance, he still received a nod from *The Courier*. Nicol claimed never to have gone through such a crisis again.

Next came *The Durable Element*, a brand new play which began a run of smaller comic parts for Nicol, followed as it was by his delusional violinist in *The Curious Savage* and his turnip-obsessed suitor, the Laird of Kettinfoot, in *Marigold*. Kate Binchy:

> Prunella Scales came up to play the lead in *The Curious Savage* and Nicol and I were inmates of the asylum. My character was called Fairy May and my illusion was that I was totally irresistable. We had this long scene playing cards and we just ad libbed it every single night because it was an easy situation to be funny in. He was terrific at that – he'd say something that you could jump on and if you gave him something, he could come straight back.
>
> *Marigold* was set in Edinburgh castle and had a huge cast, so we must all have been in it. It was the first time Brian Cox ever stepped on a stage. Somebody had got sick and he fitted the costume and on he came. He was a teenager at the time, it was before he went to drama school and he was excellent.

In the summer of 1961, the Rep staged a version of Chekhov's *The Seagull* freely adapted by John McGrath, then a promising 26-year-old dramatist in a relationship with Elizabeth MacLennan, whom he later married. Nicol was cast in the important part of Duncan (Konstantin in the original), a troubled young playwright who makes a failed suicide attempt before successfully killing himself at the end. Nicol himself became depressed during the run and one night ran off and jumped into the Firth of Tay. McGrath and some others from the theatre pulled him out. However, it does not seem to have been a genuine suicide attempt, as Kate Binchy remembered:

> I don't think he was trying to drown himself – he jumped into the river alright, but the water only came up to his knees! But he *was* a bad swimmer. If you'd done National Service, you were supposed to be able to swim, but much later when we were down in London, we all went swimming one day. We were in a pool in Chelsea and he took fright for some reason and grabbed me. I immediately went under the water. It didn't bother me because I was used to swimming, but I remember feeling how panic-stricken he was, so he must have been afraid of the water. I remember him almost using me as a stepping stone to get out, which again didn't bother me because when it's under the water there's no weight. He used to say, 'I'm such a bad swimmer.' He had a thing about it.

Lillias Walker, a Rep actress who appeared in many plays with Nicol, remembered another occasion on which Nicol suffered a fit of depression:

> He was given to mood swings and sometimes deeply depressed… one evening after rehearsal he seemed especially down and as he left the theatre I decided to follow him at a discreet distance as he made his way towards the sea. Now I don't know what he intended, but I found him sitting morosely on the beach. I sat down beside him and we must have talked for about an hour. I persuaded him to go back with me and we went to the pub.

On the other hand, *The Seagull* also had moments of humour, even if they were not always intended. Kate Binchy:

> In his disgust and angst, Konstantin goes out and shoots a seagull and then – because he wants the girl to take notice of him – he throws it at her feet. This particular night, I'm lying on a rug on a thrust stage out in the middle of the audience waiting for Nicol to come on and throw the seagull at my feet. There was a terrible long pause and eventually, on he

comes, with leaden footsteps – he was supposed to be very depressed. The seagull used to be kept in the freezer overnight and somebody had forgotten to take it out, so that when Nicol went to get it they handed him a completely frozen, rigid seagull that weighed a ton, but he had to come on with it and drop it at my feet – it landed with a thump and little chips of ice flew off it all around. Nicol's face was all screwed up in agony and I was frozen in shock – amazingly the audience were dead quiet – not a whisper – the pause seemed to go on forever but eventually we pulled ourselves together and went on and the play continued as though nothing off-putting had happened.

The Seagull was Binchy's final play at the Rep and she had fond memories of both Nicol and her time in the company:

We all used to go and have a drink if we possibly could after the show. It was quite difficult sometimes because there were very few places where you could go as a woman and be welcome to drink in those days. We were made honorary members of a ship down at the docks where we could all go and have a drink. Otherwise, on a Sunday we had to go all the way to St Andrews because in Ireland and Scotland you had to go through this farce of pretending to be a traveler if you wanted to get a drink on a Sunday! So we'd get the ferry across to St Andrews, so we were travelers, and then we could have a drink. But I wouldn't say that Nicol was a mad drinker – we all used to drink too much but we still made it to rehearsal the next day.

Nicol was very funny and clever. He'd tease you, but it was quite good value and usually accurate. His girlfriend, Sheena Howieson, was with us quite a lot. She was very nice and I'm sure she used to come with us on the trips to St Andrews. She wasn't an actress, she could have still been a student. She was Scottish – I think she was from around Dundee somewhere.

Soon after *The Seagull*, Anthony Page left the Rep. His replacement, the 22-year-old Piers Haggard, remembered:

Anthony had opened this show [*Man for the Job* by Dennis Driscoll], which was a northern comedy, and he'd gone back to London. Nicol was in the show. I'd come from the Royal Court Theatre, which was very serious, quite socially-conscious and sort of socialist art... it wasn't popular comedy. And this was a very popular, '50s or '60s working-class comedy, really simple and traditional. Nicol was playing the dad in it and with him was an actor called Gawn Grainger. Nicol was playing piano in the show – probably it wasn't in the script, but they just decided they'd do a song. It was pretty cavalier what they were doing – they were making free and easy with what was a pretty silly play, really. So they were having a good time and the audience obviously loved them. They'd been there for a long time, so they were favourites of the audience. Nicol was the favourite. He always played older because he was quite plain-looking, a bit battered-looking and he had sort of a gravelly voice. He was always uncomfortable playing anything like even a half-romantic lead... And I stood in the wings as the new director (I'd been an assistant director at the Royal Court). I was very young and I'd worked on a number of interesting productions, but I didn't have any miles under my belt. I noticed that he and Gawn Grainger were corpsing – were giggling – and I was appalled that they were so unprofessional to be corpsing on stage, and it seemed to go on for quite a long time. It wasn't my production, I was standing in the wings, and there was nothing you could do... At the end of the show I said to Nicol, 'Pity about that, bit of a bad show really – not really professional.' 'Wasn't it great?' he said, 'It was fantastic – they loved it!' I said, 'What do you mean?' 'Oh, we weren't corpsing – we were just pretending to corpse!'

Then I did my production, a middle-class comedy [*Widows Are Dangerous* by June Garland], but it was equally stupid, and Nicol played the older man... it was old-fashioned farcical theatre, and he was wonderful to work with because he was *so* talented... he could do almost anything, he was tremendously funny and sharp...

He stayed on for one show, and then he left because he'd been there with Anthony, really... I was really, really sad... he was *fucking* good – naughty, but very, very good. I tried to persuade him, I think, to stay on, but he'd had enough and he wanted to go off to the bright lights, to London...

Widows Are Dangerous was originally to be Nicol's last play at the theatre, but it seems that Haggard was successful in persuading him to remain for one further production as he played the lead in *Gaslight*, which opened on the 25th of September and closed on the 8th of October 1961. *Gaslight* enabled him to depart on a high note, and the *Evening Telegraph* reported that his final role at Dundee had turned out to be 'the one for which he will be most warmly remembered', going on to say that his 'control... is something much above the ordinary.'

Although he felt that drama school and National Service had wasted five years of his life between them, Nicol was a great deal more positive about his stint at Dundee, later saying, 'That kind of rep is good for an actor because he has to play everything. [When I] had to play a coal-black mammy with a skirt and bandana headscarf, I was awful - but it was good experience... I think that an actor must try anything and everything, otherwise he's not really being an actor.'[7] Nicol seems to have had reasonably amicable relations with the rest of the company most of the time, but even in his rep days he was already exhibiting an unpredictability that did not sit well with everyone. Clifford Hanley, author of *The Durable Element*, would later say that on opening night Nicol had 'switched to an Irish accent nobody had heard before' and that this had thrown the other actors off.[8] Some of Nicol's colleagues also discovered that his sudden changes of mood were not always harmless, as Michael Culver remembered:

> We had one of those ridiculous rows... I think it was about me babysitting for Lillias Walker, who had two small children. Sometimes she needed babysitters, and if you weren't working you went and babysat... Nicol was playing the piano and he had told me that Lillias needed me to babysit, and when I got there she didn't need me at all. The next morning I was in the green room with Nicol and I said, 'Nicol, why did you tell me that Lillias needed me to babysit?' He didn't pay any attention and went on playing the piano, so I said again, 'Nicol, why did you lie about Lillias?' and that was it! The word 'lie' and I was on my back on the other side of the room. He'd just hurled me across the room, saying *'Don't you ever fucking call me a fucking liar!*' I'd come across people who were violent before, but never in such a concentrated burst of venom.

However, Culver was grateful to Nicol for introducing him to *The Lord of the Rings*, and said that, 'I always thought Nicol was really born to play Gandalf.' He also remembered Nicol's mischievous side when he went to see Alfred Hitchcock's *Psycho* during an afternoon off, saying, 'As I came out of the cinema and was just about to cross the road, this creature came out of nowhere, screaming like in the shower sequence of the film. I practically had a heart attack and almost fell down. That was Nicol.'

After the babysitting incident, relations had been somewhat strained between the two actors. Michael Culver left first, in the summer of 1961, and the two did not remain in contact. However, some twenty years later, Culver and his then wife Lucinda Curtis, who had also been an actor at the Rep, went on holiday to the Greek island of Rhodes:

> …we were walking through Lindos, which is a typical Greek village with little narrow streets, and as we walked down one I turned to her and said, 'I've just seen Nicol!' She said, 'Don't be so silly – you're being paranoid – you see him everywhere!' – which wasn't true! Anyway, we went out for a meal that evening to a restaurant, and we were waiting for a seat when in through the door comes Nicol… he joined us for a drink, he joined us for dinner, and then he said, 'Come on back to my place and have a drink with me,' which we did… and he was charming. And I'm not sure we didn't meet up with him one more time, when he walked us up and over to a nearby village. And then I never saw him again.

Chapter 3 – As Hungry and as Generous as a Lion

It seems probable that Nicol and Anthony Page had made an arrangement whereby Page would go to London first and Nicol would join him once Page was in a position to help him find work. Page was hoping to resume his directing career at the Royal Court Theatre in Sloane Square which, since its legendary production of John Osborne's *Look Back in Anger* in 1956, had (along with the Theatre Royal in Stratford, East London) become the centre of cutting-edge British drama. The effect that Osborne had on the English theatre at this time is not dissimilar to the effect that Elvis had on popular music at around the same time, albeit on a smaller scale and with a greater seriousness of intent. The younger generation had become tired of the clichés, stereotypes, snobbery and divorcement from reality of the established theatre and wanted it to reflect working class life, giving rise to the terms 'angry young man' and 'kitchen sink realism'.

Ann Beach acted at both Stratford East and the Royal Court in the early '60s and, speaking over fifty years later, had this to say:

> I want to express how very important the '60s were for theatre. I appreciate it more now than I did at the time. I was lucky to have left RADA when I did – I had a Shakespeare scholarship there – and to find myself working for Joan Littlewood at Stratford East in *Fings Ain't Wot They Used to Be*, *O! What a Lovely War*, all those things, and at the same time at the Royal Court, with very good writers and directors. I'd go back and forward between the two. At the Royal Court they appreciated me being at Stratford East as well because they appreciated Joan. Although there were differences between the two, we were a group of people who were experimenting with a new style of acting which we felt was more real and truthful – and the plays were coming out like that too. It was also very influential on film and television.

The resident players at the Royal Court were the English Stage Company, headed by George Devine and Tony Richardson. It was run somewhat differently to a standard repertory company as actors were paid only when they worked and casting was done on a play by play basis. However, although actors came and went, Devine and Richardson gave frequent employment to those they believed in, such as, during this period, Robert Shaw and Wilfrid Lawson. Shaw was trying to make a name for himself as a serious actor after becoming a TV star in a rather silly series called *The Buccaneers*. Lawson was an eccentric, an alcoholic Yorkshireman who had been a versatile star character actor but was at this point on his way down.

Page's directing career had got off to a false start at the Royal Court in September 1958, when his production of John Arden's *Live Like Pigs* – which he had co-directed with George Devine – had received such terrible reviews that for the following year the theatre employed him only as an assistant, after which he had found himself pushed out into the world of regional rep. However, his work at Dundee in particular had impressed a lot of people and his reputation was in much better shape by the time he returned to London. Devine and Richardson promised him a second chance but were to keep him waiting a while yet.

Page still had friends at the Court, and he persuaded William Gaskill, who had been directing there since 1957, to cast Nicol in his forthcoming production of Henry Chapman's *That's Us*. Gaskill, a Yorkshireman who had been heavily influenced by Brecht, gave Nicol the unlikely part of I-ti, an Italian labourer, in what was an ensemble piece set on a building site. Such plays set in the world of unglamorous professions were at the time a new sub-genre which had been created by the new wave of playwrights who had followed in Osborne's wake. *That's Us* opened at the Cambridge Arts Theatre on the 30th of October 1961, then played at the Theatre Royal in Exeter the following week before finishing at the Royal Court, where it opened on the 13th of November and again ran for one week. Nicol's Dundee Rep colleague Edward Fox was also in the cast. The play had little plot to speak of and was not well-received on the whole, with many critics complaining they had found it 'dull'. Nicol received no mention in the majority of reviews, with most of the praise going to Ronald (or Ron) Pember, an actor who would become a familiar face on British television in the '70s playing a succession of pub landlords and small time crooks. It filled only 13.7% of the Royal Court's seats and took a mere £216 at the box office.

Nicol's London debut might have been a disappointment, but Gaskill gave him a much better part in *Arden of Faversham*, which opened in Cambridge on the 20th of November and also ran for a week in Exeter before finishing at the Royal Court. *Faversham* is a 16th-century tragic-comedy of uncertain authorship thought to have possibly been written (or co-written) by Shakespeare. The play is based on the true story of Thomas Arden, a rich businessman who was murdered by assassins hired by his wife and her lover. Ron Pember, who became good friends with Nicol, was again present as was Edward Fox, but this time Nicol made the most of his opportunity in what was essentially a comic role as Black Will, one of the two incompetent assassins. The other, Shakebag, was played by James McLoughlin. Nicol adopted a broad Lancastrian accent for the role and was perplexed during the first performance as to why he got a laugh every time he said 'Shakebag.' He subsequently realized the audience had thought he was saying 'Shitbag.' Nicol was singled out for praise in both *The Daily Telegraph* and the *Cambridge Review*, whose critic went so far as to say the evening had been 'saved' by his performance. A small personal success for Nicol, then, but the attempt at a partnership scheme between the three theatres was not judged a success and soon ended.

A few weeks of unemployment followed for Nicol before he was offered a role in Tony Richardson's Royal Court production of *A Midsummer Night's Dream*. Richardson had come a long way from his humble beginnings as a jug-eared chemist's son and gone to Oxford, where he had gained a reputation as a flamboyant theatre enthusiast.

Like Gaskill, whom he had known since school days when the two had put on amateur plays together, Richardson was from Shipley in Yorkshire, although his regional accent had long since disappeared and he had a curious lisping way of speaking which was a gift to impressionists the world over. Only 33 at the time, he had already directed both the original play and film versions of *Look Back in Anger*, *The Entertainer* and *A Taste of Honey*.

A Midsummer Night's Dream was the first Shakespeare play to be attempted by the English Stage Company. Richardson loved Shakespeare, but it was not what people had come to expect from the Royal Court. Nicol played the minor role of Flute, the bellows-mender, one of the six 'mechanicals' (or tradesmen) who moonlight as actors. Presumably, the part necessitated Nicol appearing in drag as Flute reluctantly takes the part of Thisbe, the female lover, in the play performed by the amateur troupe. Previous productions had often gone to town to create spectacular magical forest settings, but Richardson's version was comparatively modest and the stage size of the Royal Court perhaps too small for a play of its kind. The production was criticised as amateurish and surprisingly old-fashioned from such a supposedly cutting-edge talent. Kenneth Tynan in *The Observer* called it 'conventionally imagined and clumsily executed' but did concede that the mechanicals came off fairly well, although most of the laughs came from Colin Blakeley's Bottom and Nicol's 'shame-faced' Thisbe. Blakely was the one actor consistently singled out for praise; otherwise only Bernard Levin in the *Daily Express* had anything very good to say about the production or bothered to mention Nicol, 'the uproarious, trembling, stage-frighted Flute of Mr Nicol Williamson.' Peter Gill saw the production and still remembered Nicol's performance as being both 'brilliant' and 'charming' over fifty years later. By all accounts as poorly received by audiences as it was with the critics, the show struggled on for twenty-nine performances before closing to the obvious relief of everyone involved. Only 40% of the seats had been sold and the box office takings of £2408 barely covered half of the production cost of

£4201. However, anyone who did attend would have gained bragging rights a few years later as Ronnie Barker, James Bolam, Samantha Eggar, Corin Redgrave, Lynn Redgrave, Rita Tushingham and David Warner had also been featured in the cast. Some were unknown at the time, but all would become well-known by the end of the decade. David Warner remembered it this way:

> It was my first job in London and it was really a production mounted for a couple of film stars who'd started to get going in the '60s – Rita Tushingham and Samantha Eggar. It was an extraordinary cast and it was a disastrous production! It was really not very well-received at all! Nicol certainly stood out because he had an extraordinary presence. In that part you don't necessarily say, 'Oh, there's a future big star', but you just knew there was something very special. I wasn't surprised that Nicol soon after took off and became what he became – absolutely not surprised.

Corin Redgrave also spoke about the production in a 2004 interview with Ian MacKillop for the British Library's Theatre Archive, saying,

> It was critically an absolute disaster and the critics were pretty harsh on all of us. They were very harsh on Tony Richardson for even thinking of doing *A Midsummer Night's Dream* at the Royal Court because he was thought to be the sort of great godfather of all the new realist school of playwriting and why would he be doing *A Midsummer Night's Dream* they all asked. We were just hooted at and in fact we were so bruised that George Devine who was a very kind man and very good towards the young brought us all together to do a Sunday night production of *Twelfth Night* so that we'd have something to think about and take our minds off the awful notices that we'd all been given. [9]

George Devine, 51 at the time, was very much the father figure of the Royal Court. With his silver hair, thick-framed glasses and ever-present pipe, he must have seemed an unlikely member of the new wave, but he was without doubt one of the most significant. Having directed Gielgud in Shakespeare in the '30s, he was in some respects a member of the old guard who had defected, but he had not completely cut his ties and often provided a valuable link between the two generations. It had been Devine and Richardson's determination to produce modern plays by serious writers which had been the impetus behind the formation of the English Stage Company.

Devine decided to mount a one-night only production of *Twelfth Night* for two reasons; firstly, he wanted to show that the Court was perfectly capable of doing Shakespeare despite the scathing notices which *Dream* had received. Secondly, he also wished to demonstrate that it was not necessary to spend a lot of money on costumes, props and scenery if you had a solid play with strong actors. He used many of the cast from *Dream*, as David Warner remembered: 'I ended up having three or four lines but Nicol got Malvolio and he was just extraordinary. I think he did a Scots accent.' Malvolio, an unlikeable steward who is tricked into believing that his employer, Olivia, is in love with him, is the plum role in *Twelfth Night* as it provides an actor with a rare opportunity to make an unpleasant character both very funny and ultimately tragic. Devine's clout was such that he was also able to bring in Albert Finney – then starring in John Osborne's *Luther* in the West End and already a big star – to play Feste. The production was entirely without décor and, as it was performed once only, it received no reviews. However, those who were fortunate enough to see it – or be in it – all remember it as a far more rewarding experience than Richardson's *Dream* had been.

At this point, Nicol was staying – for some of the time, anyway – in a flat at 9 Highbury Crescent, with two other penniless young actors, Tom Courtenay and John Thaw, and Terry Bicknell, a TV cameraman who later married Rita Tushingham (then appearing in *A Midsummer Night's Dream* with Nicol). As the actors could not afford to do much hellraising, they apparently stayed in much of the time playing with their Scalextric set.

Nicol had garnered enough good reviews by this time to be signed by a talent agency, Peter Crouch Associates. One of Crouch's assistants, Penny Taylor, remembered Nicol as being very shy and 'shambly' when she first saw him at the office in Soho Square and said that he had been very patient when Crouch kept him waiting for an hour. However, she went on to add that he later became 'rather demanding' and 'very starry.'[10] Later, around 1965, Nicol got into a dispute with Crouch over percentages. He took his agent to court and won the case.

After appearing in two Shakespeare plays at the Court, Nicol then joined the Royal Shakespeare Company for a season of three non-Shakespeare plays at the New Arts Theatre Club in London. The first of these was to be directed by Anthony Page, who was presumably responsible for giving Nicol his entrée into the establishment. The play was *Nil Carborandum*, the title being a sort of Latin corruption of the phrase 'don't let the bastards grind you down.' It was set in the world of National Service conscripts at an RAF base, an environment Nicol knew well. Page gave him a leading part as SAC (Second Aircraftman) Albert Meakin, a cook who uses his position to finagle every unfair advantage he can think of. James Booth played Nicol's partner in crime and also featured were another three actors who had followed Page from Dundee Rep – Kate Binchy, Edward Fox and Gawn Grainger. The play opened on the 12th of April 1962 and ran for a month. Binchy, who remembered Nicol as 'a perfectionist who never thought he was good enough' later recalled that he had suffered a crisis of confidence at one point and disappeared on a train to Scotland but had reappeared the following Monday and continued without further incident. Page's direction was praised for keeping control of a large cast and a considerable amount of action on a small stage. The play itself received mixed reviews, as not all critics appreciated Livings' style, often complaining that it was 'plotless' and / or 'crude'. Nicol, however, was highly praised, although he was usually mentioned in tandem with James Booth rather than singled out. Kenneth Tynan in *The Observer* found Meakin to be 'superbly played' by Nicol 'with the full, slimy whine of a Black Country accent', while Alan Brien in *The Sunday Telegraph* said that Nicol had given the 'performance of the evening' as the 'failed Iago of the underdogs.'

Nicol's next play for the RSC, also at the New Arts Theatre Club, was a version of Maxim Gorky's *The Lower Depths* performed with regional English accents. The play examines the lives of various poverty-stricken characters who, crammed together in a cheap boarding house, are stirred up by the passing through of the kindly Luka (played by Wilfrid Lawson). The director was Toby Robertson (not to be confused with Tony Richardson), a strong personality who came from a privileged background and who had been christened Sholto David Maurice Robertson, but claimed he had gained the nickname 'Toby' due to his habit of reciting Hamlet's 'To be or not to be' speech as a child. He also claimed to have put down a Mau Mau uprising single-handed while performing his National Service with the East African Rifles. At this point, he was 33, and his theatrical experience had mainly been as an actor, although he had already directed a number of plays for television. He assembled a strong cast which also included Ann Bell, Julian Glover, Freddie Jones, Fulton Mackay, Prunella Scales and Margaret Tyzack.

At one point during rehearsals, Wilfrid Lawson failed to return from lunch. Nicol, growing impatient, began pacing the stage and launched into a tirade about what an unreliable drunk he was, when from the back row Lawson's voice rang out, saying, 'I thought that speech had been cut!'

The Lower Depths is really an ensemble piece with no obvious lead but, as Satin, the gambler, Nicol gained some quite extraordinary reviews, with Gerard Fay in *The Guardian* writing that the way he had taken control of the final twenty minutes was 'an object lesson in how an actor can keep power in reserve.' *The Sunday Telegraph*'s reviewer, Alan Brien, an early champion of Nicol's talent, said that his performance as Satin had signalled the arrival of a 'new epic actor in the making', while Roger Gellert of the *New Statesman* spoke of how Nicol had 'emerged from obscurity to appear in four fantastically diverse parts during the last few months, growing in stature with each.' Gellert went on to compliment his 'sudden brilliant impersonation of Mr Lawson', which he found to be 'the most moving moment of many.' Clive Barnes of *Plays & Players* was also deeply impressed, describing Nicol as having been 'as hungry and as generous as a lion' and praising the way he had delivered Gorki's message with 'utter conviction.'

When *The Lower Depths* had finished its four-week run, Nicol was recruited, alongside fellow Dundee Rep veterans Edward Fox and Glenda Jackson, by Lindsay Anderson to help fill out the cast of his film *This Sporting Life*, starring Richard Harris and Rachel Roberts. Anderson was also a theatre director at the Royal Court and knew Anthony Page, which is probably how these three came to appear in the film. Nicol can be seen in two uncredited, non-speaking bit parts: firstly, as a piano player at a party about one and a half hours in, and secondly, as a grinning lodger at a seedy boarding house about one hour and 57 minutes in. In the second part he is glimpsed for only a couple of seconds but, simply by scratching himself, aptly suggests the flea-infested nature of the accommodation.

Nicol's third and final play for the RSC at the New Arts was *Women Beware Women* by Thomas Middleton, for which he was reunited with Anthony Page. Opening on the 4th of July 1962, one of those in attendance was Peter Gill, who thought the play memorable for a number of reasons:

> Productions of Jacobean plays, other than those of Shakespeare, were rare then. Tony Richardson's production of *The Changeling* at the Court theatre was unusual enough and Antony's production of *Women Beware Women* was the first since its premier and was an important part of the rehabilitation of Thomas Middleton.
>
> One of the interesting things in that production was the casting of Ernest Milton as the Cardinal, a legendary actor who had seemingly completely disappeared. He was in fact American. He made his debut in James O'Neill's company – that's Eugene O'Neill's father's company.

The plot concerns a young woman, Bianca, who elopes with Leantio, a young man of little means who, out of insecurity, proceeds to keep her under lock and key. However, his concern proves well-founded when Bianca is wooed through the window by a duke who then manages to gain access and seduce her. When Leantio discovers that Bianca no longer loves him, the tragedy begins to unfold.

Nicol, with Birmingham accent, goatee beard and studded jacket, once again benefitted from one of the best parts as the clumsy Leantio and gained very favourable notices, including praise from Alan Brien in *The Sunday Telegraph* for his naturalistic delivery and portrait of a 'provincial in agony among the city slickers.' Kenneth Tynan, who became perhaps the most important believer in Nicol's talent among the critics, devoted an entire paragraph in the *Observer Weekend Review* to Nicol's performance. Tynan was especially impressed with the way Nicol played a 'conventionally pathetic role for reality instead of sympathy' and seemed to have 'a psychological justification for every word' he spoke.

The production itself received the best reviews of the season and Page was highly praised for the unfussy clarity of his direction. However, the RSC's tenancy at the New Arts had apparently not been a financial success and soon came to an end. Nicol, on the other hand, had enjoyed stunning success for a young actor fresh from the provinces, and in July he received votes from Alan Brien, David Nathan, Kenneth Tynan and T.C. Worsley in the London Critics' Ballots, which led to him being named as 'most promising newcomer' of 1962. He had become a leading London stage actor after only appearing in a handful of shows.

Chapter 4 – Not the Most Disciplined of Young Actors

After finishing his season at the RSC, Nicol played a number of parts for British television, but showed no interest in playing an ongoing character, opting instead to appear in one-off TV plays. At the time, these were mostly live broadcasts which put the actors under considerable pressure. His debut was as Beauchamp, Earl of Warwick in a version of Jean Anouilh's play about Joan of Arc, entitled *The Lark*. In the play, the English Warwick initially wants Joan tried and burned as soon as possible, but later becomes sympathetic and urges her to avoid this fate. Directed by Claude Whatham in Manchester for Granada's *Play of the Week* slot, it was shot and broadcast on the 26th of August 1962. Joan was played by Elizabeth MacLennan, with whom Nicol had acted at Dundee. Such live TV plays often utilised a number of sets and cameras, so thorough rehearsal was vital as precise timing was required and the actors would frequently have to sprint from one set to another in order to make their cue. MacLennan had a bout of gastroenteritis on the day and had to keep disappearing to vomit into a well-placed bucket during rehearsal, although fortunately she had finished by the time of the actual broadcast and proceeded to give an appropriately pale and shaky performance as the incarcerated Joan. She later spoke of Nicol as 'not at all difficult', saying that he was a 'real pro' because he dared to take risks.[11]

Nicol's next job was to reprise his role in *Nil Carborandum* for a TV version filmed in Manchester for the BBC by Vivian A. Daniels as part of a series of plays under the banner title *From the North*. John Thaw played the role of Nicol's sidekick previously enacted by James Booth. It was broadcast on the 26th of October 1962 – the night of the Cuban missile crisis – but, along with *The Lark* and many other television plays from this period, has since been lost.

The producers of *Play of the Week* became highly ambitious at this time and decided to attempt a dramatisation of the epic Tolstoy novel

War and Peace – also to be broadcast live! Based on an earlier German stage version by Alfred Neumann, Erwin Piscator and Guntram Prüfer, it made use of a narrator to replace large sections of the novel with a brief synopsis in order to cram the sprawling story into a digestible evening's entertainment. The project was placed in the care of Silvio Narizzano, a Canadian of Italian-American ancestry who had become one of the most able and experienced directors of television drama in the '50s and early '60s. Instead of the usual hour and a half, an entire evening was to be devoted to the broadcast and the running time was doubled, making it the longest TV play ever shown at the time. The producers began searching for a leading actor to play Count Pierre Besukhov – and they needed one of exceptional ability who would be unfazed by the pressure. Competition for the part was apparently fierce, with one newspaper referring to it as 'the role that every young actor in the country was ready to sacrifice his eye-teeth, his right arm, and even his agent to get'.[12] However, it is clear that Nicol excelled in audition situations and it was indeed he that won the part. The cast also included Ann Bell, Daniel Massey, Clifford Evans, Valerie Sarruf and Kenneth Griffith as Napoleon. Elaborate sets were designed by Peter Phillips, some using *trompe l'oeil*[13] techniques to give the illusion of three dimensions to flat surfaces. Rehearsals were especially complex as the many set changes had to be achieved both quickly and silently, so camera placements had to be precise and the actors were allowed little freedom of movement.

War and Peace was broadcast on the 26th of March, 1963 and became the first winner of the new Emmy award for Best International Programme. Even those critics who were not entirely convinced by the undertaking gave kudos to the producers for trying. Nicol, in period costume and wire spectacles, once more gained some impressive reviews, with *Variety* stating that it was largely for him that the production would be remembered and that his performance 'came near to greatness as it progressed.'

Around this time, Nicol rejected an offer from Peter Hall of a long-term contract with the Royal Shakespeare Company. The majority of actors in his position would have accepted without a second thought but, with a couple of notable exceptions, Nicol would always value his independence too much to commit to anything very long-term. Instead, he accepted a supporting role in a film version of Somerset Maugham's popular and highly-regarded novel, *Of Human Bondage*, to be directed by Henry Hathaway, a tough Hollywood veteran best known for a number of John Wayne films, although he had also made a handful of striking *films noir*. Laurence Harvey was cast as Philip Carey, the would-be artist with a club-foot who ends up abandoning art, studying to be a doctor and falling disastrously in love with a working-class waitress, Mildred, played by Kim Novak. In what would have been his film debut in a speaking part, Nicol was to play Carey's friend Griffiths, a fellow medical student who betrays him by seducing Mildred. However, after shooting began at Ardmore Studios in Ireland, Nicol was at some point replaced by Jack Hedley. A later newspaper article suggested that Nicol had been fired for mocking Novak's attempt at a cockney accent, but assistant director John Quested had no memory of this and thought it unlikely, saying,

> I was unaware of any acrimony between Kim and Nicol and do not think Hathaway would allow anything like that to happen. He was a very cunning old director and always knew what was going on. I think his biggest problem was dealing with Helen Goss, her dialogue coach. Also, Chris Stamp (my second assistant) would joke with Kim about her Cockney accent and she liked it because he had a true accent.
>
> [However, Nicol]... was not the most disciplined of young actors; for instance, Hathaway always wanted to see how the actors looked in their costumes. I asked Chris Stamp to get Nicol onto the set dressed. After an hour, I said, 'Where is he?' and it turned out he had gone off to Dublin without telling anybody – he was found playing the piano in a pub there.

Perhaps because the two leads, Harvey and Novak, did not get on, the production soon became a troubled one, as cast member Eamon Morrissey recalled:

When Henry Hathaway resigned/was fired there was an uneasy one or two weeks when Bryan Forbes (the writer) took over direction.

Then there was chaos. There were big script changes and cast changes. When Ken Hughes took over many characters simply disappeared, including myself…

Nicol – who seems to have put on a bit of weight at the time – can be glimpsed in a couple of scenes in the finished film, although he has no dialogue and received no credit.

The amount of money which an actor could earn from a film was considerably higher in those days than that which could be earned from theatre or television work. Although the disparity remains today, the gap has closed somewhat. Nicol was not interested in the accumulation of wealth but viewed money as a means to an end and had had an ulterior motive for accepting the role. He had come up with an idea for a one-man stage show, *An Evening with McGonagall*, and originally planned to use his fee for *Of Human Bondage* to put towards it.

William McGonagall (1825 – 1902) was an eccentric Scot and long-term resident of Dundee often described as the world's worst poet for his unintentionally amusing verse often based on real historical events. His most famous poem, *The Tay Bridge Disaster*, is about the railway bridge in Dundee which collapsed in 1879 and killed an entire train full of people. It concludes movingly:

> … your central girders would not have given way,
> At least many sensible men do say,
> Had they been supported on each side with buttresses,
> At least many sensible men confesses,
> For the stronger we our houses do build,
> The less chance we have of being killed.

McGonagall would perform his poetry at every opportunity, undeterred by the many varieties of rotten food which were flung at him as a result. He also made a number of unsuccessful attempts to gain an audience with Queen Victoria and other esteemed figures of the day, including the actor Henry Irving.

Nicol persuaded Anthony Page to collaborate on the project as director, and the two returned to Dundee together for four days to research the life and work of McGonagall at the Central Library. They planned a play of around an hour and a quarter in length, in which Nicol as McGonagall was the only cast member, although they intended to hire two Scottish folk musicians – one on accordion, the other on fiddle – to provide accompaniment on a couple of poems which Nicol would set to music. The concept was successfully sold to impresarios Michael Codron and Oscar Lewenstein. *The Rattling Boy*, as it was now called, was to open in mid-November at the New Arts, where Nicol had played his season with the RSC. He saw it as a sympathetic treatment of McGonagall, with the theme being 'the man who never made it - the little man who thought he was big and who kept coming up against the blank walls in the shape of heavy-handed bureaucracy'.[14] Nicol planned to have the audience pelt him with fruit for the finale but, for reasons which are now unclear, *The Rattling Boy* never became a reality.

Nicol next returned to the Royal Court to play the mysterious 'man at the end' in a Sunday night production of German playwright Frank Wedekind's *Spring Awakening*. Dealing as it does with the sexual awakening of the young, the play was at the time a controversial one, and the Court's was the first public performance in the UK. The director was the 29-year-old Desmond O'Donovan. Peter Gill assisted on the production and remembered,

> Desmond had no sense of time and many thought he was too unworldly (his original intent had been to be a priest) and too unfocused to be a director. But he could be a marvellous director with special gifts. He was an associate director of Bill Gaskill at the Court and I think the first ever assistant director to Laurence Olivier at the National Theatre at the Old Vic.

I can remember Nicol being striking at the end... The Lord Chamberlain was still licensing plays then. I remember going with Ian Cuthbertson to St James' Palace to ask them to reverse some of the cuts that had been demanded before the play could be licensed, but without success.

The Sunday night production was, as usual, without décor, but the decision to stage it on two successive Sunday nights at the end of April meant that it did receive a couple of reviews. Although Nicol's role was little more than a cameo in which he appeared in the final scene to dissuade the hero from committing suicide, *The Times* thought him 'brilliant' and the *New Statesman* found his part to be 'superbly clowned.' Plans to give the play a proper run a few months later in its uncut form were scuppered by the Lord Chamberlain's office. However, by 1965, the censorship rules had been relaxed and it was finally staged as intended by the author, although by that time Nicol was no longer available.

On the 1st of May, Nicol played a character named Jack Clark in an episode of the BBC's *Z Cars*, the series credited with introducing realism to the police genre. Broadcast live, the episode was directed by Anthony Page and also featured Glenda Jackson, along with series regulars Brian Blessed and Stratford Johns.[15]

At the Royal Court once more, Nicol was given the lead in a new play by Henry Livings. The author of *Nil Carborandum* was attempting a much more serious work with *Kelly's Eye*. Livings had been so impressed by his performance in the earlier play that he insisted only Nicol could play Kelly. The two became good friends and Nicol would sometimes visit Livings at his home in the village of Dobcross, near Manchester. The director was David Scase, who had come from regional rep and whom Nicol seems to have had little respect for. The story involved a murderer who has fled society to live in seclusion on a beach, only to be joined by a middle-class runaway (played by Sarah Miles). Miles had recently had a success co-starring in the film *Term of Trial* with Laurence Olivier, with whom she had embarked on an affair that would last for some years but which would remain a closely-guarded secret until after Olivier's death. While performing in *Kelly's Eye*, she also began a relationship with Nicol.

The two stars had not got on well at first – Miles was upset that Nicol kept playing scenes differently from previous nights and throwing her off, whereas he had not been amused when her dog had escaped from the dressing room one night, joined them on stage and stolen the show from under his nose. However, when Miles heard Nicol singing at the piano, she was enchanted. They became lovers and Nicol moved into her house in Hasker Street, Chelsea. According to her, he was often kind and gentle, especially in the early days of their relationship, when he would spend a considerable time in the kitchen cooking delicious stews and suchlike, but as time went on he would increasingly feel the need to go out, get drunk and start a fight. In her autobiography *Serves Me Right*, Miles remembered one occasion when Nicol was walking down the street arm-in-arm with his friend Oliver MacGreevy – an Irish actor who had lost all of his hair as a result of alopecia – and overheard a homophobic remark by a builder leaning out of an upstairs window. They got into an argument and the builder came down to the street, revealing himself to be only a little over five feet tall. Nicol mocked the man's diminutive stature – and the builder laid him flat!

Kelly's Eye was not a success with audiences. Opening on the 12th of June, it was originally scheduled to run until the 13th of July. However, reviews were mixed and only 24% of seats were sold. The play closed early, on the 29th of June, after taking only £1,178 at the box office against production costs of £3,096. Its failure did no harm to Nicol, though, and he again received excellent reviews, with Kenneth Tynan writing for *The Observer* referring to him as 'our best young actor in the vein of smouldering resentment.' John Russell Taylor, in *Plays and Players*, even saw Nicol's performance as a breakthrough, saying that it had 'effortlessly' put him 'in the front rank.'

Nicol's relationship with Sarah Miles led to his involvement in a short film entitled *The Six-Sided Triangle*, directed by her brother, Christopher Miles. The thirty-minute film presented a love triangle in six different versions, each of which parodied the cinema style of a different country. Nicol played 'the Lover' in each episode, so he appeared alternately as a Valentino-like sheikh in the American silent movie-style episode, as a sombre Max von Sydow stand-in in the Swedish episode, and so on. Sarah played the various wives and Bill Meilen the cuckolded husbands. *Triangle* was filmed over the course of a week at a studio in Chancery Lane on a budget of £6,000. On the third day of shooting, Nicol failed to appear. However, he returned the following day, offering no explanation but doing everything necessary to complete the film.

The 24-year-old Christopher Miles had mortgaged his flat and borrowed £1,000 from the Boulting Brothers to help finance it. Originally screened only at the Academy Cinema in London, it went on to be nominated for an Oscar for Best Short Film and was booked to show in a chain of 50 cinemas. A minor success for Nicol, then, who was paid £200[16] and gained a few more good notices.

After they had finished the film, Nicol, Sarah and her big white Pyrenean mountain dog, Addo, went off together to (ahem) Shag Rock in Cornwall, where her family kept a holiday home. One day they visited the nearby village of Veryan and went for a drink in a pub which happened to have a piano. Nicol, never able to stay away from a piano for long, impressed the landlord by playing a few songs, as a result of which he was hired to provide entertainment in the evening. Proving popular with the locals, a one-night booking turned into several.

While they were on holiday, Nicol revealed that he wanted to marry Sarah and even went so far as to take her to a local church where he had arranged a meeting with a vicar, but she refused to enter. Nicol's drinking became worse and she began making him sleep in the spare room. According to her, on the fourth night of this he flew into a rage and began smashing things in the spare room. He would not let her in, so she attempted to gain access via the window but when he saw her about to enter, he 'charged' at her and she fell backwards, slid down the roof and hung from the guttering for a minute before she was forced to let go when he failed to come to her rescue. She escaped with only a twisted ankle but decided then and there to end the relationship. After Miles's book had been published in 1994, Nicol denied that this had ever happened, saying that he was the one who had ended the relationship and that she would have married him if it had not been for her mother, a woman he described as a 'haughty cow' who considered him too low class to be worthy of her daughter. He also said that, shortly after their relationship had ended, she had come to the Royal Court and invited him for a drive. He agreed and they stopped for a walk in Richmond Park, where she told him she had been pregnant with his child, which she had aborted – a story which Sarah Miles flatly denies.

On his return to London, Nicol found himself a small flat in Notting Hill Gate, where he lived alone. His next acting job was the title role in *Dr Murke's Collection of Silences*, an episode of a short-lived series of half-hour dramas produced by the BBC entitled *Teletale*. Based on *Murke's Collected Silences*, a short story by Heinrich Böll, this was broadcast on the 15th of November 1963 and is now believed lost. In the original story, Murke is not a doctor but an ambitious if non-conformist young man who works for a radio station editing broadcasts. The silences he collects are pieces of recording tape which he has cut from programmes because the speakers paused for too long. Murke takes pleasure in splicing the silences together and 'listening' to them at home. He is assigned the task of deleting all references to god from the broadcast of one Professor Bur-Malottke, a highly respected public figure, and replacing them with 'that higher Being Whom we revere', a phrase which Bur-Malottke believes now more accurately describes his current beliefs. Murke must first record the Professor speaking the longer phrase multiple times and his hatred for a man he sees as boring and pompous means that he delights in making the job as difficult as possible. It is an odd, comic story, and the role could have been tailor-made for Nicol; Murke's contempt for authority figures and pleasure in making them squirm – not to mention his existential outlook – were qualities which would be found in a number of the characters Nicol would later portray so memorably.

Back at the Royal Court, Nicol was cast as Sebastian Dangerfield, the workshy antihero of J.P. Donleavy's novel *The Ginger Man*, in an adaptation by the original author. Directed by Philip Wiseman, who had staged an earlier version with Richard Harris in 1959, it first tried out at the Ashcroft Theatre in Croydon, opening on the 4th of November 1963, where it ran for two weeks. The other actors in the cast were Susan Hampshire[17] as Dangerfield's wife, T.P. McKenna as his friend Kenneth O'Keefe and Margaret Tyzack as the prim Miss Frost, who allows herself to be seduced by Dangerfield. Nicol was a natural for the part and David Pryce-Jones of *The Spectator* found him to be 'entirely dominating and self-destructive, as it should be.' Alex Matheson Cain, writing for *The Tablet*, added that he gave 'a splendidly life-like performance as he wildly runs through the gamut of every emotion.' However, although the play received favourable reviews, it was less successful at the box office than it should have been, as the assassination of John F. Kennedy shortly after it opened at the Royal Court understandably diverted the public's attention. Irish cast member T.P. McKenna was particularly upset by the news as he was an avid Kennedy supporter who had been present during Kennedy's visit to Ireland six months previously.

In early 1964, Nicol was cast by Anthony Page in *Horror of Darkness*, a bleak one-hour TV drama produced by the BBC for *The Wednesday Play* series and written by John Hopkins, who had scripted numerous episodes of *Z Cars*. Wearing his hair brushed forward and adopting a thick Scots accent, Nicol played Robin Fletcher, a struggling writer who turns up at the house of a university friend he has not seen for two years. The friend, Peter Young (Alfred Lynch), is now living with Cathy (Glenda Jackson), whom he refers to as his wife although they are not actually married. Young is a painter of rather passive-aggressive temperament who has already compromised his youthful ideals and now uses his artistic talents on whatever jobs he can get that will help to pay the rent. Fletcher moves in to the couple's home without waiting for an invitation; at first, he seems like a fun-loving, if attention-seeking, free-spirit, but we gradually come to learn that he is in fact a troubled young man desperately in love with Young. Nicol was highly effective, both in the early stages when his character's exuberance appears to be a breath of fresh air in Peter and Cathy's already somewhat stale existence, then later as he gradually reveals the hidden pain of Fletcher with the subtlest of looks. Homosexuality was still illegal at the time of broadcast and, nervous about the gay-love theme, the BBC delayed its broadcast for a year; when it was finally shown in March 1965, there proved to be very little outcry after all. Indeed, Page and Hopkins had been forced to be so coy about their theme that it is likely many viewers did not even register it.

Speaking some fifty years later, Glenda Jackson had one abiding memory of the production:

> We were rehearsing at a church hall in Chelsea somewhere and Nicol just disappeared for two days. We didn't actually quite know why. Poor Tony almost had a nervous breakdown because of his anxiety and then Nicol swanned back as though nothing had happened.

Chapter 5 – Inadmissible Evidence

By spring of 1964, Nicol had already enjoyed a remarkable degree of success. He had become a leading actor both on stage and television, impressed a lot of critics, directors and fellow actors – not to mention audiences – and done work which he could be rightly proud of. The fact that he did not have the looks of an Albert Finney or Richard Harris only made his achievements seem more impressive. He was receiving a substantial number of offers, most of which he turned down. As we shall see, this selectiveness was a trait which would remain constant throughout his career. Although Nicol was not yet famous, had very little money and no permanent home, his position was about to improve dramatically as a result of his association with both the Royal Court and Anthony Page.

George Devine had suffered a heart attack the previous October and taken three months off to recuperate. As the attack seemed likely to have been stress-related, when he returned his workload had to be lightened. He would retain his title as Artistic Director alongside Tony Richardson (who was at the time concentrating on his film career), but a third Artistic Director had to be found. The position was first offered to William Gaskill, who declined, and eventually taken by Anthony Page, with Lindsay Anderson acting as Associate Director. The arrangement was to run for one year from September 1964.

In April, John Osborne had completed a new play entitled *Inadmissible Evidence*. By this point, it went without saying that it would be staged by the Royal Court, the theatre where Osborne's game-changing *Look Back in Anger* had opened in 1956. Osborne had since proved himself a versatile, surprising and unquestionably talented playwright with *The Entertainer* (which had starred no less a personage than Laurence Olivier) and *Luther*, featuring Albert Finney – already a star after his role in the film version of Alan Sillitoe's novel *Saturday*

Night and Sunday Morning. The original productions of both of these subsequent plays had also been at the Royal Court. All three had transferred to the West End and, later, to Broadway. *Look Back* and *The Entertainer* had been made into successful films by their original director Tony Richardson, while Osborne had become a celebrity and a favourite of tabloid gossip columns. The term 'angry young man' was first used in reference to him, and his private life was a colourful one which never remained very private for long. For all of these reasons, a new play by Osborne was bound to receive a great deal of attention.

The direction of a new John Osborne play would traditionally have been the province of Tony Richardson, but as he was unavailable he asked Devine to direct. The protagonist of *Inadmissible Evidence* is Bill Maitland, a 39-year-old lawyer whose life is coming apart at the seams as he reaches the terrible realisation that nobody actually likes or needs him. The opening scene takes place in a courtroom with Maitland as a defendant accused of some vague sexual crime. This is soon revealed to be a dream and the scene segues into a typical morning at his office, in which the remainder of the play is set. Maitland cheats on his wife, has affairs with his secretaries, avoids his clients, drinks too much and rails against the state of the world. He cannot help contrasting the ideals and passions of his youth with the shabby reality that surrounds him and asking himself how he ever ended up as a second-rate lawyer representing clients whose pathetic tragedies disgust him so much that by this point he barely pretends to listen to them.

Osborne had created the character by combining a number of different inspirations. The initial spark had been lit by a letter he had read in a newspaper advice column in which a woman had spoken of how her husband appeared to be losing the affection of everyone around him despite having done nothing discernible to offend anyone. Maitland's skirt-chasing and sexual banter were characteristics which Osborne had observed in his own lawyer, Oscar Beuselinck, whereas the opening scene included a parody of Harold

Wilson's speech about the importance of technology at the previous year's Labour Party conference. There was also a good deal of Osborne himself present in the character, whose often amusing contempt for bank holiday day-trippers, politically-correct dinner party bores and sundry other types could have come straight out of Osborne's own mouth.

The role was an extremely challenging one for any actor – the character is in every single scene and has a great deal of dialogue, much of which is taken up by lengthy diatribes (often delivered in a deliberately disjointed style). The part also required an actor with the ability to switch convincingly between bullying sarcasm and self-loathing vulnerability. Indeed, the play focused almost entirely on its central character and whoever won the role would have to be on stage continually for three hours excluding the brief interval between Acts One and Two.

After Paul Scofield turned the part down, it had been offered to Peter Finch, who was taking some time to reach a decision. Meanwhile, Anthony Page had been told that he may be able to direct in place of Devine if Finch pulled out, so he gave a copy of the play to Nicol to read during a train journey. Nicol thought the play was brilliant and said to Page, 'I never want to see this again until I know if Finch is going to say yes or no.' [18] Finch, a big star at the time, would probably not have accepted the little-known Page as director, but he eventually decided not to play the part anyway, as he thought that it might tarnish his image. Page finally got the chance he had been waiting for. Since the disastrous *Live Like Pigs* in 1958 he had directed only one further play at the Court, *The Room*, which had formed half of a Harold Pinter double bill there with *The Dumb Waiter* in March 1960. The fact that he was entrusted with a new Osborne play is indicative of the extent to which his stock had risen as a result of his work both at Dundee and with the Royal Shakespeare Company. The selection of the lead was to be a joint decision between Page and Osborne. Page had Nicol in mind all along but was well aware that Osborne, Devine and Richardson may need some convincing. In fact, Tony Richardson is said to have sent a telegram from America saying 'Nicol Williamson terrible idea – nothing more than good rep actor.' Among the actors who auditioned were Nigel Davenport, Freddie Jones and Leonard Rossiter. As neither Page nor Osborne were satisfied with any of these, feeling that they had failed to bring Maitland to life, Nicol was given an audition on the 2nd of June 1964.

The theatre was being refurbished at the time and on the day of the audition all of the seats had been removed. Osborne was standing at the back of the stalls area waiting to be impressed. Nicol began. It soon became clear that he had the ability to express both the angst and the humour of the character in a way that none of the other actors who had auditioned had managed to do. As Nicol's performance progressed, Osborne found himself drawn as if by a magnet up to the very front of the stage where he watched, transfixed. Nevertheless, Nicol went through a period of anxiety which only ended when the three decided over dinner that he was by far the best option. Osborne told him, 'You bet your sweet life you've got it,' and, as Nicol later put it, 'the game was on.'

Around this time, Nicol had become friendly with Mark Boyle and Joan Hills, an artistic Scottish couple who worked at Jasper's Restaurant, where he often ate as it was situated conveniently behind the Royal Court. The couple had a flat at 114 Queen's Gate in South Kensington which they also used as a studio to create art in a wide variety of media. Nicol ended up staying with them and their two young children while learning his lines for *Inadmissible Evidence*. They were having trouble with their landlord, who wanted to evict them, and so were seeking the services of a lawyer. By pure coincidence, Michael White, a theatre impresario whom they knew, recommended Oscar Beuselinck. When they called at his office, Beuselinck proudly proclaimed that he had a lot of artistic clients, including John Osborne who, he said, had recently written a play based on him and his office. While staying with Boyle and Hills, Nicol also began visiting Beuselinck's office to help him prepare for the part of

Maitland. On the 27th of June, he took a break from learning his lines to attend the wedding reception of John Thaw and Sally Alexander, which took place at the house of the bride's father.

Not due to open at the Royal Court until September, *Inadmissible Evidence* was first to try out in Brighton, where it would open on the 13th of August at the Theatre Royal. Nicol had a little over two months between the audition and the first performance. Normally this would have been more than enough but, for a part of such magnitude, he needed it. Assisting Anthony Page on the production was Peter Gill, who, speaking over fifty years later, stressed the importance of Page in launching Nicol's career:

> It would be hard to exaggerate how much Nicol's success owed to Anthony's enthusiasm for his acting and his promotion of Nicol's talent all those years ago and for a long time after. His ability to nurse an actor through a leading part was particularly evident in *Inadmissible Evidence*. His obsession with Nicol's acting at the beginning was an extraordinary thing to witness, particularly the attention he lavished on Nicol's performance in that production.

Gill remembered Nicol as difficult to deal with during the rehearsal process:

> A different director would, I think, have found it very hard to cope. Anthony's previous experience with Nicol was vital to the success of the production. Nicol never found learning easy and Maitland was a big part. I remember going through it with him trying to get the lines into his head.
>
> Nicol was convinced he had a brain tumour throughout rehearsals. And I can remember on several occasions having to ring Russell Willett, who was a psychologist working at Maudsley hospital and married to Helen Montagu, the Court's casting director, for Nicol to see whoever he thought we should arrange for him to see, and it was clearly very real to Nicol with the consequence that he would put the heel of his hand to his temple during rehearsals, a gesture which he incorporated subconsciously into his performance.

Nobody had got the temperament of Osborne better than Nicol. Perhaps Robert Stephens in *George Dillon*, directed by Bill Gaskill or Victor Henry in a revival of *Look Back in Anger* directed by Page.

The part of Maitland's teenage daughter, Jane, was originally to be played by the 17-year-old Marianne Faithfull, who had recently had a hit with her single *As Tears Go By*. However, her manager, Tony Calder, considered it a bad career move as the part was a non-speaking one and the pay was very low, so Faithfull pulled out and was replaced by Natasha Pyne. The other cast members were Sheila Allen as Liz (Maitland's mistress), Ann Beach as Shirley (Maitland's secretary), Lois Daine as Joy (Maitland's receptionist), Clare Kelly as Maitland's three female clients, Arthur Lowe as Hudson (Maitland's head clerk) and John Quentin, who played the double part of Maitland's junior clerk Jones and Maples (a client). Speaking over fifty years later, Ann Beach recalled her experience of working with Nicol:

> I have to admit that I was warned that he was not easy to work with, and I thought at the time, 'Fair enough – that's okay.' I mean, often very, very clever, devoted actors do appear as if they're difficult to work with, but they're trying to get to grips with the part they're playing, and it was a *very* difficult part he had. But we got on fine. We didn't socialise all that much. I didn't keep in touch with him but we weren't unfriendly, we got on and I was playing a very feisty part, so if there was any mucking about I could jolly well go at him!

Aware of the enormity of the part he had to learn and the stress he was under, the other actors generally gave Nicol plenty of space and were tolerant of any outbursts.

When the play opened at the Royal Court, many critics hated it. They were offended that a three-hour play had been devoted to such an 'unsympathetic' character and derided what they saw as its lack of plot and structure and the self-indulgence of its author. However, such a strongly negative reaction was no doubt better for the box office than cool indifference would have been, and the play would be one of the Court's most successful productions, selling 98% of seats and taking £11,890 at the box office against production costs of £3,003. Nicol's performance was praised even by those critics who had not been convinced by the play. However, one reviewer who did come out in its favour was Harold Hobson of *The Sunday Times*. Never afraid to go against the grain, he championed it as Osborne's best play. He was also especially complimentary about Nicol, calling his performance a 'sensational achievement.'

A few days after the opening, a half-page article about Nicol by Helen Mason appeared in *The Sunday Telegraph* revealing that, although the play had made him a star overnight and he was already being stopped in the street by gaping fans, Nicol was still in debt to the tune of over £1,000. In an interview with Mason, he also spoke about the psychological pressures of undertaking such a role, saying he would never be the same again and that he felt he could easily end up like Maitland, the thought of which he found sickening. Although it would be a gross simplification to say that Nicol was essentially playing himself as Maitland, it is certainly the case that he shared some of Maitland's characteristics to some extent – namely, the drinking, the paranoia and the hypochondria (on having a pain in his thumb, Maitland immediately jumps to the conclusion that it must be cancer). When Nicol complained in the same interview of first night audiences, 'with their fur stoles, and their boxes of chocolates, coming to the theatre because they think it's how the gentry behave,' he sounded just like Maitland – or, indeed, Osborne.

As the run continued, the actors, encouraged by the full house and the response the play had provoked, became increasingly confident and began to 'fly.' Nicol had a vivid memory of one such performance towards the end of the run:

> … the lights went down and we all went to the front of the stage. There would usually be applause from the audience. This time we clomped, you could hear the *clomp, clomp, clomp* of all these people's shoes as they walked to the front of the stage. Nothing. And we stood in line, bowed three times quickly. Nothing. And we walked off the stage, *clomp, clomp,*

clomp. And we'd been off the stage about four seconds when the audience started to applaud. And the stage manager said to me, 'Quick – get back on!' And I said, 'No, that's theatre history – I'm not going back out there! *You* don't know what's just happened but *I* do!' [19]

After forty performances – there were matinees twice a week – the play closed on the 10th of October, but plans were rapidly being hatched for a West End transfer.

Much has been made of Nicol supposedly being too young for the part but he turned 28 during its original run and an extra eleven years is, in the history of acting, barely worthy of comment. What is more impressive is that he won the role over the heads of more famous and superficially-suitable actors, that it was one of the longest parts ever written and that his portrayal proved so definitive that it was many years until the play would be revived with another actor.

Incredibly, while playing Maitland in the evenings, Nicol was also shooting a film during the day. *The Day of Ragnarok* was a 50-minute piece John McGrath was making for BBC2 for a series of six films simply entitled *Six*. McGrath's wife Elizabeth MacLennan was also in the film, as was Pauline Boty, a 26-year-old British pop artist (and peer of Peter Blake and David Hockney) who also dabbled in acting. Some of Boty's paintings were used in the film and Nicol was cast as her lover. The other main female character was played by Tamara Hinchco, who was at the time married to David Andrews. She had been with her husband when he had appeared in *Death of a Salesman* at Dundee and remembered Nicol from that experience as being 'very ambitious and a man in a hurry', but recalled that during the time of *Ragnarok* he 'seemed very calm and easy to work with.' This may be surprising considering the daunting task of playing Maitland night after night, but Nicol was highly confident in his abilities as an actor in these early days and much of the stress had diminished after opening night. He also apparently got on very well with Boty, with whom he had a passionate love scene and shared a sense of humour. She had recently married the literary agent Clive Goodwin so, despite her famously Bardot-esque looks, her relationship with Nicol remained a platonic one. Boty was diagnosed with cancer the following year while expecting her first child. She refused chemotherapy as it would have been potentially harmful to the baby and died at the age of 28 a few months after giving birth.

Depicting a world where nuclear war is about to break out, *The Day of Ragnarok* is almost entirely without dialogue, and McGrath's oblique approach was not to everyone's taste. One disturbing scene featured close-ups of a number of deformed foetuses in jars, the point of which was presumably to illustrate the doubts that many women were experiencing at the time about the wisdom of having children with the threat of nuclear war looming. The unnamed characters played by Nicol and Boty are killed at the end, repeatedly impaled with wooden stakes by McLennan and Hinchco in Holland Park because (as Hinchco put it) 'they wanted all the women to withhold their sexual favours until men stopped going to war', although the meaning of much of McGrath's film was probably less clear to audiences. However, it was certainly well-shot and featured a striking modernist score by composer Dudley Moore, better known for his association with Peter Cook. Reviewing *The Day of Ragnarok* for *Films and Filming* after it had been screened at the 8th London Film Festival, critic David Holland was scathing:

> Supposedly an allegory of war told in Lesbian terms (!) I think I can safely say it's the worst film I've had the misfortune to see. Obscure, pretentious, badly directed and as dull as ditch-water...
>
> ... Nicol Williamson – how did an actor of such talent and integrity manage to get himself involved in such meaningless drivel?

One of Nicol's great strengths as an actor was his ability to deliver difficult dialogue, so his decision to accept a rare non-speaking role in *Ragnarok* may have been influenced by the fact that he was playing such a wordy role in the evenings. As it was the second time Nicol had worked from a John McGrath script and the third time he had worked with McLennan, it might also be assumed that he did it largely out of loyalty.

Chapter 6 – The Nothingness in the Little Eden Afternoon

The new season at the Royal Court which had opened with *Inadmissible Evidence* was originally to have been under the joint artistic direction of both Anthony Page and Lindsay Anderson. However, before the season had begun, the two had had a disagreement over the casting of the play which was to follow *Inadmissible Evidence*, a revival of Ben Travers' *A Cuckoo in the Nest*, one of the 'Aldwych farces' first presented by Tom Walls at the Aldwych Theatre in the 1920s. Anderson had thought that Daniel Massey was the most suitable actor to play the lead but Page had insisted on casting Nicol in the part originally played by Ralph Lynn, an actor who specialized in such roles. Anderson thought that this showed 'a lack of collaborative spirit' and quit, although he had agreed to remain as director for the third play in the season, *Julius Caesar*, with Nicol as Brutus. Nicol later recalled it as 'the season when Page wanted me to do *Hamlet* and Lindsay Anderson rushed forward and said, "No – I'm doing it with Richard Harris!"[20] In an acerbic aside, Page commented that in that case they should change the title to *Hamalot*. Harris never did play Hamlet and Nicol would have to wait another five years. The fourth play was to be a new adaptation of *Great Expectations*, again with Nicol, although as this was abandoned, it is uncertain whether he was going to reprise his role as Joe Gargery, as he could equally well have played the escaped convict Magwitch. The fifth proposed play was an eccentric new comedy by David Storey, author of the novel *This Sporting Life*. Lindsay Anderson had suggested it with the intention of casting Nicol in the lead, but this too would never happen, although the play would become *The Restoration of Arnold Middleton* and be well-received when it opened a couple of years later with another actor.

A Cuckoo in the Nest was a very old-fashioned farce which had not been revived in London since before the war and was, therefore, a surprising choice for the Court at this time. It seems likely that Page was keen to give his loose company of actors an opportunity to do something light after the draining intensity of *Inadmissible Evidence*. The most interesting aspect of *Cuckoo* was the cast: Nicol played Peter Wykeham and Rosalind Knight his fiancée, while Ann Beach was the woman he gets mixed up with. Her father was played by Arthur Lowe and her husband by none other than John Osborne who, it is often forgotten, had begun his theatrical career as an actor. Also appearing were Beatrix Lehmann as the landlady and Alan Bennett as the vicar.

Nicol was cast as the 'silly ass' who predictably loses his trousers, and in this case Page's pushing of Nicol did the actor few favours. Ann Beach later said, 'I never felt he was quite right in it or very happy in it.' Peter Gill concurred, saying,

> That was the only time that I saw Nicol be really terrible. It couldn't have been a piece of work less suited to Anthony and he. Arthur Lowe, on the other hand, was terribly funny in it and caught perfectly the style of the piece… Nicol was a fine comic actor in other circumstances. In this case the art of farce eluded him. He couldn't find the lightness of touch and balance to temper any realism needed for the play. The character Nicol played is forced, by circumstance, to sleep on the floor of his fiancées bedroom. But he made the discomfort so acute that you couldn't laugh at him.

Alan Bennett has also gone on record with similar comments regarding Nicol's performance, but a close look at the newspaper reviews reveals that not everybody shared this viewpoint. After the play opened on the 13th of October, Nicol found a surprising number of defenders among the critics and he received good reviews in the *Daily Express*, the *Evening Standard*, the *Daily Mirror*, *The Sun*, the *Financial Times*, the *Yorkshire Post*, the *Northern Echo*, the *Birmingham Post* and the *Glasgow Herald*, whose critic believed it was 'his absolute seriousness which becomes the very thing which keeps the plot funny'. However, his approach clearly did not fit well with most people's expectations of such light material and *The Sunday Telegraph* echoed Gill, saying that the farce melted 'like an ice-cream under his blow torch.' Meanwhile, the *New Statesman* implied that Nicol's background may have shaped his performance, which their critic found to be a 'harshly funny' caricature of a self-pitying 'public-school oaf.' *A Cuckoo in the Nest* closed mid-November after 36 performances. Although only 45% of seats had been sold, it scraped a profit, having cost £3, 629 and taken £4, 727 at the box office.

The Court's next play was to be a very troubled production. Lindsay Anderson had decided to use Richard Harris, the star of his film *This Sporting Life*, instead of Nicol, who had been the original choice. However, Harris and Anderson's relationship was a complicated one as the director was in love with his heterosexual star. Harris became uncomfortable with the situation and quit, at which point Nicol re-entered the picture, but director and actor did not see eye to eye and Nicol also left, later saying of the experience, 'It was hellish... everyone had rubber clothes on... the set looked like it had been given away with a box of Shreddies!'[21] A theatre spokesperson diplomatically told the press that his departure was due to illness, and fellow Scot Ian Bannen took over. Bannen, like Nicol, was from Lanarkshire and, although he was eight years older, the two were quite friendly.

Nicol later said that Anthony Page had approached him in the pub next to the theatre to speak about the *Julius Caesar* crisis, which had thrown the company into a state of uncertainty. During the course of the conversation, Nicol found himself suggesting they do *Waiting for Godot*, which Page thought to be an excellent idea. He cancelled *Great Expectations* and began preparing to stage *Godot* as the Court's next production, even securing the participation of Samuel Beckett himself. Nicol would later recall how, during an early rehearsal, Beckett had stopped the actors early on and 'revealed the secret' of the play, which was that 'Vladimir is always moving, Estragon never moves.' Beckett was also not initially pleased with Nicol as Vladimir, feeling that his voice was wrong for the character. Nicol had long ago lost his original Scottish accent and learned to suppress the later Brummie influence which had crept into his voice in favour of a style closer to the clear, clipped Received Pronunciation (RP) which was preferred both by the theatrical establishment and the BBC. At the time, although regional characters who were more than mere comic stereotypes were beginning to appear in theatre and film in the wake of *Look Back in Anger*, it was still the case that an actor who stuck with their regional or working-class accent would find precious few leading roles coming their way. There were one or two exceptions, such as Tom Courtenay and Michael Caine, although even they would have to 'posh up' their voices on occasion, as Courtenay did for *Doctor Zhivago* and Caine for *Zulu*. Most actors needed to speak RP when a part demanded it if they wanted their career to develop. Brummie accents in particular were held in low esteem, a phenomenon which the linguist David Crystal has attributed largely to a popular radio show of the 1950s, *Educating Archie*, which featured a slow-witted character known as Marlene, the 'Pride of the Midlands', portrayed by Beryl Reid with a caricature of a Brummie accent.

On learning that Nicol was originally from Scotland, Beckett encouraged him to play Vladimir with a Scots accent. It seems likely that Beckett believed he was getting Nicol's 'real' voice, but what he was actually hearing was the flawless imitation of an accent which had long ceased to be Nicol's natural one. The result pleased Beckett immensely but, according to Page, Nicol suffered 'a kind of breakdown' during rehearsals and again disappeared for two days. However, when he returned he had come up with a highly individual performance and he looked striking in costume with his unkempt hair and beard, dressed in a bowler hat, striped baggy trousers, a loose tie with a busted collar and a moth-eaten coat. He made quite an impression on Beckett, who felt that he possessed a 'touch of genius'. Nicol also had a great deal of respect for the playwright and the two became friends. He described Beckett around this time as 'a saintly cockatoo, a great pale bird, a breathing saint.' The remainder of the cast were comprised of Alfred Lynch as Estragon, Jack

MacGowran as Lucky, Paul Curran as Pozzo and Kirk Martin as The Boy.

As the year drew to a close, Nicol found he had made a paltry total income for 1964 of about £700[22] and was £1,500 in debt, but he was otherwise in an enviable position. *Godot* opened on the 30th of December to mostly rave reviews and proved so popular that it was held over for an additional three weeks, finally closing on the 27th of February 1965 after running for 69 performances. It had taken £14,856 against production costs of only £2,164. For Nicol, it provided the convincer he needed to follow *Inadmissible Evidence*. Harold Hobson's review was devoted almost entirely to lauding Nicol's performance, while Michael Ratcliffe – also writing for the *Sunday Times* – found that, '... besides being brilliantly funny, limbs flailing all ways, he also brings off the lullaby and the puzzled cries of pain most movingly. He is frantic hope defined.' Nicol was not an actor whose reputation was based on movement, but as Vladimir his performance was very physical and, despite the odd naysayer, it received an enormous amount of praise. Ronald Bryden of the *New Statesman* even went so far as to say that he had 'a scarecrow grace which brings to mind Chaplin.' But it was perhaps Nicol's soul-chilling screamed delivery of the line 'I can't go on!' which remained the most memorable moment for many in the audience.

During the run of *Godot*, Nicol's portrayal of Bill Maitland was voted Performance of the Year in the annual poll of theatre critics conducted by *Plays and Players* magazine. Laurence Olivier's Othello came second. He also won the *Evening Standard* award for Best Actor of 1964, which he accepted at a luncheon at the Savoy Hotel. Film offers had started to come in, but Nicol was turning everything down in order to take *Inadmissible Evidence* to the West End, although he did find time to appear on an episode of the BBC arts show *Monitor*, broadcast on the 23rd of February.

One intriguing side project Nicol had embarked upon at this time was a new adaptation of Frank Wedekind's 'Lulu' plays, *Earth Spirit* and *Pandora's Box*. These had been the basis for GW Pabst's silent film, *Pandora's Box*, starring Louise Brooks, as well as an acclaimed opera by Alban Berg. The plays depict the rise and fall of Lulu, a young dancer who is lusted after by a variety of men and women with the result that she experiences the highs and lows of society before coming to an untimely death in London at the hands of Jack the Ripper. Nicol knew little German and was therefore collaborating with a translator. Presumably, he had become interested in Wedekind as a result of his participation in the Sunday night production of *Spring Awakening* at the Royal Court. Nicol described the play as being about 'sex, strength, weakness, greed and selfishness.' The intention was to condense the two original plays into one and stage it at the Royal Court. Peter Gill remembered that 'Jeanne Moreau was proposed for Lulu, but I don't think anybody but Anthony [Page] and Nicol believed that it was really going to happen.' Unfortunately, Nicol discovered that he would be unable to proceed with the play until the copyright expired four years later, so he was never to finish the adaptation and it became another project which fell by the wayside.

The new production of *Inadmissible Evidence* opened in Brighton on the 8th of March for a one week try-out before opening in the West End at Wyndham's on Charing Cross Road on the 17th. Wyndham's could accommodate around 300 more patrons than the Royal Court had been able to. Nicol was being paid £200 a week. Although it was not comparable to what he might have received from film work, it was considerably more than his Royal Court salary had been and would enable him to finally pay off his debts.

Ann Beach and Clare Kelly returned from the original cast. John Quentin was replaced by John Hurt as Jones / Maples, Arthur Lowe by Cyril Raymond as Hudson, Sheila Allen by Eleanor Fazan as Liz, Lois Daine by Coral Atkins as Joy and Natasha Pyne by Imogen Graham as Jane. Anthony Page was again the director. The production was highly successful – surprising, perhaps, for such an uncomfortable play, but there was little doubt that the main attraction was the virtuoso lead performance. Indeed, a few weeks after it opened, *Variety* stated that Nicol's performance had become 'as big a London box-office draw as Laurence Olivier's *Othello*.' Meanwhile, Alan Brien of *The Sunday Telegraph* doubted 'whether any new actor in the West End can have made such an impact since the young [Charles] Laughton' over thirty years previously. However, the pressure Nicol felt himself to be under became all too obvious on a number of occasions.

During the evening performance of the 19th of March, Nicol suddenly stopped and addressed the audience, saying, 'I'm sorry, but I can't go on. We've been working very hard and I'm not prepared to give a 75% performance. You'll get your money back.' He then walked off. After a few minutes, the stage manager came out to ask the audience to wait and, ten minutes after that, Nicol reappeared and finished the performance. It was the first time Nicol stopped a play and walked off, but it was not to be the last and while on this occasion there were no serious consequences, such would not always be the case. The high standards he set himself were undoubtedly part of the cause, as was his professional pride, which meant that he would rather walk off than have people say he had given a second-rate performance. Unfortunately, walking off was to become a habit, a sort of safety valve he would use when he was in trouble and one which would understandably make producers nervous.

On the 6th of May, Nicol was distracted a few minutes into the play by a group of noisy latecomers. He walked to the front of the stage and addressed the audience, saying, 'I'm not prepared to continue until everyone is settled. The noise is upsetting my performance and spoiling your enjoyment.' This was a highly unusual thing for an actor to do no matter who they were, but in this case it worked and, when the curtain rose again a few minutes later, the audience were on their best behaviour.

Two weeks later, another performance was interrupted when Nicol, convinced he was having a heart attack, staggered off stage clutching his chest. His understudy was Arthur Cox, who cast member Coral Atkins later recalled as 'trembling every night in the dressing room wondering whether he was going to have to go on or not!'[23] Cox took over for twenty minutes, after which Nicol felt sufficiently recovered to be able to continue. At the end of the performance, he again walked to the front of the stage and spoke to the audience, this time offering to refund their money. Fortunately, nobody took him up on it and he then told the audience that the management were overworking him and 'behaving like a second-rate Mikado with a whip'. Nicol's agent, Peter Crouch, explained to the press the following day that his client had requested the Wednesday matinee performances be dropped three weeks previously as they were tiring him out. The management had agreed, but had not cancelled the matinees immediately due to the number of tickets they had already sold. Nicol thought they were being too slow to do so, and his curtain speech had the desired effect of speeding up the process.

During the Wyndham's run, Nicol was rising at around midday in his Kensington flat, then visiting a nearby pub for lunch and a pint before making his way to his dressing room at the theatre, where he would sleep on a sofa until shortly before performance time. Afterwards, he would go alone to a restaurant until about 2 a.m. before returning home. He was careful to conserve his energy as he considered each performance the equivalent of a 15 mile hike. The result was that his life was a lonely one at this time and he suffered from insomnia.

Despite the pressure, Nicol managed to put in a couple of other appearances during the run. One of these was on the ABC television arts show *Tempo* in an episode entitled *Look Back at Tomorrow*, which featured Nicol and George Devine performing excerpts from a number of Osborne plays, including *Look Back in Anger*, *The Entertainer*, *Luther* and *Inadmissible Evidence*. The programme was broadcast on the 4th of April.

Another was a Sunday night production at the Royal Court of *Miniatures*, a first play by David Cregan. Set in the staffroom of a modern comprehensive school, it was directed by Donald Howarth.

Nicol led the cast as Joe Johnson, a kleptomaniac music teacher who makes a bungled suicide attempt. Peter Gill remembered:

> Mary MacLeod was in it. Nicol had been in college with her in Birmingham. It was he I think introduced her to the Court. It was a very enjoyable evening partly because the headmaster was played by George Devine and the rebellious teacher was Lindsay [Anderson].

The other cast members were Graham Crowden, Bryan Pringle, Roddy Maude-Roxby, Miriam Brickman and Jane Birkin, a then-unknown 18-year-old making her debut as a sixth form girl and apparently arousing a lot of interest from the male members of the cast. Bernard Levin, reviewing it in *The Daily Mail*, singled out 'another of Mr Williamson's wildly gangling, shambling performances'.

Nicol had Sundays off while appearing at Wyndham's and this enabled him to take part in another one-off event. T.S. Eliot had died in January and a tribute night, *Homage to T.S. Eliot*, had been organised for the 13th of June at The Globe Theatre.[24] Among those reading Eliot's poems were Paul Scofield, Laurence Olivier, Peter O'Toole, Ian Richardson, George Devine, Alec McCowen and Groucho Marx. Nicol was to play the title role in Eliot's unfinished verse drama *Sweeney Agonistes* and also to read *The Hollow Men*. He consulted Lindsay Anderson for guidance on the latter, an occasion which Anderson recorded in his diary. He wrote of his dismay that Nicol had taken the opportunity during his visit to belittle the abilities of a number of his fellow actors, including Alfred Lynch and Tom Courtenay, and to say that he 'saw through' Anthony Page and Tony Richardson.

Sweeney Agonistes was directed by Peter Wood with some colourful projections by Bridget Riley and jazz music by Johnny Dankworth, whose wife Cleo Laine also appeared, along with Anna Quayle, Roddy Maude-Roxby, Bernard Cribbins, Clive Revill, Alec McCowen and John Le Mesurier. The character of Sweeney appears at a small party in the flat of two young women. Sweeney says he would like to take Doris to a 'cannibal island', make her into a stew and gobble her up. She takes this as a flirtatious joke, but later becomes disturbed when Sweeney starts talking about a man he once knew who 'did a girl in'. Nicol's Sweeney, comic and sinister by turns, partly sung and partly spoken in his inimitably nasal, rapid-fire style, was widely felt to be one of the two highlights of the evening, the other being Groucho's reading of *Gus the Theatre Cat*.

Nicol was also asked to participate in *An Evening of Samuel Beckett*, which would take place on Sunday the 22nd of August as part of the Stratford-upon-Avon Poetry Festival. The invitation came from Beckett's publisher, John Calder, who had been present during rehearsals of *Godot* at the Royal Court. Nicol was keen, but only if he could get some direction from Beckett himself, who was then living in Ussy in northern France. He decided to cancel his performance of *Inadmissible Evidence* on Saturday the 14th and hand over to his understudy so that he could visit Beckett. The trip turned out to be an influential one for Nicol and he was so affected by it that he later wrote a 6,000 word piece about the experience.

Nicol flew to Paris and then had to endure a long car journey out to Beckett's secluded home with Calder at the wheel. On arrival, a quick tour of Beckett's house filled Nicol with consternation as he found it austere to the point of perversity, a comfortless cell in which relaxation was impossible. For lunch, Beckett served up a mouldy loaf of bread, after which he (in Nicol's words)

> ... returned with a book, which he placed on the table. 'This is something that I particularly want you to do, Nick.' It was the very end of *How It Is*, a favourite of his own, and he wished to demonstrate himself the attitude and the manner in which he felt it would be best performed. 'This is how it should be done,' he said and, taking up the book, he began to read at once almost in a drone, a faithless, clicking incant, a cheated, contemptuous, tired accusation running through the chant, which made it fascinating, riveting... The voice ran on, acknowledging the nothingness in the little Eden afternoon... [A] grim endorsement of the sentence of death forever...[25]

After this bizarre lunch, Beckett drove them out to visit his friend, Henri Hyden, an 81-year-old painter. Nicol insisted they stop at a pub on the way so that he could neck a few pints of beer in order to quell the existential angst he was feeling as a result of Beckett's performance. When they finally arrived, they had dinner with Hyden and a few other guests, after which Beckett coaxed Nicol into making use of the piano. Meanwhile, the wine continued to flow and at one point Beckett placed his hand on Nicol's shoulders and said 'I love ye, Nick... I want ye to know that I really love ye.' In his own words, Nicol felt 'euphoric' on hearing this, but was later shocked when they went out to the garden and Beckett deliberately trampled on his host's flowers.

Beckett's reading of *How It Is* struck a deep chord with Nicol. The fear, not of death *per se*, but the death of the ego, the knowledge of a future state of non-existence, is something that would trouble him throughout his life. *How It Is* became a piece he would frequently perform in the future to stunning effect.

After returning to London, Nicol disappeared for a week and Arthur Cox had to play Maitland. He then turned up at John Calder's flat to rehearse the day before the Beckett evening. In addition to *How It Is*, the evening would also feature extracts from *Godot*, *Endgame*, *Watt*, *Molloy* and *The Unnamable*, many of which would be performed as a duo with the Irish actor Patrick Magee, another favourite of Beckett's. However, although Nicol was a huge hit with the audience, he did not entirely stick to the plan. This made life difficult for Magee, who swore he would never work with him again.

Nicol continued to play Maitland at Wyndham's until around the end of September, after which he was replaced by Alan Dobie. He then took a few weeks holiday before he began preparing for the play's Broadway run.

At some point in 1965, Nicol had become the subject of a black and white portrait taken outside his Kensington flat by the famous photographer Bill Brandt. The photograph shows an unsmiling, shadowy-featured Nicol in the foreground, his eyes two black pools, with a lock of hair flopping down over his furrowed brow. The use of light and monochrome made it appear that he had dark hair greying at the sides and front, with the result that it almost looks like someone else.

Chapter 7 - Broadway Bound

According to a *Daily Mail* article dated the 15th of July 1965, Nicol was adamant that 'he would go [to Broadway] on the best terms offered to a British actor for a straight play in the past ten years. Or he wouldn't go at all...' This seems uncharacteristically venal, but it is possible that Nicol priced himself high because he would have been secretly relieved if his terms were not met. After all, he had just played Maitland for six months in the West End so it was no wonder that he had doubts about the wisdom of committing to a further six months in the States. On the other hand, he believed passionately in the play and felt understandably territorial about the part, believing that, 'What Jason Robards was to O'Neill, I am to Beckett and Osborne.' In any case, Nicol must have been satisfied with the terms he was offered as the production went ahead.

Anthony Page was again the director and was accompanied by the Royal Court's costumer and scenic designer, Jocelyn Herbert. The producer was David Merrick, a 54-year-old former lawyer from Missouri turned impresario, who had previously produced John Osborne's *Look Back in Anger*, *The Entertainer*, *An Epitaph for George Dillon* and *Luther* on Broadway. Apart from Nicol, the Broadway cast were new with the exception of Lois Daine, who had also played Joy in the original Royal Court production. Peter Sallis was cast as Hudson; he later became very famous in the UK both for his portrayal of Clegg in the long-running television comedy *Last of the Summer Wine* and for providing the voice of the cheese-loving inventor Wallace of *Wallace and Gromit*. However, most significant from Nicol's point of view was the casting of the young actress who was to play Jane Maitland.

Jill Townsend was a 20-year-old Californian from a wealthy family whose father, Robert Townsend, had recently been CEO of the car rental company, Avis. Jill had spent two years in London at RADA but her role as Bill Maitland's daughter in *Inadmissible Evidence* would be her first professional job. Her agent was Lionel Larner, an Englishman who had been a casting director for the BBC before coming to New York and forging a career as an agent. Larner thought the part a fairly thankless one as, not only was it a non-speaking role, but Jill would be sitting in a chair with her back to the audience most of the time. He managed to persuade the producers to turn the chair around so that she would at least be seen if not heard. Larner, who was soon to become Nicol's agent in the USA as well, later recalled, 'Jill had the perfect look for the swingin' sixties, Carnaby Street time. She had that Susan George look, the blonde fringe, she was adorable. I could see anyone falling in love with her.' Jill was blue-eyed and petite, nearly a foot shorter than Nicol. Speaking over 50 years later, she remembered how their relationship began:

> I met Nicol in New York when I went in for the audition at the Belasco Theatre. We started rehearsing there before having our out of town opening in Philadelphia. He had a huge presence and one that I really didn't quite understand, having been to an all-girls boarding school and then off to RADA in England and then back to New York. All of a sudden this larger than life character was in my life.
>
> He asked me out straight away. I was so sheltered that, if ever I went out, I would just order a bowl of spaghetti and a glass of milk. He took me to an Indian restaurant in New York City – I'd never had Indian food before – and he treated me to lime pickle, saying, 'This isn't spicy – trust me!' So I said, 'Well, it'll be hard to trust you for a very long time after that one!'

The play tried out at the Forrest Theatre in Philadelphia, where it opened on the 9th of November. It was a much bigger venue than either Nicol or Page were used to, with a seating capacity of over 1,800. The opening night performance went smoothly enough, but trouble was brewing backstage. David Merrick felt the play was too long – an observation which had been made by a number of critics in London. Merrick announced to Osborne and Page that he wanted cuts to be made. Osborne's profitable association with Merrick meant that he had no desire to alienate his producer and so he raised no objection, or at least not a strong one. Page, on the other hand, refused to cut any of it. Merrick – by all accounts something of a tyrant used to getting his own way – told Page that if he would not cut the play, he would be replaced. At this point, Nicol, also present, said that Merrick would also need to find another actor to play Maitland if he fired Page. The situation then escalated with the result that Nicol threw his glass of Budweiser in Merrick's face and socked him on the jaw. Nicol later said that he was trying to emulate José Ferrer at the end of *The Caine Mutiny* when he contemptuously empties his drink over Fred McMurray. In some versions, Nicol picked the producer up and put him in a dustbin, even rolling the begarbaged Merrick around in it, but this is certainly an exaggeration, although it may be that Merrick collided with a dustbin after receiving the blow. In any case, shortly after punching one of the most powerful figures in American entertainment, Nicol said he was returning to London and left the theatre, with Merrick's threat that he would never work again ringing in his ears. The incident became an instant legend.

The next day, the parties concerned had calmed down somewhat. Nicol was found at the railway station in the morning about to go to New York and then fly home. He was persuaded to return to the theatre and there was an uneasy reconciliation. Page was retained and the cuts were made after all. Jill had not been present during the contretemps as she had already left to drive back to her parents' place on Long Island, but she thought that the press attention given to Nicol as a result was to have an unfortunate lasting effect:

> It changed a lot, because after the incident the press came out with the 'hellraiser' and lumped him with Richard Burton and Peter O'Toole. I wondered if this was something that Nicol would feel he had to live up to or if he would be able to get over it.

Jill also recalled that David Merrick 'never came around again' and 'wasn't going to do anything to help the play.' Nevertheless, theatres had been booked, tickets had been sold and Merrick was committed, so the run continued as planned, closing at the Forrest on the 27th of November before opening on the 30th at the Belasco Theatre on Broadway after one preview the night before.

The Forrest had been a big theatre to fill, but the new venue had a more manageable seating capacity of around 1,000. There were matinees twice a week, but these were played by Nicol's understudy, James Patterson. *Inadmissible Evidence* was not the smash hit in New York that it had been in London and it was perhaps to be expected that a culture obsessed with success would not take so kindly to staring failure in the face for three hours. Despite this, Nicol's performance was as talked about as ever and it was by no means a complete flop. However, Merrick used the disappointing box office returns to justify giving everyone a 30% pay cut – 'part of Merrick's revenge' according to Jill Townsend. Nicol only agreed to the reduction with great reluctance at the urging of Page.

Meanwhile, Nicol and Jill moved in together. Jill Townsend:

> This was a huge thing because I was hiding it from my parents. They were very old-fashioned and very strict with me. We lived at the Gorham Hotel[26] in New York so, to me, this was now, 'I'm a woman and I'm living in sin!' But I just loved Nicol, I really did.

Peter Sallis was a great admirer of Nicol's talent and, according to Jill Townsend, 'they had a similar sense of humour and there was always something going on onstage which the audience wasn't aware of' with which they amused one another. Both actors also had a taste for Dixieland jazz. Sallis had already been living in New York prior to *Inadmissible Evidence* as he had been appearing in another play there, so he was familiar with many of the city's jazz spots. One night, he took Nicol to a jazz bar called Jimmy Ryan's on West 54th Street. [27] Nicol sang a couple of songs and received an enthusiastic response from audience and musicians alike. He fell in love with the place and it became his favourite hangout whenever he was in New York until its closure in 1983. On arrival, he would be warmly greeted by an eccentric figure sitting outside wearing an official-looking cap. This was Gilbert J. Pincus, who had been the club's self-appointed doorman since 1942. Known as the 'Mayor of 52nd Street', he was one of New York's famous characters until he was killed by a truck on his way to the club in 1980.

In mid-January Nicol left the play temporarily and his understudy went on. The reasons for his absence are unclear but it seems that he returned to London during this time as he was present at the funeral of George Devine, which took place in Golders Green, with Samuel Beckett also in attendance. He later wrote the following poem about the occasion:

Samuel Beckett - The Signal Red Man

How well I remember the signal red man
He danced with me once when the springtime began
As we reeled in a polka, his streaming scarf ran
Like a long, scarlet ribbon of blood

I ran into him at Golders Green once at nine
In the hushed crematorium he made a beeline
To stand stiffly beside me wrapped up in his wine-
Coloured scarf, a dark ribbon of blood

To those staring at him he gave not a sign
As his gaze fastened onto the casket of pine
Which obscured the dead body of old George Devine
And in silent observance we stood.

'De ye smell anything Nick?' he breathed in quiet talk
I said, 'No – like what?' and with the eyes of a hawk
He cocked his head sideways and whispered, 'Like pork.'
It sounds crazy, but I understood.

The last time we met: 'Nick, de ye still feel the same?'
I said yes. 'Ego-death makes a mockery of fame.'
He smiled, 'Still, we're obliged to express all the same.'
And we stood, two odd brothers in blood.

For reasons now unclear, *Inadmissible Evidence* closed at the Belasco on the 5th of February and transferred two days later to the larger Shubert Theatre, a little further along the same street. A few cast changes were made, with Christine Pickles taking over as Shirley, Susan Tabor as Joy and John Harkins as Nicol's understudy. It ran until the 23rd of April, breaking even after a total of 166 Broadway performances. Nicol departed two weeks before it closed, leaving Harkins to step in. Jill Townsend also left the production early in order to appear in a film, but shortly before doing so she had received an unwelcome surprise, as she later recalled:

> One morning Nicol said to me his girlfriend from London was coming so I would have to move out. I was heartbroken. His girlfriend's name was Ruth Myers. She was a costume designer, so they must have met on a production somewhere. A lovely woman, yet I didn't know he had been going out with anybody and when we first met he had told me, 'I knew the moment I saw you from the wings of the theatre when you came into audition that that's the woman I'm going to marry.'

The New York critics' response to Nicol's portrayal of Maitland was largely as positive as it had been in London, with *Time* magazine calling it 'the most bravura performance by a newcomer that Broadway has seen in over a decade'. On the 8th of June he won his third award, the Whitbread Anglo-American Award for Best Actor. He was also nominated for a Tony award, but lost out to Hal Holbrook, who won for his performance in the title role of *Mark Twain Tonight*.

Although it had been a triumph for Nicol, he learned from the experience that long runs were not for him. What he enjoyed most was the anticipatory phase of rehearsals, previews and opening nights – once these had passed he found it an effort to sustain his interest.

He swore he would never commit to such a long run again and, with one exception, proved true to his word, although such would not always be the case, as he also told a reporter at the time that he had no wish to ever play Hamlet as 'Any no-talent bum can do that part and get away with it.'[28]

It was natural that, when Nicol returned to London, he would want to take a break before resuming his acting career. However, his break turned into rather a long one, the reasons for which are obscure. He had not made his fortune on Broadway, although he had probably saved enough not to have any immediate worries. It is likely that many of the parts offered to him seemed lacklustre in comparison to Maitland, and certainly he and Page were determined to make a film of *Inadmissible Evidence*. He appears to have decided that his official feature film debut would be in the role which had made him famous. It was around this time that he was approached by the American actor Mel Ferrer, who was producing a film version of the hit play *Wait Until Dark* as a vehicle for his then wife, Audrey Hepburn. She would star as a blind woman terrorised in her apartment by a trio of villains who are later revealed to be one person. Nicol was offered the three-roles-in-one part of the master criminal, but rejected it because he was too obsessed at the time with putting Maitland on film to become excited about anything else. He would later regret this decision as *Wait Until Dark* became a highly successful film and did wonders for the career of actor Alan Arkin.

Nicol made an appearance at the Old Vic on the 13th of June performing extracts from *Inadmissible Evidence* with Jill Townsend (in town for a short visit) as part of a gala to raise money for the George Devine Award for new playwrights. Jill enjoyed chatting with Noël Coward during the course of the evening – he had known her grandfather, Frank Tours, a composer and arranger with a long list of Broadway credits. Coward shared his dressing room with Nicol and, according to Jill, he 'went to the wings every time Nicol was on stage.' Other performers included Lindsay Anderson, Jill Bennett, Samantha Eggar, Alec Guinness, John Osborne, Laurence Olivier,

Lynn and Vanessa Redgrave, Robert Stephens, Sybil Thorndike and Rita Tushingham. The event was filmed by David Frost.[29]

There was some talk around this time of Nicol doing *King Lear* at the Royal Court, an idea which had most likely been proposed by someone else on the theory that Nicol was good at playing older. At some point anyway, the idea was dropped.

Meanwhile, Jill Townsend returned to the States to play a leading part in the TV western series *Cimarron Strip*. She remembered:

> Nicol flew out to California to ask me to marry him and I refused to see him, then he went back to England. I just needed some time on my own. When we were doing the play in New York I was out of my depth. I don't drink and I never have, so the alcohol was an issue. However, I believe I just couldn't find my footing. He was wild and unpredictable, something I'd never known before. The first thing I ever did as a professional was *Inadmissible*, then I got spotted and taken out to California. Sam Wanamaker was the director on that episode and he spent time with Nicol trying to calm him down. I didn't want the upheaval, I just wanted to focus and see what I could do.

Nicol tried to forget about Jill and went back to London, but she remained very much on his mind.

When Nicol finally returned to the stage, it was with another *tour-de-force*, a one-man version of the Russian writer Nikolai Gogol's classic short story *Diary of a Madman*, which had been adapted for the stage by Belgian theatre director, writer and translator Walter Eysselinck. The play was first tried out at the Sussex University Arts Centre, but it was decided that major changes should be made before transferring to the West End, so Anthony Page came aboard as director, electronic sound effects were added and the sets and costumes became more detailed. The full production opened on the 13th of March for a limited run of four weeks at the Duchess Theatre. Located on Catherine Street in London's West End, the venue had a very similar capacity to that of the Royal Court. The show now ran for around an hour and three quarters and was produced by the impresario Peter Bridge with some additional financial support from

Sean Connery, who was at the time married to Diane Cilento, a friend of Page.

Nicol played Alexei Ivanovitch Poprichtchine, a civil servant who, unable to accept his lowly position as a clerk, retreats into a fantasy which eventually develops into full-blown madness. In the Gogol story, he is infatuated with the chief's daughter, who barely registers his existence. Ultimately, he comes to believe he is the unrecognised king of Spain, stops going into work and is incarcerated in an asylum. In the final scene, Nicol appeared wearing a skin-coloured cap to give the illusion that his head had been shaved.

Hilary Spurling, writing for *The Spectator*, was one of many critics who again heaped praise upon Nicol, saying that his performance had 'an uncanny shapeliness and grace.' *The Glasgow Herald*'s critic found it 'a virtuoso performance, inventive, clever, brilliantly controlled' and noted Nicol's 'high speed' delivery and 'incredible nasal sneer'. Nicol was apparently so convincing in the role that he was even asked to give a special performance of the play for an audience of psychiatrists.

On the 30th of April, Nicol was briefly back at the Royal Court to take part in *An Evening of Music and Reading from the Work of Samuel Beckett and Bertolt Brecht*, a gala benefit in aid of the Free Art Legal Fund. Presumably, Patrick Magee must have forgiven Nicol for throwing him off on their previous Beckett evening, as the two once again shared the stage.

The film of *Inadmissible Evidence* finally began shooting on the 5th of August. Apart from his earlier uncredited bits, it marked Nicol's feature film debut, and was an unusually belated one as he had already been a star for nearly three years – a delay which was partly due to Nicol's commitments to the stage productions, but also to his own selectiveness in choosing scripts. The film was produced by Tony Richardson's Woodfall company, which was in effect a cinematic extension of the Royal Court. Anthony Page directed once again despite having no previous experience in the film world. The budget was low and the film was shot in stark black-and-white, mostly on location in London. John Osborne himself wrote the screenplay and Peter Sallis was invited back to play Maples. The device of having Jones and Maples played by the same actor and the three female clients by the same actress was dropped so, although Clare Kelly was again featured, on this occasion she played Mrs Anderson only. The remainder of the cast was new and included Eleanor Fazan as Anna, Eileen Atkins as Shirley, Ingrid Boulting as Jane and John Osborne's soon-to-be wife Jill Bennett as Liz.

Page came in for some rather unfair criticism for opening the play up and some reviewers gave the impression that they would have been happier if he had just pointed the camera at a stage. The film is, of course, a different experience from watching the play, but that is obviously as it should be. However, there were some who appreciated the qualities of the film, notably the critic of *Time*, who said that the play had 'made a triumphant transition to the screen, with all of its claustrophobic intensity, venom and quinine-bitter laughter intact' and even went as far as to say that the use of close-ups had made *Inadmissible Evidence* even more powerful than it had been on the stage.

Unfortunately, some filmgoers found the use of flashbacks confusing and seemed unable to comprehend that Maitland was never intended to be likeable, or that the beginning in which he is apparently on trial is actually a dream sequence. The film was not a hit, although the budget had been low enough that it cannot have lost the producers much financially. Yet it remains not only an invaluable record of a deservedly famous performance, but a very well shot, atmospheric film in its own right with solid performances all round and a brilliantly disconcerting music score composed, rather surprisingly, by a moonlighting Dudley Moore.

Nicol had moved again at some point and was now living in a five-room flat off Gray's Inn Road in London. In the winter of 1967, Kenneth Tynan filmed an interview with Nicol at his home for an American arts documentary entitled simply *The Actor*, presented by Alec Guinness. Tynan reproduced most of the interview, albeit in slightly misquoted form, in the long piece he wrote for *The New Yorker* a few years later. In the interview, Nicol expressed his disdain for actors who chased awards, worked their way through the 'great parts' so they could tick them off the list and tried to keep continually busy as this supposedly helped to 'keep the instrument in tune.' He went on to make the extraordinary assertion that 'anything that I do you won't fault me on – you won't like it, but you won't fault me on it.' It is perhaps worthy of note that Nicol said 'you *won't* like it' rather than 'you might not like it.' Nicol's readiness to be disliked is one of the characteristics that marked him out from other actors and gave his performances an unsettling strength. For people in general to be unconcerned with whether or not they are liked by others is unusual, but for an actor it is almost unheard of and may have been the source of much of Nicol's power, a secret weapon that was impossible to imitate.

It was at this point that Nicol received some unwelcome news. Jill Townsend had married Tom Sutton, an American rancher who had been working on *Cimarron Strip* as the stunt double for the star of the series, Stuart Whitman. The two found a house together in Woodland Hills, an affluent area just outside of LA. Surrounded by beautiful scenery, it was perfect for the horse riding they both enjoyed and probably more appealing than anything Nicol could have offered at the time.

Nicol's next job was to play Lennie, the strong but slow-witted itinerant farmhand, in a version of John Steinbeck's depression-era classic *Of Mice and Men* for the American TV channel ABC. Dressed in a battered hat, dungarees and crumpled ill-fitting suit jacket, he gave a surprisingly affecting performance in a role to which he was perhaps not obviously suited. George Segal portrayed the travelling companion who tries to keep him out of trouble, and the two played very well off each other. The script was written by John Hopkins, who had also written Nicol's earlier TV play *Horror of Darkness*, so it may well be that the idea of casting Nicol came from him. The director was Ted Kotcheff, a Canadian who went on to make the remarkable *Wake in Fright* as well as *First Blood*, the first and easily best in the series of films starring Sylvester Stallone as Rambo. The production was widely acclaimed, with *Time* saying that Nicol had been 'extraordinary' as Lennie and played the role with 'touching insight'. Shot on videotape, *Of Mice and Men* ran for two hours including commercials and was broadcast on the 31st of January 1968.[30]

Chapter 8 - The Sign of the Cross

A couple of years previously, John McGrath had written a play based on his own experience of doing National Service in the '50s entitled *Events while Guarding the Bofors Gun*. McGrath knew that Nicol had also been a conscript at around the same time, and he wrote one of the main characters with Nicol very much in mind – an Irish gunner named O'Rourke who is the dominant personality among a group of reluctant soldiers guarding an obsolete piece of military equipment on a base in Germany in 1954. The other main character is an acutely homesick bombardier named Evans, who has been placed in charge on what is to be his last night in Germany before he returns to England for officer training. The story unfolds during this one night in which O'Rourke – reaching a peak of disgust with the petty concerns of those around him as well as with what his own life has become – goes on a drunken, self-destructive rampage. The situation is made worse by the ineffectuality of Evans, whose attempts at placating O'Rourke with an assortment of platitudes only provoke him further.

The play had originally been staged at the Hampstead Theatre in 1966. The unavailability of Nicol at the time meant that O'Rourke had been played by Irish actor Patrick O'Connell. James Bolam had played Evans. Nicol had received a great deal of press for *Inadmissible Evidence* and so at this point in time there were many people who were very keen to entice him into a film. One of these was Otto Plaschkes, an Austrian with a taste for serious drama who had worked in films as an assistant director before forging a new career as a producer. His producing partner was Robert A. Goldston, a New York lawyer who had represented a number of people in the film business. Plaschkes and Goldston were both fairly new to the world of film production, but they had enjoyed one previous success together, *Georgy Girl*. Although McGrath's play was not the most promising of commercial prospects, it had the advantage of requiring only a low budget in order to be done well. Jack Gold was chosen as director after the producers had viewed his 1967 BBC film *The Lump*, which used a documentary approach to a drama about the exploitation of workers on a building site. Gold was a 37-year-old Londoner who had begun his career making documentaries for the BBC before switching to drama. In 2013, he remembered,

> I'd seen Nicol on stage in *Inadmissible*. I thought he was terrific. *Bofors* was my first feature. They told me who was in it, and when I told people Nicol Williamson would be in it, they almost put the sign of the cross over me. I'd heard a bit about his reputation. We met in a pub in Notting Hill, which is near where he lived at the time, and we had a couple of quiet drinks and talked about music mainly. He was a great jazz fan, as I was. We went back to his flat round the corner and he started playing records – Billie Holiday, The Mamas And The Papas, and all that stuff that was going round at the time, and we had a good time. So I sort of connected with him on that level, and we then had tense rehearsal for a couple of weeks.
>
> He had a great mate that he shared his flat with, which was John Thaw,[31] which helped a lot on the film. Some of the other actors he knew, and some he didn't, but he was dynamic with the other actors – he gave *everything*. And they had to respond. No-one could coast along in a scene if Nicol was involved. There was this tight bunch of actors, all of whom were together with two weeks rehearsing, and then four or five weeks in this hut in the middle of winter out near Bushey, so things were very intense and claustrophobic. There was nowhere to go! Outside the hut it was *bleak*. And cold. So it was a very close, compact, highly intense piece thematically, with a lot of humour in it, and a lot of physical activity, and it worked... I was given this great crew by producer Otto Plaschkes, and everybody professionally around me was wonderful – I was very, very lucky.
>
> It was, certainly from Nicol's point of view, a great success – terrific reviews. Nicol was up for Best Actor at whatever the equivalent of the BAFTAs were at the time. He didn't get it. It went to Spencer Tracy, who'd just made his last film, as a sort of honorific tribute to him. Ian Holm got the Best Supporting Actor. But Nicol should have had the Best Actor that year, I think – he was tremendous. And we stayed

friendly, you know, and there'd be parties and things like that that we'd go to, but his was a sort of drinking culture, and mine not [laughs], but I was certainly with him on the music, so we could talk about jazz people together.

When we were filming, he came on to the set one morning and gave for about fifteen minutes a diatribe about the production or the producer which had everybody in fits. Totally improvised! But it was devastatingly wicked and funny, and he had the demon in him. And this was in the morning – he wasn't drinking or anything. So there were a lot of very attractive things about him, I felt. I enjoyed being with him, but a lot of people didn't. I always had a good time working with him.

Rehearsals took place at Panshanger Aerodrome in Hertfordshire in an aircraft hangar. A Regimental Sergant Major from the Brigade of Guards had been hired to teach the actors how to march. RSM Britten stood a formidable 6' 6" and had the booming voice to match. Nicol put his National Service training to use by executing the first march perfectly, unlike the rest of the cast. He managed to convince Britten he had been an officer and required no training, thus gaining the rest of the day off, but not before suggesting to Britten that he put the other actors through four hours of close order drill. Parts of the film were shot at Panshangar, where the actors slept in barracks and filmed throughout the night. There was some location work in Germany without Nicol, while interiors were shot at Rayant Studios in Bushey, north-west of London – probably the oldest, smallest and cheapest studios in the country at the time.

Nicol related strongly to the character of O'Rourke, seeing in him a fellow non-compromiser, and said that, 'what I also like about him is that I have just as much self-loathing and scorn for myself as he has.' He made a memorable entrance in the film. The other actors are lined up on the parade ground awaiting inspection when Nicol and John Thaw arrive to join them, marching with rifles over their shoulder and screaming command responses in an exaggerated manner which leaves no doubt that they are laughing in the face of authority while ostensibly behaving in a perfectly correct military fashion. Nicol also pulled off a very convincing and consistent Irish accent, and punctuated his dialogue at appropriate moments with snatches of traditional Irish songs.

Despite his lack of experience with professional actors, Gold obtained flawless performances from his cast, and it seems that it was partly due to his naivety that he was able to do so. His documentary work had often involved filming real people and encouraging them not to play to the camera. When dealing with actors, if he found a performance unconvincing, he would simply tell them that he did not believe it, make a few suggestions and ask them to try again. Otherwise, he gave his actors little direction other than was necessary in order for them to hit the marks required by the camera and so on. Gold was a believer in casting the right people, trusting them and then keeping out of their way. He subsequently became a director with a reputation for handling actors well and went on to work with most of the great British actors of the '70s. It is no coincidence that it was Jack Gold who would work with Nicol more times than any other film or television director.

Nicol became friends with Ian Holm during the shoot but later attempted to seduce Holm's partner, Bee Gilbert, falling out with him in the process. Barry Jackson, who played Private Shone, joined Nicol in the pub on one occasion when Nicol proposed a game of darts in which one player had to place their hand against the dart board without flinching while the other tried to hit the board but not their hand. Nicol put his hand on the board first, Jackson threw and then they changed places, at which point Nicol threw his first dart straight into Jackson's hand. Not wishing to appear weak in front of Nicol, Jackson merely laughed it off.

David Warner, on the other hand, did not remember much socialising on or off set:

> Our two characters were chalk and cheese just like Nicol and I were chalk and cheese. I was quiet and withdrawn and Nicol was Nicol! We were cast with that in mind, I imagine. We met on the days we worked and I never saw him socially at all.

> I don't remember any extensive talks during rehearsals – our generation just got on and did it. There were never long discussions about interpretation. For those exterior scenes it was freezing cold, absolutely freezing, so that made us a grumpy lot.

Indeed, the breath of the actors is clearly visible in many shots and Gold later recalled how Nicol, stripped to his waist for the final scene, insisted despite the freezing temperature on doing a number of takes until he was completely satisfied. Gold was also greatly impressed by Nicol's dedication in giving his all even when simply feeding lines off camera to other actors, and felt that Nicol wanted the whole cast's performances to be just as good as his own.

On release, *The Bofors Gun* ran into trouble for a number of reasons. The publicists were uncertain how to sell a film with 'gun' in the title which contained no shooting. Its portrait of military life was not an appealing one to say the least, so it was also apparently banned from a number of British army bases. However, most ludicrous of all was the controversy over the line, 'He's having a crafty J. Arthur!' (cockney rhyming slang for a 'wank'). One of the distributors was the J. Arthur Rank organisation. The film opened in low-key fashion Rank's Odeon in St Martin's Lane but received only minimal distribution, a fact which some attributed to the unfortunate colloquialism.

According to *Variety*, upon its American release in September 1968, the film received six favourable reviews and only one (in *Time* magazine) which was unfavourable. However, even the *Time* review had good words to say about Nicol's performance.

While shooting *The Bofors Gun*, Nicol had signed up for another film, *The Love Department*, based on William Trevor's comic novel of the same name. It was to co-star Lynn Redgrave and be directed by Silvio Narizzano, who had directed *War and Peace* featuring Nicol, as well as the aforementioned *Georgy Girl*. Unfortunately, Narizzano had just made a western called *Blue*, starring Terence Stamp, which had gone considerably over budget and was to fail at the box office. He also overspent on his script budget for *The Love Department* with the result that the producers became nervous and the project collapsed.

In the spring of 1968, Nicol was contacted via Lionel Larner by Mike Nichols, the American comedian-turned-director who had had Broadway success with the Neil Simon comedies *Barefoot in the Park* and *The Odd Couple* and film success with *Who's Afraid of Virginia Woolf?* and *The Graduate*. At this time, Nichols was directing another Neil Simon play, *Plaza Suite*, which had opened in February at the Plymouth Theatre on Broadway. *Plaza Suite* comprised a trio of one-act plays all set in suite 719 of the Plaza Hotel. George C. Scott and Maureen Stapleton were starring as three different couples. The play was having a highly successful run but Scott would have to be absent for six weeks in order to undergo urgent surgery for a detached retina. The period of time involved meant that using the understudy was not an acceptable solution, so Nichols and Simon had brainstormed a list of name actors who they felt could reach the necessary quality of performance in a short space of time. When all of the American actors on their list rejected their offer (perhaps fearing unfavourable comparisons to Scott), Nichols began to think of actors outside the States.

Nicol was excited to be offered not just one but *three* juicy comic parts in a well-written play which was already a hit. He dropped everything and arrived in New York three days later for a week's worth of rehearsals. In Act One, he played a middle-aged businessman whose wife has booked the suite to celebrate their wedding anniversary; during the course of the evening she discovers that her husband is having an affair with his secretary. In Act Two, he was a Hollywood producer with an appalling hairstyle attempting to seduce a star-struck old flame. In the final act he portrayed a father about to give his daughter away in marriage. The most farcical of the three acts, it focused on his attempts to cajole his daughter out of the bathroom she has locked herself inside due to a severe case of cold feet.

Nichols' decision to cast a British actor proved controversial. Equity protested that an American should have been found although, once Nichols and Simon had shown they had already approached every suitable American actor, their choice was reluctantly accepted. However, despite the agreement, a number of Equity members with placards picketed the theatre on Nicol's first night. One of them even went so far as to buy a ticket in order to continue the protest inside, and ruined Nicol's entrance by singing 'The Star-Spangled Banner' before being escorted out by a police officer. The actors began again and proceeded without further interruption. The remainder of the audience were clearly on Nicol's side as he received a standing ovation at the end. In contrast to his earlier comic lead, the poorly-received Whitehall farce *A Cuckoo in the Nest*, on this occasion Nicol received excellent notices, with *Variety* praising his American accent and ability as an 'adept farceur'.

Lionel Larner remembered telling Maureen Stapleton at one point that Nicol loved her, to which she responded, 'All my leading men love me. They don't want to fuck me but they all love me!' Scott returned to the play on the 17th of June 1968 and Nicol took a holiday in the south of France.

Nicol was at this point also a client of the agents Robin Fox and Laurence Evans[32] in England, the former of whom was the father of actors Edward and James Fox. While Nicol was on holiday, they were contacted by Tony Richardson, who was two weeks into shooting *Laughter in the Dark*, a film based on Vladimir Nabokov's novel and starring Richard Burton. Curiously, it was Robin Fox who had proposed the project to Richardson in the first place. Richardson had decided to update Nabokov's story and set it in the world of contemporary art in swinging '60s London. Burton was playing Sir Edward More, a distinguished art critic and collector, who becomes infatuated with a cinema usherette named Margot, played by Danish actress Anna Karina, well known from her starring roles in a number of films directed by her former husband, Jean-Luc Godard. Margot turns out to be a gold-digger who forces Sir Edward to leave his wife.

She has a lover whom she manages to persuade Sir Edward to employ by convincing him that the man is homosexual. When Sir Edward loses his sight in a car accident, Margot secretly installs her lover in his house and the two connive to gain control of his considerable fortune.

Richardson had just fired Burton for continual lateness and then decided that Nicol was the person to replace him – at least, that was the official version. Nicol later said that he felt it may have been a 'set up,' by which he meant that Richardson had used Burton's name in order to bankroll the film but had wanted Nicol all along. Although there is no hint of this in Richardson's posthumously-published memoir, the fact that he carefully avoided any mention of his well-known bisexuality suggests that the book is hardly the frankest of autobiographies. It should also be noted that, despite the telegram in which he dismissed Nicol as merely a 'good rep actor,' Richardson had made at least three attempts to cast him after their first collaboration on *A Midsummer Night's Dream*.

Nicol had been offered the role of the scheming, hypocritical Blifil in Richardson's film of *Tom Jones*, but he did not think it much of a part. He later recalled that, when producer Oscar Lewenstein had pressed him to accept and asked him why he would not do it, his answer to the exasperated Lewenstein had been, 'Because I think Tony Richardson is a liar and a cunt.'[33] The role was eventually played by David Warner. Presumably, Lewenstein did not repeat what Nicol had said to Richardson as the latter approached Nicol about another role about a year later. When he asked Nicol if he would be interested in playing Konstantin in a production of *The Seagull* he was planning to direct at the Queen's Theatre, Nicol was more positive. However, when Nicol mentioned that he had played the part before under the direction of Anthony Page at Dundee, Richardson abruptly changed his mind and cast Peter McEnery instead. Nicol also later remembered how Richardson had attempted to entice him away from the American run of *Inadmissible Evidence* by offering him the male lead in his film *The Sailor from Gibraltar*. Nicol thought that Richardson had made the offer in the hope that it would be 'one in the eye' for Osborne and Page.[34] However, he was not interested and Ian Bannen was cast instead. There is considerable evidence to suggest that Richardson could be a manipulative, even devious person (although undoubtedly not without his good points). Nicol's suspicion that the firing of Burton was another of Richardson's manipulations is not entirely implausible, then – but, if such were the case, it would prove to be an expensive one.

Richardson, needing to contact Nicol urgently, was dismayed to find that no-one could tell him where he was, only the approximate area in France in which he was likely to be found. However, Richardson owned a home in the south of the country and had a lot of friends there, some of whom he was able to persuade to mount a search. One of these amateur detectives found Nicol among a group of Englishmen at a café in Ramatuelle and put him in touch with Richardson via telephone. Nicol agreed to take over from Burton, returned to England immediately, quickly obtained a script and appeared on set a couple of days later word perfect. However, according to Anna Karina, the situation was no better than it had been with Burton as, not only was Nicol frequently late and / or drunk, but he and Richardson screamed at each other throughout the shoot. Nicol was apparently on a thirtieth of Burton's $1 million salary, so he would have received around $33,000 – a still not inconsiderable sum in 1968, although much of it probably went to the Inland Revenue. Burton sent Nicol a good luck telegram to which Nicol later admitted he had forgotten to reply.

Nicol's first day of filming took place at Farringdon House in Oxfordshire – then owned by English eccentric Robert Heber-Percy – which was doubling as the residence of Sir Edward More. According to Peter Bowles, who was playing Sir Edward's brother-in-law, when the company sat down to lunch, Nicol turned to Richardson and asked him loudly why he spoke with 'that ridiculous false whining camp accent'. Richardson was embarrassed but laughed it off. Nicol would sometimes use this kind of tactic when he was beginning a project and for some reason felt insecure or unsure whether everyone was on his side. He wanted to send a clear message that he was not to be trifled with – and it usually worked. When they were filming the scene in which Bowles comes to the rescue of the blind Sir Edward, Nicol unexpectedly improvised a violent attack on Bowles with his stick and was astonished to find himself suddenly flying through the air as a result of Bowles' judo skills. However, the two actors otherwise enjoyed a good relationship.

Much of the film was shot on location in Majorca near the village of Deià, where the writer Robert Graves lived. Richardson was interested in making a film of Graves' *I, Claudius* and took the opportunity to visit Graves. He was accompanied by Nicol and Edward Bond, the screenwriter of *Laughter in the Dark*. There was talk of Nicol playing Claudius but, for a variety of reasons, the project was abandoned, although Richardson later turned it into a stage play starring David Warner.

Nicol had obviously not had the luxury in this case of considering for long whether or not he should accept the part of Sir Edward. Unfortunately, he was not ideal casting for the role, and the story would have been more effective with an older and suaver actor such as George Sanders. Having said that, although Nicol has little to challenge him in the first half of the film, once his character loses his sight, he pulls off a number of memorable moments – the excruciating scene where Sir Edward first realises he is blind; the moment when he cries, his eyes suddenly welling up with tears which overflow and stream down his face; a number of scenes where, in his blind exploration of the rented villa, he seems genuinely to be at risk of imminent injury. The callous treatment of his character by Karina and her lover, who entertain themselves at the expense of his blindness, is at times difficult to watch and, while it may be hard to have much sympathy for Sir Edward in the first half, we certainly feel pity for him once he becomes so pathetically vulnerable in the latter stages.

The film has some good moments, but they are outweighed by its flaws. For example, the only apparent consequence of the collision between a group of cyclists and the car containing Sir Edward and his mistress is Sir Edward's loss of sight. The implausibility of this makes it difficult to escape the conclusion that lazy film-making is to blame. Furthermore, the fatal illness of Sir Edward's daughter is dealt with in a very perfunctory fashion, and the ending, while it may be logical enough, is unsatisfying and clumsily shot. In fact, the film suffers from a lack of visual style throughout, while Raymond Leppard's music, intended to provide an ironic counterpoint to the action, often sits uneasily with the events onscreen. Actor Peter Gale, who would subsequently appear in Tony Richardson's production of *Hamlet* with Nicol, later said that, 'Tony was a dreadful director, but the most amazingly clever producer, a great "getter-onner" of things.' This is an opinion which has been echoed by others, although some of Richardson's films remain impressive. However, perhaps his greatest talent was in creating a sense of excitement which made people want to get involved. One illustration of this facility is the presence of Oscar Beuselinck and David Hockney in *Laughter in the Dark*, both of whom can be glimpsed as extras.

Filming was completed in October 1968 and the picture opened the following May in the USA and (as one of the first X-rated films) in August in the UK, at which time it received mixed reviews and the public stayed away. However, Nicol did win a Best Actor award for the film at the San Sebastian Seashell Awards in July.

Variety reported in October that Nicol was in discussions with playwright Ben Maddow to star in *Window on the River Rouge*, a romantic play set in a Detroit hotel room, but this came to nothing.

At the end of November, Nicol appeared on David Frost's highbrow talk show, *Frost on Saturday*, to discuss the subject of death alongside the poet John Betjeman and other guests. Betjeman had been deeply impressed by *Inadmissible Evidence* and claimed to have felt an affinity with the character of Maitland. Nicol performed his reading from Beckett's *How It Is* with his usual harrowing intensity and then spoke about his fear of sudden death and the state of non-being.

Shortly after *Laughter in the Dark* had finished shooting, Nicol was once more before the cameras in a leading role. John McGrath had written a screenplay based on a novel called *The Harp that Once* by Patrick Hall. The book had not been notably successful but McGrath saw in it a perfect vehicle for Nicol. The title seemed too literary for a film, so he changed it to *A Matter of Honour*, but this working title was also abandoned and the film would be released as *The Reckoning*. The story revolves around Michael Marler, who has grown up as the son of working class Irish parents in Birmingham (changed to Liverpool for the film) and gone to London to make his way in the world, which he does with great aplomb and considerable ruthlessness as a marketing executive for a big company. Substitute Irish for Scottish and marketing executive for actor and the parallels between Marler and Nicol are obvious. Marler regards the majority of his colleagues with contempt, viewing them as back-stabbing hypocrites, while he himself favours a full frontal attack.

Nicol's view of his theatrical colleagues could be similarly contemptuous – he once said, 'Most of the people that you meet in this profession – like directors, actors, actresses – are self-indulgent, boring, conceited and largely unintelligent…A hateful breed of people, on the whole, to me.' He was also known to sometimes publicly deride the abilities of his contemporaries, although he only did so with star actors and was also capable of being complimentary.

Although Marler is only genuinely at ease among those of his own class, he enjoys the luxuries his job affords him, which include a large house in Virginia Water, a Jaguar and a posh, sexy wife. As a result, he has become estranged from his family, but when he learns that his father is seriously ill, he is forced to return to Liverpool for the first time in five years. When his father dies, he discovers that it was actually as a result of a beating he had received at the hands of a young thug. His family are not the kind to go running to the police, so it is a 'matter of honour' for Marler to mete out his own form of rough justice. Marler's vengeance provides him with some motivation to return and helps to hold the attention of the audience, but the more important question is whether or not he will reject his materialistic lifestyle and return to his roots. He feels drawn to people of his own class, but ultimately his memories of poverty and struggle prevent him from re-entering their world. He successfully out-manipulates a rival at work and is reunited with his wife, who had left him after he had become *persona non grata* in their world by drunkenly causing an embarrassing scene at their party. The final scene sees them together in his Jaguar as he fails to stop at a red light just for the fun of it and nearly crashes the car into an approaching lorry in the process. 'If I can get away with that, I can get away with anything!' he gloats, and the image freezes on his view of the sky as he drives up a hump in the road. Neither Marler nor the audience know what lies on the other side of the hump, but we do know that he has forsaken his one opportunity to change and that, although he has chosen the world of wealth, luxury and status, he has not by any means been tamed. The ending has some intriguing parallels with that of the later *Taxi Driver*.

The film was originally to have been directed by J. Lee Thompson, but he had to withdraw – probably because post-production problems on his previous film, *McKenna's Gold*, made it impossible for him to make the start date. Admiring the job he had done on *The Bofors Gun* and knowing he worked well with Nicol, John McGrath suggested Jack Gold, who later remembered:

> Columbia were happy because I'd made my first feature, so Nicol and I were together again very quickly. It was an American producer, Ron Shedlo, working in England. There was a device in the script, which was a voiceover, a lot of narration by the chief character, which Columbia didn't like. They said voiceover like that never works in films – forgetting *Sunset Boulevard*, *Double Indemnity* and a lot of other films where it works wonderfully! Anyway, it had to be adapted to please Columbia, so it lost all the voiceover. But it was Nicol's film. Columbia had quite a lot of money, so it had great actors in it – Rachel Roberts, Ann Bell, Zena Walker, Paul Rogers – and a terrific cameraman, Geoff Unsworth,

who was one of the leading British cameramen – he'd done *2001*, for instance.

Nicol used to be devastating on film sets – he could imitate the voice of the Assistant Director, and suddenly people would be scurrying around doing things. I remember at the end I had the chippies build an eight-foot wooden spoon which we all signed, because he was a great stirrer, he used to like causing little problems, little *frissons*, and teasing. He used to tease the producer terribly…

Some actors adored him and some didn't, but I found him always very engaging, incredibly intelligent about performance and people and characters, a very acute observer of people. I'm told he did a very good impression of me, but thank god I never saw it! But he could be terrifyingly funny.

Luke Williamson also later recalled how Nicol's performances were influenced by close observation of those around him:

He was a great people-watcher and if there was something about somebody's character that made them do something physical, when they weren't comfortable, when they'd pick something up and play with it or light a cigarette or cross their legs, he would file away these things and he would attach that somehow to a character.

A great deal of the film was shot on location in areas including Liverpool, Birkinhead, Wallesley, Slough, Virginia Water and various parts of London, but the scene in the smoky workingmen's club was actually filmed on a highly convincing set. Nicol was featured in every single scene and he related to the character of Marler to such an extent that it was as close as he ever came to playing himself, with the result that *The Reckoning* remains the quintessential Nicol Williamson film. Marler may not be the most pleasant of characters, but he generates sympathy partly because his anguish at the death of his father is clearly genuine and partly because the types he attacks are so insufferably smug. For these reasons, one cannot help but cheer him on as he behaves scandalously, destroying the careers of his colleagues and punching a guest at his wife's dinner party. It is one of the strengths of Nicol's performance that at no point does he appear to be *playing* for the audience's sympathy. The script allowed Nicol ample scope to demonstrate his range and be by turns funny, aggressive and melancholy, as well as giving him an always welcome opportunity to sing. He also cried for the camera once more, as he had done in both *Laughter in the Dark* and *Inadmissible Evidence*, an ability which seemed to come easily to him. However, Jack Gold soon discovered that there was one thing Nicol could not do which would have been very useful – he could not drive. This created some problems as the script featured a couple of important scenes with Marler driving, but Gold successfully managed to make it appear that Nicol was in control of Marler's Jaguar through careful use of back projection and other techniques. Nicol later said that it was the only film he had ever really enjoyed making, and he loved his final line about being able to 'get away with anything' so much that he enjoyed repeating it on appropriate occasions for years to come.

The film ran into some censorship problems in post-production, and the opening sex scene between Nicol and Ann Bell had to be toned down. Reviews of the film were mixed, with some critics unfairly writing it off as just another 'angry young man' movie. As the film is very much concerned with the British class system, it also stood little chance in America, so the box office was disappointing, as Jack Gold recalled:

> It didn't take off the way they wanted it to. It came out at the same time as *Get Carter* [in America].[35] Both were about a man returning to his hometown, both tough people, and one was a gangster film and one wasn't. And for whatever reason, *Get Carter* took off, while *The Reckoning* was quite successful but never zoomed up. We had brutal moments in *The Reckoning*, but I didn't want to linger on them, I had them very short and sharp – not extended beatings-up or anything, whereas *Get Carter* was quite a violent film.

The Reckoning was to some extent an attempt to turn Nicol into a film star. In this it failed. This may have been partly because American film companies were severing their ties with the British film industry at the time, so Columbia's promotional campaign for the film was minimal. However, Jack Gold felt that there may have been other reasons:

> Nicol was uncompromising in his performances, so there was no sort of Paul Newman / Robert Redford twinkle in the eye, 'I'm playing a bad guy but I'm not really.' He was nakedly the character, for better or worse. So I'm not sure whether you would consider him sexy – I don't mean necessarily in sexual terms – but perhaps audiences didn't warm to him as they did to major stars. I think he sort of dared audiences to not like him, but understand him or appreciate him.

Chapter 9 – Hamlet

Anthony Page had wanted to do a version of *Hamlet* with Nicol for some time, but he now found himself competing with other directors of considerable reputation for the services of the star he had himself created. Tony Richardson was also keen to do *Hamlet* with Nicol, and he had the greater power and influence. Nicol had shown a considerable degree of loyalty to Page in the past, notably in the David Merrick incident, but the two now began to drift apart and it would be a long time before they worked together again. Letters between Page's friends Christopher Isherwood and Don Bachardy[36] reveal that Page felt Richardson had stolen Nicol away from him and was far from happy about it. Speaking many years later, Nicol seemed to downplay the role that Page had played in his career, saying,

> Directors are very important for actors. They adopt actors sometimes, like Lindsay Anderson adopted Richard Harris, Malcolm McDowell and Frank Grimes, Anthony Page in his early days adopted James Booth and Alfie Lynch because he had a very personal relationship with them. I never had or encountered a director early in my life who said, 'I want to do things with you.' I always had to fight for what I got. I was never given anything on a platter… [37]

Tony Richardson now attempted to adopt Nicol, but he was to find him an unruly charge to say the least.

Richardson wanted to get away from the traditional proscenium arch type of theatre and decided to stage his *Hamlet* at the Roundhouse, an unusual venue in the north London borough of Camden. The circular building had originally served as a railway shed in which trains had turned around, but it had been utilised as a theatre since 1964. Peter Brook had recently staged *The Tempest* there, and it had also been the site of a number of concerts by some of the era's most happening names in rock music, including The Doors and Jimi Hendrix. However, the fact that it had never been designed as a venue presented a number of challenges in terms of acoustics and seating. As a result of this, Richardson decided to block off the outer circle. This reduced the capacity but meant everyone who was in the audience would be able to see and hear the actors properly. The division between actors and audience would also be less sharply delineated than in a proscenium arch theatre as the audience would be sitting around the stage rather than in front of it. Richardson brought Jocelyn Herbert from the Royal Court to make further adaptations to the space and design the costumes. There was little in the way of scenery as Richardson wanted to focus on the actors and the text.

A formidable supporting cast was assembled. Marianne Faithfull, who had almost played Bill Maitland's daughter in *Inadmissible Evidence*, was cast as Ophelia, and surprised many with the naturalness of her performance. Nicol later said that 'she was brilliant because she was totally vulnerable.'[38] However, although she was better known as a singer than as an actress, her voice broke one evening as she was performing Ophelia's song, causing Judy Parfitt as Gertrude to corpse uncontrollably. Anjelica Huston had also read for Ophelia but, known only at the time as John Huston's daughter, had ended up as Faithfull's understudy, although she was also given a bit part. She later said in her memoir that she had been flirting with Nicol throughout the production. Claudius was played by Anthony Hopkins, then one year younger than Nicol and just beginning to emerge as a star. Horatio was played by Gordon Jackson and Laertes by Michael Pennington, while veteran film star Roger Livesey appeared as both the gravedigger and the first player.

Osric was played by Peter Gale, a former child actor who had made his debut playing David opposite Nigel Green's Goliath on live television. He later recalled:

> It was a very clever choice of venue. The Roundhouse was in a pretty rough and ready state and it was kind of an edgy thing to do, to go and

see this dangerous *Hamlet* in that old turntable house for trains, and it was a very exciting event to be a part of. It brought the most wonderful kind of fluid ambience to the production and there was the sense of an *event*. It was very refreshing for an audience.

Lots of people came. Jocelyn Herbert went to watch the play to find that Barbara Streisand had sat down in the next seat and put her coat on Jocelyn's. She said, 'Excuse me!' and Streisand very reluctantly lifted this huge fur coat which looked like it had cost a fortune!

The production opened on the 17th of February 1969 and was a huge hit with both critics and audiences, and especially popular with the younger generation of theatregoers. One measure of the attention it received can be seen in the fact that it was reviewed by *Time* magazine. This was unusual for a play being staged in London with a limited run. Their reviewer found Nicol to be 'a Hamlet who scoffs and snarls and wields the soliloquies like a switchblade.' Nicol's Hamlet was clearly not the weak, vacillating character that had often been portrayed in the past. The ghost appeared only as a bright light and its voice was provided by Nicol himself, clearly implying that it was a manifestation of his own troubled subconscious rather than the supernatural.

Living actors who had been notable Hamlets in previous years included Laurence Olivier, Peter O'Toole and Richard Burton, but it was John Gielgud's Hamlet at the Aldwych in the '30s which had cast the longest shadow. Gielgud was known for his mellifluousness, a quality which Nicol and Richardson were entirely uninterested in. Richardson felt that the key to understanding Hamlet was to focus on his irony. Nicol loathed the approach to Shakespearean acting in which the words were recited as if they were holy scripture. He felt very strongly that an actor must understand every word he is saying and why he is saying it, and that the purpose of the words was not to sound beautiful but to convey meaning.

Nicol's 'bad boy' image was fuelled by various incidents and backstage shenanigans during the run. One of these was the affair he had with Marianne Faithfull. Nicol later said 'she used to come to my dressing room to smoke a joint' because he was the only actor who did not have to share his room. Their trysts mainly took place there before performances or between acts. Faithfull was at the time still in a relationship with Mick Jagger. Both she and Nicol later said that they felt they had been manipulated into having a relationship by Tony Richardson. Nicol was also not controlling his drinking as much as he had been for *Inadmissible Evidence*. Michael Pennington later said that it was not unusual for him to have consumed a couple of bottles of wine before taking the stage, but that it did not seem to affect his performance. Anthony Hopkins was also drinking heavily during this stage in his career and was unhappy as he did not much care for Tony Richardson, although he seems to have had an amicable rivalry with Nicol. On press night, Nicol poked his head around Hopkins' dressing room door after the show and said, 'You're good… but I'm *brilliant!*' and walked off. Peter Gale remembered another occasion when Nicol enjoyed a joke at Hopkins' expense, saying that 'One night, in the final tense scene, Nicol was acting with Anthony Hopkins and as he finished his line, he added under his breath, "You cunt." Anthony had terrible trouble trying not to laugh.'

Nicol was the undisputed star at this point and rarely tempered his behaviour. Gale remembered how wary of him others became as a result:

> My teacher came to the show one night. I told him later that she thought he was wonderful and he said, 'Well, why didn't you bring her round?' I said, 'Well, I thought you'd have lots of friends here,' and he said, 'I sit here night after night and nobody comes near me!' I thought, well, surprise, surprise! If you behave like a cactus, nobody's going to touch you, are they?
>
> It's very compelling to watch somebody like that. It's like being in the presence of an animal that you don't quite know what it's going to do next. Although he was a very, very disciplined performer. He didn't mess around, he didn't suddenly decide to do a scene coming on from a different angle. Some people are like that, but he was very, very consistent. He never messed me about at all, he was wonderfully consistent to work with and very dangerous.

Nicol seems to have walked off on at least one occasion at the Roundhouse, although he did return, and he was also known to interrupt the play from time to time, to the consternation of his fellow actors and the delight of the audience. Richardson felt that Nicol had begun to overact after only a few performances and attacked him for it. Nicol responded by telling Richardson in no uncertain terms that he was never to speak to him like that again. Their relationship became strained as a result and *Hamlet* would mark the end of their professional association.

Richardson decided he should film the play but did not want to simply point a couple of cameras at the stage during a live performance. Instead, he saw a way in which he could utilise the venue by filming some of it in other parts of the building, such as the cellars. He would also do away with the need for any elaborate sets by shooting the actors at close range and focusing on their faces. Seats would be removed after performances to allow the film crew space to work the following day. Richardson raised $350,000 through producer Marty Ransohoff and made the film over ten days, shooting every day until around 4 p.m., when the seats were replaced for the evening show. The production was already a heavily cut version of the text, running at around three hours, but Richardson made further cuts to achieve a running time of under two hours for the film. The film would be released in September in the UK and on the 21st of December in the US. Not all critics would consider Richardson's experiment a success, but many were positive, including *Time*, who found it thoroughly appropriate that the film had focused its attention on the actors and the words they spoke rather than on 'some grandiose castle.' As the budget had been so low and the publicity so strong, the film was instantly profitable.

Meanwhile, plans had been afoot to take *Hamlet* to America. Richardson knew Broadway producer Norman Twain from previous New York visits and asked him to produce. Cast changes were made, as not all of the Roundhouse actors were keen to cross the Atlantic. Anthony Hopkins was replaced by Patrick Wymark, Judy Parfitt by

Constance Cummings, and Marianne Faithfull by Francesca Annis – a 'wonderful actress' in Nicol's opinion. The rest of the cast remained unchanged.

Nicol travelled to New York on the 30th of April and the production opened on the 1st of May at the Lunt-Fontanne Theatre on West 46th Street, a large venue which could accommodate 1,400 people. Unfortunately, the production had been designed to suit its previous venue and some of the life evidently went out of it now that it had been placed in exactly the kind of proscenium arch setting Richardson had been at pains to avoid in the first place.

It was not as well-received as it had been in London, and American critics in particular accused Nicol of mangling Shakespeare with his nasal, Brummie-accented delivery. Much was made of this Birmingham accent which Nicol supposedly adopted, but it is not evident in the film version. Certainly, Nicol wanted to get away from the plummy-voiced Gielgud style, but it seems unlikely that he adopted a hard Birmingham accent for the role. He was an actor well capable of delivering a wide range of accents convincingly, although he was not one to focus on this at the expense of feeling. It seems more probable that he was aiming for a fairly neutral accent and the Brummie in him occasionally revealed itself in moments of passion. Clive Barnes of *The New York Times* was unsure at the beginning of the opening night performance, but had become a convert by the end, saying, '... the poetry takes on new wings in this strange, compulsive voice' and that Nicol had 'banished John Gielgud's sweet prince and established... a Hamlet for a new generation.' However, although more than one reviewer referred to Nicol as the 'Hamlet of his generation', it should be noted that his interpretation had nothing whatever in common with the hippy culture for which this period is so famous. Instead, he was an earthier, more forceful Hamlet, one which was informed partly by the working-class breakthrough which had happened in English theatre and partly by Osborne's influence, but also very much by Nicol's individual temperament and outlook. It was probably less informed by its director, as Nicol and

Richardson rarely saw eye to eye. Nicol told the *Reno Gazette-Journal* at the time that acting was a 'sort of therapy' for him and that without it he 'might even become a recluse.' He did, in fact, become somewhat reclusive when he stopped acting many years later, but at this point he was far from it.

Nicol's salary during the run was $250 a week. It was not much, but he enjoyed being in New York again and was once more frequenting Jimmy Ryan's Bar, where he would continue to jump up and sing at every opportunity. He also became in demand as a chat show guest and found time to appear on one episode of *The Mike Douglas Show*, two episodes of *The Merv Griffin Show* and made his first appearance on *The Dick Cavett Show*. Lionel Larner remembered:

> They had begged me for him and he never wanted to do it and then one day they asked him one more time and he said yes. And in those days – thank god – the interviews were taped at around 5 or 6 o'clock and they went out later at 11. I forget who was on, but it was a ballet dancer who had just had a baby, and Dick Cavett said to Nicol, 'Would you like to have a baby?' And he said, 'Yes, I would, but I'd be so afraid it'd be a little girl.' And Cavett said, 'Why would you be afraid? Most fathers would love a little girl.' And he said, 'Oh, I'd be afraid that she'd look exactly like her mother and I'd want to be the first to slip it in.' The audience just gasped! Fortunately, they were able to take that out but they yelled at me afterwards, and I said to them, 'Look – you begged for him and you got him!'

Nicol's remark was no doubt calculated to shock. Somehow, like the character he portrayed in *The Reckoning*, he 'got away with it' and was invited back on a number of occasions, becoming good friends with Cavett in the process. He delighted in testing the boundaries but, while at this stage in his career he usually seemed to escape any dire consequences, in later years such behaviour would not be treated so indulgently.

The Broadway production of *Hamlet* closed on the 14th of June after a total of 52 performances. When it transferred to the Colonial Theatre in Boston shortly after, it initially suffered from low ticket sales, partly because it was on during the summer. The venue was also even larger than the Lunt-Fontanne, with a capacity of around 1,700.

Shortly into the opening night performance, Nicol provided some additional drama. Peter Gale remembered it this way:

> He chose the court scene, in which every single member of the company was on the stage, to suddenly throw his goblet across the stage and say, 'I'm giving an effing poor performance. You can all have your money back, but I can't do it,' and walked off! We were astounded – it was like that cutaway shot in *The Producers* where they cut to the audience and they're sitting there with their mouths agape! Patrick Wymark improvised and said, 'Come – let us withdraw into the antechamber!' and so we all piled off, except I thought I would do the nice thing and wait for Connie Cummings to go, but she stayed! And then she walked forward and said, 'Ladies and gentlemen, I must tell you that Nicol has played more consecutive performances of *Hamlet* in the history of blah, blah, blah...' Whether it's true or not, I don't know, but she said, 'I'm sure if you're patient and stay in your seats he will be persuaded to continue. Thank you so much for your patience.' It was a lovely and gracious speech, and I was like the conjuror's assistant, and then we went off together. And in the little room between the back stage and the dressing room, Nicol suddenly appeared, and she said, 'You really should get yourself together!' and he said, 'Oh fuck off!' to which she said, 'No, I'm *not* going to fuck off!' She was a woman of certain years and she didn't take any of that kind of nonsense from anybody! Connie Cummings was the only person I ever saw stand up to him. Everybody else was terrified of him.
>
> It was so interesting, waiting on the stage while they brought the curtain down and you'd see all these suits coming from the auditorium, across the wings and down into his room – the money boys! Saying, 'You've got to get back out there otherwise we've got to give all that money back and we're not giving it back – you'll have to give it back!' So he was always persuaded to continue.

One of the people rushing backstage was Lionel Larner, who also had a vivid memory of the night over forty years later:

Nicol, in the middle of the play-in-the-play scene, threw the goblet across the stage and said, 'This is a load of *shit!*' And the audience couldn't believe it, *I* couldn't believe it, and the actors just filed off the stage. I ran back and they said, 'You can't go back there.' I said, 'Oh yes I can!' I went into his dressing room, his head was in his hands and he was crying. I said, 'Nicol, what's the matter? Let's have a glass of champagne.' So we opened some champagne and I said, 'Now, tell me what the problem is.' He said, 'Well, it was down, and the actors were down and I couldn't get them to come up. I have to give all of myself and I didn't feel I was doing it.' I said, 'They've brought the curtain down and all the critics are sitting there – you've got to go out and talk to them and give them an explanation.' So I coaxed him back out on stage, and he said to the audience, 'I apologise, but I wasn't giving you my all.' He didn't blame the other actors, he blamed himself, and this was the horrible part – he said, 'I will finish the play but this is my last performance on any stage.' And there was a tour booked! But he finished the play and he got a standing ovation. Afterwards, I went backstage and the press all came back, wanting to speak to him, and I went out and said, 'Look, the man is exhausted. If Maria Callas did this in *Tosca* you wouldn't be at all surprised. What is the difference? The difference is she plays *Tosca* once every ten days, Mr Williamson's been playing Hamlet in London for a long run and he's been in New York for a long run. The man's nerves are raw, he's exhausted and you can't see him tonight, but if you give me this time I promise you can have a press conference with him at the Ritz at noon tomorrow.' I don't know where the thing about Callas came from but it seemed a very rational thing… but she probably didn't go out and booze all night either – *he* did!

We went out to dinner alone and went up to his suite and picked up the paper and it was a rave. They said something like it was the greatest performance since Barrymore. And I said to him, 'You were very lucky!' And he said, 'No, I wasn't.' I said, 'Nicol, you *were* – you said it was a load of shit and they could have agreed with you!' And he laughed and that was that.

The next day, they asked me about him saying it was his last performance, and I said, 'I'm sure he meant it when he said it, but he's enough of an actor that when a provocative part comes along he'll find it challenging and he'll do it and I'm sure he'll fulfil the tour.'

The general consensus was that Nicol's performance had been extraordinarily good when he returned. He received wildly enthusiastic applause at the curtain call, and his walk-off attracted a great deal of publicity which, in this case, resulted in dramatically increased ticket sales and most of the subsequent Boston performances being sold out.

By the time the Boston run finished in early July, some of the actors had had enough and further cast changes were made[39] before the tour moved on to the West Coast. Richardson was not involved in these and had left the production to look after itself. The play ran for two weeks at the Greek Theatre in Berkeley, then transferred to the Huntington Hartford[40] in Los Angeles, opening mid-July. Lionel Larner followed his client to L.A. and remembered:

> The only thing he was concerned about that opening night was whether or not Jill would come. It was very important for him – he was living for Jill.[41] I left the day after the opening and came back to New York. Either the next day or the day after, he went to a party in L.A., met a girl, was drinking, didn't drive, offered to drive her home, drove a car off Sunset Plaza Drive and landed in somebody's yard. She had to have facial surgery, he broke his arm, and at this point I called Oscar Beuselinck, his attorney in London, and I said, 'Oscar, I can't handle it – this is going to involve the authorities. He's on an H1 visitor's visa, he's broken the law by driving without a licence, he *has* to have an attorney deal with this.'

Norman Twain remembered Nicol as a bad driver without a licence who often insisted on driving anyway. Considering the fact that Sunset Plaza Drive is a road with many sharp bends and Nicol was by his own admission drunk at the time, it was fortunate that he was not killed. Instead, he spent several days recuperating in the Cedars-Sinai Medical Center and was replaced by his understudy, Welsh actor Clive Graham, for five consecutive nights. The press were told that Nicol was unable to perform due to exhaustion, but the story came out anyway. Ticket sales predictably dropped as a result.

The tour ended on the 9th of August. Nicol had received a number of film offers during his time in L.A., all of which he turned down, including an offer of $400,000 to play Enobarbus in a version of *Antony and Cleopatra* directed by and starring Charlton Heston. The role went to Eric Porter instead. However, there were a number of other potential projects around this time which he did not reject, but which would not come to fruition – or, at least, not with his involvement. One of these was a London production of the Greek tragedy *Prometheus Bound*, which would have involved Nicol being naked and chained to a rock throughout the play.

The Scottish writer Troy Kennedy Martin had been one of the creators of *Z Cars*. He was a tremendous fan of Nicol's and wanted him for the role of Bridger in the film of his script *The Italian Job*. However, the director, Peter Collinson, had other ideas and gave the part to Noël Coward instead, a piece of casting which completely changed the concept of the character.

Back in April, Nicol had signed on for a film entitled *A Mouthful of Gold*, based on a novel of the same name by Michael Baldwin. The screenplay was by Peter Barnes, best known as the writer of the play *The Ruling Class*. Nicol would have played a con-man newly released from jail, but the film was never made.

Another potential project was *Tiger, Tiger Burning Bright*, a film version of *The Old Man and Me*, a blackly comic novel by Elaine Dundy. The author had previously written *The Dud Avocado*, which had been a best-seller a few years earlier, and also happened to be the ex-wife of Kenneth Tynan. The book had been turned into a screen play by Isobel Lennart, an established writer who specialised in such adaptations. The story involved a young American woman who comes to England to seduce and attempt to kill off an English poet who she believes has cheated her out of her inheritance. Despite the efforts of producer A. Ronald Lubin, the project never made it off the ground. Presumably, Nicol would have played C.D. McKee, the poet.

Perhaps the most tantalising of Nicol's still-born projects at this time was *Macbeth*. It had always been on the cards that he would play the role, and the first planned attempt was a theatrical version scheduled to open at the Royal Court in December 1969 and to be followed by a West End transfer. This was to be produced by Norman Twain, directed by Anthony Page and would have co-starred Gordon Jackson as Banquo and possibly Rachel Roberts as Lady Macbeth. Plans were hatched simultaneously for a film version to be directed by Jack Gold and produced by Filmways in association with Columbia and a new company which Nicol had formed with Gold and a few others. Nicol began scouting for locations in Scotland with Gold, and they were given a budget of $700,000. However, Gold felt that the amount was insufficient as, although it was to be a stark version without elaborate sets or costumes, it would be expensive to light the locations which he and Nicol had in mind. He pushed for a budget increase, Columbia refused, and the project was cancelled, as was the Royal Court production. A year or so later, Nicol was in the running to star in Roman Polanski's film of *Macbeth* alongside Francesca Annis. Polanski had co-written the screenplay with Kenneth Tynan, who was keen to cast Nicol. However, the director eventually decided that Nicol was not suited to playing kings and should instead play 'ordinary men who are extraordinary.' He cast Jon Finch instead. Nicol predictably ignored Polanski's unsolicited advice and went on to play a number of kings in the years to come.

Returning to New York for a few days before flying back to London, Nicol appeared once more on *The Dick Cavett Show* alongside the folk singer Arlo Guthrie. He also hosted a midnight preview of *The Reckoning* for special guests including Andy Warhol and fellow actors George C. Scott, Alec McCowen and Pearl Bailey.

Chapter 10 – Corridors of Power

On the 15th of October, Nicol visited 10 Downing Street to meet the astronauts of Apollo 11, who were then engaged on a world tour. His invitation had presumably come from the Prime Minister, Harold Wilson, who had been to the Roundhouse to see *Hamlet* and become an enthusiastic fan. Nicol later recalled how Wilson had told him, 'I'm going to make you the youngest knight in British theatre!'[42] While at Downing Street, Nicol was approached by a stranger who asked him who he thought had been the best socialist leader. When Nicol replied, 'Hugh Gaitskell,' according to Nicol, the man screamed at him in 'a total loss of control' before running from the room. The man in question turned out to be Anthony Wedgwood 'Tony' Benn, the former Lord Stansgate, who was Minister of Technology at the time.

Towards the end of October, Nicol was interviewed for television by Mary Marquis on the first ever episode of *First Person Singular*, a BBC Scotland programme which was similar to the more famous *Face to Face* in that it consisted of an intense thirty minute interview with just one guest. According to the *Glasgow Herald*, when 'gently but inexorably needled' by Marquis, he 'confessed himself to be a man with perhaps more than his fair share of belligerence, and inclined to be impatient.'

Nicol was to be strangely inactive in the worlds of film and theatre over the next two years. There were a number of reasons for this absence. As we have seen, around this time his name was frequently attached to projects which were abandoned. Although he was seen as a desirable name who would bring prestige to a film, in the world of cinema he was not considered bankable and therefore his name alone was never enough for a film to receive the green light. Another reason is that the British film industry had undergone a sudden downturn towards the end of 1969. Many films had been receiving a considerable financial boost from American companies in return for the stateside distribution rights, but at this point the Americans withdrew *en masse* from London taking their chequebooks with them. Looking back at their association with the British over the past decade, they had concluded that their financing had simply not been profitable enough to make it worthwhile for them to continue.

The other reasons for Nicol's low profile were more personal, and he confessed to Jane Watts of the *Arts Guardian* a few years later that after *Hamlet* he had been 'so fed up with the stage' he had been unable to 'work up any enthusiasm for anything.' He went on to blame this state of affairs on exhaustion as a result of working 'for two years practically non-stop every day.' Nicol had also achieved so much in the space of ten years that he must have thought he could afford to bide his time. His *Hamlet* had been named as one of *Time* magazine's top ten theatrical experiences of the decade and earned him a Drama Desk Special Award as well as an *Evening Standard* Award as Best Actor of the London Stage 1969.

In January 1970, Kenneth Tynan took Nicol to lunch at the latter's favourite London restaurant, l'Etoile in Soho, and offered him a place in Laurence Olivier's National Theatre Company, which was then based at the Old Vic, where Tynan was employed as literary advisor. The offer included meaty roles in a number of classics, including those of Judge Brack in a version of *Hedda Gabler* to be directed by Ingmar Bergman, and Jamie in *Long Day's Journey into Night*, which would have been directed by Mike Nichols and co-starred Laurence Olivier. Nicol enjoyed the lunch and said he would sleep on it. The next day, he phoned Tynan and turned him down. Nicol placed a very high value on being his own man and it is his extreme individualism that best explains what may seem to be some quite perverse career choices. He needed to feel that his decisions were entirely his own and did not much welcome the help of others when it was unsolicited.

Meanwhile, Nicol had become something of a regular on *The David Frost Show* and, during one of his appearances, was given the opportunity to sing. His ability surprised many and it is indicative of his status at the time that it led to a recording contract with CBS Records. The cover of the resultant self-titled LP featured a pink-tinted extreme close-up of Nicol's face with his new drooping moustache. Nicol crooned a dozen easy-listening songs over the lush, string-laden arrangements of Ray Cane and David Lindup. Cane became a good friend and long-term musical collaborator. Nicol opened the album with Jimmy Webb's *Didn't We*, which had previously been the opening track sung by Richard Harris on *his* debut album. This seems a bizarre choice as Harris had played the title role on stage in adaptations of both *The Ginger Man* and *Diary of a Madman* before Nicol, so one would expect Nicol to have avoided encouraging any further comparisons. The record also featured no less than three songs by Kris Kristofferson, as well as others by songwriters such as Hoagy Carmichael and Tim Hardin. It was very competently produced but hardly ground-breaking, and it seems ironic that a man who was something of a firebrand as an actor made an album full of rather corny songs treated in such a conventional manner. Nicol was a strong singer when he was not reaching too high, but he was a great deal less distinctive as a singer than he was as an actor. His image was also a long way from Frank Sinatra's, so it seems doubtful that he would have been able to do more than scrape a living singing in pubs or on cruise ships had he chosen this career path. The album sounds rather dated today, although it remains a pleasant enough listen. Nicol was himself not entirely satisfied with the result, but he had clearly enjoyed making it and begun to say that he preferred the company of musicians to that of actors as he found them less pretentious.

At this stage in his career, Nicol had dispensed with the services of a theatrical agent in the UK and was using Oscar Beuselinck, who had become his lawyer, to also field any offers that came his way. On the 11th of February, Nicol received a call from Beuselinck asking if he would care to perform *Hamlet* at the White House at the invitation of Richard Nixon. The offer had come about as a result of a meeting between Nixon and Harold Wilson during which the latter had enthused about Nicol's performance at the Roundhouse. Nixon had subsequently become genuinely interested in Nicol and mentioned this to the press. A Columbia Pictures publicity man had taken note and proposed the idea of Nicol's visit to the White House.

On this occasion, Nicol accepted the offer without hesitation, later citing curiosity as his prime motivation. He must also have been aware that such an offer would almost certainly never come his way again as he was, in fact, the first actor ever to have been invited to the White House to perform. As it would probably have been impractical to stage the whole play and tedious to merely perform excerpts, Nicol decided to put together a one-man show consisting of extracts from *Hamlet* and other plays along with a few poems and songs – the sort of show he had been longing to do for years, in fact. He recruited Kenneth Tynan to help him devise the show. Tynan managed to make an arrangement with *The New Yorker* to write a profile of Nicol focusing on the preparations for the White House evening. Lionel Larner remembered:

> They did not want Tynan. They said to me, 'Oh, isn't he something to do with *Oh, Calcutta*?'[43] So I said, 'You can't dismiss Kenneth Tynan as something to do with *Oh, Calcutta*. A lot of important writers wrote for *Oh, Calcutta* – he's a dramaturge of the National Theatre of England, and he's here doing a profile for *The New Yorker*, and he has to come.' And they finally said to me, 'Well, he can come as a member of the press but he cannot come as a guest of the president.' I said fine, he just wanted to be there. So Ken Tynan came and followed us around the whole time. Whenever we went to dinner, Ken was there making copious notes.

After accepting an award from the Variety Club of Great Britain for Best Film Actor of 1969 at the Savoy on the 8th of March, Nicol flew to New York with Tynan on the 11th. The evening was to take place on the 19th. Despite having a massive amount of material to learn in a few days, Nicol was often out until 4 a.m. singing at Jimmy Ryan's, although he quite likely felt that he needed an opportunity to focus on something other than the big night which was fast approaching. He was also continually advised by friends such as Penelope Gilliatt that he must use his opportunity to make some subtle kind of political statement, a suggestion which he considered but ultimately rejected. The programme was to have run as follows:

1. Hamlet's speech to the players
2. Poem by Samuel Beckett
3. Song: 'Blow, Blow Thou Winter Wind' (from *As You Like It*)
4. Hotspur confronts the King from *Henry IV, Part 1*
5. Poem: extract from 'Little Gidding' by T.S. Eliot
6. From *Inadmissible Evidence*
7. Poem: 'may i feel said he' by e.e. cummings
8. Song: 'Sigh No More' (from *Much Ado About Nothing*)
9. The dagger speech from *Macbeth*
10. Song: 'Dunsinane Blues' by Johnny Dankworth
11. Song: 'South Rampart Street Parade' by Bob Haggart (band without Nicol)
12. Malvolio's letter speech from *Twelfth Night*
13. Song: 'Winter' (from *Love's Labour's Lost*)
14. 'A man is not a piece of fruit' (speech from *Death of a Salesman*)
15. Song: 'Baby Won't You Please Come Home?'
16. 'The Treasurer's Report' by Robert Benchley (comic sketch)
17. Song: 'Darktown Strutter's Ball'
18. Poem: 'The Second Coming' by W.B. Yeats
19. Extract from *How It Is* by Samuel Beckett
20. Song: 'Savoy Blues' (band without Nicol)
21. 'Oh what a rogue and peasant slave am I' (speech from *Hamlet*)
22. Poem: extract from 'The Lovesong of J. Alfred Prufrock' by T.S. Eliot
23. Prospero's 'our revels now are ended' speech from *The Tempest*

After a rehearsal in front of an invited audience at the Roosevelt Grill in Manhattan riddled with fluffed lines and dropped cues met with a muted response, the Malvolio speech was dropped and replaced with the 'now is the winter of our discontent' speech from *Richard III*. The 'to be or not to be' soliloquy from *Hamlet* was also added. Nicol,

Tynan and Larner flew to Washington the evening before the big night.

The evening took place in the East Room with 270 guests in attendance in black tie. The musicians were also formally attired, but Nicol himself was able to get away with a light blue sweater, grey slacks and a silk scarf. He was introduced by Nixon himself, who it emerged later had had the film of *Inadmissible Evidence* screened at his Camp David retreat shortly before. Nicol was backed on the musical interludes by The World's Greatest Jazz Band, a nine-piece led by Yank Lawson and Bob Haggart. Nicol had gone to see the band when he had been in Boston playing Hamlet, dragging several other members of the cast along with him to the Jazz Workshop, where he ended up singing a few songs and becoming friendly with the musicians. When he began putting the presidential show together later, the White House wanted Nicol to use the Marine Corps Band but he insisted on using the band he had met in Boston.

Considering how shaky the rehearsal had been, fortunately the old showbiz maxim 'it will be alright on the night' proved true in this case, with one exception, as Lionel Larner remembered:

> There was security all around the room, and we were sitting almost directly behind the president. It was the night Cambodia fell. Nicol had a programme of what he was doing and he went out of sequence and Ken said to me, 'Lionel, go back and tell him!' And I said, 'I'm not getting up out of my seat – I'm behind the president!' I would have been frogmarched out! I said, '*You* go back and tell him!'

Tynan also proved reluctant to move, but Nicol got back on track without anyone having to leave their seat.

The World's Greatest Jazz Band played their own set in the State Dining Room after the main performance had ended and the Nixons had gone to bed. Nicol sang 'I Can't Give You Anything but Love, Baby' with them and unveiled yet another hidden talent by contributing a trumpet solo to their rendition of 'Tin Roof Blues'.

The show was very well-received and all of the critics present gave positive reviews. Lionel Larner remembered the aftermath:

> It was a triumph. When Nixon introduced him, he said that Wilson had called him the finest Hamlet of his generation. I said to Nicol, 'Wasn't that a wonderful thing for him to say that Wilson had said that?' He said, 'No, because if I fell on my arse it would have been Wilson's fault.'

However, although Nicol also initially seemed to feel it had gone well, when asked some years later by *Penthouse* magazine how he would rate his performance, he replied, 'It stank,' and went on to say that he had a tape of the performance which he would occasionally play to remind himself that 'a red face is sometimes good to wear, privately.'

Another person present at the White House was Ro Diamond, who was at the time Lionel Larner's associate. She and Nicol became quite close for a while to the extent that one newspaper reported them dining together in early April 1970, and a few weeks later another referred to her as Nicol's 'constant companion lately.' Diamond later remembered:

> The first time I met him was at the St. Regis in the Cecil Beaton suite with him ordering Tattinger champagne by the case. Columbia Pictures were paying for everything because Nicol's appearance at the White House was huge publicity for his *Hamlet* film. I didn't date him but just hung out with him a lot - I was totally enthralled and captivated by his craziness. It was addictive.
>
> I remember sitting in the green room with him at *The Dick Cavett Show*, waiting for him to go on. He had just returned from a trip to Mexico & had these chili peppers in his pocket. He convinced me to eat one by taking a bite first. It set my mouth and brain on fire! I was choking and gagging and he was laughing. Lionel was upset that I was so stupid. I remember Lionel saying 'Monkey see, monkey do!'

Back in England, Nicol had again been nominated for a BAFTA, this time for the film of *Inadmissible Evidence*, but lost out to Dustin Hoffman, who won for *Midnight Cowboy*. However, he did accept an award for Film Actor of the Year from David Hill, the editor of *Weekend* magazine.

Manhattan had by now become something of a second home for Nicol, and he began to go back and forth between New York and London quite frequently. In May, he was interviewed at the King Cole Bar in Manhattan's St. Regis hotel by a journalist from the *Sarasota Herald-Tribune* for their 'Celebrity Cookbook' column. The headline was 'Nicol Williamson Likes American "Hot-Dog" Mustard'. Readers whose interest had been piqued by this controversial revelation could read on to discover Nicol's recipe for potato-corn cakes and learn that, although Nicol enjoyed the taste of oysters and snails, both foods made him nauseous.

With the proceeds from his film work, Nicol had bought John Osborne's former home, The Old Water Mill at Hellingly in East Sussex. It later became a Grade II listed building and may have been a good investment but, as it was not a convenient location for someone who did not drive, Nicol never lived there and seldom visited. His base in London at this time was a small house in Notting Hill. He had become a member of the nearby Mount Street Football Club, which met every Sunday in Hyde Park. Fellow actors Richard Harris, Tom Courtenay, Ian McShane, Marty Feldman, John Alderton and David Hemmings were also members, as was a restaurateur known as Alvaro, and Douglas Hayward, a Mayfair tailor whose client list included many famous names. In June 1970, the team was flown out to Mexico for a friendly match with the England World Cup team. A half hour documentary was made about the event, entitled *Today Mexico, Tomorrow the World!*

In July, Nicol travelled to Spain to be one of the jury members for the Seashell Awards at the San Sebastian Film Festival along with Fritz Lang and others. Shortly after arriving, he did his by now familiar disappearing act and had to be replaced by a Uruguayan critic. On another occasion during this period, Nicol was again invited to appear as a guest on *The Dick Cavett Show*. However, he got bored while waiting in the green room and departed, leaving Cavett and his only other guest, Nora Ephron, struggling to fill the airtime.

Meanwhile, Nicol had heard from mutual friends that Jill Townsend's marriage had not been a success and was delighted to learn that she had divorced her husband. Determined not to let her slip through his fingers a second time, he devoted his energies to winning her back permanently. As a result of this, Nicol's career – which he had perhaps begun to take a little unwisely for granted – became further neglected. Jill Townsend:

> In the summer of 1970 I was in London. My parents had rented a flat in Goodwin's Court, a little alleyway in Covent Garden. There were a lot of theatre agents in there. I had been with my parents sailing the Aegean in a boat belonging to a friend of theirs because my father was about to turn 50 and he didn't want to think about it so we went sailing – my sister, myself, my mum and dad. Then we went back to London. My parents returned to the States and I stayed in the flat. I was only going to stay for a couple of days. The phone rang – this is the biggest mystery to me – I picked it up having no idea who it could be and said, 'Hello?' A man's voice said, 'Hello?' I said, 'Hello? Who is this?' and he said, 'Nicol.' I said, 'How did you get this number?' and he said, '*You're* calling *me!*' I said, 'I'm not calling anyone!' and that's how we got together. He must have planned it somehow but I don't know how, and that's when we started going out again.

Not long after they had resumed their relationship, Nicol moved into Jill's basement flat in Chelsea's Markham Square.

Nicol's first acting role for some time was in the title role of *Terrible Jim Fitch*, an episode of *Thirty-Minute Theatre* broadcast by the BBC in January 1971. The play was written by James Leo Herlihy as part of a trio of short plays with the umbrella title *Stop, You're Killing Me*. Herlihy was the author of *Midnight Cowboy* and, like that more famous work, *Terrible Jim Fitch* is also a close-up look at the seedy side of life, in this case the life of a petty criminal who makes his living robbing church charity boxes. Set in a motel room, the play is a monologue directed at his sulking girlfriend, Sally, who has just discovered she will be permanently scarred as a result of a beating from Jim. Although Jim is certainly a nasty piece of work, it becomes clear not only that he is also suffering but that he is actually a rather pathetic figure. Sally was played by Marianne Faithfull and her role was remarkably similar to that of Bill Maitland's daughter, which she had very nearly played back in 1964. Like Jane Maitland, Sally has not one word of dialogue and is there as a sort of receptacle for the outpourings of the main character. The director of the episode was James Ferman, who abandoned this career a few years later to become director of the British Board of Film Classification.

Lionel Larner decided he had to drop Nicol as a client around this time, as he later explained:

> I was always dragging him out of pubs and brawls. He'd have to be somewhere in the morning and the phone would be ringing and he'd knock the phone off the hook. I was running over to the hotel and barging into his room and dragging him out of bed and getting him to meetings with studios and things – it was a full-time job! I had a whole agency to take care of, so it was really 'Do I take care of Nicol and lose all my other clients or do I protect my agency?'
>
> He treated me like a best friend. He would wake up in the morning if he had nothing to do, stroll over to my office where I was busy. I had a Chesterfield sofa in the reception room and he would lie down on it and read magazines – and sometimes they were alarming, he was reading *Screw* magazine! My clients would come in and say, 'Is that Nicol Williamson out there?' because he was very celebrated, he was really the great white hope and he had enormous – *enormous* – talent and he could have been the successor to Olivier.
>
> The success did come, but he was tortured. He was very envious of what he called the 'pretty boys', the guys that got the girls. He didn't seem to have too much problem, but he was envious of the Robert Redfords and people like that.
>
> He called me one day and said, 'Lionel, I was dreaming about you last night. I want to ask you a question: would you lend me some money?' I said, 'Yes, of course – how much?' And he said, 'No, I don't need any money. That was just a test… would you take me back?' I was

dreading it, and I said, 'Oh Nicol, we've done all that, we're just going to be friends now.' But I did love him a lot.

He loved all the 1930s music. I had an LP of Gertrude Lawrence and Noël Coward where they do the balcony scene from *Private Lives* and he would sit there and listen to it and say to me, 'You know, I believe every word of it.'

We would go to Jimmy Ryan's on 52nd Street. He wanted to see me all the time – as friendship, it was fun. He went out with Camilla Sparv, a promising movie star of the time, beautiful! They were at PJ Clarke's and I thought, 'Oh great, I've got the night off!' Then the phone would ring and he'd say, 'I'm just sitting here with Camilla and I was telling her about you – why don't you come and join us?' And I'd say, 'Oh Nicol, I'm in my pyjamas now!' But he always wanted me along and if anybody spoke sharply to me in a bar or pushed me or anything, he was ready to have a fight! It was exhausting. I was very proud to represent him and I liked him a lot, but it was too demanding and suffocating. He could have had the world. He was self-destructive. Nicol was up there with Peter O'Toole and Richard Harris – he could do everything those guys could do.

In February, Nicol lent his voice to a recording of *Lessness*, a work by Samuel Beckett which was being produced by Martin Esslin for Radio 3. *Lessness* is not so much a play as a prose poem. According to Esslin, 'Mr Beckett indicated how he wanted six voices to share in the reading – not as different characters or persons, but as indicators of different groups of images.' The 25 minute piece was recorded at the Royal Court and the other voices were provided by Patrick Magee and Harold Pinter among others. It is not a very accessible work even by Beckett standards, and the number of people who listened to the end must have been small indeed. However, for those with the requisite patience, it is an effectively unsettling experience.

In May, Nicol had lunch with Kenneth Tynan at l'Etoile once more, was offered King Lear, and again politely declined.

Chapter 11 – Domestic Bliss

On the 10th of May, Nicol was back on *The Dick Cavett Show* in an episode filmed in London, which also featured actors Laurence Harvey and Adrienne Corri along with former spy Eddie Chapman. On this occasion, Nicol had a different kind of surprise in store for his long-suffering host. Jill Townsend:

> I was sitting in the audience in my hip-hugger jeans and a white, long-sleeved T-shirt which had the Superman emblem on it. Nicol was up there being interviewed by Dick Cavett, saying, 'I'm getting married!' I had no idea – he hadn't proposed to me – and he said, 'And there she is, sitting in the audience!'

Nicol spoke of his plan to marry in July at his parents' farmhouse, East Hazeldean, just outside the small town of Stonehouse in Scotland.

In order to help provide Jill with a comfortable home, Nicol decided to make a film. Of the various scripts available, he selected one called *Jerusalem, Jerusalem* by Troy Kennedy Martin, a thriller set in 1967 just after the Arab-Israeli Six Day War. The part of an archaeology professor struggling to keep his students out of danger attracted him because, as he told the *Evening News*, all his other characters had been 'men hell-bent on driving themselves to destruction,' whereas this one was 'hell-bent on saving something.' Indeed, it was about as close as Nicol would ever get to playing the hero but, while he may have found the novelty of this stimulating, few others would see the part as a good use of his talents. Still sporting his drooping ginger moustache, he had little to do but look concerned and stride purposefully down corridors. The cast also included Donald Pleasence as a police major and American actor Bruce Davison in the leading role as a student flirting dangerously with politics.

The film was shot on location in Jerusalem and Tel Aviv on a budget of $1 million. The director was an American, John Flynn, who had previously directed only one feature, *The Sergeant*, starring Rod Steiger. Flynn would later make a couple of films which became cult classics of the '70s (*The Outfit* and *Rolling Thunder*) before finishing his career directing vehicles for the likes of Steven Seagal and Sylvester Stallone. He was forced to work under difficult circumstances, having to put up with sudden changes in the Israeli crew as some members had to leave at short notice to do military service. His cinematographer was the highly respected Frenchman, Raoul Coutard, but the fact that the rest of the camera crew were also French (due to Coutard's lack of English) caused further difficulties. Flynn also had no right to final cut, and when he later arrived in London to do the dubbing he was shocked to find that the film had been drastically edited by someone else into something he no longer understood, which may explain why the characters all seem underwritten. When the film was released as *The Jerusalem File* on the 2nd of February 1972, some critics saw it as Zionist propaganda, but there is little real justification for this – if the film had a message, it seemed more to do with the dangers of idealism in a world ruled by revenge.

For some of the shoot, Nicol was staying at the American Colony Hotel in Jerusalem, where Bob Dylan was a fellow guest. Nicol was apparently not always on his best behaviour and tended to burst into song at ear-splitting volume late at night. According to John Flynn, when Dylan complained, Nicol threatened to throw him off the balcony. This incident aside, Nicol apparently behaved well and had a good relationship with the cast and crew. Jill Townsend joined him for part of the shoot, and recalled:

> Nicol and I rented the *Time Life* correspondent's apartment. He was in Vietnam at that time. One funny story that I remember was when they were filming a scene in the old walled city and they had to go out and get extras. They found all these guys and told them, 'Ok, we're going to give you some money and you just have to stand along the walls here to

give us some local colour.' Then John Flynn turns to Raoul Coutard and says, 'Are you ready to shoot?' and all the extras fled!

Nicol's parents flew out for a while and spent much of their time exploring the city with Jill. John and Anna Morrell, a couple who were close friends of Nicol, also came out for a visit. John Morrell was a banker who worked for Barings and Anna was apparently an actress or dancer who had known Nicol for many years. When Nicol returned with Jill to London in July, they abandoned the plan of marrying in Scotland and were instead married on the 17th with a notable lack of ceremony at Chelsea registry office. The only guests in attendance were the Morrells and John Thaw. Jill Townsend:

> John Thaw was about Nicol's best friend when we were together. I loved John. He had a great sense of humour. When we arrived, I didn't want to get out of the car because all the press were there. I didn't like press attention – I was happy for Nicol to have it all. Afterwards, we went to his favourite little Irish restaurant in Soho for lunch, where we had Irish stew.
>
> Later, when my parents came over, we had a blessing at Chelsea Old Church on Cheyne Walk in London. Then we had a party at Meridiana, an Italian restaurant, where all our wedding gifts were stolen during the party. It was terrible because we couldn't thank anybody. Our guests arrived at Meridiana, left their presents downstairs and went upstairs to the restaurant, which was closed to the public that night. Somebody pulled up with a truck and just took them all!
>
> We had our wedding night at the Ritz hotel and the fun thing is, the night before the wedding, Nicol stayed at our house and I went and stayed at our cousin's, so we didn't see each other until we got to the church.

In interviews at this time, Nicol had begun to speak of giving up acting in favour of singing. During 1971, he appeared as a singing guest on two television shows hosted by Tom Jones and one hosted by Harry Secombe. The album he had made a year earlier was finally released, but despite this exposure, sales were not brisk enough for him to seriously contemplate such a move.

Nicol and Jill purchased an attractive yellow-shuttered three-storey terraced house known as Woodfall Cottage at 12 Woodfall Street, a cobblestoned cul-de-sac in Chelsea. Jill had found it when she visited a nearby Indian restaurant and saw the 'For Sale' sign being put up. Only later, when she took Nicol to view the property, did she discover it was on the same street in which John Osborne and Mary Ure had lived at number 15 before it became the offices of Woodfall Films. By the time Nicol and Jill moved in, Woodfall Films was no longer active.

Nicol and Jill shared their new home with Ellie and Fred, two lovebirds Jill had bought and then housed in a large Victorian birdcage in the dining room. There had always been a conventional side to Nicol, and he had been yearning for a stable home life with the woman he loved and with whom he wanted to have children. He told the *Daily Mail* that he had suddenly realised that his true nature was that of a 'complacent, middle-aged, backgammon playing, nest building, house painting, happily married man.' It was a new role for him and one which he would enjoy playing for a while, but in reality he was fooling himself and the novelty would soon wear off. Although Nicol mostly ceased his late-night bar-crawling, he was not an entirely changed man, as Jill Townsend remembered:

> He still had his moments of drinking. I used to refer to them as 'horror shows'. But we went to a bridge school and learned how to play bridge, which we used to play with the neighbours. We were homebodies and that was how I thought it was going to be for the rest of my life.

Enjoying his new-found domesticity, Nicol continued to stay away from acting for the next few months. It was also around this time that Jill introduced him to a place which was to become very important in his life:

> When I was sailing with my parents in 1970 we went to many of the Greek islands and I discovered this little place called Lindos on the island of Rhodes. Later, Nicol had asked me, 'What's your favourite

place you've ever been to?' and I said, 'Lindos,' so he found somebody he knew, Mary Clow, who had a place there and we would rent it. After he and I separated, he started going back and taking Luke with him.

Lindos (photograph by author)

Mary Clow had been an assistant to Tony Richardson on the films *Laughter in the Dark* and *Hamlet*. Located on the east coast of the island, the village of Lindos is dominated by the ancient acropolis which sits at the top of a very steep hill. Whitewashed houses adorn the lower slopes and the village is blessed with both a sandy beach and a rocky bay with clear blue water. It is a very attractive place which has inevitably become more tourist-dominated over the years, but was at this time something of a well-kept secret. Lindos had become a colony for artists and drop-outs in the '60s and attracted a number of famous people over the years, including several members of the band Pink Floyd, whose David Gilmour still owns a house there at the time of writing. Nicol was to revisit it many times and would eventually end up living there.

In January the following year, Nicol accepted the lead role in a film based on the book *Hostage in Peking* by journalist Anthony Grey.

The book was a non-fiction account of the two years Grey had spent as a captive of the Chinese government. The film was never made. Another role which fell by the wayside was that of Chief Inspector Oxford in Alfred Hitchcock's *Frenzy*. The reason for this is unclear, but the part was eventually played by Alec McCowen. In April, Nicol did a screen test for the role of the aviator in Stanley Donen's musical film of the enduring children's classic *The Little Prince*. The test showed him dressed in 1930s flying gear, singing one of the songs which had been written for the film. However, Donen's associate producer, A. Joseph Tandet, was not convinced and the part went to Richard Kiley.

Back in 1966, Luis Bunuel had written a screenplay with his frequent collaborator Jean-Claude Carriere based on Matthew Lewis' gothic novel *The Monk*, a favourite among the surrealists, perhaps because of its attack on religious hypocrisy and the fact that almost none of the characters are what they appear to be. Bunuel ended up abandoning *The Monk* and making *Belle de Jour* instead but gave the screenplay rights to his friend Ado Kyrou a few years later. Kyrou, a Greek who had been living in Paris for decades, was a film critic with a penchant for surrealist and avant-garde cinema and had written a book on Bunuel. He had directed only one previous feature and jumped at the chance of helming a film based on a script by his idol. He persuaded a couple of enterprising producers to finance a version with himself as director. One of the producers was Howard Zucker, an American who was better known as an actor under the name of Zack Norman. The other was Henry Lange, a Frenchman who specialised in producing exploitation films. The film was to be an Italian-French-German co-production, which meant that an actor known throughout Europe was required for the lead. The role was taken by Franco Nero, the star of the hit spaghetti western *Django*. The female lead went to French actress Nathalie Delon, while Nicol agreed to play the Duke of Talamur, a part which did not exist in the original novel and had been created by Bunuel and Carriere. Jill Townsend accompanied him for the filming and remembered:

I had to read the contract in French and translate it to Nicol. We arrived at Le Bourget airport to find our luggage had been stolen then we got into this Citroen DS taxi and went way out into the country where they were filming. We're in the back of the taxi and all of a sudden we hear a sound and I know that the windscreen is gone, so I throw Nicol onto the floor and cover him. But when we arrive at wherever we're staying, we're covered in glass and had to pick it out of our hair and our clothes. We had a tiny little bedroom, it was very cold and the toilets were outside holes in the ground. It only took about three days for him to make that film, but it was three days of, 'Are you kidding me?' It was not an easy production!

Franco Nero played Ambrosio, a monk so devout that 'they say he can't tell the difference between a man and a woman.' However, when Ambrosio finally succumbs and is seduced by a woman disguised as a monk, he rapidly becomes depraved to the point of using witchcraft to take advantage of a young girl. Nicol's Duke is a bearded, apparently jovial nobleman who takes in orphans under the guise of charity. In reality, he is a paedophile who abuses then kills them and has them cooked in a stew for his dinner (thankfully, this is implied rather than shown). Unfortunately, budgetary constraints had forced Kyrou to make changes to the script and, as a director, he was no Bunuel. Nero was also fatally miscast and in the English version his strong Italian accent at times renders his dialogue barely intelligible. Nicol gave a witty performance as the unctuous monster but it is difficult to see the film as anything other than a failure. Shot in 1972, it was not released in the UK until two years later when, touted as 'the most audacious work of Luis Bunuel' it received a very limited release before vanishing into obscurity along with *The Jerusalem File.*

Kenneth Tynan's long piece about Nicol had finally been published in *The New Yorker* in January. Tynan focused on Nicol's eccentricities and let the witticisms flow. It was an entertaining read, but Nicol did not appreciate the way he had been portrayed and treated Tynan coldly from this point on.

Meanwhile, Nicol's old school friend from his Birmingham days, Tony Garnett, had abandoned acting to become a successful producer, mainly for television. Despite his often controversial subjects and hard left outlook, Garnett had produced a number of works which had been seen by huge numbers of people and much discussed. Among these were a number of collaborations with director Ken Loach, including *Cathy Come Home* and *Kes*. A lesser known work was *The Lump*, which had marked director Jack Gold's first foray into drama. Garnett had recently become interested in the work of German playwright Bertolt Brecht and had particularly enjoyed a West End production of Brecht's *The Resistible Rise of Arturo Ui* he had seen starring Leonard Rossiter. Written in 1941 and depicting the rise of a Hitler-like figure and his cronies in 1930s Chicago, the play was clearly intended as an attack on the Nazi regime. Garnett decided he wanted to make a version for the BBC and retitled it *The Gangster Show* to avoid alienating the non-intellectuals. He hired Hungarian writer George Tabori to turn it into a screenplay. Tabori, whose father had been a victim of the Nazis, had already translated the play in 1964. Garnett chose Jack Gold to direct and asked him for suggestions for the lead. Gold thought that Peter Sellers would be perfect and, when Garnett discovered that he was interested, producer and director went to see him at his home in Dublin, where he enthusiastically acted out the part in his living room and expressed indifference about money. Garnett and Gold thought they had been very lucky to secure such a huge star for a tiny BBC fee but, as the weeks passed, Sellers became unreachable and they realised he was not going to commit after all. At this point, thoughts turned to Nicol, as Garnett explains:

> It was Jack's idea to have Nicol. I had grave doubts about it. What we were trying to do was the equivalent of a Warner Brothers gangster movie recreating 1930s Chicago in London with a big cast on a BBC budget, which was a ridiculous thing to try to do in the first place! We had a very good crew. Jack's a very disciplined, responsible director... I thought it was a smart idea for Nicol to play the part, but I couldn't

afford the slightest delay. I couldn't afford any temperament or spoiled actors who were irresponsible. And by then his reputation was pretty incendiary and I thought, 'We're totally fucked if he plays up!' But, on the other hand, he'd worked with Jack before, and actors don't play up with Jack. He doesn't create antagonism, he's the sweetest man in the world. And he's very grown-up, he gets on with the job and he's honest with people and I thought, 'Well, if anyone can handle Nicol, it'll be Jack.' So in the end I said okay – with my heart in my mouth, really – but I said, 'Let's do it.' And of course Nicol arrived – I hadn't seen him for some years – and he was very friendly and he behaved impeccably from start to finish.

Jack's too modest to say that that was probably down to him because on a whole lot of other things Nicol did, there *were* problems. I think it might have been his own insecurity… when actors are spoiled, as they call them, it's because literally they have been *spoiled*. Because it's a shitty job and they're treated badly, and there they are offering themselves up for scrutiny and they develop all sorts of defence mechanisms to deal with it, and when they get – as occasionally some do – into a position where they've got a bit of power, they play up, which is exactly what little children do if they've been spoiled – that is, treated badly, not loved enough, not trusted enough, not believed in enough. That's what actors do and, I think, what Nicol did. I don't know what the cause of his insecurity was, but the life of an actor was probably quite difficult for him in terms of his own self-belief, although of course he could put on a pose of being the most imperious, confident person. But Jack just cut through all of that and as soon as any actor walked on the set – or before they got to the set – they just chatted with Jack, and they relaxed – they just *knew* this would be okay. I did two films with Jack and it was just like the easiest ride in the world.

One of the aspects of Nicol's reputation which had concerned Garnett had been his alcohol consumption, but in this case he need not have worried, as he goes on to say:

On *Arturo Ui* there was not the slightest sign of alcohol. He was always on time, he always knew his lines, he behaved courteously with everyone else. He actually behaved like an impeccable pro, to be fair to him. I knew he had a drink problem as a grown-up, but when I met him way before *Arturo*, and I said, 'You're looking well, Nicol,' he said, 'Yes, I've given up drink completely!' I said, 'Really? Goodness me, Nicol, that's an achievement – well done. No wonder you're looking so well.' He replied, 'Oh yes, just a couple of bottles of wine a day, that's all!' And he said it as though he was not making a joke, this is a serious statement, an amplification of what he'd just said – that he'd given up drink. Because for him, drink was spirits and a couple of bottles of wine a day was just, well, not really drinking. It wasn't bravado, I think it was just a statement of fact, so he probably could take it. It probably didn't do his health any good in the long-term, but… I think he put it away in big quantities, but I never heard of him being incapable, and I certainly never heard of him missing a performance from it.

Nicol gave a brilliant comic performance, playing Ui as Hitler with a Brooklyn-ese accent as he bribes, blackmails, bullies and wheedles his way to control of the cauliflower trade. It seems likely that he studied footage of Hitler in preparation as he replicated the dictator's mannerisms and odd gestures perfectly. He also threw in a few moments of slapstick for good measure. The supporting cast was strong, despite the difficulty in finding enough available actors who either were American or could do a convincing American accent. Bruce Boa, the Canadian actor from the Dundee Rep production of *Death of a Salesman*, also appeared, as did Sam Wanamaker, an American actor-director who had come to England twenty years previously to escape the McCarthy witch-hunts. In 1970, Wanamaker had founded the Shakespeare Globe Trust to rebuild the Globe Theatre at its original location. There was also a good part for Jill Townsend as a woman who dares to stand up to Ui. She had one abiding memory of the production:

> We were filming somewhere in Earl's Court and Nicol was dressed like Hitler. It's lunchtime and there's a little old-fashioned hotel with a dining room where the residents eat. Nicol said, 'Come on, let's go in and have lunch here,' and, of course, he does the whole Hitler thing as he goes in there! It's so terribly embarrassing and very funny at the same time! He's ordering food like he's Hitler and the patrons in the

restaurant were terrified! I think I excused myself because I just couldn't stand the torment of those people there! He could be very, very funny, but how he had the courage to do something like that, I don't know.

Jack Gold remembered the production as having been shot in '23 or 24 days' and said that he 'never thought of it as a television film, just as a film which happens to be shown on television.' Filming in black and white, Gold and crew pulled off a highly impressive pastiche of the American gangster film which belied its low production budget. The audience may not have been huge, but the reviews were uniformly excellent and *The Gangster Show: The Resistible Rise of Arturo Ui* is a film which deserves to be much more widely seen, especially as the satire remains so relevant decades later. Nicol was nominated for a BAFTA for his performance but lost out to his old sparring partner Anthony Hopkins, who won for his portrayal of Pierre in a major new television production of *War and Peace* – the same part that Nicol had played ten years previously.

Towards the end of October, Nicol attended a charity boxing night in aid of care for the elderly at the Hilton Hotel in London alongside other celebrities including Peter Sellers and Michael Caine. He apparently lost a not inconsiderable amount through betting on some Scottish boxers before returning home with Ian Bannen in tow and singing until 3 a.m. The following day, nursing a hangover, he learned that Jill was expecting a baby.

In November, the BBC's Radio 3 broadcast an uncut audio version of *Othello* which had been pre-recorded at some point after *Arturo Ui* had been shot. The title role was portrayed by another Shakespearean giant, Paul Scofield, and it was to be the only occasion on which he and Nicol worked together. Nicol had the perhaps more interesting role as Iago, the two-faced villain who, merely because he has suffered a blow to his vanity, orchestrates Othello's downfall by manipulating those close to him. The radio play was directed by John Tydeman, who remembered it this way:

Nicol was a quirky man – you didn't know which way he was going to jump, but we got on relatively well as director and actor. He had his own individuality, as indeed had Scofield, which is partly why I cast them both. I knew Paul Scofield very well but I didn't know Nicol, although I'd met him. I thought they'd spark the right things off against each other as Iago and Othello and I think it's an exceptionally good rendition of the play – not because of any part that I played – but because they were so right together in conflict. They were two very unalike personalities, but alike in a sense as actors insofar as they both had a very individual way of approaching things. They were both unusual actors and both spoke in an unusual way.

They had a conflict, actually, as types of actor *and* as people because Nicol was wild and Paul was safe and respectable by this age. Anyhow, when we came to do it, it was done not as one usually does a radio play in bits and pieces and so on. The first act of the play is set in Venice and stands apart, so we recorded that alone. I then said to the cast that we were going to record the rest of the play – the other four acts – from the arrival in Cyprus to the end in one long, long take, which is very unusual, i.e. to do it as though one were doing a stage play and then to pick up any mistakes that were made afterwards by doing retakes. If anyone made a mistake of which they were aware, then they stopped, went back and started again because it could easily be edited later.

We had a read-through of the whole play and about halfway through we had a break and I was aware that Paul and Nicol sounded a bit alike. The *timbre* of their voices was similar and they did and could sound really quite alike which, when you're doing radio, is not a good thing! So I told this to them and Paul said, 'Well, I can go darker and deeper and I think I can Moor it up a bit!' So Paul lowered his voice and added a slight African-ish accent, whereas Nicol retained his slightly nasal way of talking. Anyhow, we did the first act, which was fine, then they arrived in Cyprus and went through to the end of the play and it was fairly good and exciting. I said from the control room, 'That was excellent ! We'll have a little pause and then we'll do the retakes.' And Nicol said, 'Retakes?' I said, 'Yes, there were bits that weren't right, bits that could be better, etc., so we edit those in.' Nicol said, 'I'm not fucking doing that!', threw his script down on the floor and walked out of the studio. The other actors were rather surprised! Paul said, 'I don't know what you're going to do, John!' I said, 'Don't worry – I'll get him!' I found Nicol somewhere in Broadcasting House – in the canteen, I think – and I said, 'Now, come on, Nicol, I told you exactly what was going to happen.' He said, 'I can't do it again the same!' I said, 'You can! An actor always does. You have a retake and you think it's not the same, but it's there somehow, it's printed in your voice and in your memory and you will do it the same. I'm sorry, but you've got to get the words right, the pronunciation right and certain things should be better.' There were quite a lot, but not a *huge* number – very few considering the length of what we had done. Anyhow, I finally managed to woo Nicol back on side and he said, 'Okay, if you say no-one will notice,' so we did it and it ended not unhappily.

Afterwards, it was recognized by the whole cast, even Nicol, that this was really rather a special occasion and could be a very good production on stage and be very popular with an audience. Both Paul and Nicol became keen on doing it in a theatre with me as their director. Paul had always been on my side, but it was not until afterwards that Nicol said, 'You're bloody good, John – I've never been better directed' and so on. So, in the end, outside forces came into play and Nicol spoke to his agent and Paul to his and they said yes, they would do it together if they had the right management or producers to put it on. Nicol said, 'I promised Sam Wanamaker that the next production I did would be for him and it would be to make money to build The Globe.' Paul, who never spoke ill of anybody, said, 'I refuse to work under Sam Wanamaker – I think he's a snake! I think we should go to the best impresario that I know. He's got the money and he's got the production company behind him and that man is Michael Winner. We can put it on at Her Majesty's Theatre.' Paul also said, 'If I do do it, I'd like you to see that Nicol is kept as far away from me as possible off stage because I find him very irritating!' Anyhow, it all finally fell apart. I think both of them were frightened a bit of the other. It was damned silly and it was a big shame for everybody, including the audience, who missed what could have been a most exciting stage production.

Nicol signed on for a rather odd film project in November. Canadian-based British director Eric Till planned to make a film of *La Guerre, Yes Sir!*, a comic novel by Roch Carrier about a dead soldier brought back to his Quebec village to be buried during World War Two. French and English language versions were to be shot back to back in Canada in January, but it was to be yet another unrealised project. However, it is difficult to see a suitable part for Nicol in the book anyway, although it is of course possible that the screenplay was substantially different.

In December, Nicol appeared as a guest on the ITV chat show *Russell Harty Plus*... in an effort to plug the one-man show he was debuting at the Queen's Theatre for one night only. The show consisted of various songs and poems and was similar to the one he had performed at the White House but without the dramatic monologues. He called it *Midwinter Spring* and would revive it (with slight variations) a number of times in the years to come.

The beginning of 1973 was a quiet one for Nicol until he received a phone call from Mike Nichols, who had employed him back in 1968 to replace George C. Scott for six weeks in his hit production of *Plaza Suite*. Nichols had been given *carte blanche* by Theodore Mann, the artistic director of the Circle-In-The-Square theatre, and decided to tackle Anton Chekhov's *Uncle Vanya*, first published in 1897. The theatre, on West 50th Street in Manhattan, was relatively new at the time, having first opened its doors in 1970. One of the smaller Broadway theatres, it had a capacity of around 650 and, as its name suggests, an open stage on which the actors were surrounded by the audience. In collaboration with Albert Todd, Nichols co-authored a new translation of the play. *Vanya* is set in the house of Serebryakov, a celebrated but pompous academic who has retired and returned to the country estate he inherited when his first wife died. He brings with him his second wife, Yelena. She is much younger than him and her beauty stirs up passions in both Dr Astrov, a visiting friend of the family, and Vanya, the first wife's brother, who has been maintaining the estate. Vanya has come to the conclusion that he has wasted his life in service to Serebryakov, whom he once admired but now considers a fraud.

Nichols had worked with George C. Scott on a number of previous occasions and persuaded him to play Dr Astrov. Scott had appeared in several hit films and become a world famous Oscar-winning movie star for *Patton* in 1969, although he had declined the award. This had made him highly sought after despite the fact that his reputation for drinking and difficult behaviour trumped even Nicol's. Nichols thought Scott perfect for Astrov due to his 'ability to play intelligence and a certain jadedness' and he had pulled off an undoubted coup by enticing the actor back to the stage after a five year absence. Nicol, the director's first choice for Vanya, hesitated at first as he thought it would be rather a dreary, depressing character to play, but when he re-read it, he discovered new dimensions of passion and irony which interested him, so he agreed. He would surprise many critics by bringing a considerable amount of humour to the role. The other important male part of Serebryakov was to be played by Barnard Hughes, a less famous but nevertheless distinguished American actor. Elizabeth Wilson was cast as the professor's plain daughter, Sonya, and silent film star Lillian Gish as Maryina, the nanny. Veteran British actress Cathleen Nesbitt, who had made her debut in 1910, was given the part of Vanya's mother, while Nichols' other major coup was the casting of Julie Christie as Yelena. Christie had been a major film star since *Doctor Zhivago* and had not acted on stage for ten years.

Five weeks of rehearsal began in mid-April. Nichols' used some unusual techniques including, at one point, bringing beds into the rehearsal room and having the actors rehearse their lines lying down. Nicol, sceptical at first, admitted that this had been a good idea which enabled the cast to feel more relaxed about their performances.

Many thought Nichols had been asking for trouble by casting both George C. Scott and Nicol, and it is clear that Scott was envious of the younger actor. He was accustomed to being the dominant personality and, feeling his position threatened, he charged into Nicol's dressing room shortly before the first dress rehearsal was to take place and verbally attacked him, then approached Mike Nichols, saying he did not want to go onstage with 'that cunt'. Surprisingly, Nicol does not appear to have risen to this provocation and even told Elizabeth Wilson that he felt intimidated by Scott. The dress rehearsal was postponed as a result of the spat while Nichols tried to persuade Scott to temper his behaviour. Nicol later said that Scott had made things so difficult that he thought he might have to quit the production. Although he came close to doing so, Nicol ultimately decided to stay, and the two actors gradually developed an amicable if uneasy relationship, even dining out together twice a week. However, tension was never far away with Scott and one night, jealous of the laughs which Nicol was generating, he smashed the speaker which had been installed in his dressing room so that he could listen for his cues.

Despite the rivalry, there was one occasion on which Scott came to Nicol's rescue. The two were walking through the streets of Manhattan one night when Nicol gave the finger to a couple of policemen who were driving past. They immediately stopped their car and went to arrest him but Scott intervened and, giving them his best General Patton air of authority, dissuaded them. Talking to Joyce Haber of the *Los Angeles Times*, Nicol later spoke of Scott as 'a tortured man, given to outbursts of rage and extraordinary behaviour,' and went on to say that he found the extent of his self-loathing to be 'quite staggering.' The irony, of course, is that very similar comments were also made about Nicol throughout the course of his career.

Previews began on the 21st of May, continuing until the official opening on the 4th of June. The play ran for 64 performances before closing on the 28th of July. Unsurprisingly with such a cast, every night was sold out, but many in the audience were clearly there to gawp at the stars rather than appreciate Chekhov, and Scott stopped the play on more than one occasion in order to threaten audience members who were busy snapping away with their cameras.

Playing a character ten years his senior, Nicol merely added a little grey to the beard he had grown to suggest the extra years. Reviews were highly favourable, especially for Nicol. *Time* magazine's T.E. Kalem praised him for the 'mischievous, sardonic, self-mocking wit' that he brought to Vanya and added that his scenes with Scott had 'the charged intensity of *mano-a-mano* contests between bullfighters,' while Mary Campbell of the Associated Press was impressed by the 'masochistic delight' he had brought to the character.

During the run of *Vanya*, Nicol also began a run of his one-man show, now entitled simply *Nicol Williamson's Late Show*. Produced by Norman Twain, it ran from the 26th of June until the 28th of July almost every night at 10.45 p.m. at the Eastside Playhouse on East 74th Street. The 90 minute show featured Nicol backed by a six-piece band. On one occasion, he was even joined on stage by Dick Cavett, who sang a song with him. The show was a success, despite a negative review from the *Village Voice*'s Michael Feingold, who found it 'mediocre and overlong', although he admitted to being impressed by the excerpt from Beckett's *How It Is*. However, Nicol again received a rave review from *Time*'s T.E. Kalem, who saw 'an effervescent mirth, irony, mischief and intelligence emanate from every tone and gesture.'

Norman Twain also produced a one-hour special based on the show for cable TV. Entitled *A Night with Nicol Williamson*, it was filmed not in the Eastside Playhouse, but at The South Street Seaport Museum, also in New York. Director Peter Levin recalled:

> It was shot in one night down at the East River. We started shooting multiple cameras (three, probably) at about 7 p.m. and quit at 7 a.m. The South Street Pier looked much differently then than it does now. The Fulton Fish Market was there then and the whole area was a real working area. Now it's a tourist mecca and all built up with shops and restaurants. Then it had a rough feel about it, a genuine dock for working fishermen.

This unusual location works well and undoubtedly makes the programme more interesting than it would be if it had been shot on a traditional stage or in a studio. It contains the following performances:

'I Ain't Gonna Give You None of My Jellyroll' – Spencer Williams
'Something' – The Beatles
'Fern Hill' – Dylan Thomas
'Everybody's Talkin'' – Fred Neil
'A Subaltern's Love Song' – John Betjeman
'The Second Coming' – W.B. Yeats
'I Can't Give You Anything but Love, Baby' – Jimmy McHugh & Dorothy Fields
'The Joke Was on Me' – Bee Gees
'Mia Carlotta' - Thomas Augustine Daly
'Chantilly Lace' – The Big Bopper
'Gunga Din' – Rudyard Kipling
'Sunday Morning Coming Down' – Kris Kristofferson
'The Owl and the Pussycat' – Edward Lear
'Not Waving but Drowning' – Stevie Smith
'Me & Bobby McGee' – Kris Kristofferson
'Poem in October' – Dylan Thomas
Extract from *The Tempest* ('Our revels now are ended…') – Shakespeare
'When You're Smiling' – Shay, Fisher & Goodwin

Nicol is somehow more convincing when belting out a jazz standard like the opener – in which he also contributes a piano solo – than when tackling ballads by The Beatles and Kris Kristofferson. As far as the poems are concerned, the undoubted highlight is 'Gunga Din', which is not so much a poetry recital as a one-man performance from Nicol as a nostalgic old soldier paying tribute to the Indian who served as water boy to his regiment.

During the run of *Uncle Vanya* in June, Jill had given birth to Nicol's son, Luke, at a hospital in Manhattan. Nicol was thrilled and it is likely that this period was, for him, the happiest and most fulfilling of his life. However, for Nicol it was usually easier to find something to be unhappy about, as Jill Townsend recalled:

> I remember walking down the King's Road hand in hand – life is beautiful, we sing while we're walking… but that wasn't inherent in his life and I think one of the reasons is because, unbeknownst to Nicol,

when he was sent to Scotland as a child, his mother was pregnant, so when the war was over and they all got back together, suddenly he's got a sister who was never sent away. I think Nicol's problem was not that he was borderline or manic depressive, it was a result of the war and he felt he'd been thrown away. I think that's also why it was hard for friends of Nicol to become successful and still be friends. When we were married I thought I'd be able to help him get over it, but I couldn't.

He was with me at my parents' house out on Long Island when Laurence Olivier called and said he was stepping down as Artistic Director of the National Theatre and he would love it if Nicol would step into his shoes. Nicol was rude to him, and said, 'How dare he insult me?' I said, 'That's not an insult, sweetheart – you don't have to get angry with him because he offered you that.'

When he'd argue with people or say something unkind about somebody, I'd say, 'Nicol, you're bigger than that, don't be disparaging.' There was a party at Kenneth Tynan's house where he reduced Olivier to tears. I think it's also why he stopped seeing John Thaw – John began to have a really successful career and all of a sudden Nicol felt that was a threat to him somehow. Instead of being glad for somebody else's success, he felt like it was taken away from him.

Chapter 12 – A Coiled Cobra

Nicol's next move was something of a surprise. After consistently rejecting a number of similar offers over the past decade, he had accepted an offer early in the year from Trevor Nunn to return to the Royal Shakespeare Company. Nunn had just directed a version of *Coriolanus* at Stratford-upon-Avon with Ian Hogg in the title role, but it had not been a success. He decided that Nicol was the man to bring *Coriolanus* to life for the London transfer and was willing to wait until he was available. Nicol was at first not especially interested in the part but had remained very keen to play Macbeth, so he allowed Nunn to persuade him on the basis that they would later collaborate on the Scottish play. Nicol was to be paid £150 a week.[44]

Under the umbrella title *The Romans*, Nunn was staging a season of the four Shakespeare plays set in ancient Rome (the others being *Julius Caesar*, *Antony and Cleopatra* and *Titus Andronicus*). As this was too ambitious an undertaking for one man alone, he was working across all four plays with two co-directors – Euan Smith and Buzz Goodbody (the company's first female director). Smith was apparently more akin to an assistant than a co-director, but Goodbody supervised some rehearsals when Nunn was otherwise occupied. Nicol would appear only in *Coriolanus*, which was to open the London season as Nunn thought that Nicol's return would immediately grab the attention of critics and audiences alike. *Macbeth* was to be reserved for the following year.

Caius Martius Coriolanus was a Roman general who may or may not have been a real person. In Shakespeare's play, he is a military hero who has been instrumental in saving Rome from an attack by the Volscians and consequently wins the position of consul in the Roman parliament. However, scheming politicians soon turn public opinion against him and he is smeared as a traitor and sent into exile. In revenge, he joins forces with his former enemy, Aufidius, and leads an attack on Rome. His mother, Volumnia, is sent by the Romans to dissuade him from destroying the city. He eventually capitulates but Aufidius sees this as betrayal and has him killed. Margaret Tyzack, who had acted alongside Nicol in *The Ginger Man* and *The Lower Depths*, would play Volumnia, while the part of Aufidius went to Trinidadian actor Oscar James.

Conscious of his status as an outside star with a reputation for being difficult, Nicol was apprehensive about joining an established company. When he first met the rest of the cast he said that he sensed them all giving him 'the eyeball', and decided to ask for a read-through, which was not usual practice in the RSC at the time. He said at the time that he felt the read-through had helped to break the ice and spoke in glowing terms about the other actors and how happy he was to be working with them. However, actor Anthony Rowlands, who played one of the citizens, painted a different picture:

> He'd disappear in a flowing cardigan the moment the performance was over... He hated the fawning adulation he got from quite a lot of his fellow actors... he had this wonderful, wilful rejection of the life of the actor and the world he was forced to participate in to make a living.

Nicol later spoke of Coriolanus as being the 'most exacting' role he ever had to play and said that the fact that 'the first big fight is only fifteen minutes in' made it 'frighteningly exhausting.'[45] In order to prepare as thoroughly as possible, he spent two hours every night in the Donmar Warehouse – then in use as a rehearsal space rather than a theatre – with the Aldwych's stage manager, Michael Joyce, grilling him on his lines. Nicol was pleased to be playing a role which provided a sharp contrast to Chekhov, although he retained his *Uncle Vanya* beard for the part of Coriolanus. In place of the tweed he had worn for *Vanya*, his costume now consisted of a black leather cloak, pants, skirt, corset, belt and sandals, although he wore a toga in some scenes and at one point in the play even appeared dressed in rags with a dead fox on his head.

Coriolanus opened on the 22nd of October at the Aldwych Theatre in the West End. The Aldwych had a capacity of around 1,200 and had been the Royal Shakespeare Company's London home for some years by that point. Nunn had trimmed the play to give it a running time of three hours. The performance began with the ominous sound of a drum being beaten loudly for nearly two minutes. Even from an audio-only recording made on the 6th of December, it is clear that, when Nicol makes his entrance nine minutes in, he *owns* the role. Although the character is often seen as one of Shakespeare's least sympathetic protagonists, Nicol makes him sympathetic by revealing how his apparent harshness is actually born out of an innate, uncompromising sense of honesty. Nicol's Coriolanus is proud, scathing and contemptuous, but also modest and incapable of boasting. It is his misfortune to be an idealist in a world with little time for ideals. He believes in actions and distrusts words, especially those of politicians, and as a result he is temperamentally incapable of playing the public relations game required to succeed as consul. It is difficult to imagine any other actor's voice dripping with contempt to the degree that Nicol's does as he delivers the line, 'You common cry of curs!' However, he also managed to get some laughs in the scene where Volumnia persuades him to go back and beg the forgiveness of the people for having spoken so harshly and, exasperated, he furiously agrees to speak 'MILDLY!!' Although the dialogue is extensive, in contrast to Shakespeare's other plays, there is very little soliloquising. There is, on the other hand, a considerable amount of fighting between the characters, for which a choreographer had been specially hired. One evening during a fight scene a steel pole which was part of the scenery came crashing down and struck Nicol above the eye, causing a gash which bled profusely. Nicol, momentarily stunned, was forced to pause briefly but soon recovered himself, roaring, 'COME ON!' before continuing the fight with extra gusto. Alarmed by the blood pouring down Nicol's face, Trevor Nunn attempted to stop the performance as soon as the scene ended but Nicol brushed him aside, insisting that his wound was not as bad as it appeared and that, anyway, that was 'what it was all about.' Jill Townsend remembered it as her 'favourite production that Nicol ever did' and went on to say that, 'It was breathtaking. The opening night was unbelievable and one of the reviews made the front pages.'

Reviews were indeed extremely enthusiastic, particularly for Nicol, with Kenneth Hurren of *The Spectator* writing that, 'in the famous scene in which his mother pleads for Rome' he had come 'within range of the greatness that Olivier touched in an earlier Stratford production...' Alan Brien, writing for *Plays and Players*, noted that, 'Only once does Mr Williamson pause – and what a pause, a single shot held even longer than Harold Pinter or John Ford would dream could grip an audience – when his mother begs him to spare Rome...' Many other critics also singled out this moment, which consequently became a famous one in the history of Shakespeare performance. Irving Wardle of *The Times* wrote that, 'The pause... seems to stretch out into minutes while Williamson's face visibly turns to pulp. ... the tone he produces, of a tearful enraged child, humiliated beyond bearing... makes it painful to look at the stage.' On the audio recording which survives, the pause is held for 47 seconds. The only major criticism levelled at Nicol by reviewers was of not speaking clearly enough at points when his performance was perhaps carried away by passion, but his voice is certainly clear throughout the recording and he was otherwise almost universally acclaimed.

During the run, Nicol participated in a political protest, not something he was generally known for. On the 6th of November, he joined a demonstration led by Laurence Olivier outside the Russian embassy to protest the unfair treatment of two ballet stars who were on a hunger strike as they had not been permitted to leave the country.

Towards the end of the run, Nicol also resurrected his one-man show. Reverting to the original title of *Midwinter Spring*, it was performed at the Aldwych on three consecutive Sunday nights, with Nicol backed by a band featuring many of the musicians from the New York production, who were now calling themselves Heavy Feather. A minimal set featuring a set of steps and a street lamp was provided. Nicol had expanded his repertoire to include three songs by Carl Perkins ('Blue Suede Shoes', 'Restless' and 'That's Right') and two by Randy Newman ('God's Song' and 'Political Science') as well as 'The Old Music Master' (Hoagy Carmichael), 'Twenty-One' (The Eagles), 'Mack the Knife' (Brecht and Weill) and, for an encore, 'Great Balls of Fire' (Jerry Lee Lewis). He also added some new poems: 'Unholy Marriage' by David Holbrook, 'Argument' by Iain Crichton-Smith, 'I Paint What I See' by E.B. White, 'Onos' by Spike Milligan, 'Poetry of Departures' by Philip Larkin, 'Apocalypse' by D.J. Enright and 'At Lunchtime – A Story of Love' by Roger McGough. Nicol's outfit was casual but loud – he wore a shirt but no tie and a pair of vertically striped trousers.

As such a wide range of material was tackled during the show, the mixed nature of the reviews was unsurprising, but they were mostly in Nicol's favour, although few were convinced that he succeeded in everything he attempted. Writing for *The Times*, Irving Wardle found it a 'refreshing experience' to 'see an actor refusing to adopt a mask and slowly feeling his way into honest contact' with an audience.

1973 had been a vintage year for Nicol. *Time* magazine placed both *Uncle Vanya* and *Nicol Williamson's Late Show* in their top ten theatre events of the year and he won a special Drama Desk Award for Outstanding Performance for *Vanya*. The same play also resulted in both Nicol and George C. Scott being nominated for a Tony Award. Typically, when the awards ceremony was held in April 1974, both actors stayed away. Equity-related resentment of Nicol being a non-American may have been a factor in the final decision, but whatever the case, the award ultimately went to Michael Moriarty. However, back in the UK, Nicol was named Best Actor of 1973 for *Coriolanus* by *Plays and Players* magazine.

Early in the new year, another version of Nicol's one-man show was recorded for the BBC, for which he was again backed by Heavy Feather. The director was Robert Knights, who remembered:

> Until about '69 I was working in the theatre. I'd been an assistant director at the Royal Court, which was very much a place where all the

directors wanted to work with Nicol Williamson. Anthony Page, whom I had worked with, had had plans to direct Nicol in *Hamlet*. Then (I believe) there was a battle with Tony Richardson, who had lined up a production at the Roundhouse. Not a production you'd ever forget if you were lucky enough to catch it....

Nicol could be like a coiled cobra on stage and was a very, very powerful actor. In 1970 I started making television dramas and in the very early '70s there was a time when Christopher Morahan was head of plays and what he really wanted to do was a number of shows out of the plays department of BBC London which would be cheap, and not take forever to get written or rehearse or shoot, and then to get on air. And one of the productions that Mark Shivas came up with the idea of putting on tape was Nicol Williamson's one-man show. I went with him to see it and then I met Nicol and worked out what was going to be included from the stage show and what was not. We arranged a day when a studio was free and rehearsed it through the day, probably from about 10 o'clock until about 4 or 5 o'clock, just the cameras and walking through it, then broke, then the audience came in and we went straight through and recorded from about 7.30 or 8 until 10. There were probably about two or three hundred people in the audience.

I remember there was one occasion when Nicol absolutely couldn't remember what the hell he was doing next, so he just said, 'Look, can we stop for a moment? Sorry Rob.' Because at that time when you taped you would tape on to a very broad band of tape and the BBC were always very keen on shows being done as live so you didn't cut the tape and it had a second life and could be recorded over.

You get out of that show a really good idea of what Nicol really enjoyed doing. He's an actor who seems almost not to have a skin, he's very, very intense and you have a very strong sense of him, the actor in the role. You have an electric presence in the way he acts.

He wasn't a comfortable man ever in the way that you might say of Anthony Hopkins or Jeremy Irons whom I worked with later. Working with him was great fun because some actors' fingerprints are very light – they disappear into a role and they don't naturally show much of themselves, but he certainly had his own stamp.

He was disciplined in those days – I don't know what he was like later on. He was very well known in England, because England likes to look for its Albert Finneys and its Tom Courtenays and this very hard working-class background which they carry with them.

Nicol was approached around this time by Harley Usill, whose label Argo records, a subsidiary of Decca, specialised in recordings of poetry and steam trains. Usill wanted to produce an audio book of Tolkien's *The Hobbit*. He had the approval of the author himself and had heard that Nicol was a Tolkien enthusiast. Nicol was delighted to be given the opportunity to bring Tolkien's characters to life. The result was a *tour-de-force* in which he gave a distinct voice to around twenty different characters, switching between a variety of accents – cockney for the trolls, West Country for Bilbo, and so on. The undoubted highlight was his hissing, sibilant Welsh Gollum, although his throaty Smaug was also memorable. The original version was six hours long, which would have required at least six vinyl records and been too expensive. Usill and Nicol eventually managed to edit it down to three and a half hours and produce a box set of four LPs. The resultant audio book has remained popular with Tolkien enthusiasts throughout the decades since.

In the early '70s, British film director John Boorman, who had made two striking films in America, namely *Point Blank* and *Deliverance*, also had Nicol in mind to play Gandalf in his proposed film version of *The Lord of the Rings*. It was an ambitious project which required a large budget and was eventually abandoned, but it was also the seed which later led to Nicol's role as Merlin in Boorman's *Excalibur*.

In February, Nicol travelled to Kenya, accompanied by Jill and Luke, to appear in a film entitled *The Wilby Conspiracy*. Interiors would be shot later at Pinewood. The other two stars were Sidney Poitier and Michael Caine, the presence of whom guaranteed a substantial budget. Nicol and family were accommodated with the other stars in their own private bungalows at the luxurious Mount Kenya Safari Club, which was part-owned at the time by the film star William Holden.

Set in South Africa, the plot involved a black activist and a neutral white Englishman who find themselves on the run together after getting into a fight with a couple of policemen. It combined two popular formulas: the odd couple buddy movie and the chase thriller, and threw in an anti-apartheid message for good measure. The latter ingredient meant that there had never been any chance of it actually being filmed in South Africa.

The director, Ralph Nelson, was an American who had started in television but had a dozen feature films to his credit by this stage in his career, the best known of which was the controversial western *Soldier Blue*. Given that Nelson was a workmanlike director with no great critical reputation and the film was based on a bestseller by Peter Driscoll, it is clear that this was a commercial proposition for Nicol. However, he would not have accepted if he had not been intrigued by the role of Major Horn. Nicol received many offers to play heavies over the years and very rarely agreed, but there was something about the part of the Afrikaner policeman in pursuit of the two fugitives that interested him. The appeal seems to have been the opportunity to give the character a certain integrity, no matter how disagreeable his views. The producers were also willing to indulge Nicol in developing the character and changing some of the dialogue. Nicol portrayed Horn as a man who believes so passionately that his people are 'a civilised Christian minority' under threat that he is prepared to go to any lengths to preserve the power of the whites in South Africa. It is clear that he takes no pleasure in brutality – for him it is purely a means to an end – although he finds it useful to have a sadistic sidekick around who enjoys the dirty work. The result was a villain so persuasive that at times he almost sounds reasonable and is all the more dangerous as a result. Nicol added a few memorable surface touches too, doing a convincing Afrikaner accent and playing Horn as a chain-smoker who likes to say 'alrighty?' as if he actually cares whether anything is alright with anyone who does not share his agenda. Nicol was so effective in the role that many audiences reportedly cheered when he received his comeuppance at the end.

The Wilby Conspiracy is entertaining enough, but it is difficult to take its political message seriously when much of the film is so frivolous. The plot becomes very silly indeed around half way through when Poitier and Caine enlist the help of an Indian dentist to recover some diamonds hidden in a sinkhole. The film was not a big hit but critics and public alike frequently singled out Nicol's performance as the most memorable aspect.

Back in London, Nicol received a request from the Royal Court Theatre for help in raising money to repair the roof. Although he had not performed there himself for many years (with the exception of recording *Lessness* at the theatre for BBC radio), he put on a Sunday night fundraising concert at the Court on the 8th of March, backed by his regular band, who were now calling themselves Parachute.

Nicol's next role was as Richard Nixon – still in office at the time, although impeachment hearings were underway for his part in the Watergate scandal. At the end of April, over 1,200 pages of transcripts of the Nixon tapes had been released and it was these which provided much of the source material for *I Know What I Meant*, a television play starring Nicol as his former host. The production company may have been hoping to capitalise on Nicol's connection with Nixon. Nicol, on the other hand, had received a great deal of criticism for entertaining the unpopular president four years earlier, but he had never been a Nixon supporter and had gone to the White House in a spirit of adventure. He was not without qualms about mocking the man whose hand he had shaken, but ultimately he welcomed the opportunity to make it clear that he did not share Nixon's values. The play saw Nicol once again working under the direction of Jack Gold, who remembered it this way:

> Granada had started a series of late-night dramas and the producer, Michael Cox, had this idea of the Watergate tapes. I'm not sure whether David Edgar had suggested it or whether he commissioned David Edgar to write it. And again I don't know where the idea of Nicol came from,

or whether they thought Nicol would be great and they'd got in touch with me because I'd worked with him. I met with them a few times, and Nicol said he wanted to do it. We got an all-American-speaking cast, which I thought was important. When Nicol agreed, we talked about not using make-up and hair-pieces. There was an occasion early on before we went up to Manchester to do it when Nicol had decided late one night *not* to do it, and I remember panicked phone calls with his agent and Granada, but anyway, it was all sorted out, but it was one of those things Nicol could be difficult about sometimes – he may decide *not* to do it! Anyway, he did it and we went up to Granada and had a good time.

It wasn't an eyelash-copy of the real Nixon, but certainly Nicol had met the man at the White House, and there was a mass of material about Nixon that we had to look at. He absorbed things very well, Nicol. And he was great as Nixon. We did it in a very short period, a day or two maybe at the most, so it was intense. I don't know what the audience size was, but the reviews were very, very good – particularly for him, so in that sense it was a success. And it was quite good for Granada as it kicked off their little drama series and was – I don't know how accurate this is – one of the few times where the actual transcripts were used word-for-word. They were obviously edited by David Edgar to create a narrative in the forty minutes, but every word of it is authentic.

The set was a painstaking reconstruction of the President's Oval Office. One unusual and amusing device Edgar employed was the incorporation of phrases covering missing words in the transcripts, such as 'expletive deleted' and 'unintelligible' into the actual dialogue. Broadcast on the 10th of July 1974, the programme was well-received in the UK but attempts to sell it to American networks such as CBS, NBC and NET all came to nothing, undoubtedly because a British satire about an embarrassing American political scandal was not entirely welcome at the time. The programme still survives but has not aged well.

Chapter 13- Company Man

For the next year, Nicol focused on his work with the Royal Shakespeare Company, beginning with a role he had played once before in a one-night production at the Royal Court. Peter Gill, who had been an assistant at the Court during Nicol's time there, was at this point working as a director with the RSC. He remembered:

> I think Nicol had only been contracted to play Macbeth when Trevor Nunn asked me to do *Twelfth Night* in the same season, so when I knew he was going to be in the company I jumped at the opportunity to get him to play Malvolio. I don't remember Nicol being in any way particularly difficult. I remember there was a lot of chopping and changing accents as he created the part and I never found Nicol particularly easy, but that was beside the point as compared to what I knew he would bring to the production. He was well-matched in the company – a marvellous contrast to Jane Lapotaire and Mary Rutherford and particularly in the company of the older actors like Frank Thornton, who was a great comic actor,[46] Ron Pember, who was an old friend of his, as Feste, and Patricia Hayes as Maria, but then she had worked with every important comic in the country, some of whom made Nicol look like a beginner as far as difficulty in handling was concerned.

There had been no fancy costumes available for George Devine's Sunday night production of *Twelfth Night* back in 1962, but this time Nicol was able to make a memorable visual impression. He had shaved off his beard to play Nixon and remained clean-shaven for Malvolio, which somehow served to make the ruff he wore around his neck even more ridiculous than it otherwise may have done. Streaks of grey were added to his hair, which was swept back, and he was dressed in stockings, high-heeled boots and a vertically-striped top with cross-hatching on its padded sleeves and cuffs. He also carried a black walking cane with a straight handle. An audio recording which survives has him speaking with a strong Welsh accent, although some participants have remembered him performing the role in a Scottish accent, so it is possible that this varied during the run.

Malvolio, the pompous steward who is tricked into believing that his beautiful young employer (Olivia) is in love with him may not be a leading role, but is easily the choicest part in the play, and one which had previously attracted such heavyweight actors as Henry Irving, Herbert Beerbohm Tree, John Gielgud and Alec Guinness. Malvolio's journey goes through three distinct stages. Initially, he is seen as an officious bore attempting to prevent Olivia's uncle, Sir Toby Belch, and his cronies from drinking and singing into the night. One of the cronies is Olivia's maid, Maria, who has noticed that Malvolio harbours unrequited feelings for Olivia. In revenge, she fakes a letter from her mistress in which she supposedly confesses her love for Malvolio and requests that he be 'opposite with a kinsman, surly with servants,' smile at her and wear cross-gartered yellow stockings, all of which have actually been well-calculated to offend. Malvolio is baffled when every attempt to please Olivia has the opposite result and he becomes a figure of mockery. However, the joke goes too far when he is eventually incarcerated as a lunatic, and so at the end of the play the humour turns to pathos.

Nicol's understudy was 28-year-old London-born Paul Moriarty, who remembered how Nicol initially kept his distance from the rest of the company during rehearsals:

> Nicol tried out a few different voices. He obviously wanted to do it very puritanical, so he tried it Scottish and then he did it Welsh. Peter Gill said, 'You know, you just let him get on with it.' And Malvolio was an outsider anyway, so that first rehearsal down in London we didn't really get to know him. He just turned up and did it, and we could see what an amazing actor he was, and he just played Malvolio right down the line.
>
> Once I remember Nicol coming up to Peter Gill towards the end of rehearsal and saying, 'I wonder if you mind, I've got to go to New York so I won't be here for a couple of days,' and Peter Gill said, 'Yes, that's fine Nicol, you go,' and he said, 'Oh well, I don't have to go,' and Peter

said, 'No, no, you go.' So he handled him by not handling him or by not treating him as this incandescent bloke who was going to explode at any moment.

When asked about this incident, Gill said that 'inconvenient as it certainly was and not a request you like be landed with in the middle of rehearsals, I think I thought it better to just let him go without any fuss.' The trip to New York was probably part of the doomed attempt to sell *I Know What I Meant* to American television.

The play opened at the Royal Shakespeare Theatre in Stratford-upon-Avon on the 22nd of August 1974. Peter Gill:

> I can still remember on the first night the energy and focus and concentration in the moment with which he delivered his first line and the unusual enthusiasm of the audience's response.
>
> It's very difficult to describe exactly why Nicol was so very good in the theatre considering that on first sight, for many, he could hardly be described as having much charm in any conventional sense of the word... It was to do with real skill, brilliant speaking, speed, living in the moment, a talent for comedy, extreme emotional intensity and being alive in a way that only very great performers are.

Working from an uncut text, the performance ran for around two hours and 45 minutes, with Nicol making his first appearance around 20 minutes in. In the surviving audio recording, his Malvolio comes across as an utterly charmless and ridiculous character. Nicol is very funny in the famous, nearly ten-minute letter scene, especially when he tries to make sense of the acronym 'MOAI', and he receives an enthusiastic round of applause from the audience as the scene finishes.

Paul Moriarty thought that Nicol's performance was all the more effective for being played straight:

> He didn't do any cheap tricks or laughs, which a lot of actors do when they play Malvolio, he was just this man who was in love with this woman and was a puritan, and it was all the more funny for that. There

was something about this six-foot-two man with this lugubrious long face, terribly intense, saying 'My lady loves me!' It was hysterically funny. But disturbing as well… and at the end, of course, Malvolio goes mad.

As a colleague, Moriarty remembered Nicol as a man with a mischievous sense of humour and a generous nature:

> One night in the green room, he came running in and said, 'Quick everybody – get into the wings! Frank Thornton's asleep in his dressing room and he's on next!' I said, 'Well, didn't you wake him up?' He said, 'No, no – this'll be much funnier!' And there was this huge long gap of course while there was no Frank Thornton playing Andrew Aguecheek, and then he turned up with his wig all over the place, panting, and dashed on stage. And Nicol thought this was hysterically funny!
>
> We didn't have line-runs or rehearsals in those days for understudies. You were just expected to know it. I turned up on a Monday night at 6 o'clock and they said, 'Nicol's not going to be here - you're on!' I remember sitting in the dressing room in his costume – he's six foot two or something, I'm five foot nine, and I could just hear over the tannoy, 'For tonight's performance Nicol Williamson can't be here,' and a huge groan went up from the auditorium… but I did it alright, I got good applause, and when he next turned up he said, 'I think I owe you a meal,' and I said, 'Well, a pint will do, Nicol.' And he said, 'No – I owe you a meal!' And we went out. He never said why he was off. He just said, 'I hear you got on quite well,' and I said, 'Yeah, I did,' and he said, 'I bet you were scared,' and I said, 'I was! I was scared that I wouldn't get laughs and I'd let the play down,' and he said, 'No, no, Shakespeare does all that for you, so you just have to go on there and do it as you mean it and the laughs will come,' and he was absolutely right. So I went on twice for him, once when we got down to London as well, when again he just disappeared, then he came in the next night to my dressing room and he said, 'Oh, they left these shoes they gave me for Malvolio, they're rather a nice pair of boots, do you want them?' And I said, 'Well, I can't,' and he said, 'Course you can – put them in your bag.'

One of the other leading actors in *Twelfth Night* was the 29-year-old Jane Lapotaire, who would work with Nicol on a number of occasions and go on to win a Tony Award for her performance as

Edith Piaf on Broadway. Lapotaire played Viola in *Twelfth Night*, the young woman who disguises herself as a man and causes a great deal of sexual confusion. She remembered her first experience of working with Nicol this way:

> The accent [he used] gave him a kind of primness and therefore he didn't have to play at being a puritan, it came naturally with that rather precious Edinburgh accent, but it was a joy to watch. We all used to crowd round at most performances and watch him do the letter scene. He was a brilliant comedian and he was very funny off stage too.
>
> He used to do dreadful things to me as Viola – I mean dreadfully funny, lovely things! He'd hold me in the wings and not let me go on when my cue came! I'd struggle and struggle and he'd ruffle my hair and put his knee up my bottom! He was great fun, but I was absolutely terrified of him because he was this huge talent and an enormous personality and, not only that, a brilliant pianist. If there was a piano in the rehearsal room, at every possible moment Nicol was at it playing blues and jazz and singing along.
>
> I think Nicol had a very flippant reaction to work at times – if he thought it was getting too serious or too heavy he'd send it up and make everybody laugh. Although now, in my 70s, I can see what a vulnerable man he was, he gave off an aura of being so confident and so sure of himself.

Nicol again won excellent reviews. Michael Billington of *The Guardian* was among those who praised his ability to 'blend high comedy and deep emotional pain' and B.A. Young of the *Financial Times* found Malvolio's ending especially memorable, observing that Nicol 'can move a house to heartbreak at a stroke.'

Twelfth Night transferred to London's Aldwych theatre the following February with the same cast and no major changes.

After *Twelfth Night*, Nicol finally got the opportunity to play *Macbeth*. He told the *Evening Standard*: 'I have to say this [role] is the big one for me... I've secretly stalked him like his murderer... [and] I don't care who knows it.' For this production, he would work very closely with Trevor Nunn, who he said was 'able to take the cork off me better than anyone I've ever known.'

As Lady Macbeth, Nunn cast Helen Mirren, who was 29 at the time and had already worked extensively with the Royal Shakespeare Company. Unfortunately, this proved to be an unlucky choice and there was a great deal of friction between her and Nicol. It has often been rumoured that the two had an affair, but there seems to be no real evidence for this. Paul Moriarty, who was playing Lennox and once more doubling as Nicol's understudy, remembered:

> Nobody knows what went on there. When somebody said, 'Look to the lady!' he'd go up and put his arms round her shoulders and say, 'Fucking slag!' I don't know whether it was a thwarted affair... I doubt it, because he was very much with Jill Townsend and into being a family man by that time. Some chemistry wasn't working and it definitely showed that there wasn't much going on between the two of them. I don't know whether Trevor Nunn, being a great Macchiavellian, thought that this antagonism might work, but it didn't and it's a shame.

Jane Lapotaire, who was playing a number of small roles in the production, had this to say:

> I wouldn't like to assess what the relationship was between Nicol and Helen, but a group of us had gone out to eat one night and they were in the same restaurant and at one point there was a big hiatus at the sound of a ringing slap across Nicol's face! I have no idea of why. From what I could see, it wasn't a comfortable relationship with him and Helen, but I think Helen had decided by then (she stayed in the house I rented in Stratford) that she wanted her name on the back of a chair and she wanted to work in films, and I think she was probably very one-minded about her working life, and Nicol – I think it was a cover for huge shyness. I know it sounds like a cliché, but it is actually true that a lot of actors are very shy people. You put them in a costume and they're fine, but you take a photo or interview them as themselves and they don't know where to put themselves. I think there was something very vulnerable [about him]... And I suspect Nicol was a great big softie

under all that – although I would never have realized it at the time because I was so blinded by the *power* of the man.

Film director John Boorman later said that Mirren told him Nicol had wanted to sleep with her and she had turned him down and that Nicol told him Mirren had wanted to sleep with him and *he* had turned *her* down.

Nunn had some unusual ideas about how he wanted to stage *Macbeth*, as Paul Moriarty remembered:

> On the first day of rehearsals at Stratford, Trevor said, 'We're not going to rehearse today. It's an unlucky play, so we're going to go to the church to have a look around and decide,' and the next day we came in and he said, 'This is the set.' And it was inside a church with a chandelier over the top where the witches were going to be hanging…

One of the witches was Jane Lapotaire:

> It was the first of Trevor Nunn's attempts to do the play and I had the joy, because of having had my hair cut short for Viola, of playing Banquo's son Fleance as well as the second witch and Lady McDuff! And the second witch makes an exit as Lady McDuff comes on! So they had three people in the wings to get me out and get me on again! That first dress rehearsal of *Macbeth* on stage at the Royal Shakespeare Theatre ran something near four hours because there were only a handful of actors and we were all changing hats and trousers and running on playing umpteen other parts! It's one of Shakespeare's shorter plays, so it was very, very tightened up by the time it got in front of an audience.
>
> I lived next to the house Nicol rented and he and Trevor used to work late at night sometimes and I heard this godalmighty shouting and sound of furniture being thrown. I think they were having a rehearsal of the Banquo's ghost scene.
>
> I also remember him saying to Trevor when he was rehearsing the scene with the two murderers he persuades and bullies into murdering Banquo that he wanted to play it like Nixon and he did indeed play it behind a desk as a kind of politico and it worked brilliantly…

Paul Moriarty also had some interesting stories to tell about the rehearsal period:

> Nicol had spent a lot of time with Trevor Nunn and actually stayed with him at Stratford in the same house. There's a story of Trevor Nunn waking up in the middle of the night to find Nicol straddling him. Trevor said, 'What the hell are you doing?' Nicol said, 'I just want to know what Duncan looked like!' There were just so many stories about him… apparently, Trevor Nunn invited some people round for dinner and in the middle of it, Nicol suddenly jumped up on the table and pretended he was seeing Banquo! That was his way of trying something out!
>
> I remember they were trying to find out how to kill young Siward in rehearsals. Trevor's got all these different ideas and Nicol's stretched out on the floor a bit hungover and then he looks up and he says, 'I've got an idea, Trevor!' And Trevor says, 'Yes, what?' Nicol says, 'Why don't you come on stage, take the boy into a corner and bore him to death!' And, again your heart went, Huh! You don't say that to Trevor Nunn! He's a very witty man, too, and he said, 'Thank you, Nicol, that's very helpful, but I don't think I could do that *every* night.' So they obviously got on extremely well together and at the same time there was this frisson that this man could be very, very dangerous. And yet, obviously, physically, I never saw him do anything violent off stage at all, but you had that feeling of some electricity around him all the time, which again you don't tend to get with English actors all that often. Of course, he was Scottish, so maybe it was that Celt thing that he had.
>
> I remember the night before the opening, he was having lunch or dinner and I walked through and he said, 'I can't wait for tomorrow – it'll just be me and those critics!' And I said, 'There'll be others with you,' and he said, 'Oh, of course, you lot will be there as well, but really it'll be me.' And so when he said 'It'll be me,' I thought, 'Is this mad egotism or is he really so entrenched in this part of this man who self-destructs?' – which is what Nicol did all the time, of course.

Trevor Nunn wanted to focus on text and performance, so Nicol's costume was far from elaborate. He made his entrance dressed in a scarlet cloak, later switching to a black shirt. Rehearsal stills show him clean-shaven apart from short sideburns, and his hair is uncharacteristically neat. The dark, simple costume he wears seems designed to make his face and hands stand out, and sometimes these are all that is visible. A photograph of the set model shows a large candle in each corner, pew-type seats on the left and right-hand side, a font, a table and a statue with a crucifix in the centre. Suspended above the set is a chandelier holding three sinister figures representing the witches.

The play opened on the 29th of October to mixed reviews. Nunn's church setting in particular came in for a good deal of criticism. Milton Shulman, in the *Evening Standard*, felt that Nicol 'flounders about in this mish-mash of ideas' and was 'surprisingly unconvincing as either a soldier or a philosopher.' Michael Billington of *The Guardian* also thought that Nunn had made a mistake by 'trying to work in too many conflicting references' but found much to admire in Nicol's no-holds-barred portrait of the 'decline and fall of a human being' in which he underwent 'total transition from securely confident soldier to unhinged, raving despot.' The most positive review, however, was probably that of Irving Wardle who, writing for *The Times*, was deeply impressed by Nicol's ability to take the audience inside his head and concluded by saying that, 'If you see Macbeth as a man of action with a tormenting imagination, this is the definitive reading.'

During a matinee performance on the 4th of December, an incident occurred which has become part of the Nicol Williamson legend. Jane Lapotaire remembered it this way:

> He had what I thought was an absolutely brilliant idea – when he sees the dagger in the air, he didn't move a muscle, but he took the stool out from under him and threw it through the space where he saw the dagger. Brilliant idea. Well, of course, on a schools' matinee they thought it was the funniest thing they'd ever seen and he stopped the play and walked to the front of the stage and said something along the lines of, 'Surprising though it may seem to some of you, there are people in this theatre that want to hear this play. Those of you who don't, leave now!'

Nobody left and the audience remained silent for the rest of the play. While this incident is often cited as an example of Nicol's difficult behaviour, the schoolchildren had apparently been noisy and disruptive from the beginning and many in the audience must have been grateful that someone had finally given them a proper reprimand.

Lapotaire had one further vivid memory to share:

> I was playing the second witch, who we developed as a sort of channel for the information that the witches had, and she was pregnant with ankle socks – like a child, but pregnant – and in one of the witches' scenes, Nicol came up to me very close and said, 'I s'pose a fuck's out of the question…' [laughs]
>
> I think he got bored very easily. There's a huge hunger and need of people who have a dependency on alcohol, and there is something very broken in them and the spirit replaces whatever spirit they've lost. That's a very kind of facile statement but no-one is an alcoholic who isn't very, very badly hurt inside and I think his bluster and his 'I'm not scared of anyone or anything' attitude was a huge defense.

While *Macbeth* was still running, Nicol began rehearsals for a new production of *Uncle Vanya* with the RSC and with himself as director. The play was to be staged at The Other Place, the RSC's intimate 140-seat theatre in Stratford-upon-Avon. In the part of Astrov, he cast Patrick Stewart (already bald at 35), who had been a member of the company since 1966. Jill Townsend was cast as Yelena and Jane Lapotaire as Sonya. Lapotaire remembered:

> When we were doing *Uncle Vanya*, his wife was in it, so those were happy times for him. When he got us all together for the very first rehearsal he said, 'Look, I've cast you lot because you can do it so, with *Macbeth* killing me at night, let's meet up at 11 and work till 1 and then go to the Duck.' So that's what we did, although not all of us went to the Duck![47]
>
> It was a very comfortable, very easy time. I loved the play, I loved playing Sonya and I remember him saying to me, 'Sweetheart, don't worry if you can't get real tears on the first night, because nerves often

stop them.' And I thought, what an extraordinary thing for Nicol to say – and of course he was absolutely right! I think my fear of him was probably what kept our working relationship in a very easy balance. I never felt threatened by him as an actor, ever, but then I was always very aware of the space he needed and, let's face it, Sonya is subservient to Vanya and Lady Macbeth is subservient to Macbeth.

Jill Townsend wasn't a member of the Royal Shakespeare Company. I liked the woman, we got on well. It must have been really hard for her being brought in as Nicol's wife.

I never saw Mike Nichols' production, so I don't know how much was taken from it. I think we mostly blocked ourselves. It was *too* easy in a way. Not starting until 11 and finishing at 1, which was just heaven for those of us who'd got performances in the evening. But the thing that really worried him was that, at the end of the play – with that demanding nature for the male lead – he then has to do this bloody great fight. He hated the fight, he *loathed* it and was frightened of it. Nicol was such a contradiction in lots of ways. He was very scared physically of that...

Jill Townsend downplayed the difficulty of being the star's wife and also remembered the experience as a positive one:

I loved working with Jane Lapotaire and Patrick Stewart, it was a joy, and Nicol was a good director. He had his own little quirks that he put in, some things he would have loved to have done before but which Mike Nichols wouldn't have wanted.

The play opened on the 17th of December to enthusiastic reviews and it is clear that critics and audiences alike were pleased to have the opportunity to see Nicol play Vanya in the UK. Garry O'Connor, writing for *Plays & Players*, considered Nicol's performance to be 'a masterpiece of comic neurasthenia' which, despite a 'sarcastic undercurrent' was nevertheless a 'very cheerful piece of character playing.'

Nicol gave one performance of *Midwinter Spring* at The Royal Shakespeare Theatre in Stratford on the 19th of January, shortly after which preparations began to take Trevor Nunn's production of *Macbeth* to the Aldwych. Given that the Stratford production had not been altogether well-received, it was decided to make some major changes. The church setting was abandoned and the text was cut further so that it now ran for two hours with no interval. Jane Lapotaire had decided she did not want to continue, and Barry Stanton was replaced by Gordon Jackson as Banquo, but otherwise the cast was the same as it had been in Stratford. Paul Moriarty, again understudying Nicol and also appearing as Lennox, remembered:

> For some reason, he and Trevor decided they'd do the stripped-down version at the Aldwych, which didn't work as well, and we were sitting on boxes in a circle round the stage. Later, Ian McKellen did that version with Trevor at the Other Place and they got all the credit for it, but a lot of that was actually Trevor and Nicol working it out, sitting on boxes and doing a thunder sheet on stage and all that. The one at Stratford was epic and he was huge in it, as you can imagine. He was also terrific at the Aldwych. This man had obviously sold his soul to the devil and didn't really care, he was still going to go on fighting till the last. It was really shocking.

Macbeth opened at the Aldwych on the 4th of March, and an audio recording was made on the 27th. The play begins with the sound of church organ music, then the witches start to wail and a sheet of metal is shaken to simulate the sound of thunder. The next sound we hear is a male screaming in a thick Scots accent. Nicol makes his first appearance ten minutes in, also adopting a Scots accent and rolling his 'r's. The production is fast-paced and there seems to have been little restraint in the acting. Scottish actor Gordon Jackson makes a fine Banquo, but Helen Mirren seems incongruous playing Lady Macbeth with an English accent.

Writing for *The Times*, Irving Wardle said that, despite the fact that some of the details of Nicol's performance had been lost in the new version, 'the reading stands as one of the most minutely studied and rethought that we are ever likely to hear of an over-familiar text.' Lawrence Malkin, writing for *Time* magazine, praised his 'iron control over the poetic rhythms' and noted how Nicol's scrutiny of Richard Nixon had informed his performance in the scene in which he 'instructs Banquo's murderers with a flat naturalism that echoes the White House tapes'.

While it is clear from such reviews that his collaboration with Nunn was by no means a critical disaster, Nicol always remembered it as having suffered a hostile reception, telling Michael Kernan of *The Washington Post* that, despite being 'the best and truest thing' he had been involved in since *Inadmissible Evidence*, 'there was no way London would accept it…they HATED it and HATED us for doing it.'

During the Aldwych run of *Macbeth*, Nicol was having to deal with two personal crises. His mother, a non-smoker, had been diagnosed with lung cancer in September and told she would probably only live for another two months. At the same time, his relationship with Jill Townsend was rapidly disintegrating. This is how Jill remembered the situation:

> I didn't drink, so there were a lot of nights that were lost to me because, if we went over to somebody's house, we'd be there until 5 o'clock in the morning and he'd be having drunken conversations while I'd be asleep on the sofa. After Luke was born I couldn't do that. I think he was probably having a few affairs at that time too. I only knew about the ones he told me about and I remember saying to him, 'I can love you and I can hate you, Nicol, at any given time, but when I don't care about you, that's the warning sign, so be careful – you're pushing it!'
>
> He loved the idea that he had a son but he was very demanding of attention. When it was time for me to feed Luke, he would all of a sudden say, 'I have to go to Harrods to get a tennis racket – you have to drive me.' I'd say, 'Well, let's feed Luke first,' and he'd say, 'No, let's go get the tennis racket now.' I think it was a little difficult for him to share the spotlight and I'm not sure he knew the role he was supposed to play as a father, so he would imitate his own father sometimes. Nicol's parents were quite strict with him – they wouldn't take bad language, or if he'd had too much to drink and yelled at me they would kick him out of the house. My sense is that he would take on this role of being the disciplinarian to this infant who, if he cried, had to leave the room. I

think Nicol didn't know what he was supposed to do because he wasn't given a script.

Nicol kept the news of his mother's illness to himself, but the company soon became aware that his marriage was in trouble. Paul Moriarty:

> Nicol had just found out that Jill didn't want to be with him any more. I came in on a Monday to the Aldwych, and they said, 'Nicol's not going to make it, he's in a bit of a bad way, so it looks like you're going to have to go on!' and I said 'Oh God!' He turned up and he had a scar under his eye, he'd banged his head on something, and I said, 'Shall I get you a coffee?' and he said, 'I don't want a coffee, I want a pint of beer!' And I said, 'Oh, I'll get you a pint of beer then,' and he said, 'I'll come with you.' And there we were in the Opera Tavern. After three pints it was nearly quarter past seven and I said, 'Look Nicol, I'm your understudy, *one of us* has got to go back!' and he said, 'Oh, I wouldn't do that to you,' and grinned maniacally at me. We went back and he put forty minutes on the play that night. I was playing Lennox and when we had to go into the wings to see what the murderers had done to Duncan, he grabbed me by the back of the neck and said, 'It's just a movie, kid, we'll just do it scene by scene and we'll get through it – come on, we're on!' And he lurched from scene to scene, virtually, but he got through it.
>
> He got right to the end and he said, 'Tomorrow and tomorrow and tomorrow...' and his face went white. He sweated and looked out at the audience and said, 'You all know the line – what is it?' And somebody shouted out, 'Creeps in this petty place!' and he said 'Thank you!' It was the first time I'd seen an actor blow that part, and he must have been thinking, 'Tomorrow there will be no baby, no wife there, there'll be nothing...' The next night he just went on and did it and it wasn't alluded to again.

Nicol and Jill did have a reconciliation after this, but it was the beginning of the end and their marriage was not to last for much longer.

Paul Moriarty remembered Nicol as a highly individual actor who was neither old school nor method and appeared to rely largely on a combination of instinct and experimentation:

> There were very few actors like him – maybe Brian Cox and Mark Rylance, but very rarely do you see that kind of danger on stage. Most of the English actors are too polite – they're very intelligent and they do it like they know exactly what they're talking about and they never surprise themselves, but with Nicol it looked like it was all happening in his head as it was happening. It was great.
>
> Another actor who was a friend of mine, Alfie Lynch, did *Godot* with Nicol, and he said he didn't know what he was doing in rehearsal and he went missing for a week, and then when he turned up he had this performance of windmilling arms and the strange running round the stage and everything. He'd gone away and something had happened to him and he just came back in with the performance. It was very hard to see how he did things, but he did them with all his heart and sinew. He reminded me of actors like Gene Hackman and Al Pacino, who put in everything and were totally gone in the part, which makes it all the more frightening because you don't know where they are. Nicol wasn't an intellectual actor, you didn't see him go, 'Oh, I know what Macbeth was thinking here!' He just went out and tried things in rehearsal.
>
> I used to go out and have a drink with him and he was affable, friendly, good fun, but you were never quite sure how the evening was going to end up, whether he would suddenly throw a brick or something and go running down the street laughing. He was slightly out of control and I think most actors *aren't* slightly out of control, and I think that was because of these demons he had. Macbeth was *the* great part for him.
>
> He was certainly a drinker, like a lot of those famous actors in those days, although god knows why, but Burton, O'Toole and Harris all did that self-destruct thing. But however late he was out at night – and he'd be out sometimes until 4 in the morning – he would always turn up the next day and he always said he gave a better performance because he was kind of relaxed and loose when he went on. He was only drunk on stage that one night when his wife left him. Otherwise, he was extremely disciplined. And I think he just loved it – he *loved* performing. He was like a gladiator going on, getting ready for the fight, standing there in the

wings and just looking. I remember he had a look in the play upstage to me and none of the audience could see it or anybody else on stage, it was just him looking at Lennox and it was absolutely terrifying, I can tell you! He could have crossed his eyes and mucked about but no...

There was something ghoulish about him and maybe a frustration that he never really made it in the films. He was always talking about these film scripts he had, but they weren't great film scripts, and he kept saying, 'I don't think they'll make this, it's too weird, or it's too off-key – why else would they ask me to be in it?' I think that was a huge frustration for him that all these other people were getting on and being lauded by everybody and he had this sort of fight and struggle, and I think he was slightly distrusted by the establishment. He wasn't an Oxford / Cambridge actor who intellectually thought things out. He was nobody's idea of Hamlet, but his intensity of everything he says when you see the film of it is extraordinary. He really is somebody in extremis. Maybe the way he threw himself into all those roles and never coasted exhausted him by the end.

He was fearless, I think that's the other thing, absolutely *fearless*, he would just have a go, throw himself into the roles. And fearless with directors as well. On the production we did, there was just us twelve plus him. And that was Trevor's thing, that it was completely pared down so that you'd just see him, and instead of seeing hundreds of soldiers going on, you'd just concentrate on the text, which Trevor obviously knew very well.

I remember somebody said to him, 'You never go up for the voice classes, Nicol.' And he said, 'Well, I think if they did anything with my voice it might finish my career altogether – my voice is unique and I want to keep it that way!'

He was obviously a very intelligent man and knew what he was doing and why he was doing it, and all this added up to his greatness. It was just such a privilege to be on stage with him. And to be part of his company – he was fantastic company. He played jazz, he loved Randy Newman and he could sing most of Randy Newman's songs. He was an entertainer and he brought something to life – he *was* life! But he gradually burnt himself out.

Chapter 14 – Little John and Sherlock

1975 saw the release of Nicol's second LP, entitled *Nicol Williamson Live in London with Parachute*. An eclectic mixture of songs and poetry from *Midwinter Spring*, the title was slightly misleading as five of the songs featured were actually recorded in the studio. The remaining tracks were from Nicol's shows at the Aldwych and at the Queen's Theatre. The cover featured a tube map made out of Nicol's face and the LP was issued by the Decca label on both vinyl and cassette. The segueway from John Betjeman's 'Hunter Trials' into the rock'n'roll song 'Chantilly Lace' has the dubious distinction of being one of the most jarring on record. Sales were negligible but the album does feature Nicol's quite astonishing performance of the extract from Beckett's *How It Is*, a disturbing piece of work delivered with a pace, clarity and intensity that has rarely – if ever – been equaled.

Now that Nicol's second stint with the RSC had come to an end, he returned to film work. James Goldman, an American, was the elder brother of the more famous William Goldman and the author of *The Lion in Winter*, a hugely successful play about Henry II. He had planned a play about Robin Hood but decided to turn it into a screenplay instead. The idea was commissioned by Columbia Pictures, for whom Goldman completed a screenplay entitled *The Death of Robin Hood* in 1971. When Columbia ran into financial difficulties shortly after, the project was put on hold, but by 1974 the company was recovering and Goldman was able to revive it. He initially approached a number of directors without success, including David Lean, John Frankenheimer and Lindsay Anderson.

Meanwhile, Richard Lester – an American who had based himself in England and was best known for directing two films starring The Beatles – received a visit from Peter Guber, a Columbia executive. Guber gave Lester seven cards, on each of which was written a story idea owned by the studio, and asked him to pick the one he wanted to direct. On one of the cards was written 'Robin Hood as an older man', and this was the one which Lester chose. Lester had recently had a success with his version of *The Three Musketeers* and its sequel, *The Four Musketeers*. The Musketeers films had shown an impressive ability to blend comedy, action and romance, tinged with a certain wistfulness, in a story set in the past. *The Death of Robin Hood* was somewhat different in tone because the first three elements, although present, were downplayed, and the wistful quality was brought to the fore. Nevertheless, Goldman had no objection, Lester was assigned to the project and the budget was set at $5 million.

Goldman's script was of a very high calibre for an original screenplay, and Lester was able to assemble a formidable cast. Albert Finney was offered the role of Robin Hood and Sean Connery the part of Little John. However, Finney dropped out and Connery wanted to play Robin Hood, which Lester decided could work well as Connery was prepared to look his age (44) in order to convincingly portray the aging Robin of the story. Richard Harris was to play Richard the Lionheart and Nicol would play Little John. The idea of being the hero's sidekick seems to have appealed to him, and was certainly not the type of part he had played before. Richard Lester was pleased with the choice, and later remembered:

> I didn't meet Nicol in advance but, as a friend of Tony Richardson, I did know his work fairly well. As far as I remember, Nicol was a perfect professional during the shoot. What you see on the screen is what Nicol could do so very well. I merely helped create the atmosphere for him to do his work, and tried to keep the filming process quick and interesting. In general, from my point of view, the cast were all a director could wish for; I was very pleased with the result, and the scene at night between Audrey [Hepburn] and Nicol showed what a fine actor he was – it was a privilege to have worked with him.

Audrey Hepburn was cast as Maid Marian, her first film role since *Wait Until Dark* in 1967, and Robert Shaw as the Sherriff of Nottingham. Shaw was paid $100,000 and absolutely insisted on sharing star billing above the title with Connery and Hepburn, as he had previously done on *The Sting*, for which he had managed to get himself billed alongside Paul Newman and Robert Redford. *Jaws*, the film which would make Shaw a bona fide film star, had not yet been released when shooting began. We can assume that Nicol was paid considerably less than $100,000 and, unlike Shaw, he never made such demands about billing. In fact, he frequently accepted alphabetical billing which, with a surname beginning with 'W', often led to his name being far down the cast list even when, on a number of occasions, he was playing the lead.

The film was mainly shot in and around Pamplona in northern Spain, beginning in early June, 1975. The Musketeers pictures had also been shot in Spain and it was a popular country in which to make a film as the budget stretched further there than it would have in England or many other countries. Another reason for the choice was that several members of the cast had to limit the amount of time they spent working in the UK in order to avoid being hit with a massive tax bill. Denis Healey, then Chancellor of the Exchequer, had recently increased the top rate of income tax to 83%. A 15% investment income surcharge meant that some high earners were obliged to hand over 98% of their income to the government. The inevitable result was that many of the UK's most famous people fled the country during this period, and it was one of the reasons why Nicol spent most of his time outside the UK from this point on.

Additional scenes were shot in Burgos, the historic capital of Castile, while other sequences made use of the castle at Villalonso. Although the locations were chosen partly for pragmatic reasons, there can be little doubt that they worked in the film's favour. The Urbasa Range in western Navarre doubled as Sherwood Forest and was said to more closely resemble the Sherwood Forest evoked by the legend than the real one did.

The film follows the middle-aged, battle-scarred and weary Robin Hood and Little John as they return from the Crusades to Sherwood Forest after an absence of around twenty years. The Sheriff of Nottingham is still in power and seems pleased by Robin's return as he has clearly been without a worthy adversary for a very long time.

Maid Marian has become a nun but her love for Robin is soon reawakened. It's very much an autumnal film, and the effects of age on the protagonists are subtly emphasized. We see Robin and his men waking up after a night in the forest, joints stiff from the cold. After kneeling down to pray while wearing his armour, the Sheriff has difficulty getting back up again. Mounting a horse has become a struggle and the fights are graceless and ungentlemanly. Robin is not above kicking a man below the belt. He and the Sheriff are trying to recapture their youth, but their agility has gone. In the climactic fight between Connery and Shaw in particular, the heaviness of the swords is emphasized and every swing of the blade is an effort punctuated by a grunt.

Perhaps surprisingly given the number of hard-drinking alpha males in the cast, shooting went fairly smoothly, and one suspects that the presence of Audrey Hepburn may well have been responsible for putting the men on better-than-average behaviour. Lester worked very quickly, often shooting just one take, which he covered with multiple cameras. Nicol's former friend Ian Holm had a small part as King John. During the shooting of one of his scenes he had been totally unprepared as he had not heard Lester shout 'Action!' He was astonished when Lester then congratulated him on his performance and dismissed him. Holm was not impressed, and Audrey Hepburn was also unhappy about working at such a pace. Ronnie Barker, Nicol's former colleague from the 1962 Royal Court production of *A Midsummer Night's Dream*, had a supporting role as Friar Tuck and thought it poor direction on Lester's part to be told to 'do something funny' just before a take. Nicol, on the other hand, seems to have found Lester's refusal to spend time massaging the egos of his stars both amusing and refreshing, and he adapted to Lester's methods more easily, as he himself remembered:

> Sean Connery and I had to have this big battle against all the Sherriff's men. Lester had said to me before the film, 'You know how I shoot, don't you? I use four cameras mainly, sometimes five.' Now, I see this fight and I see these cameras lined up … there's a long range, a medium

range and a close-up on performance and I have to computerize that... It doesn't matter to me – I understood that, I got it all, it was fine.

He worked with Malcolm McDowell[48] after Lindsay Anderson had had him in *If...*[49] Lindsay was like [speaking softly], 'Are you ready? Everyone – please be quiet, Malcolm is gathering himself for this wonderful scene... alright, Malcolm?' He goes on to this next film with Richard Lester, five cameras, he goes on and asks the questions he would always ask Lindsay. He said, 'What do you want me to do?' Lester says, 'Well, I don't know – you're the fucking actor!'

To Lester, technicians were the tops... He would set out all these tables groaning with a cornucopia of meats for the technicians while Sean and I and the rest had to sit apart and take second best. Sean said to the Spanish location manager, 'What do you mean we can't shit there? Why not?' He said, 'Well, that's for Mr Lester and the camera crew.' He said, 'Bollocksh to that, we're shitting there!' So he sits down, I sit next to him and we're scoffing away. Lester comes round this bend through this little copse of trees and stops. And he couldn't come over to Sean or me and say, 'You've got to go...' Sean would have said, 'Pish off!' So he said, 'Set another table up over there every day.' From that day on there were two tables. But it shows how Lester had no real time for actors...[50]

Nevertheless, such an apparent lack of attention to performance is nowhere evident in the finished film. Lester knew what he needed and that performances could be improved during the post-production process of looping the dialogue track. Sean Connery also enjoyed the experience on this occasion and worked with Lester again a couple of years later.

Ronnie Barker later recalled that Nicol and Denholm Elliott (who played Will Scarlett) had constantly been 'at each other's throats' during the shoot,[51] but the reason for this is unknown and Luke Williamson had a clear recollection of his father telling him that the only person he had had a problem with during the shoot was Ronnie Barker. Lester seems to have been unaware of any clashes among the cast, although he confirmed a story that, when Nicol discovered a Columbia Pictures spy reporting the events of the day over the phone to the producer, he pulled the phone out of the wall and attempted to flush it down a toilet. However, such problems were relatively minor ones, and shooting was completed in a mere five and a half weeks despite a heatwave and an outbreak of dysentery. In fact, *Robin and Marian* holds a strong claim to be the best film Nicol ever appeared in. It benefitted greatly from the beautiful cinematography of David Watkins as well as a subtle John Barry score.[52] Both Connery and Hepburn, while not the most obvious casting for their roles, gave career-best performances, and their eyes express a great deal more than is actually said, with the result that their love is completely convincing.

Nicol played the part of Little John with a Scots accent, which was chosen in order to be consistent with Connery. He had a great deal of screen time, but not always a great deal to do, although he did feature in a couple of notably moving scenes. One of these is when he is talking to Marian one night and tells her that, if she had been his lady, he would never have left Sherwood Forest. Nicol's restraint makes the scene all the more effective, and Hepburn is equally good. She resented Lester for making her shoot it when she had laryngitis, but he apparently believed this would add to the emotion, which it probably does. Little John's grief when he realizes that Robin is dying is another touching moment from Nicol.

When the film was released as *Robin and Marian* the following year, reviews were mostly favourable but, although it was well-received in Europe, it was a commercial disaster in the U.S., grossing only $4 million. There can be little doubt that it remains one of the most mis-sold films in history. The studio had elected to advertise it as an upbeat romantic adventure story, which it decidedly was not. The predictable result was that those who did go to see it had a completely different experience to the one they had expected, whereas those that might have appreciated it for what it was had been put off by the way it was advertised. *Robin and Marian* is a film of many fine qualities, but the original title of *The Death of Robin Hood* would have been far more appropriate as it is an elegiac film which has a surprising amount in common with *The Wild Bunch*. While Lester's film may not be as violent as Sam Peckinpah's (which he had not seen), both works feature a gang of ageing outlaws hoping for one last triumph who, while being fully aware they may not survive, deliberately place themselves in danger. What they are really afraid of is not death, but old age.

On the 30th of June, during the shooting of *Robin and Marian*, Nicol's mother, Mary, died of lung cancer which had progressed to the point of infecting her bones. She had lasted eight months longer than the doctors had predicted but her death had been a slow and painful one and by the end she had lost a great deal of weight. Nicol later said she had never complained but 'you could see the pain in her eyes'. Jill Townsend:

> I was at the rehearsal rooms at the BBC at the time [doing *Poldark*] and I got a call saying that Nicol's mother had died. I called Dick Blodget – his agent in London at the time – and I said, 'Whoever tells Nicol that he needs to come home must have his plane ticket ready and take him to the airport.' He came back for the funeral and then went back to finish the film and Luke and I went back with him.
>
> Nicol resembled his mother and her father more [than he did those on Hugh's side of the family]. His mother was very gracious, very loving and kind. She had a beautiful singing voice. Hugh absolutely worshipped her. She was very elegant. She had a great sense of humour but she would never swear.

Nicol's father, Hugh, was never quite the same again. Added to the burden of grief was the guilt that he felt at having smoked in her presence throughout their 39-year marriage. Luke Williamson later said that he felt that this was the source of his grandfather's 'overwhelming sadness.' Nicol stopped smoking not long after his mother's death and, after a couple of relapses, eventually managed to kick the habit for good.

Nicol and Jill decided in August to sell their house at 12 Woodfall Street as they had begun to find it too small once Luke had begun to walk. They bought a larger house at 77 Castlenau in Barnes.

In July, Nicol had signed on for a film, *The Seven-Per-Cent Solution*, to commence shooting in October in London, Vienna and the Italian Alps, with interiors shot at Pinewood and a modest budget of $4 million. Based on a bestselling novel by Nicholas Meyer, who also wrote the screenplay, it would star Nicol as a drug-addicted, paranoid Sherlock Holmes. Nicol was not Meyer's first choice for the part, as he later recalled:

> It was [the director] Herb Ross' idea to cast Nicol (Alan Arkin as Freud and Robert Duvall as Watson were my contributions). I had initially urged Peter O'Toole, but he and Herb had a falling out making the musical version of *Goodbye, Mr. Chips*. I remember Herb calling me and asking me what I thought of the Nicol idea.

Nicol had recently turned down a cameo as Sherlock Holmes in Gene Wilder's spoof *The Adventure of Sherlock Holmes' Smarter Brother* and claimed never to have read a Holmes story or seen a Holmes film. Contradicting himself somewhat, he told *Time* magazine that he intended to portray Holmes as 'lovable, magnanimous, charming, witty and irresistible — not the aesthetic creep we all know and can't stand.' The director, Herbert Ross, was a New Yorker who had directed vehicles for Barbra Streisand and Woody Allen and had seen some of Nicol's Broadway performances.

The story involved Dr Watson (Robert Duvall) luring Holmes to Vienna in order to cure him of his cocaine addiction with the help of Sigmund Freud (Alan Arkin). Once there, they become involved in a case concerning one of Freud's patients, played by Vanessa Redgrave. The strong cast also included Laurence Olivier as a meek Professor Moriarty and, in a flashback sequence, Jill Townsend in a very brief (and appropriately Freudian) appearance as Holmes' mother. This involved Moriarty and Mrs Holmes being caught in bed together. Jill Townsend later remembered Olivier asking her just before the scene was shot if she thought Nicol would be jealous.

The Seven-Per-Cent Solution was a well-made, entertaining film. Nicol may not have been an obvious choice for Holmes, and it seems surprising that it was not even felt necessary to dye his hair for the part, but he proves remarkably likeable and effective in the role as a peculiarly neurotic version of the Conan Doyle character. The first meeting of Holmes and Freud gave Nicol an excellent opportunity to demonstrate his verbal dexterity in a long scene in which, unaware of the identity of his host, he makes a series of impressive deductions about Freud after what appears to have been the most casual glance around Freud's study. Nicol also appears to have performed at least some of his own stunts during the climactic train chase sequence.

While the actors played it straight for the most part, the film also has its comic aspects, which Nicol saw as being in keeping with the 'comedy of circumstance' which he enjoyed. However, Robert Duvall adopted a rather charmingly absurd English accent which could be taken as tongue-in-cheek, although Nicholas Meyer felt that this was not the intention:

> Like the novel from which it was derived, the idea was to make audiences re-look at these famous characters, to blow the cobwebs off their more familiar (and to me, frequently inaccurate) portrayals. I was never part of the discussions as to whether Nicol should or shouldn't dye his hair, wear a different nose, etc., but I definitely wanted Duvall, anything to get away from Nigel Bruce's[53] totally preposterous Watson. Bruce may have had a genuine English accent, but I could never understand why a genius would hang out with an idiot. And Bruce was never the narrative voice I heard when I read the original Doyle, whereas Duvall's stolid, dependable doctor came much closer. I certainly think Duvall was doing the best accent he could; tongue in cheek was not his style at all.
>
> Holmes was a real change of pace for Nicol, but Holmes in this instance was a greatly troubled man and Nicol never played him less than genuinely tormented. My encounters with Nicol were in Vienna, where shooting began. My impression was - and remains - of a desperately unhappy, lonely and anhedonic[54] man, more or less trapped in a melancholy world from which he seemed unable, indeed, perhaps unwilling to escape. Alan Arkin thought him enormously talented - as he did Duvall... [but] I don't recall the three actors spending much down

time together. They had, ultimately, little in common except the work and there they met on terms of perfect synchronicity.

Vanessa Redgrave had become an evangelist for the Workers' Revolutionary Party, Palestine and a number of other causes, and irritated several of her colleagues, including Nicol, by attempting to convert them, but this seems to have been the only notable case of friction among the cast. On one occasion, Nicol even presented camera assistant Cedric James – who had also worked on *The Reckoning* – with a birthday cake. Nicol later spoke about working with Alan Arkin:

> Alan had come on playing Freud and it came out as Jewish schtick. Herb said, 'Alan, would you just walk out the door and come in again?' So, he walks out and comes back in again. Herb said, 'I don't believe it, Alan.' If someone said that to me, I'd say, 'Well, why? What do you want me to do?' But it wasn't humiliation, he was actually saying to him, 'You'd better dig deep down in this and find out what it is because this isn't working.'... [but it worked out alright and] Alan was generous. We had a drink on the last day and he said, 'You really made me work my *ass* off on this movie!' [55]

Notices for the film were mixed when it was released in October the following year – Vincent Canby gave it a glowing review in the *New York Times*, but others felt that it had slightly missed its mark. Box office receipts were disappointing, although the film retains a loyal following to this day. Nicol seems to have been positive about the film – to help its promotion, he made an appearance on *The Tonight Show*, where he was interviewed by David Brenner (standing in for Johnny Carson). Nicholas Meyer went on to work as both writer and director on two of the *Star Trek* films, as well as his own *Time After Time*, which featured Malcom McDowell's H.G. Wells pursuing David Warner's Jack the Ripper through time. Meyer remembered one further encounter with Nicol:

The last time I glimpsed Nicol Williamson stands out very much in my memory. It was some years after the film, though I can't pinpoint how many. I was driving West on Sunset Blvd, just crossing through the green traffic light at Sunset and Horn Avenue (Tower Records was then on the northwest corner of the intersection). There I briefly witnessed Nicol standing on the center island, alone, waiting for the light to change. I presume he was on his way to Tower Records. He looked like the loneliest man I'd ever seen.

On the 7th of December, Nicol participated in *The Actors Are Come Hither... Buzz, Buzz*, a memorial tribute to Buzz Goodbody, who had been one of the co-directors of the RSC's production of *Coriolanus* featuring Nicol. She had also been the first Artistic Director of The Other Place, but had committed suicide in April. The evening took place at the Aldwych and featured many members of the RSC. Nicol performed some items from *Midwinter Spring*.

Chapter 15 – Nic Wrecks Rick's Rex

Nicol's next project was a dream that turned into a nightmare. It was the brainchild of Richard Adler, a 54-year-old New Yorker who, with his collaborator Jerry Ross, had written the songs for the hit musicals *The Pajama Game* and *Damn Yankees*. After the early death of Ross, Adler had found it difficult to repeat his early success and had begun to dabble in production. He wanted to produce a musical about Henry VIII and approached Richard Rodgers to ask if he would be interested in composing the music. Rodgers, a Broadway legend, had enjoyed an astonishing run of hits with his collaborator Oscar Hammerstein, including *South Pacific*, *The King and I* and *The Sound of Music*. Even though his heyday was over and he was now 73 and in poor health, the name of Richard Rodgers still counted for a great deal, and Adler was thrilled when he agreed. Adler also hired Sheldon Harnick as lyricist, a decision which pleased Rodgers as he had been impressed by Harnick's lyrics for *Fiddler on the Roof*. Meanwhile, playwright and screenwriter Sherman Yellen was hired to write the book. Yellen, a 44-year-old New Yorker, had previously collaborated with Harnick on another Broadway musical, *The Rothschilds*, for which he had been nominated for a Tony award.

Adler hired Edwin Sherin to direct. Sherin's 1969 production of the boxing play *The Great White Hope* had won both a Tony Award for Best Play and a Drama Desk Award for Outstanding Director. The play's star had been James Earl Jones, whom Sherin had also directed as King Lear, so he was an able and experienced director of drama but perhaps not the ideal choice for a musical. Another problem was that Rodgers was known for sunny, optimistic musicals, but a different tone would be required when dealing with the subject of a monarch famed for having two of his six wives executed.

For the part of Henry, Adler reportedly first approached Richard Burton, Albert Finney and Peter O'Toole, all of whom turned him down. He then thought of Nicol and flew to England in the spring of

1975 to meet him. Nicol, who loved to sing and had never appeared in a musical – let alone a Richard Rodgers Broadway musical – agreed terms with Adler over lunch. If the musical was a success, Nicol would potentially be tied up for as long as a year. The fact that he had not agreed to such a contract since *Inadmissible Evidence* shows how enthusiastic he must have been about the idea.

Future star Glenn Close was cast as Princess Mary, but the female lead was Penny Fuller, who played a twin role as Ann Boleyn in Act 1 and Henry's daughter, Elizabeth, in Act 2. She had previously been nominated for a Tony Award for her performance as Eve Harrington in *Applause*, the Broadway musical version of *All About Eve*. Fuller later remembered:

> I had an *extremely* difficult time. And Nicol had a difficult time. He was in one of his I'm-not-drinking-only-white-wine phases (we all know what that means) … but when we started I was thrilled because he was who he was. I had not seen his *Hamlet*, but Norman [Twain] had told me how wonderful it was. And Norman, who was a hero of mine in those days, he thought Nicol was great, and he told me how he picked David Merrick up and put him in a trashcan. Now I happen to love David Merrick but that's another thing… It was in that era when young women loved rebellious, dark, angry poets, so it was fine. I was not in love with Nicol at all. We were actually kind of pals, and later on I saw him and we hung out for a night or two, and I think he kind of respected me…

After two years of planning, rehearsals of *Rex* began on the 19th of January, one month before it was due to open at the Playhouse Theatre in Wilmington, Delaware. It soon became clear that a number of key problems had yet to be solved, with the result that a process of rewriting both songs and book continued right up until the Broadway opening at the Lunt-Fontanne Theatre on the 25th of April. Meanwhile, the musical transferred from Wilmington to the Opera House in Washington's Kennedy Centre and then to the Shubert Theatre in Boston, running for a fortnight in each. Box office receipts were actually healthy throughout the tour, with a number of shows being sold out, but the same could not be said for the reviews. Adler knew that it was one thing for a show to sell out when it was playing for only two weeks in cities which were culture-starved in comparison to Manhattan, but that for *Rex* to survive on Broadway, he needed the support of the New York critics. A number of songs were discarded entirely and new ones hastily written, while everyone involved struggled to find the right tone. Nicol reportedly felt that the writing did not put Henry's point of view across sufficiently, with the result that the audience saw him as too unsympathetic. He was even booed on at least one occasion for Henry's shameful treatment of Katherine of Aragon. When changes were made at Nicol's insistence to address the issue, others in the cast complained that Henry had become absurdly nice.

Penny Fuller later stated that Nicol 'wasn't particularly difficult throughout, but then when it became obvious that we were in a turkey he got difficult' and that this had become apparent by the time the company arrived in Washington – where Nicol, unable to escape the ghost of Nixon, was staying at the Watergate Hotel. During his stay, Nicol was invited to dinner at the White House by president Gerald Ford but, due to his commitments with *Rex*, arrived too late to attend.

Interviewing Nicol at the Jockey Club, journalist Herbert Kretzmer felt that he was already on the verge of a nervous breakdown. Nicol told Kretzmer in no uncertain terms not only that he regretted taking the part but that he hated being the lead in a musical and would never appear in one again under any circumstances. After having quit cigarettes some months previously, he was now chain-smoking and he said that he dared not take a drink or he would never be able to force himself back on to the stage. Penny Fuller:

> The first town, you don't know what kind of trouble you're in till you have your audience. And really good producers like David Merrick would listen, not just to the laughs of the audience, but to the tenor of the laughs, and they would know and tell the directors what they needed

to fix. But this was so big and there were so many kings, if you will – Richard Rodgers, Sheldon Harnick who was doing obeisance to Richard Rodgers, and Richard Adler, it was like a great, heavy piano that nobody knew how to carry and nobody knew how to play. So Nicol was okay to begin with, but as he became endangered, like a trapped animal, he fought back.

Richard Adler and Edwin Sherin became understandably nervous at this point and came very close to replacing Nicol with American actor Jon Cypher, who was of a similar build to Nicol and was also an able singer. Shortly after Kretzmer's interview, Jill – who had remained in England – agreed that she and Luke would join Nicol when *Rex* opened in New York, and this news may have helped to calm him and avert the crisis.

Meanwhile, the press continued to circle as vultures do on sighting a wounded animal. Adler insisted the show merely had 'a cough, not cancer.' In Boston, he managed to persuade Hal Prince – the producer-director of a number of hit Broadway musicals – to come in as advisor in an unofficial capacity. Prince performed some fairly major surgery on a variety of aspects, but it would prove to be too little too late. The actors were often in the difficult situation of having to rehearse new scenes during the day while performing the older versions in the evening. Nicol sometimes refused to co-operate, even insisting that one of the strongest songs, *The Pears Of Anjou*, be dropped as it was 'too taxing'. When *Rex* closed in Boston on the 10th of April, there remained only five days of grace before Broadway previews began.

Sherman Yellen had found Nicol to be very difficult throughout both the rehearsals and subsequent tour, later recalling how Nicol had thrown his gold-plated crown (an expensive prop) across the stage during one rehearsal, destroying it in the process, as Richard Rodgers looked on in dismay. When the company arrived in New York, Yellen, worn-out and having a couple of drinks at the bar in Sardi's to soothe his nerves, was approached by a journalist acquaintance who asked him what a 'nice Jewish boy' was doing drinking on Passover. Yellen replied that, after a month on the road with Nicol Williamson, he 'no longer believed in god.' Unfortunately, he found himself quoted in the press the following day with the result that Nicol refused to appear at the opening without an apology in front of the cast. Yellen, suffering at the time from a polyp on his vocal chords, managed to croak out an apology for his indiscretion rather than for what he had actually said, but Nicol was apparently satisfied and the opening went ahead as planned.

With the notable exception of George Oppenheimer in *Newsday*, the reviews were largely unfavourable. Some critics thought that a musical about Henry VIII was a fundamentally flawed idea, others that the talents involved were hopelessly mismatched. The writing came under attack for trying to cram in too much history into the time allotted, while certain reviewers felt that Rodgers had lost his touch. In comparison, the actors were let off lightly and both Nicol and Penny Fuller received good notices, although this was something of a double-edged sword, with T.E. Kalem of *Time* magazine comparing Nicol to 'a marauding shark becalmed in a suburban swimming pool'. Clive Barnes of the *New York Times* made a similar observation, reporting that Nicol 'walks through the musical like Gulliver through toytown' and that, although his stage presence was 'fantastic,' and technically his singing was hard to fault, 'when he sings his voice loses its character... suddenly the genius leaves him.'

Adler posted a full-page ad in the same newspaper the following day in which he quoted ten 'favourable' reviews, but the reality was, they were more mixed than favourable and he had quoted selectively.

There was some unintentional but no doubt welcome humour along the way. At one performance, one of Nicol's shoes flew off, which he chose to ignore despite the fact that everyone in the audience had noticed and were now watching the shoe rather than him and wondering how he would manage to retrieve it. Eventually, at the exit, one of the other actors scurried across the stage and recovered it.

It has been said that more songs were written and subsequently dropped than those that made it into the finished show. One of these, entitled simply 'Rex', was apparently abandoned because it sounded like Nicol, singing 'Rex! Rex!' was attempting to summon a lost dog. During another rehearsal, Nicol reduced both himself and Penny Fuller to fits by repeatedly fluffing a line so that it came out as, 'Madame, you dimish the throne I thit on.'

Although *Rex* was to become famous as a notorious flop, an audio recording of one of the performances has survived in which the house sounds as if it must be at least fairly full and the audience laugh readily, applaud enthusiastically and generally appear to be having a good time. Despite the fact that it had not been an immediate smash hit and some of the reviews were embarrassing, the situation was not necessarily beyond salvation, but trouble was waiting in the wings.

Nicol was still unhappy and wanted out. It is highly likely that he was hoping to be fired and that was the real reason he had not bothered to behave well and was being so uncooperative. As the star of a show in which a great deal of time and money had been invested and changes were constantly being made, he was naturally under a great deal of pressure. In addition to this, he was heading a large company who had been relocating to a new city every couple of weeks and having to adjust to a different theatre. His energies had also been consumed by recording the album of songs from the show and with looping sessions for *The Seven-Per-Cent Solution*. Meanwhile, his relationship with Jill continued to deteriorate, and she later recalled that 'He came back from *Rex* one night telling me he'd just slept with Liza Minnelli. I don't know if it was true but I said, "You don't have to share that information." He was self-destructing.' At the end of a performance on the 12th of May, Nicol finally snapped.

Jim Litten, a young dancer who was a member of the ensemble, had already irritated Nicol by being over-familiar and had apparently tried to persuade Nicol to join him for a drink and made other unwanted overtures of friendship. During the day of the 12th, Litten had participated in the shooting of a television advert for the show.

Nicol had refused to take part and his understudy had played Henry in long shot. When the television crew completed the shooting of the advert, Litten later claimed he had heard one of them say, 'It's a wrap!' After that evening's performance of *Rex*, as the company came out for their curtain call, Litten repeated the phrase, 'It's a wrap!' Unfortunately, Nicol heard this as 'It's crap!' and delivered Litten a stinging slap across the face in full view of the audience, allegedly also threatening him, 'Keep your mouth shut or you'll get the same again!' The severity of the assault is not entirely clear, but actress Barbara Andres later recalled that, 'The wives tried to get Nicol offstage and away from Jimmy, who was on the floor.' [56] Penny Fuller did not witness the actual slap, but remembered the incident this way:

> So I come out from my curtain call and I'm bowing, and then I hear behind me [nonsensical shouting] and I grabbed Nicol and pulled him into the line. We took the bow and those two started swearing at each other, or people started swearing, and I went up to my dressing room and, as I climbed the stairs I thought, 'Is this what the Germans did, they just turned their backs?' [laughs] That's what I thought.
>
> The next day I had some kind of interview and I was told, 'Don't talk about the slap!' And I said, 'Oh, is that what happened? I didn't even know!' So then I find out that there was some contretemps and I get to the theatre and I have to play with Nicol. And I *like* Nicol, and I get it, and I think, 'What the hell am I gonna do?' And I see the press at the stage door, so I go through the front of the house and – where I got this I don't know – I go up to Nicol's dressing room and knock on the door. 'Come in!' I said, 'You sonofabitch! You want this play to close and you pull a stunt like this! We're gonna run forever!' It was brilliant because it let him off the hook. We laughed, we talked, we didn't go into it but... I don't know where it came from – I didn't know I was gonna say it when I knocked on the door! But it was not forgiving him, it was calling him on it, but it was a way to get on and continue to act with this man.

The incident received a great deal of publicity. Litten complained to Equity, who filed charges against Nicol for unprofessional conduct. Penny Fuller felt that Equity relished the opportunity to humiliate the actor who had controversially replaced George C. Scott in *Plaza Suite*, supposedly at the expense of an American actor. Along with Glenn Close and Tom Aldredge (who played Will Somers), Fuller attended the Equity hearing not to defend Nicol, but to provide some friendly support as the ensemble members had all banded together in support of Litten. This created a schism among the company from which it never recovered, with the result that any motivation to continue despite the production's other problems was greatly dissipated. Penny Fuller believed that Nicol's anger was an essential part of what made him an exceptional actor:

> I've seen a lot worse behaviour, except for the slap. But you could imagine the state he was in to do that – he was *so* miserable, he wanted it to close so bad, he wanted out, it was no fun to do… but he knew he'd been an asshole.
>
> Nicol's anger and dark side was the seed of his genius that he could pull from and be in those plays that he did, in *Hamlet* and *Inadmissible Evidence*. Of course, his best scene in *Rex* was the one in which he got to be angry as that was what he did best because it tapped into his dark side. Jocular, I wouldn't call him. Funny guy, but funny in an intellectual, dark way…
>
> If you were going to write a novel about a tortured Scotsman with a lot of talent, that'd had the wisdom to put the anger and the torture into his work, then there's nothing that he did that was that much of a surprise. He was a winner and he didn't win, so he ended up something less than a winner and I think that's part of what the anger was too.

Rex continued to run for a few more weeks after the slap, but if the publicity generated by the incident helped ticket sales, it did not help enough, and the show finally closed on the 5th of June after 48 performances. Somewhat surprisingly under the circumstances, both Nicol and Penny Fuller were nominated for Drama Desk Awards for *Rex* but, less surprisingly, neither actor won. Nicol lost out to Ian Richardson, who won for his performance as Henry Higgins in a revival of *My Fair Lady*.

Chapter 16 – A Series of Unfortunate Events

Nicol accepted a film role shortly after it became clear that *Rex* was to close early. Steve McQueen, keen to be taken more seriously as an actor, had badgered Warners to let him play the lead in a version of Henrik Ibsen's play *An Enemy of the People*. The studio agreed as they were desperate to get one of their most popular stars in front of a camera again after a long hiatus. McQueen – with full beard and glasses – would play the doctor who discovers that the water supply in his town may not be safe. For the part of the doctor's brother, the mayor who attempts to suppress this information in order to protect local business interests, McQueen first approached Charlton Heston, who declined, then considered Oliver Reed before deciding against him and offering the role to Nicol instead. Jill Townsend:

> Nicol signed a contract to do *An Enemy of the People* but the film company couldn't insure him because of his walking off movies or theatre, so they did a deal whereby he could do the movie but he had to sign over everything that he owned in order to be in the production to keep him from walking off. He flew out there and I think he did one reading and then disappeared. I got a call that our home was going to be taken away and we were going to lose everything because he'd walked off the production. Edward Oldman from Oscar Beuselinck's office used to advise Nicol financially. I asked him where Nicol was but he didn't know. I said, 'If you hear from Nicol or if you find him, tell him that Luke and I will be on the streets.' Nicol's reply to that was he didn't care, he just didn't want to do this production, that was the most important thing. Edward Oldman had said to me, 'File for divorce and that'll stop them from taking the house away from you.' And I said, 'Well, will you tell Nicol that this is what I'm doing?' so I filed for divorce and the next thing I know it's all revenge and retribution – all the things I was afraid would happen, but we didn't lose the house. He was never going to forgive me for filing for divorce in order to save the house. Then I got the threats: 'I'll make sure you never work again, I'm

going to ruin your reputation.' Then it was five years of threats and interviews in the press he would give saying I was living in a commune in Cornwall or that Luke was a lovechild. I just knew not to respond. He was going to accuse me of having affairs with everyone I'd ever worked with, he was going to take Luke away from me and sue me for alimony! But it didn't come to anything.

I liked and respected Edward Oldman, so if I needed to tell him something about Luke I would always do it through him. It was friendlier that way. I didn't want to make an enemy out of my son's father.

When Nicol disappeared, he seems to have gone to Lindos, which became a sort of retreat for him and where he began to spend an increasing amount of time. Mary Clow threw a party for him at her house, but Nicol found it boring and wandered outside, where he ran into fellow escapee Emma Hamelynck, a striking blue-eyed blonde. The two began chatting and got on extremely well. Emma was the wife of Karel Hamelynck, a doctor who specialised in sports injuries. The couple, both of whom were Dutch and resided in Amsterdam, had been regular visitors to Lindos for a number of years. However, Emma was separated from her husband by the time she met Nicol, although they remained good friends. Nicol and Emma began a relationship which lasted a number of years before it too changed into an enduring friendship. Emma Hamelynck later said that the reason it lasted was that neither party made any claims on the other.

Nicol's other friends in Lindos included a number of colourful locals, such as Dimitris Mavrikos, a restaurateur, and Socrates Tsouvilis, an extroverted ex-policeman and womaniser turned bar owner. Other frequent companions were John O'Kane, an American linguist, and Henry Blofeldt, the cricket commentator, whose stammer and upper-class demeanour made him something of a stooge for Nicol, but who could nevertheless match him for drink for drink.

It is not known exactly why Nicol became adamant that he was not going to do *An Enemy of the People*, but it seems that he had taken against Steve McQueen for some reason. He was quickly replaced on the production by Charles Durning. As far as the film was concerned, it had not been much of a missed opportunity as the shooting went way over schedule and, when it was finally finished, Warners barely released it. Having said that, it was a well-made effort and McQueen gave a good account of himself.

During this period, Nicol also reportedly tried for the part of Fredrik Egerman in Hal Prince's film version of *A Little Night Music*, the Stephen Sondheim musical. Prince already had one difficult star to contend with – Elizabeth Taylor, who had insisted that he fire the original leading man, Robert Stephens, after only an hour of rehearsal because she had taken an instant dislike to him. Prince, no doubt remembering what had happened on *Rex*, eventually cast the original Broadway actor, Len Cariou, instead, but *A Little Night Music* was also not a film which would go on to be successful.

Playwright Trevor Griffiths later recalled meeting Nicol in Los Angeles around this time and going on a 'working pub crawl' during which they discussed the possibility of him playing Eddie Waters, a retired comedian who teaches stand-up, in a Mike Nichols Broadway production of Griffiths' play *Comedians*. However, Nicol ultimately decided against it and Irish actor Milo O'Shea was cast.

On the 10th of October, Nicol was issued with a B1 visa, which would allow him multiple entry into the USA for business purposes. These were usually valid for ten years, but Nicol's was valid indefinitely. The day after obtaining his visa, he arrived back in New York.

In November, Nicol signed on to play Guy Burgess in *Philby*, a film based on a screenplay by Arthur Hopcraft. Burgess, along with Kim Philby, was one of the Cambridge Five, who had sold secrets to the Soviets and subsequently defected. Robert Shaw was to play the title role and the cast would also include Christopher Plummer and Vanessa Redgrave. The director was to be Mike Hodges, best known for *Get Carter*. Interiors were to be shot in the UK and locations in Israel, Vienna and Washington, beginning in March 1977 on a budget of $5 million. However, producer Benjamin Fisz ran into problems with the financing and the project was delayed until the following January when a new director, Don Sharp, was assigned as Hodges was no longer available. The film finally collapsed when Robert Shaw's American agent, John Gaines, persuaded the star to renege on his agreement with Fisz and make *Avalanche Express* instead as it would earn him his highest salary to date of $750,000. With Shaw gone, Fisz lost his backing – a pity, as the screenplay was said to be of a high quality, a claim which nobody would ever make in regard to *Avalanche Express*.

Jill Townsend had by this time begun a relationship with Alan Price,[57] with whom she had co-starred in the film *Alfie Darling* two years previously. On the 23rd of December, Nicol flew to Los Angeles, but returned to Lindos early in the new year. 1977 was not to be a good year for Nicol. There was also a dramatic shift in the cultural landscape at this time. As the corpse of Elvis Presley stiffened on a Graceland toilet and the Queen celebrated her Silver Jubilee, the punks of London and New York were doing to prog rock and hippies what Nicol Williamson had done to John Gielgud's Hamlet back in 1969. Yet the punks would not have considered the trad jazz-loving Nicol to be one of their own any more than Nicol would have worn a ripped T-shirt and bondage trousers. Nicol was an individualist and had never seen himself as being representative of the so-called 'angry young man' movement – or any other movement, for that matter. This was to be the year when he became in danger of becoming yesterday's man. *Rex* had flopped, *Robin and Marian* had flopped, even *The Seven-Per-Cent Solution* had failed to turn a profit. The big hits at the cinema would be *Star Wars* and *Close Encounters of the Third Kind*, films that relied more on special effects than actors and would change the industry entirely. As far as the theatre was concerned, Nicol was still considered a major prize, but by now it was clear that many in the film industry felt that he had had his chances and that he never had been and never would be a name that was going to draw people into cinemas.

Presumably as a favour to Herbert Ross (director of *The Seven-Per-Cent Solution*), Nicol flew from Greece to L.A. at the end of March to play an uncredited cameo in Ross' film *The Goodbye Girl*, a romantic comedy written by Neil Simon. It starred Marsha Mason as a single mother in New York who is forced into sharing her apartment with struggling actor Richard Dreyfuss, whom she initially detests but eventually becomes romantically involved with. Nicol appeared near the end as Oliver Fry, a successful American film director who visits Dreyfuss' character backstage to offer him a part in his new film. Although his screen time came in at under a minute, Nicol was a striking presence as the confident, well-dressed director wryly amused at Dreyfuss' lack of cool. Despite a superficial realism, *The Goodbye Girl* was a rather schmaltzy affair, but it nevertheless became a runaway hit, taking over $100 million at the box office. It is somehow typical of Nicol's film career that the most financially successful film he appeared in would also be the one in which he had the shortest screen time.

Meanwhile, Jill was granted a *decree nisi* back in London, which meant that she and Nicol would be divorced within six weeks unless Nicol made a case as to why it should not proceed. Nicol decided not to do so and the divorce was finalised in April, but his personal problems had clearly exacerbated his drinking. Towards the end of May, he was arrested in Hollywood for allegedly driving while drunk. He was taken to County Hospital for an examination and released after six hours on a bail of £290.

On the 18th of May, the *Evening News* had published an article by Nicola Tyrer which featured a lengthy interview with Jill about the collapse of her marriage to Nicol. Jill held little back and, although she made it clear that Nicol had never hit her, she said that 'his verbal attacks did enough damage' and that Nicol had told her that he would rather see his family out on the street than continue with a project he was not happy about. When the article came to Nicol's attention, he was furious and consulted his lawyer. On the 20th of June, as Nicol arrived in Los Angeles, a writ was issued on his behalf alleging that Jill had libelled him, but the allegation was dropped before it went to court. Meanwhile, the house at 77 Castlenau was sold and Jill and Luke moved into a house on Scarth Road, also in Barnes. In the wake of the divorce, opportunities for Nicol to spend time with his son became limited, as Luke remembered:

> Dad had to work very hard to see me as a kid. He always tried to make sure that it was a special experience and we did something fun. I was football mad as a kid and I used to just want to play football all day. We would go to the park if he was in London and I would run him ragged and in Greece we played on the beach and there was a cave we used as a goal. I made him play football all the time, but he never complained – he was just so happy to spend time with me. There were nights in Lindos when he would pull the mattresses out on the roof and he would sing 'Swinging on a Star' and point out the constellations to me. With the time that he had he always did the maximum he could possibly do and he always wanted to see me.
>
> I remember once I was put on the plane from boarding school to go and see him in Greece and either on the plane or from school before I left I got headlice, so when I arrived I was scratching my head like crazy. Dad took me to the doctor, who said, 'Just shave his head.' Dad freaked out saying, 'I can't do that – I'll never be allowed to see him again if I send him back to his mother with a shaved head!' So, somehow he managed to find that special shampoo and then he spent about two hours every day combing dead lice out of my hair.

In order to raise funds for expenses incurred as the result of the divorce, as well as to contribute financially to Luke's upbringing, Nicol accepted a guest-star part in an episode of the enormously popular feature-length American TV series *Columbo*, entitled *How to Dial a Murder*. He played Dr Eric Mason, a wealthy American self-help guru whose wife has died six months earlier in suspicious circumstances. The 'doctor' is also a film buff who has a large collection of movie memorabilia including W.C. Fields' bent pool cue and the sled from *Citizen Kane*. Mason murders his wife's lover by training his two Dobermans, Laurel and Hardy, to attack anyone who says the word 'rosebud' while talking on the phone in his kitchen. Nicol gave a strong performance, but it was not the kind of material to be taken too seriously, although it was a pleasure to see him match wits with Peter Falk's Columbo and he had a good opening scene in which he delivers a seminar to a hall half-filled with gullible Californians while drawing amusingly incomprehensible diagrams on a blackboard. The script left little doubt that his character was little more than a fancy snake-oil peddlar, but there is one instance of quintessential Nicol when he gleefully delivers the line, 'I never felt better in my life!' after having his wife's lover torn to pieces; with these words, his character seems to express his bottomless contempt for the values of 'civilised' society. However, it was not a role that Nicol would have accepted had he not needed the money, although perhaps the irony of playing a 'life control' specialist and wife-murderer in order to pay for his own divorce appealed to him. Years later, author Mark Dawidziak attempted to interview Nicol about the episode for his book *The Columbo Phile* only to find that Nicol claimed to have no memory of making it. Given the popularity of *Columbo* and the number of repeats the series enjoys on television to this day, Nicol's performance as Eric Mason is almost certainly his most widely seen.

Shortly after his *Columbo* appearance, Nicol again appeared opposite Peter Falk in *The Cheap Detective*, a rather obvious spoof of the Humphrey Bogart classics *Casablanca* and *The Maltese Falcon*. Written by Neil Simon, the script strained relentlessly for laughs, of which there were far too few, and failed to provide much in the way of a story or any kind of character development. Nicol played what was essentially a rehash of the Conrad Veidt role from *Casablanca* and had some fun with a comic German accent. As the all-star cast was listed alphabetically, his name appeared towards the end of the cast list – not the last time the disadvantages of having a surname beginning with 'W' would become apparent.

In August, Nicol made another money-motivated decision to accept a role, this time as co-star to Robert Shaw and Harrison Ford in *Force 10 from Navarone*, the belated sequel to the 1961 hit *The Guns of Navarone*. However, Nicol's involvement came to an abrupt end. Luke Williamson recalled his father's side of the story:

> He was supposed to play the demolitions expert. In the script they have to blow up this bridge and Robert Shaw's character goes, 'I don't know if we can do that,' and the demolitions expert gives a detailed explanation of how they can do it. A few days in and all of a sudden Nicol's character is saying, 'I don't think we can do it' and Robert Shaw is telling the explosives expert how he can blow up the bridge. So Nicol walked. He was willing to walk off over stuff like that.

This certainly sounds plausible given Shaw's obsessive competitiveness and the fact that $50,000 of Shaw's $750,000 fee was supposedly for screen writing services. However, after Nicol's old Dundee Rep colleague Edward Fox was hired to replace him, George Macdonald Fraser was hired to rewrite the script, partly to tailor the role to Fox's rather different characteristics. Fraser later wrote in his book *The Light's on at Signpost* that Fox had been a last minute replacement for an actor he refers to only as 'a volatile Scot', whose participation in *Force 10* had ended when he 'wrenched the phone off the wall' during a heated conversation with the producer. Some film buffs have mistakenly identified the actor concerned as Ian Bannen, but a member of the crew (who had no memory of any stories about a phone being wrenched off a wall) confirmed that Bannen had never been involved and also said that Nicol was replaced before shooting began because the producers had heard he had a drink problem and did not want to take a risk on him. Although it is quite possible that the telephone argument was over Shaw's alleged dialogue theft, it is also possible that Fraser, who worked with Richard Lester on several occasions, had confused the story about the *Robin and Marian* phone-wrenching incident with something that had happened on *Force 10* prior to his own involvement. It would also be reasonable to surmise that Nicol was not replaced *because* of his 'drink problem', but rather that the producers did not attempt to pacify him after the argument because they had become nervous about having to deal with both

Nicol and Robert Shaw, whose drinking had become a serious problem by this stage in his life. The difference was that Shaw was the star of *Jaws* and they would not have been prepared to lose him as they were to lose Nicol.

Nicol's next role was also doomed, and there was to be further phone-wrenching involved. William Peter Blatty, author of *The Exorcist*, had written a highly unusual screenplay entitled *The Ninth Configuration*, based on his own novel, *Twinkle, Twinkle Killer Kane*. The central character, Colonel 'Killer' Kane, is a highly decorated American marine-corps guerrilla fighter with a fearsome reputation for being lethally effective in the field of battle. He has been assigned to take charge of an asylum for members of the armed forces who are apparently suffering from various kinds of mental problems but are considered by some to be malingering. It emerges that Kane has his own problems, although his unconventional approach in indulging the whims of the inmates appears to be having a positive effect, especially on Cutshaw, an astronaut who suffered a nervous breakdown and aborted a rocket launch as a result.

Blatty began as a writer of comedy and there is a great deal of comedy in *The Ninth Configuration* but, as in *The Exorcist*, he was largely preoccupied with questions of faith, especially in regard to the existence of life after death. It is this blend of wise-cracking comedy with drama which attempts to tackle the big questions that makes the script so daring. After a number of studios decided the film was too unusual to risk financing, Blatty managed to raise a budget of $4 million by persuading Pepsi to co-finance it with him. Blatty had earned a huge amount of money from both the book and film of *The Exorcist*, and so was able to contribute $2 million personally.

For the role of Kane, Blatty had initially approached Charlton Heston, who accepted but later bailed out when he discovered that the film was to be shot in Hungary, as he was not prepared to work in a communist country. Blatty had long been an admirer of Nicol's, and was convinced he could play virtually any part, so he asked Nicol and was delighted to receive a positive response. Nicol arrived in

Budapest on the 2nd of January 1978 for rehearsals, along with 21 other male actors. There were no female cast members, alcohol was cheap and there was soon an enormous amount of drinking going on, as a result of which actors Jason Miller and Joe Spinell got themselves into serious trouble with the police for starting a bar-room brawl.

According to Blatty, on the final day of the two week rehearsal period, Nicol returned to his hotel in the evening and attempted to make a telephone call to his father in Scotland, but was finding the operator in Budapest unhelpful. As this was happening, a waiter arrived bringing room service and Nicol lost his temper, called the waiter some names, kicked him and wrenched the phone out of the wall, which he threw out of the window. He then went down to retrieve the phone, slammed it on the reception desk and demanded to be reconnected. The hotel made a complaint with the result that the authorities in Budapest insisted that Nicol could not remain in the country. Blatty not only managed to keep the story out of the press, but suppressed it until after Nicol's death. Meanwhile, Nicol was quickly replaced by Stacy Keach.

The official reason for Nicol leaving the picture was that both Blatty and he had reached the conclusion that he was not right for the part, and it is true that Blatty had begun to have doubts about Nicol's suitability as he felt that he may not have possessed the requisite physique to make a convincing guerrilla fighter. He also felt that Nicol may have sensed his doubts and misbehaved deliberately. However, if the incident was a deliberate move to get out of the picture, it may equally have been the case that Nicol was beginning to have his own doubts. Blatty was a novice director who was also having problems with his other lead, Michael Moriarty,[58] so it could be that Nicol foresaw a disaster and that was why he chose once more to wrench a phone out of a wall. The fact that he did this on the very last day of rehearsals, a Friday, before shooting commenced on the Monday, also suggests that there may have been an element of calculation on Nicol's part.

The film eventually turned out well, although it lost money as no-one had any idea how to sell it. Stacy Keach is extremely effective as Kane, perhaps more so than Nicol would have been. Nicol was a very expressive actor but the plot made it necessary for Kane to be inexpressive for the majority of the film – not a quality usually associated with Nicol.

In February, Nicol flitted back and forth between Los Angeles and New York and accepted a role in an eight-hour American mini-series entitled *The Word*, based on Irving Wallace's doorstep bestseller of the same name. He later admitted that this was another part he had agreed to purely for monetary reasons. A pre-*Da Vinci Code* religious thriller, it told the story of an American PR man working for a powerful publishing company who takes on the job of verifying the authenticity of a newly discovered gospel which claims that Christ did not die on the cross after all. Nicol, with ginger goatee and Dutch accent, played Maertin de Vroome, the head of the Dutch Reformed Church, who wants to prevent publication. For some reason, he is introduced Blofeld-style, stroking a cat in a sinister fashion. It was a decent enough part in a so-so production; Nicol was an imposing and somewhat ambivalent presence as the religious authority figure, and gave an admirably subtle and restrained performance, something which could not be said of many in the cast (most notably Ron Moody, the extent of whose overacting is quite astonishing). Less than two years before his early death, David Janssen as the lead looked tired, not entirely sober, and much older than his 46 years, making his character's apparent irresistibility to the opposite sex rather implausible to say the least. Today, *The Word* has sunk into an obscurity it probably deserves and from which it seems unlikely to be rescued.

Chapter 17 – Letting the Buggers Suffer

It had been a while since Nicol had acted in something he felt passionately about and was not doing because he needed money. Earlier in the year, he had been approached by Stuart Burge, who had become Artistic Director of the Royal Court the previous year. The Court was facing bankruptcy and Burge was determined to rescue it. He decided to see if it would be possible to entice Nicol back to the theatre. Despite a meagre £65 a week salary, Nicol signed on to appear in two plays, each for a limited run. One of these was a revival of *Inadmissible Evidence*, the first time it had been staged in London since Nicol had appeared at Wyndham's. The other was a play entitled *Sam Sam* by Trevor Griffiths, in which he would be cast as two brothers living on opposite sides of the class barrier, although this was subsequently cancelled. The reasons for this remain unclear, but may well have been related to Nicol's tax status, which meant that he could only work in the UK for a limited period before being obliged to hand over most of his earnings to the Inland Revenue.

Burge did not want to direct *Inadmissible Evidence* as he understandably had no desire to be in the position of instructing Nicol how to play his most famous role, so the task went to John Osborne himself. Although Osborne had remained productive throughout the '70s, his run of successes had dried up some years previously and he welcomed the opportunity to direct a revival of his earlier hit, especially with Nicol on board.

Since his divorce from Jill, Nicol was without a permanent home, so he went to stay with Osborne, who was residing at Christmas Place, a nine-bedroom detached property located in the tiny hamlet of Marsh Green near the town of Edenbridge in the Sevenoaks district of Kent. However, the two had a falling out almost immediately, with the result that Nicol marched off into the night, vowing never to spend another night under Osborne's roof. Fortunately, they made it up the following day, agreeing that it had been the result of a little too much wine on both sides, and Nicol stayed on both during rehearsals and throughout the run. Osborne was quoted at the time as saying that Nicol was 'without doubt... the greatest actor since Marlon Brando' and added that he was in the process of writing a play especially for Nicol, which would be the first time he had ever written a part for a specific actor. This was not to be, but Nicol's respect for Osborne's talent was equally high.

Both actor and playwright had their portraits painted in watercolour by the renowned English artist, Patrick Procktor. Nicol is depicted in a white polo shirt, drink in hand, gazing into the distance with his mouth partially open. He felt that Procktor had made him look 'like something from *The Wizard of Oz*', but this did not prevent the Royal Court from using the image on their posters advertising *Inadmissible Evidence*. Much was also made of the fact that Nicol, in his own words, was by this time 'the exact age' that Maitland was – although Nicol was in reality nearly three years older. But he was certainly a lot closer than he had been the first time around, and was himself convinced that the additional life experience he had gained over the past decade helped him to give a better performance, even to the extent of wondering how he had got away with it the first time. Nicol also remarked in an interview that he had been unable to remember the lines after a ten year gap and so had been compelled to learn the part again from scratch, something he found more difficult to do than he had when he was younger. He added that he felt it may be his final stage performance. But despite these complaints, Nicol was often to be seen chatting casually to people in the pub next to the theatre five minutes before the performance was due to commence. In the same interview, he also said that he considered himself to be a craftsman and that the word 'genius' should not be applied to actors as their job is to transmit words written by someone else. He did, however, believe that the word could be applied to Osborne.

The role of Maitland's head clerk, Hudson, was played by Clive Swift, an actor well-known for a variety of roles on British television.

Swift kindly provided the following memories from his unpublished autobiography:

> Osborne invited the cast to his Edenbridge home before we started rehearsing… [At one point he suddenly] put on a record of Mozart's *Don Giovanni* 'Champagne' aria, announcing to everyone and to no-one that 'that's how Theatre should be!' Meanwhile, Williamson was in the garden playing Frisbee.
>
> After lunch, our host and his wife led us to a local show, where the bearded polemicist behaved quite squire-like towards the populace attending the produce-stalls and pony-jumping…
>
> J.O. was similarly distant in rehearsal, forbidding any queries about his play or characters, and saying that it was a 'classic text to be spoken, Oh! Like Chekov or Shakespeare.' His concentration was almost wholly upon Nicol, and he ordered me, on-stage throughout the first Act, to do nothing to distract from Mr Williamson. So I sat, listened and responded, though I felt that good old reliable Hudson would have been working, for sure as hell his boss wasn't! He was too busy spilling out his tortured soul. Perhaps it wasn't surprising then that, with three days to go before the first performance, Osborne asked why I was sitting there doing nothing. 'Because you told me to.' 'But can't you sign a few cheques or something?' I felt mild panic. Was he implying the integration of a whole Act's 'business'? Such choreography should have been incorporated much earlier. Improvisation now would be sure to distract from Nicol. 'You can do *something!*' hissed Osborne. 'Any cunt could do *something!*' 'Not this cunt,' I replied, stung by his epithet and sticking to my guns. In the end I remained sedentary, scanning a brief.

Previews began on the 6th of September, press night was on the 12th, and the production ran until the 4th of November. Swift also recalled that Osborne had gratefully left champagne in Nicol's dressing room every evening and that Nicol had 'behaved impeccably throughout the engagement'[59] despite being under pressure from a number of directions.

On one occasion (for unknown reasons) the Royal Court's press officer felt compelled to cancel all interview requests with Nicol, and gossip columnists from the *Daily Express* were calling the theatre repeatedly in the hope of discovering something about the state of his private life. On the 24th of October, Nicol had to attend a hearing at the High Court regarding non-payment of £24,000 he had promised Jill to pay off the mortgage on their home in Barnes. As Jill was concerned that any chance of obtaining the money would be lost once Nicol left the country, she requested that he be jailed for failing to pay, but the judge refused to do so and gave Nicol more time. Nicol said that he had used to average around £70,000 a year but that recently his average earnings had only been around £25,000.

But none of this could detract from the fact that the production was a great success, selling out its 60 performances almost entirely. However, there was some concern that it was overlong, and Swift remembered that 'Audiences who at 10.45 p.m. were spell-bound, by 11.15 were stupefied. Both Nicol and Stuart Burge begged for cuts, but Osborne refused: "Let the buggers suffer," he said.' However, reviews were mostly enthusiastic, and it was frequently said that Nicol was even better in the part than he had been the first time around. Michael Billington, writing for *The Guardian*, was particularly impressed and found Nicol's delivery to have become 'much more Beckettian.'

An audio recording of a performance from the 10th of October 1978 (running around two and a half hours) has Nicol rattling through much of the dialogue at a tremendous pace, but without sacrificing any of its impact. He is astonishingly close to being word-perfect considering the number of words involved. During the courtroom scene he delivers many of the more humorous asides in a lower register as if giving vent to an inner voice. Indeed, he generates quite a few laughs from the audience and it is clear that his portrayal is far from unsympathetic. Despite the fact that Maitland is often viewed as an appalling character, he nevertheless has a number of appealing traits, such as an absence of self-deception and a contempt for platitudes, not to mention the sheer fluency of his invective. Of course, such characteristics were also true of John Osborne himself.

Osborne was reportedly hoping for a West End transfer, but this was out of the question for Nicol as he would have had to pay a crippling amount of tax if he worked in the UK for too long. The *Evening Standard* published an article claiming that there had been a rift between Nicol and Osborne as a result of this, but Nicol threatened legal action and they were obliged to print a retraction. However, he later admitted that there had been a falling out and said that after the play closed Osborne sent him a bill for £800 worth of champagne. The possibility of reviving *Inadmissible Evidence* on Broadway was also discussed, but American Equity insisted that it could only proceed on an exchange basis whereby an American company could present a play in the West End. Although an exchange involving a play called *First Monday in October* was arranged, the plan fell through when its star, Henry Fonda, cancelled at the last minute.

When *Inadmissible Evidence* closed, Nicol went to Paris, taking along a copy of Graham Greene's latest novel, *The Human Factor*, given to him by John Osborne. Nicol became thoroughly absorbed in the story of Maurice Castle, who works at a hush-hush job in an obscure division of the Foreign Office dealing with African affairs. Castle, previously posted in South Africa, compromised himself by taking a black lover; during the time in which the story is set he has been back in Britain for several years, is married to his former lover, and longs only for security and the chance to quietly finish the few years of service remaining before he can retire.[60] However, his world falls apart when a friend and colleague is suspected of being the source of a leak. *The Human Factor* is a suspenseful, funny and moving book which also has things to say both about the state of the world and the human condition.

After Paris, Nicol went to Lindos with Luke for a holiday where, to his surprise, he received a telegram saying that he had been offered the part of Maurice Castle in a film version to be directed by Otto Preminger, the famously irascible veteran director of Hollywood classics such as *Laura*, *The Man with the Golden Arm* and *Anatomy of a*

Murder. The offer was dependent only on meeting Preminger. Nicol flew to London to meet him and the deal was done.

Preminger had quickly snapped up the film rights for the book for an undisclosed six-figure sum before it had even been published. Fortunately for him, Greene had a rare talent for consistency and the novel was both a critical and commercial success. Given that a number of Greene's novels had already been successfully adapted for the screen, Preminger may have thought he had a ready-made hit on his hands – especially as, given the rather mundane locations in which most of the story takes place, a high budget was not required, and this would help to compensate for the amount paid for the film rights. He hired Tom Stoppard – the Czech-born British playwright best known for *Rosencrantz and Guildernstern Are Dead* – to write the screenplay, and had initially approached both Richard Burton and Michael Caine for the central role but, when neither actor accepted, had turned to Nicol. Although Nicol was not a 'bankable' film star like Burton and Caine, Preminger must have thought he had enough selling points to risk casting an actor primarily for his suitability and prowess. For his part, Nicol was excited about the prospect of working with Preminger and thrilled to be offered the lead in an adaptation of a book he loved, especially as it would give him a rare opportunity to play an almost entirely sympathetic character. He told Michael Owen of the *Evening Standard* that most of the characters he had portrayed had been unlikeable, with the result that 'You find people look on you as being unlikeable yourself,' before going on to complain that 'Mike Caine and Peter O'Toole get to play all the nice guys. Wherever I go I'm regarded with frozen stares of horror…'

The rest of the cast was filled out with an impressive array of British character actors, including Richard Attenborough, John Gielgud, Derek Jacobi, Robert Morley and Ann Todd. The part of Castle's wife proved more difficult to cast and, unable to find a suitable black actress who was also a 'name', Preminger looked outside the acting world and cast Iman, the Somali model.

Shooting began on the 30th of May 1979. Much of the film was shot in Berkhamsted, a town northeast of London, where Castle's home is located in the novel. Preminger hired a house in the town to serve as Castle's. The scenes of Castle at work were shot at a Victorian house in London, and the final scene (featuring a rather unconvincing Moscow backdrop) at Shepperton studios. As the political situation would have made shooting in South Africa problematic, the African sequences were shot in Kenya in late July to early August.

Predictably, Nicol clashed with the director early on. Nicol told the story himself in a later interview:

> It was a scene with Richard Attenborough. It wasn't scheduled for that day and it was a long scene... I had to learn it in an afternoon – well, I'm not *that* speedy! So I was sitting outside with Richard Attenborough and we're going through it... then we went in and I knew the scene just didn't have the power that it should have and it wasn't right... so I said, 'Right, that's it – pull the plug. Would you get my car?' to the First Assistant. He looked at Otto. I said, 'Would you *get* my *car*?' Otto comes over and says, 'Vot are you doing?' I said, 'I'm leaving the set, I'm going home. We've been here for twelve hours doing a scene that wasn't scheduled until eleven days from now. I'm tired, I can't remember it and it's not good and I'm not doing it!' He went red. 'I shall sue you!' I said, 'Go ahead, I've got no fucking money!' I walk down the path to the car and hear behind me, 'Nicol! Nicol! *Please!!*' I said, 'Tomorrow! If there is a tomorrow – I'm going to talk to my agent and I might not *be* back tomorrow!' So of I went, and that was that.[61]

From that point on there were no more fireworks between the two and Preminger later conceded that Nicol had not been at fault. However, the director soon found an easier target for his wrath:

> Richard Attenborough walked into a scene that we were doing in Chelsea... we had to stand by a fireplace and the room was full of extra people – twenty or thirty of them... Otto couldn't pronounce 'Attenborough.' He called him 'Attaboro.' Attenborough was talking to

me – not very loudly… and Otto turned around and said, 'Attaboro! Be quiet!' Then he talks to me again and Otto says, 'Attaboro! Be *quiet!*' Attenborough says, 'I'm sorry, dear.' Then two minutes later he continued quietly and Otto says, 'ATTABORO! I TOLT YOU! ATTABORO, BE QUIET! ATTABORO, SHUT *UP!!*' They're all looking like, 'Is he going to say anything?' Then Otto comes over a minute later – he would change like this – and he looked at Attenborough and said [benignly], 'Is zat your own coat?' 'Er, well… no, dear, it's one they've given me.' We go out on the stairs again, the door's closed and I couldn't resist it – it was just too funny – and I said (perfect Otto), 'Is zat your own coat?' Attenborough turned round to me and said, 'You *bastard!*' and I was covered in this spittle! I wiped it all off and said to him, 'That's what *you* should have said to *him!*' It had rattled him completely. Everyone was terrified of Otto. He used to say to me every morning, 'Zey call me Otto ze Monster,' then he would smile and say, 'It's not true.' Of course, it *was* true!⁶²

Nevertheless, Nicol began indulging in affectionate impersonations of the director to the delight of visiting journalists. However, there continued to be friction between Nicol and some other members of the cast and crew. Emma Hamelynck remembered that, 'He often had problems when he was making films. He always started hating someone and got into arguments and didn't like it any more. I remember Otto Preminger said it would be good if I could come over to Africa because he was much more mild and nice when I was around!'

The atmosphere on set must have been frosty at times – Nicol was no admirer of Gielgud and vice versa, and it was perhaps fortunate that they had only one scene together. While preparing to play Hamlet, Nicol had said he had no intention of delivering an 'Aldwych bad-breath-of-the-thirties performance', a clear reference to Gielgud's famous Hamlet of that era. Gielgud, on the other hand, had once dropped a clanger when John Osborne was a dinner guest at his house by referring to Nicol as a '*most* unattractive' actor who had been in a 'terribly dull' play. He had been referring to *Inadmissible Evidence* before realising that his guest had written it. Also in the cast was Gielgud's fellow stick-in-the-mud Robert Morley, who once wrote a list of things that he felt defined hell, including among these 'Hamlet acted by Nicol Williamson'.

One would have thought that the distinguished combination of talents involved in *The Human Factor* would have made for a fine film, but a number of issues prevented this from being the case. It had been well over a decade since Preminger's last unqualified success and his age had clearly taken a toll on his creative energy, even to the point of diminishing his mental faculties, as Nicol subsequently recalled:

> His mind was not quite on the ball. He knew what he was doing in the filming, but... we'd been staying in the Knightbridge Tampax,[63] then we went to this hotel in the country which had one floor. He'd been on the 17th floor in Knightsbridge. One night, he said to me at the dinner table, 'Vot are you drinking?' I said, 'Port.' He said, 'Vaiter! I too vill have!' One of the assistants leaned over to me and said, 'He's not supposed to drink! His memory's going and his memory goes even more...' I said, 'Well, *you* tell him!' Anyway, he has a couple of ports, then he goes out and there is huge consternation in the lobby – shrieks and gasps – so we all troop out there. There's this girl behind the desk and Otto is wrenching his script from her and saying, 'You stupit girl! Give me my script!' The hotel manager comes bounding round the corner and says, 'What's going on?' The girl's in tears by now and she says, 'He's got the hotel register and he won't let it go!' He had no idea what his script looked like, then he turned round and said, 'Nicol! Nicol! Zey hev lost my room! Vere ist ze elevator?' He thought he was still in the Knightsbridge Tampax![64]

Most of the cast were excellent, notably Attenborough and Morley, but Iman's lack of experience was all too obvious throughout. Stoppard's screenplay was perhaps too faithful to the book – a spy story with little action in the anti-glamour mould of Le Carré and a million miles away from the world of James Bond. The complex narrative had worked perfectly as a novel in which the intricacies of the plot and the motivations of the characters had been clear, but for the most part the film merely translated this into a succession of actors talking a great deal in drab-looking rooms. This may not have been fatal in itself if efforts had been made to stage such interior scenes in an inventive manner (as Preminger had done brilliantly in earlier films such as *Advise and Consent*), but here the director almost seemed determined to shoot the whole thing in as unimaginative a way as possible, perhaps as a result of the pressure he was under to shoot as quickly and inexpensively as he could.

The reason for this was that, during production, a large part of the financing had collapsed. By the time the African sequences were to commence shooting, cheques were beginning to bounce and many of the crew refused to work until money was forthcoming. Nicol, who had gone on ahead to Nairobi five days before everyone else in order to get a tan appropriate to the flashback scenes, was determined to work on regardless and worry about the money later. However, he was not being entirely selfless in this as he felt that he could not afford to let the project collapse after his involvements in both *Force 10 from Navarone* and *The Ninth Configuration* had come to abrupt endings. Preminger owned a number of valuable paintings by artists such as Matisse and Picasso and began selling these in order to continue, eventually putting a great deal of his own money into the picture in order to finish it. Meanwhile, Nicol had apparently burned his lips in Nairobi, so the delay caused by the financial problems allowed him time to heal before shooting resumed. The crew left Nairobi on the 9th of August and returned to London, where shooting was finally completed on the 24th of August.

Nicol's performance in the film is excellent. Known for his intense performances and criticised by some on occasion for supposedly going 'over the top', he proved conclusively in *The Human Factor* that he could do 'understated' as well as anyone and, by means of a simple look, gesture or vocal inflexion, frequently managed to communicate a great deal about the inner anguish of Castle which was not present in the dialogue.

However, the end result was that *The Human Factor* was a dullish film with some good performances in it. As far as Nicol was concerned, it was another disappointment, and he told *Sight & Sound* that, although he felt he had done some of the best work of his film career on *The Human Factor*, the end result was 'flaccid.' Reviews were by no means universally negative, but they were certainly mixed, and the film did not do well commercially, taking a mere $376,050 at the box office. Somewhat ironically in the light of previous events, the film's poster (designed by Preminger's regular collaborator, Saul Bass) featured a telephone receiver dangling from a frayed cord. It was to be Preminger's final film and it took Nicol a long time to receive his full fee.

Earlier in the year, Nicol had been at a party held by Philip Kingsley, a well-known hair and scalp specialist, and his wife, Joan, in their condominium in the Apthorp, a grand apartment building on Manhattan's Upper West Side. While there he met Marcelle d'Argy-Smith, who later became editor of *Cosmopolitan* magazine but was at the time editor of the *Antiques Yearbook* and living in London. The two became friends and subsequently embarked on a casual affair. Marcelle d'Argy-Smith:

> I knew the name, but he was just this very attractive, tall man across the room. Eventually we caught each other's eye and started talking. We talked for most of the evening, then he said, 'Would you like to have dinner?' It was very simple and unaffected. He was lovely. We had dinner every night for a week. I remember him being such an easy conversationalist – he was like a very well brought up boy! He didn't make any moves, he'd just say at the end, 'I'll call you tomorrow.'
>
> I loved walking down the street with him in New York – he'd kind of stride and I loved that. I found him easy, charming, deep – but I did notice that evenings involved a huge amount of drinking! I've never really been a drinker.
>
> Meanwhile, I was seeing somebody in London, but I just thought, 'You don't meet men like this every day!' I wanted to know more. He was warm and nice to be with – one of those trips to the moon that you

do, but you don't attempt to harness such a beast, I don't think. He was a fantastical creature and he couldn't control himself, so nobody else could control him, I'm sure. He was careless. I couldn't imagine him doing anything ordinary – he wasn't destined to be ordinary and I don't think he knew the first thing about it! He had more style than anybody but, as for structure, not even a matchstick! He didn't have any sense of self-protection or survival.

When I came to New York again shortly afterwards I was shocked when he said, 'I need somewhere to live.' I thought, 'You're one of the world's greatest actors – what do you mean you've got nowhere to live!' He was like somebody on a high-wire with no thought for his own safety. He didn't have any idea of consequence. Anyway, I said, 'I'm sure the Kinglseys would be thrilled to have you – they've got this huge apartment and they're very generous, they always have people staying there.' So he moved in with them for a few weeks.

Sometimes we'd go to jazz bars such as Jimmy Ryan's, which made me swell with pride because he would sit down at the piano and could easily fit in with these half a dozen seriously fabulous musicians and just become one of them. Sometimes he'd pick up a clarinet and play that as well.

I never saw him what you would call 'drunk.' He didn't do that, he didn't trip and fall over, he just went on being broader and funnier and more expansive and madder. After he moved out of the Apthorp, one night we had been drinking and Nicol said he'd left some clothes there. I still had a key to the apartment, and we sneaked in at 2.30 in the morning to get his clothes back. There was a piano in the hall, which of course Nicol could not resist playing. My heart was thumping – I thought they're going to wake up and they think I'm in London! If they find me in their apartment with Nicol I'll get killed. They didn't, but they later told me how they had heard the piano one night when there was no-one else there!

It wasn't really a love affair, but maybe it was better because there was no drama. He would hint or insinuate [about his personal problems] or after a few drinks he would say a bit and I thought, 'He's really going through it.' He seemed to be terribly lonely. He had a vulnerability about him too – if it was all just being that gloriously attractive, tall man, it wouldn't have been so interesting, but you wanted to put your arm round him and say, 'It's going to be alright, Nicol.'

I remember I was living in Westbourne Grove and he turned up at my flat one evening and said, 'Do you want some dinner?' and he was drinking too much and he was a bit difficult then. It could have been the last time I saw him and I think he was off to make some film. He was suffering and the charm was less…

Due to her work commitments, D'Argy-Smith was not always available to see Nicol. After around a year and a half they drifted apart and what seems to have been for both parties a casual, long-distance relationship with no strings attached came to an end.

Chapter 18 - 'A dream to some, a nightmare to others...'

Nicol's next film looked set to be a Merchant-Ivory production of the Jean Rhys novel *Quartet*, in which he would play H.J. Heidler alongside his former Ophelia, Francesca Annis, but the project was announced too early before either actor had committed. Both withdrew and the film was eventually made with Alan Bates and Maggie Smith. However, a better opportunity was just around the corner.

John Boorman, the London-born director of the tough American classics *Point Blank* and *Deliverance*, had been obsessed since childhood with the King Arthur legend and of one aspect in particular – the figure of Merlin, the magician. Seeing the story as an allegory of mankind's loss of spirituality in the blind pursuit of progress, Boorman felt it had a timeless relevance and made it his ambition to put it on film. Basing his version mainly on Thomas Malory's *Le Morte d'Arthur*, he spent countless hours working on a screenplay with his regular collaborator, Rospo Pallenberg, in order to somehow condense the entire story into a movie of reasonable length. When they were finished, Boorman pitched the script to a number of studios without success. Then *Star Wars* was released and the climate changed – the plot of George Lucas' surprise hit had, after all, been largely lifted from myths such as the King Arthur legend and given a science fiction makeover. Boorman suddenly had offers from four different studios on the table. He accepted an offer from Orion Pictures as they were also willing to give him full creative control. The budget was initially set at $8 million, which Boorman knew was less than he really needed, but he managed to have it increased to $10 million.

Boorman had wanted Nicol to play Gandalf when he had been trying to make a film of *The Lord of the Rings* some years earlier. He considered Gandalf to be but a minor variation on Merlin, so it was natural for him to think of Nicol as Merlin. However, his casting of

Nicol met with fierce opposition from Orion, whose executives had been involved in a number earlier pictures he had featured in, none of which had made a profit. They begged him to cast anyone apart from Nicol, but Boorman was unable to imagine any other actor in the role and stuck to his guns. He wanted to dissociate his Merlin from the magician's former incarnations, which had generally been as an avuncular, absent-minded old man with a long grey beard, and he was convinced that only Nicol could embody the comic, melancholy magician that he envisioned, which he described in further detail for *American Film*:

> Merlin fascinates me because he's a mixture of real, awesome power and foolishness. He gets things wrong. He's both less human and more human than ordinary people. He has enormous power and knowledge, and yet there are simple things he doesn't grasp or understand.

According to Boorman, Nicol nearly pulled out when he heard that Helen Mirren was to play Morgana, the sorceress Merlin mentored as a child who turns against him. Mirren had the same reaction on learning that Nicol had been cast. It has sometimes been said that the director deliberately cast two actors who detested each other to maximise the on-screen friction, but it seems to be more the case that Boorman was being pragmatic and cast them because he felt they were right for their roles, while hoping that the problems between them would add to, rather than detract from, the film itself. Nicol remembered it this way:

> Boorman asked me at the very beginning, 'Do you want to play with this woman?' and my answer was, 'I don't really have a great deal of respect for her as an actress and I don't like her as a person but you can't ask me that question. You're the director of this film and you must choose your cast.' And that was the only conversation. [65]

Mirren later said that the problems between them disappeared during the making of *Excalibur* and they ended the film as good friends. The fact that Emma Hamelynck accompanied Nicol for part of the shooting may have helped to avoid any major friction.

Although Nicol had known that he was to have his head shaved for the part, when it came down to it he refused, as he had become concerned that his hair might not grow back. Various solutions were attempted before Terry English, the armourer, made a silver skull-cap for Nicol which not only solved the problem but also helped him in some mysterious way to find the character. Nicol had been struggling at first and, when Boorman decided to replace the cameraman after the first week of shooting, Nicol gained a week's respite before the replacement could take over. He went away and asked himself, 'Who *is* this character?' and then had an epiphany: 'I know who he is – he's my old English master! He is the teacher and young Arthur is the pupil.'[66] Nicol based his characterisation largely on Tom Reader, his literature teacher from Birmingham Central Grammar School. In an interview with Michael Owen of the *Standard*, he described Reader as a 'magical, mythical man… the first one who thought I might make some sort of actor,' and went on to say that, for the part of Merlin, he had used 'his personality, his speech pattern, even some of his favourite lines.'

Filming took place over the course of sixteen weeks during the summer of 1980 at the National Film Studios of Ireland near Boorman's home in County Wicklow. Exteriors were shot at nearby locations. During the shooting of one battle scene, a large branch came crashing down on Nicol's head and apparently knocked him out, but when Boorman suggested dressing someone else as Merlin to get the shot needed to complete the sequence, Nicol 'suddenly made a miraculous recovery.' However, Nicol also had some fun during the shoot mocking the Dublin accent of Gabriel Byrne who, in his first major film role, was playing Uther Pendragon, the king who rapes Igrayne, making her pregnant in the process. Nicol claimed that Byrne's delivery of the line 'Just give me one night with Igrayne!' sounded like 'Just give me one night with your gran!' He also found much to laugh at in the attempts at horse-riding by the other actors, including former colleagues Patrick Stewart and Clive Swift, but when it was suggested that he exit one scene on horseback himself, he demurred.

The film was originally to be entitled *Merlin Lives*, but there were copyright problems with the name 'Merlin', so the working title became *Knights* before finally being changed to *Excalibur* for release. When released, the film was very successful both critically and commercially. Although it was not a hit on the scale of *Jaws* or *Star Wars*, it grossed over $35 million. At last, Nicol had scored a substantial success. His performance was extremely well-received, despite being his most eccentric to date. However, as Nicol was the only actor in the film not to play his part entirely straight, there have been naysayers who do not appreciate his performance, but it would be a mistake to assume that Boorman simply indulged him. The director himself later said that, 'Nicol's performance is wonderfully quixotic and quirky and sharp and full of wit and humour and guile… [It] is exactly what I was trying to achieve…'[67]

Nicol was equally complimentary about Boorman, but it was to be their only collaboration. He was nominated for a Saturn Award, presented by the Academy of Science Fiction, Fantasy and Horror Films, but lost out to Burgess Meredith, who won for his performance as Ammon in *Clash of the Titans*. However, *Excalibur* had in many ways put Nicol back on the map as a contender and the number of film roles he was offered increased considerably as a result.

Towards the end of the year, Nicol accepted one of these, largely for the money, although he also liked the part as it was closer to a hero than a heavy. *Venom* was based on a novel by Alan Scholefield and was an early example of what has come to be known as a 'high-concept' thriller. The plot involves a gang of kidnappers holding a young boy hostage in a house in which a deadly black mamba is loose. Nicol was cast as Commander William Bulloch, the policeman in charge of negotiating with the kidnappers. He opted for a Scottish accent and added a lot of authority and a little dry humour to the role as a man both feared and respected by his men. *Venom* also reunited Nicol with Sarah Miles, who was playing a toxicologist. The impressive (if slightly past their prime) cast also included Oliver Reed, Klaus Kinski, Susan George and, in his last film appearance, Sterling Hayden – the American star of film noir classics *The Asphalt Jungle* and *The Killing*.[68] The director of *Venom* was Nicol's former Dundee Rep colleague, Piers Haggard, who had since moved into film and television, enjoying success with *Pennies from Heaven* and the cult classic *Blood on Satan's Claw*. *Venom* proved to be a memorable experience for Haggard, although for all the wrong reasons, as he later recalled:

> I took *Venom* over from Tobe Hooper, who'd had a nervous breakdown, and when I started to do the film I realised why! Because I had Klaus Kinski and Oliver Reed and Nicol, Sarah Miles, Sterling Hayden stoned out of his mind... They'd stopped production and they wanted me to take it over at short notice, which I did – terrible mistake! I was unable to make it my own. I just ended up *doing* it, really. As I got involved in it, I learned that there'd been ructions.
>
> I met Klaus Kinski and changed his costume and met Oliver, who played a weird game with me, trying to scare me – he was an amusing bully, if you like. I had a hellish time on that film – Klaus Kinski was a bastard, really, a sort of insane egomaniac, and Oliver Reed was pretty fucking awkward when he wanted to be. However, at least he had a sense of humour! He spent most of his time trying to annoy Klaus Kinski...
>
> Nicol behaved like an angel. I was amazed because, by that time, he had quite the reputation as being hard to handle, and both Nicol and Sarah Miles when they came on said, 'Listen. Piers, I know you've been having trouble, and I promise you I'm going to be as good as gold. Don't worry about me.' When push came to shove, Klaus Kinski was so horrible to Sarah, that actually she got a bit stroppy, but Nicol was completely impervious to everything... actually, he didn't have to work with them because he was the copper and they're inside the house, so it was just Nicol and me and the camera really, and he behaved absolutely impeccably – he knew his words, he was there on time, he didn't complain even though we shot through the nights at Elstree and it was

fucking cold. He was an absolute angel and he was no trouble at all. The part doesn't remotely test or use his particular qualities, it was just a job of work for him – it was just a job of work for me, really, but I was trying to make it in movies, so I took it. I thought it might be worth taking it on as a big film, which it was not – it was a big mistake.

Much of Nicol's stuff was done in two weeks on the lot in night shooting. He played it as this sort of rough-tongued, humorous, grumpy Scottish character. He brought something very specific to it, he created a specific character. He'd have got two fees because they'd have had to rehire him because the thing was put back. He was really, really nice on it, and I was very grateful to him. So I'm one of the people who say, 'Well, he may have been a difficult bastard, but he was an ultra, super-professional' – probably, partly for old times' sake out of sympathy, because I was having a hard time with the other people, because he'd have found out by the time he came on the film that Klaus Kinski was a cunt, really, you know… [laughs] which he certainly was!

Nicol was one of the absolutely outstanding figures of his time; maybe a narrow range in that, unless he was playing in character, he never to me seemed really comfortable, but if he had something really difficult and particular to play, he was wonderful, but when he was straight, he was less convincing… there are actors who know that they are good-looking and the camera likes them and they just feel good in front of the camera. He wasn't one of those. He was possibly a more fantastic stage actor than a screen actor, really – his best work is in some of the difficult classics, I think.

Luke Williamson remembered a story his father told him about *Venom*:

Dad pretty much kept himself to himself during that film, but he said one day they were having lunch and Oliver Reed told him, 'I'm much stronger than you.' Dad said he just looked at him and said, 'Yeah, but I'm fucking certifiable,' and Oliver Reed never spoke to him again after that.

Tobe Hooper had shot for around nine days before leaving the film, but it appears that Nicol was not in any of his footage, none of which was used in the final cut. Haggard had been unable to take over immediately due to other commitments, so the production had been put on hold for two weeks. Although he did not like the set and certain aspects of the script, Haggard was given little opportunity to make changes but, despite a rather silly premise, it remains an extremely pacy and entertaining thriller with a number of effective moments. However, a big release in America failed to push it into profit and what had been a $6 million production took a disappointing $5.2 million at the box office.

At the beginning of 1981, Nicol returned to New York to star in another revival of *Inadmissible Evidence* at the Roundabout Theatre on West 23rd Street.[69] He seemed happier about the idea of reviving the play in this off-Broadway venue than he had been about John Osborne's attempts to persuade him to bring it back to Broadway, perhaps because he was confident it could be a small-scale success and had no wish to risk a large-scale failure. The director was Anthony Page, which marked their first collaboration since 1967. Elaine Bromka, who played the part of Shirley, remembered them working well together and described her own experience of working with Nicol:

> Anthony understood Nicol very well; there was no friction. Nicol and Tony were both there choosing people and it was just done quietly. Tony was at the helm, but he allowed Nicol to revisit that character on his own terms.
>
> The most memorable thing about him was his brilliance. His mind worked fast and he cared so much about the work and he was actually – wild man though he was – incredibly humble in the work. He never upstaged someone else or cared about how much he was being seen at every moment and, in a play where he has essentially everything to say, you don't need to push for that, but there are other actors who, even if they've had every single word of the play, still don't feel that they get enough attention!
>
> He needed to feel that his cast believed in him and he wanted comrades. He was not someone who was acting at other people's expense. He could exhibit a wild temper, but not in the work. Sometimes, he would just turn upstage for a long time while I did my

stuff. He was saying, 'Take it.' That's unusual with a star. When you looked into his eyes on stage, they were very open and possible and he was a dangerous performer, which was thrilling.

Making her New York debut as Maitland's silent daughter was an unknown 19-year-old actress, Andrea Weber. In a curious case of history repeating itself, Nicol fell in love, just as he had done with Jill Townsend when she played the same part in 1965. Weber, from Bloomington, Indiana, was a gymnast, so she was extremely fit physically as well as being a highly attractive green-eyed blonde. Spurred on by her mother, she had apparently been acting since the age of 10 and had studied ballet at the Jordan College of Music in Indianapolis before appearing in a handful of plays in Mexico City when her family moved there in 1976. She competed with the Mexican National Hurdling Team before returning to Indianapolis to complete her education. Her mother, Jeannie, was 'well-known in Indianapolis musical and theatrical circles' according to *The Indianapolis Star*, which also stated that Andrea had given a 'remarkable performance' as Cleopatra in George Bernard Shaw's *Caesar and Cleopatra* at the city's Christian Theological Seminary Repertory Theatre in 1980. Nicol was 44 at the time and, despite his concern about the age gap, he took her out to a jazz club followed by hamburgers at P.J. Clarke's and confessed his feelings for her. He later wrote about the evening in a poem entitled *Hindsight*, from which the following is an extract:

> ... we began under the lamp on 52nd Street
> After the shock of an abandoned meal
> She stopped me, *made* me kiss, *made* our lips meet
> And the unthinkable at once was real
>
> Disarming in its weaponless surprise
> The grip that took my wrist
> And turned me round
> The first time I had stared into her eyes
> The first time New York traffic had no sound.

Inadmissible Evidence was once more received enthusiastically by the critics, with T.E. Kalem of *Time* magazine describing Nicol's performance as 'incandescent,' and going on to say that he 'intuits every mock-marked desolating crevasse in Maitland's character.' Meanwhile, in the *New York Times*, Frank Rich wrote of 'pain that is raised by brilliant acting to the level of art.' The box office receipts were also healthy, but there had been some trouble behind the scenes. Nicol had an argument with one of the producers who had been delaying the start of the play in order to sell subscription tickets outside. One night, when the delay reached twenty minutes, Nicol went to the front of the stage, explained the situation and told the audience he was also feeling impatient to begin. He subsequently told the producer that if the curtain were ever delayed by more than five minutes again, he would refuse to perform.

In an interview for the *New York Times*, Nicol spoke of how the additional years and the disappointments he himself had suffered had helped him to understand Maitland better, and made his portrayal more human and sympathetic as a result. He downplayed his reputation for being difficult, claiming that he had had 'only three explosions in 15 years, so one every five years isn't bad.' He also complained that he had never made any money in the theatre, apart from the first time he had done *Inadmissible Evidence*, by which he must have meant the Wyndham's production and possibly the American run. The production ran for 49 performances and was to be the last time Nicol played Maitland.

During the run, Nicol filmed a short tribute to his old friend John Thaw, which was used in an episode of *This Is Your Life* celebrating the life and career of his fellow actor. He also appeared as an interviewee on the BBC programme *Barry Norman on Broadway*.

After the play closed, Nicol had a holiday in Greece then returned to England for a while. He accepted a role opposite Jill Clayburgh in the Paramount film *I'm Dancing as Fast as I Can* and returned to New York on the *QE2* at the end of July, where the film was to be shot.

Also on board for the six-day voyage was Nicol's former colleague, David Warner, who explained:

> I happened to be travelling with my pregnant wife from the United States to England and on that ship was Nicol as the special guest. On a ship like that they always have a celebrity or two on board who would get a free first class passage in return for showing a film or giving a lecture or whatever. That was the last time I saw Nicol.

I'm Dancing as Fast as I Can was based on the memoir of the same name by Emmy-winning TV documentarian Barbara Gordon, and dealt with Gordon's recovery from Valium addiction. Nicol played her boyfriend, defence lawyer Derek Bauer (a fictionalised character), who shares her Manhattan apartment. Bauer turns out to be a less than ideal person to help her through an excruciating withdrawal period. Attempting to deal with the situation without the help of a doctor, he finds himself completely out of his depth and his alcoholism and suppressed violence come to the surface. It was a fine performance and the climactic scenes in which the two are holed up in the apartment driving each other increasingly further from sanity are the best in the picture. However, one suspects that the real *raison d'etre* for the film was to finally win Clayburgh the Oscar she had twice been nominated for but not yet won. Indeed, the script seems designed to allow her to run the entire gamut of emotions and she certainly grasps the opportunity. Unfortunately, no further Oscar nominations were forthcoming; the film was not well reviewed, with critics saying that it failed to make the motivations of its heroine clear or explain why she became addicted in the first place. Audiences seemed to agree and it flopped spectacularly at the box office, taking back less than $300,000 of its $6 million budget. It probably did not help that it resembled a TV movie rather than a cinema film, while audiences seemed to have little sympathy for the drug problems of someone with a high-flying media career. In an interview for *Horizon* magazine, Nicol said that he had enjoyed working with director Jack Hofsiss but the film had been 'wrecked with injudicious cutting and self-indulgent acting.' It's certainly true that his character's transformation from slightly odd nice guy who worries about what waiters think to abusive alcoholic feels too sudden in the finished film, and his abrupt disappearance after Clayburgh's character is finally placed in a hospital also suggests that his part may have fallen victim to the editing.

After shooting had been completed, Nicol returned to the UK briefly before once more travelling back to Manhattan on the *QE2*, this time in the company of his then agent, Milton Goldman, a well-known and influential figure. In New York, Nicol did a week's worth of interviews with journalist James Delson (for a feature to be published in *Penthouse* the following year) in which he explained how he liked the idea of 'putting everything on the line for each performance' and that the energy such an approach required was the reason why he had sometimes been absent from the stage for long periods and would only commit to limited runs of a month or so. He went on to name Spencer Tracy, Marlon Brando and Montgomery Clift as the three film actors he most admired, saying of the latter that he had 'never known a screen presence more compelling than those eyes in that face.' Typically, he downplayed both his drinking and his reputation for trouble; more unusually, he talked at length about politics, attacking members of both the right-wing (Reagan and Thatcher) and the left (Tony Benn, Corin and Vanessa Redgrave), but expressing support for the American peace activist William Sloane Coffin and world nuclear disarmament while describing himself as a 'slightly left-of-centre, an old-fashioned Socialist.'

Chapter 19 – The Curse of Mac B

As a result of his roles in *Excalibur*, *Venom* and *I'm Dancing as Fast as I Can*, Nicol was financially secure in a way he had never been before. Not being interested in the accumulation of wealth for its own sake, instead of concentrating on his burgeoning film career, he used his new-found security to return to the theatre and do work he was passionate about. The success of the off-Broadway revival of *Inadmissible Evidence* led to talk of another collaboration with Anthony Page. Nicol was keen to try a new production of *Macbeth* on Broadway with Page as director. Presumably at Page's suggestion, Lady Macbeth would be played by Glenda Jackson. The venue was to be the Circle in the Square, where Nicol had appeared in *Uncle Vanya* eight years earlier. The theatre's Artistic Director and co-founder was Theodore Mann, whose career stretched back to the 1950s when he had enjoyed a notable success with a number of Eugene O'Neill revivals. However, a letter written by Page to Mann in October 1981 reveals that Mann had become spooked by something he had heard about Page and had approached another director behind his back. Negotiations broke down and Page was out of the picture, as was Jackson. The result was that Nicol found himself not only starring in *Macbeth* but directing it as well. The fact that he had done the play before with Trevor Nunn and had also successfully directed *Uncle Vanya* himself for the RSC may have given him the confidence to agree. Nicol's contract stated that he would receive a salary of $6,313.50, first choice of dressing room and a 50% royalty plus four house seats in the first ten rows per night for his guests. He was entitled to star billing in the advertising but elected to have his name listed with the rest of the cast alphabetically, meaning it appeared at the bottom of the list.

Nicol cast the play himself, choosing Sigourney Weaver for the role of Lady Macbeth because he had been impressed by her performance in the hit film *Alien*. Weaver had not appeared on

Broadway before, but her leading role in *Alien* two years earlier had given her a reputation as a strong actress who could more than hold her own among the men. Two other actors in the cast who would later become well-known in Hollywood films were J.T. Walsh, who auditioned for Nicol as Macduff and cancelled a prior commitment in order to accept the part, and Christian Slater (just 11 years old at the time), who was cast as Macduff's son. Elaine Bromka, who had appeared alongside Nicol in the revival of *Inadmissible Evidence*, was cast as the First Witch.

Nicol moved into an apartment at 353 West 56th Street and rehearsals began on the 8th of December, one month before the play was to open. Elaine Bromka:

> When he went into *Macbeth* he called me and said, 'I want you to do this – what do you want to play?' He wanted friends that he trusted.
>
> He said to us [the witches], 'Why don't you go off and work on your own scenes? Seeya later.' And we did, we directed ourselves. Then it came to the run-throughs and he said he liked what we did. So there was little first-hand opportunity to form an opinion of him as a director, but he put a lot of trust in us.
>
> His interpretation of the role was absolutely wonderful but it was just too much for someone to play that title role *and* direct it. That's why he delegated our scenes. He felt the critics would be gunning for him, saying, 'Who do you think you are, doing this and directing it?' so there was always the feeling from day one of circling the wagons.

Nicol's conception of *Macbeth* was based largely on the production he had done with Trevor Nunn at the Aldwych and again the text was cut so that the play ran for around two hours with no intermission. Nicol later said, 'It was like a racing express train – I got it to one hour forty, one hour thirty-eight!'[70] Ray Dooley, who played Malcolm in the Broadway production, provided further detail:

> The Circle in the Square space is a large ¾ thrust stage, and the play was done with very little scenery—just some furniture for the indoor scenes. The principal scenic idea was that, as Macbeth becomes more and more

isolated, the furniture was piled higher and higher (it looked quite precarious to some) and he was perched upon it, alone.

The set consisted of a flagstone floor, a stairway and some gothic arches. A harsh religious environment was suggested at the outset by a large Celtic cross placed in the middle of the floor which was removed before the witches made their entrance and performed their ritual in the manner of a black mass. Macduff's murderers were clothed in clerical robes and wore black stockings over their heads. Otherwise, the male actors carried sabers on their belts and were dressed in grey tunics, jodhpurs and riding boots, while the women wore gowns. The lighting was mainly grey and green, while ominous thunder and funereal organ music were the key features of the sound design. Nicol again played the scene in which Macbeth enlists assassins to despatch Banquo in a manner that recalled Nixon, and Banquo's ghost remained unseen (as Hamlet's father's had also been), making it clear the vision is pure hallucination. In the final scene with the witches, they appeared to burn inverted crosses into Macbeth's forehead and cheeks. Nicol also chose to have Macbeth's demise occur off-stage as it does in the original, a decision for which he would be much criticised in the reviews.

Three weeks into rehearsals, Nicol fired Sigourney Weaver. He explained in a later interview that he felt he had made a mistake in casting someone as a result of one film role and that her talent 'didn't translate' to a theatrical setting.[71] Within a few days, he had replaced her with Laurie Kennedy, who had recently been acclaimed for her performances in two Bernard Shaw revivals at the Circle in the Square, *Man and Superman* and *Major Barbara*, and was also the daughter of the well-known film actor Arthur Kennedy. As a result of the change in casting, the first public preview was not held until the 12th of January. On the 18th, while the production was still in previews, Nicol fired Laurie Kennedy because in his opinion she 'wouldn't do what was necessary in the time to get it done.'[72] As had been the case with Weaver, the official explanation was that she had left the production due to 'artistic differences'. The other cast members seem to have been given no explanation, or even to have known whether the two actresses had been fired or had quit. Ray Dooley recalled that, 'After the day off we arrived at the theater to find the entrance to the theater itself closed. Nicol was working with Andrea inside. When we entered the space later we learned that Andrea was to take over the role.'

Nicol's replacement of Kennedy with Andrea Weber led some to conclude that Nicol had wanted to cast his girlfriend all along. However, it would have been out of character for Nicol to be so Machiavellian, so such an assumption would probably be unjust, as Elaine Bromka believes:

> Sigourney was a great match for him and Laurie really had Shakespearean chops... But Nicol wants to do what he wants to do and one could call it ego but it's his vision, he was always driven by his passion for what he believed should be. It was a great shock to everyone. But all three were very good.
>
> Andrea had very little prep but she's strong by nature – a gymnast and an actress, she went into it with an Olympic attitude. Her steadiness was admirable.

Another indication that Nicol may have been pursuing his own vision regarding Lady Macbeth is provided by director Leslie Megahey, who worked with him some years later and remembered,

> ...when I told him my highly original (I thought) idea for *Macbeth* (middle-aged man who might otherwise have been content with the Thane-dom, but is led on by the venality of sexy, much younger wife) Nic said he'd already done it on the stage with Andrea.

Indeed, Nicol later said that he saw Macbeth as someone who has 'what other men don't have – this amazing, beautiful creature.'[73] John Beaufort, writing for *Christian Science Monitor*, felt that such an approach to Lady Macbeth was valid but that Weber was not the right choice because she 'lacked the experience and emotional maturity for the part.'

Before the 3 o'clock matinee on Sunday the 24th of January, Nicol instructed his cast to perform the play as speedily as possible without omitting anything so that they could all go to watch the Super Bowl, which was to begin at 4 o'clock. Shortly after Nicol's death, his dresser on *Macbeth*, Mark Burchard, published a magazine article in which he wrote that the resultant performance was farcical and also highly damaging as there had been critics in the house. According to Burchard, on one occasion Nicol also substituted the water the actors drank during the banquet scene with white wine and, on another, with vodka. Among other examples of unprofessional behaviour he cites are that Nicol had attempted to auction off the contents of an audience member's handbag he had nearly tripped over when exiting a scene and that he had bawled a line directly into a woman's face when he heard her asking her companion what he had just said.

However, if such stories give the impression that Nicol did not care what anyone thought, there are numerous others which show that he cared deeply, although he was certainly misguided at times, as Elaine Bromka recalled:

> He said, 'Okay, I want everyone to go out half an hour before the show and just mingle. Don't get trapped into talking to one another – I want you to encounter the audience.' And we were all saying, 'What are you talking about?! In character, out of character? I'm a witch – am I supposed to be walking around smiling?' He said, 'No, just welcome the audience.' He wanted them to be positively predisposed. It was, needless to say, very difficult! People started being later and later in going out. And he kept saying, 'Come on now, at half-hour you've got to be out there!' That came from his need to be accepted.
>
> Starting with our walking around for half an hour smiling at them, the audience were a little confused! But once it got later in the play – he stood up on top of this table at one point and you really heard him in his glory, the clarity of his thoughts as Macbeth. It was wonderful. So they would have to have been impressed by him as a performer but bemused by the whole concept.

The official opening was delayed until the 28th of January, by which time there had been 19 previews – an unusually high number. Opening night attendees included Theodore Bikel, Vincent Gardenia, Lee Strasberg and Christopher Walken. The 650-seat theatre was full and the performance received an ovation, but the following day's review by Frank Rich in the *New York Times* proved disastrous. Rich complained that Nicol had played Macbeth as a 'quivering wreck' at the outset and, having given himself nowhere to go, had plunged 'into a series of increasingly odd readings, some of which fracture the cadences of Shakespeare's poetry or submerge them in nasal, Peter Lorre-like hisses and guttural effusions.' He described Weber as a 'prancing, if over-aged, schoolgirl' and the rest of the company as 'so much Birnam wood.' Rich had given Nicol a glowing review for *Inadmissible Evidence* less than a year previously and his review of *Macbeth* was not entirely negative – he did find Nicol effective in certain scenes – but it was perhaps all the more wounding for that, and New York was a town in which critics could more or less make or break a play. Ray Dooley remembered Nicol's reaction:

> Nicol was very angry, and, I think, hurt by the critical response to the show. He asked the producers to have the *Times* review posted in the lobby. His strategy was to give a speech after the performance (this started after the review was published) in which he said to the audience, basically: 'You've seen the play and you've read the review. If you think the review is wrong, please tell your friends to come see the show,' etc. He would start the speech 'Now that you've had your Nicol's worth, I'll have mine...' obviously punning on his name.
>
> Once the reviews came out and the show was not doing well in attendance, a game was started in which we drew running times for the show out of a hat, I think in thirty second increments. When the performance was over, the one closest to the time won the prize (perhaps just bragging rights, as I don't remember any actual prizes). This did not have much effect on the quality of the show as the show played well at pace, and few of us had enough lines to substantially alter the running time. The show ran about 1:45 – 1:50 as we played it, and we might have cut some time off that if Nicol was moving particularly

fast. In my view this was something of a device to keep spirits up in the face of the disappointing reviews.

There was much to like about the production. Nicol was a brilliant speaker of Shakespeare's language. He had a gift for making the language clear and immediate. Nicol's performance, the clarity and forcefulness of the language, was a principal virtue of the production. The late J.T. Walsh was effective as Macduff and the cast was, generally, quite capable.

Not every review was negative, and the production was highly-praised by the *The Record*, *The Star-Ledger*, and *WNEW TV* and the *New York Daily News*, the last of which praised Nicol's 'lean, muscular Macbeth' and 'thrilling' final soliloquy, going on to say that he had given 'the entire current theatre scene a shot in the arm.' Unfortunately, even this was not enough to save the play, which had been scheduled to run until the 14th of April but closed two months early, on the 14th of February. Despite the problems, Elaine Bromka's memories of Nicol are largely positive:

He was very generous. He would always go out afterwards and buy drinks for everyone. He could go on for hours afterwards – he had so much energy!

He was never seen walking through it or not caring ever. He was pretty crazy but he cared a great deal and I learned so much from him. He came to visit us when we had our first child and sat at the piano and played music for him. More than anything, he loved the camaraderie that he sought in those late nights when he would sit at the piano and play forever.

His energy fed his work but he couldn't listen to anything. He wanted to share *his* stories with *you*. So he would have the whole cast around him and buy them drinks and hold forth with stories. He wanted us to care through his stories. He didn't listen to your stories, but you knew that going into it and it felt different from others with what one might call huge ego. There was something hungry about him and he didn't know quite how to relate to others. He was perhaps not cut out to direct other people and to receive what they were doing and see it.

My experience of him was that he was a needy, brilliant man who cared about the work and wanted comrades around him so that he could do the work, and everything emanated from that. And he trusted me, which was very touching. He'd say, 'Let's go out for drinks!' and then he'd just unload with everything that was going on. He saw the whole institution, the critics, the scene, as obstacles and he had a tendency to feel misunderstood by people. He was the outlier. And that's why the feeling of *Inadmissible Evidence* was so quiet, so, 'we are off to the side of New York, we are doing our own thing'. Because he needed that. But when we got to *Macbeth*, it was like Rome was burning all around us but we're gonna do this, this is gonna be fine... He was a fighter and as soon as he sensed a fight he came alive because he expected it – 'Here we go again!' It was an embattled production.

He just really followed his inner demons – or tried to escape them – but that's what kept him busy. He was neither mean nor vindictive but he was paranoid and had a lot of demons. Actually, *highly* paranoid. Between the alcoholism and the paranoia there was a lot going on. Something was driving him and you can hear it in the rhythm of his work. But it really wasn't ego – he loved the art.

He stated that he never drank before and he felt very strongly about that. He said, 'I'll go out and have something afterwards but not at work.' Because of the love of the work [he was able to control his drinking] – he was definitely an alcoholic, there's no question. But he had respect for his audiences and his work... He was never sloshed on stage or anything. As a co-worker I had tremendous respect for him and I felt his pain.

Nicol's mentor, Tom Reader, died during the production, fuelling his belief in the Macbeth 'curse' – a superstition he seems to have taken surprisingly seriously, refusing to refer to the play by its full name, although opting for 'Mac B' rather than the more traditional moniker of 'the Scottish play'.

Later in the year, Nicol finally had the opportunity to put his *Macbeth* on film for the BBC under the direction of Jack Gold, who remembered,

It was part of the BBC Shakespeare season, which wasn't overwhelmingly liked, I don't think. One of the things was that you had to do uncut versions for the American market, so there was no editing of the text, and it also had to be done in period costume, there were no modern-dress versions, so what you got was sort of straight-down-the-middle, traditional costuming, full text, no editing for audience expectations, it was almost like a schools production, it was a sort of representative production of Shakespeare, but they did every play in the canon.

I'd seen him do *Macbeth* at the RSC, so I didn't have to explain the play to him! He was great at Shakespeare – he made it intelligible, I think. I was responsible for the staging of the television production, and the blocking of it – everything that was to do with the cameras as opposed to the theatre.

In his stage portrayals of Macbeth, Nicol had been clean-shaven and wore his hair fairly short but, in both his own production and Nunn's, period detail had been ignored in favour of deliberate anachronisms, presumably because both directors had wished to emphasize the play's contemporary relevance rather than nail it to a specific time and place. To fit in with the traditional approach favoured by the BBC as well as the probable difficulties involved in being well-groomed in 11th-century Scotland, Nicol grew his hair long and resurrected his drooping moustache of the early '70s.

The BBC wanted British actors with plenty of Shakespeare experience, so there was never any possibility of casting Andrea Weber. Jane Lapotaire, who had also worked with Gold before, was given the part of Lady Macbeth. She later recalled the experience:

It was shot in five days. Horrendous, which is why I feel robbed of the role, although it was a joy to work with beloved Jack again. We would have rehearsed it, of course, for three weeks or whatever. I don't think Jack would have been comfortable in the studio – he was a film man, he needed to be on location. And, however good the set was – and it doesn't look too bad, at least not as bad as the set for *The Tempest* (poor old Michael Hordern, clambering over those polystyrene rocks!), you're aware all the time it's in the studio.

> I think Nicol found the cloak and the crown and all the accoutrements of kingliness quite difficult. Physically, he wasn't an expansive actor. He was tall but I wouldn't say his physical expression of a role was on a par with his emotional or characterization level. Unusually for an actor, he never struck me as someone who was comfortable in his own skin. The most relaxed I ever saw him was when he was at the piano singing and playing – all without music – quite, quite brilliant.
>
> When you look at his face on film, there is such a vulnerability behind those eyes. I don't think his BBC Macbeth comes into its own until he plays the setting up Banquo's murder scene with the two killers. It was almost as if he'd got back on track then and he could play the politician, the wheedler... but I don't think he was happy in the long robes and the crown, that's not Nicol at all.
>
> He insisted we had real blood, so there were trays of cat's lights[74] in the studio and the make-up girls were in a terrible quandary because, of course, blood doesn't look like blood on film, it goes brown very quickly. And the smell was absolutely appalling! But dear Jack indulged him and we *weren't* covered in paint!

Nicol was going through some emotional turmoil during the filming because his relationship with Andrea Weber was in trouble and, as she had remained in America, he could do little to remedy the situation. He would later cite this as another example of the 'curse' at work. The cast also included Ian Hogg (as Banquo), who had this to say:

> ... in the case of Nicol I see a fine actor dirtied by gossip. An aura of arrogant bullying behaviour preceded him. I have belligerent Scottish blood in my veins as did he and after two years army service mostly with a Highland regiment I was well able to deal with bullies and handle a dram or two if necessary. That was the image I had of the man I was to rehearse and act with. Bloody gossip! The Buddhists are right: Gossip ye not 'tis top of the list of 'wrong actions'. In my experience he was an open and generous actor and a quiet and thoughtful conversationalist who said he envied me my life style. He was very isolated in England at the time and the BBC had put him up in a hotel and he was very lonely. He kept his cool throughout most of the work and only 'blew his top'

once when pressured by the studio-hustle of the BBC and its shadowy gentleman producers…

I value the contact I had with Nicol; the acting contact especially and also listening to him talk of his Greek island and his wishing that he had the mind and patience to enjoy it.

Both the production and Nicol's performance met with a mixed response. A larger budget and a longer schedule would undoubtedly have enabled Gold to produce a better film. As it stands, the BBC *Macbeth* is too obviously studio-bound, being frequently overlit and without a single breath of wind in evidence in the outdoor scenes. The performances are good, especially that of Lapotaire as a Lady Macbeth who becomes increasingly terrified of her husband as he descends into madness. There is a strong score by Carl Davis and the staging, camera movements and editing are all well thought out. However, it is unfortunately not one of Nicol's finest achievements on film. Gold probably deferred to Nicol too much and there was insufficient time available in which to hone the performance. As Lapotaire has said, his best scene was perhaps the one in which he persuades the two minions to kill Banquo. Nicol makes it very clear in his performance that the dagger, Banquo's ghost, etc, are all hallucinations brought on by madness and his playing of these scenes as a man who has become completely detached from reality and is experiencing some kind of fit is full-on but convincing. But there are other sequences in which his performance is writ too large. These may have worked on stage, but on television, shot in close-up, they feel misjudged. This may be part of the reason why, despite the fact that Nicol made several attempts at *Macbeth*, his interpretation would never have the impact that his *Hamlet* had done.

Chapter 20 – Normal and Quite Happy

Nicol managed a reconciliation with Andrea Weber, but their relationship would continue to be shaky for the following few months. Towards the end of 1982, he returned to New York to star as Archie Rice in a revival of John Osborne's *The Entertainer* at the Roundabout, where he had appeared the previous year in *Inadmissible Evidence*. The director was William Gaskill, who had directed Nicol's first two plays at the Royal Court over 20 years previously. However, for unknown reasons, Gene Feist, Artistic Director of the Roundabout, took over the reigns from Gaskill at some point, although Gaskill retained sole credit as director of the production.

The part of the down-at-heel music-hall entertainer had been a massive success for Laurence Olivier on both stage and screen, so any actor attempting the role in his wake would be bound to suffer endless comparisons (as would any actor attempting the role Nicol had made his own in *Inadmissible Evidence*). For this reason, *The Entertainer* had only rarely been revived, and the Roundabout production was the first to be staged in New York since Olivier had starred as Archie on Broadway in 1958.

Nicol did away with the hat, cane and grotesque make-up Olivier had used. Most critics gave Nicol credit for trying but did not think he was as effective as Olivier had been. Writing for the *New York Times*, Frank Rich felt that Nicol had softened the role too much with the result that he seemed 'more a Willy Loman than an Archie Rice.' However, in this case the production survived the reviews. Opening on the 21st of December, it ran for 96 performances before closing on the 12th of March, 1983. Nicol again had his portrait painted by a well-known artist during the production – this time, by Claude Marks, who was known for theatrical portraits and also as a long-time lecturer at the Metropolitan Museum of Art.

Nicol and Andrea Weber moved in together around this time, sharing a rented apartment at London Terrace, a huge building which took up an entire city block in the Chelsea area of New York. Nicol dubbed the place 'Folsom' after the famous prison.

During the run of *The Entertainer*, Nicol had received an offer from Joseph H. Shoctor, one of the producers of Nicol's Broadway *Hamlet*. Shoctor was now Executive Producer of the Citadel Theatre in Edmonton, Canada and in order to entice Nicol there he offered him the opportunity to star and direct in a play of his choice. Nicol chose Jean Anouilh's *The Lark*, a play he was familiar with from the 1962 live television version in which he had played Warwick. It seems highly probable that he chose it because he felt that the leading role of Joan of Arc would be perfect for Andrea Weber. Intriguingly, on this occasion Nicol chose not to play Warwick, but to take on two contrasting parts. In Act 1 he would appear as Robert de Beaudricourt, a squire whose vanity Joan plays on in order to obtain a horse, an armed escort and some men's clothing, thus enabling her to undertake the perilous journey necessary to deliver her message to the king. In Act 2 he would play the Spanish Inquisitor impervious to Joan's charms. This choice involved a very slight amount of trimming as there were points when both characters were on stage at the same time. It also seems to have been an entirely original idea of Nicol's. It is tempting to theorise that these two opposing parts reflected his own sometimes ambivalent feelings towards Andrea Weber. He was without doubt either in love with or obsessed with her (whichever way one cares to phrase it) and it is also clear that, although it endured for several years, Nicol never felt quite secure in their relationship. However, Weber was not the only other cast member from *Macbeth* to accompany Nicol to Canada, and Ray Dooley once more found himself under Nicol's direction, as he explained:

> My memory is that Nicol was allowed to bring two actors with him from the U.S. He asked me to come (I suppose based on my work in *Macbeth* and our working relationship, which was respectful on my part) and included as the second actor my then-wife, Diana Stagner. This was, obviously, tremendously kind of him. Diana and I often, perhaps most evenings after the show, went to Nicol and Andrea's apartment to play

bridge, drink wine (Nicol liked German white wine from the selection in the Canadian government stores) and eat snacks that Nicol would prepare (a spicy lobster paté and crepes suzette come to mind).

If memory serves it was a reasonably smooth rehearsal process and we opened on time and played the full run. The Citadel would have relied on subscriptions rather than being a commercial house and relying on single ticket sales based on reviews.

I had the great luxury of knowing Nicol during those weeks in Edmonton when things were normal and quite happy. Games of bridge, and all that sort of thing. He always treated me well, even warmly, and was unfailingly generous.

The play was presented in the Shoctor theatre, the Citadel's main stage, which had a capacity of 680. The theatre's management were ambitious and had previously managed to attract a number of other British stars including Peggy Ashcroft, Ron Moody and Glynis Johns. *The Lark* was chosen to open the theatre's 1983-84 season on the 24th of September 1983 for a limited run of four weeks. Luciano Iogna, who worked on *The Lark* as Assistant Director, told the story of the production:

> The Citadel had an arrangement with an apartment hotel and Nicol got the best suite available that they would give the big stars coming in, but he wasn't all that pleased with it. But I'm not quite sure whether that was a manipulation on his part…
>
> Within two days Nicol found great displeasure with Nesbitt Blaisdell, who had been cast as Cauchon, the bishop – and this was a prominent American actor, who has since had a tremendous career character acting in films such as *Dead Man Walking*. There was something about his style, and I guess he was a little too American for what Nicol was looking for and so there was a bit of a kerfuffle there when Nicol decided to release him, which was something which was not done at the Citadel.
>
> It was a factory, basically, and Nicol had a way of putting crimps into processes like that. The one that stands out most for me was in the design – it was a very simple design – essentially it was a raked stage, extremely raked, something like 12 or 14 degrees, so it was quite steep and then they would just bring in iconic set pieces to represent locations.

He'd okayed it and I remember going into a production meeting with him and everything was fine, and then when they had the superstructure of the rake put onto the stage he went out to have a look at it, took a walk on it and he went, 'No…no, this won't do at all.' And the production manager, Rick Schick, was having conniptions because it was like $10,000 in supplies and labour to put this on and all of a sudden Nicol was saying, 'No, it won't do – take it out!' I was known as a lighting designer and a technician at the time as well and so I had a good relationship with Rick, who was pulling out his hair. I went to him and I said, 'Look, I'll have a talk with Nicol and I'll figure out what's going on and we'll see what we can do.' I tried to pour oil on the troubled waters, so to speak, so Nicol and I went out and had lunch and I said, 'Well, you know this is a pretty major decision…' and he said, 'Yeah, I know! I'm just a little annoyed today but it'll be fine.' So after lunch I went back to Rick and I said, 'Everything's going to be okay, don't worry about it, he just had to reassess certain things in the staging, so we should be fine.' But it was just his way of shaking things up a little bit, I think. There are positive and negative aspects of that. Certainly, at the Citadel they needed some shaking up and he had the pedigree to be able to do that and get away with it. In the end the stage remained as it was, but he certainly put people on their toes, and in that way people were ready to listen carefully and they were going to contribute their best – certainly the cast, because if he was ready to release someone like Blaisdell then everyone knew that, no matter what position you had, your job was on the line and you were going to give your all! So whether he was playing a psychological game or whether that was just his personality or whether it was intentional, sort of indirect manipulation, he certainly got the best out of everyone and I had tremendous respect for him for that.

The stories preceded Nicol. Because I'd worked with Jean Gascon[75], I think that's why they stuck me with him as well, because I've always been a sort of mediator and that's sort of what I do now! So I was expecting a certain amount of that. I had a lot of lunches during rehearsals where there was a fair amount of alcohol consumed but it never affected his work, unlike other directors I've worked with. He was *sharp* and that gained my respect for him and certainly he never (in my presence) overdrank at functions.

I think that he was trying to be really protective of Andrea at the time as well. He was not going to tolerate any criticism, and so he didn't want to hear any gossip around that or their relationship or about her casting at the time, so I think, also in an effort to protect her, he wanted to get her away from there as well, but I certainly don't recall any instances where he was over the top, but you could tell that he was one of those mean drinkers. You could see that in him, that if he did drink too much he would go to dark places, but I never saw him abuse a cast member, I never saw him come in in the morning hungover, so he was on best behaviour to the best of my recollection.

Mostly what got his rankles up was Joe Shoctor because Joe was the impresario and he wanted to be perceived that way. There were certain requests by the management and by Joe for Nicol to attend certain events. Nicol did not show up or flatly got into arguments with him. There were never really large public scenes – it was generally out in the lobby after rehearsals. When there were public functions, with these meet-and-greet members of the Citadel, ticket-holders and people who'd made huge contributions and so on, I guess Nicol was contractually obliged to show up but he wasn't contractually obliged to be polite to people, so he would say, 'How do you do?', turn his back and walk away to another corner. He'd have his four or five glasses of wine, and be out the door. He'd fulfilled his contractual obligations and no more, so that certainly rankled Joe Shoctor and the administration certainly didn't know how to deal with him.

I like to think I didn't put on airs because of my working class background, so that may have been something going for me at the time which allowed me to benefit from his warmer side. I may be looking back through rose-coloured glasses and being a little bit nostalgic, but I don't think I'm that naïve to think that...

He certainly had the potential of being cruel. I know that when he wanted something he wasn't going to let anything get in his way, so I'm assuming that he got most of what he wanted because there weren't many fireworks during the production, other than with Joe Shoctor, and I wasn't witness to many of those things that one could hear – you know, sort of raised voices and he'd come in with this very dark mood for about two minutes and then it was gone, it was back to business and in to rehearsals.

I remember the lunches I had with him were marvellous. I don't know whether he used me as his audience. There were very few other people who would have lunches with him, other than Andrea. But more often it would be, 'Luc! We're going to lunch!' and maybe that was his time to be warm. And, again, at those sort of meet-and-greets, the first two drinks he would be all fine, and then after the third or fourth drink the darkness would begin to appear and his patience would run out and enough's enough and time to go. But this is what alcoholism does and you either have those types who get really warm and outgoing and then you get the really dark and abusive and violent. I never really saw that side to him. I saw the edge to it, but I was never witness to when he went in as in the stories that preceded him. Just that sharp, quick temper and then gone.

Although Beaudricourt is supposed to be rather corpulent, Nicol chose not to wear padding and simply adopted a change of costume and performance to differentiate between his two roles. As the inquisitor he was dressed in a dark cowl with a scarlet cross emblazoned on the chest. Iogna went on to comment on the response to Nicol's casting of Andrea Weber:

It was a surprise because certainly everyone was expecting a name as Joan but it wasn't a disappointment as far as the production went to my recollection. With Andrea's youthful energy and her background as a gymnast, the physicality that she brought to the role was tremendous. You know, the background sniping and gossipers, as there will be in theatre, were questioning if she was right for the role and saying, 'She's only there because of so-and-so.' I could tell in rehearsals that she lacked a little confidence, but once the show was up and running, she certainly grew into it. She might not have been the brightest candle on the stage at that point in her career, but she certainly held her own and got along well with the rest of the cast.

As a result of his Broadway *Macbeth*, many in the New York theatre world had come to the conclusion that Nicol had no ability as a director, but Iogna's memories of *The Lark* paint a different picture:

I think the cast really enjoyed working with Nicol and learnt a lot through the process with him... He was very well prepared and was able to get what he wanted across without demeaning anyone. Because they knew him as an actor as well, they could talk to him in an actor's language and they were able to give him what he wanted. I don't recall any problems with any of the other actors other than Nesbitt Blaisdell.

I think there were people who were already contracted to perform for the piece, so I don't know that he had full control over casting. Peter Curtis, who played Cauchon, was originally English but spent many, many years in South Africa and was a wonderful, lovely gentleman who had memory problems and a huge role in the play! Because I'd had experience with Peter in past productions I was able to tell Nicol to be aware and Peter had this physical trait where you knew when he was going to blank because he would go to his wedding ring so, as soon as he went to his wedding ring everybody in the cast was on their toes but you wouldn't know whether it was just going to be this long lapse or whether he was going to wander wherever. And Nicol was very patient with him. Peter was not a great actor. He was competent, he certainly had a presence on the stage, although not like Nicol. When Nicol took the stage, your eyes were riveted to him. He was phenomenal. There was a light there which was unbelievable. But in dealing with Peter – who Nicol could have easily dismissed – he was very patient and stayed with him through the whole process. So I learned a lot from him as a director, certainly, and he was able to talk to actors as an actor as well as a director.

The Lark seems to have been counted neither as a failure nor as a notable success and Nicol's followers in the UK and the USA remained largely unaware of his Canadian sojourn. Iogna felt there had been a lack of qualified drama critics in Edmonton at the time and offered his own evaluation:

From my perspective, most of the shows on the main stage at the Citadel were never that moving to begin with. Even when you had brilliant performers in powerful pieces, like James Whitmore in *Death of a Salesman*, who was *phenomenal*, but sitting at the back of the house you'd watch this and walk away going, 'Okay, that was an okay show.' In that context, for me, *The Lark* was up there with the best of them. Because the subscription series was so strong there, even a show that was not artistically well-received was already sold out anyway for the run. To the best of my knowledge, certainly amongst the theatre community, people enjoyed it, there weren't any major criticisms of it. There was still the question of, well, if they're bringing in an unknown like Andrea Weber, they could have picked an unknown actor from here in Edmonton, so there was some pettiness in that regard, but as far as production quality, I don't recall any large negative response, but at the same time I don't recall any overwhelming, glowing review or praise for it.

Despite having mainly positive things to say about Nicol, Iogna admitted also feeling some resentment towards him, which he explained as follows:

Here's a guy with such incredible talent who had so much going for him and yet he self-sabotaged himself all along. I'm envious of people who have his ability – it seems to come so easily and naturally to them – and yet they take it for granted in many ways, and so I sort of resented him for that. To see the waste of that skill and that talent... He could have spent more time in terms of teaching as well. It seemed that it only came out when there was a problem. He had so much that he could have shared with us. But I think the world needs to know about this man and what a tremendous artist he was, and the legacy that he left us in his film work.

Shortly after *The Lark* closed on the 22nd of October, Nicol went to London to play Malyarov, a senior KGB agent in *Sakharov*, a film Jack Gold was making for television about the Russian physicist of the same name. Andrei Sakharov played an important role in the development of the hydrogen bomb and later became a human rights activist, speaking out about political persecution in the USSR – an act for which he himself was persecuted despite having won the Nobel Peace Prize for his efforts. The film was intended to draw attention to the plight of Sakharov who, at the time of production, was in exile in Gorky suffering from poor health as a result of a hunger strike and forbidden to contact anyone outside the USSR, including members of his own family. The American actor Jason Robards had the title role and Glenda Jackson was playing human rights activist Yelena Bonner, who became Sakharov's second wife. It was a worthy project and screenwriter David Rintels perhaps understandably prioritised historical accuracy over dramatic license, but the film suffered somewhat as a result, feeling overlong and underpowered as a piece of drama. Topical at the time, it is largely forgotten today.

Nicol had only two scenes, the first being the opening in which he delivers a mini-lecture to his KGB minions explaining the significance of Sakharov – a sort of prologue clearly intended to bring the audience up to speed rather than for any dramatic purpose. In his second scene he played opposite Robards, another actor with a reputation for being 'difficult.' However, Gold remembered them getting on well together and had the impression they had met before – not unlikely, as they were both prominent in New York theatre. Nicol's role gave him little to do and it is clear that he accepted it solely because Gold was directing. It was to be their final collaboration.

Chapter 21 - Odd Choices

Nicol's next role was as King Ferdinand of Spain in the big-budget 6-hour mini-series *Christopher Columbus*. Shot in the Dominican Republic, Malta and Spain in late 1983 – early 1984 and featuring an exact replica of Columbus' ship, the *Santa Maria*, it was not broadcast until 1985. Directed by veteran Italian film-maker Alberto Lattuada, it featured a cast of international stars which also included former colleagues Gabriel Byrne (as Columbus) and Oliver Reed, as well as Max von Sydow, Eli Wallach, Rossano Brazzi, Virna Lisi, Raf Vallone and, as the Queen of Spain, Faye Dunaway. Each actor spoke their own language while filming and recorded their dialogue later or, in some cases, were dubbed by other actors. Nicol did his own dubbing for the English language version. This approach was standard practice in Italy and, although it was an international co-production, it was very much an Italian-dominated one in which Columbus' Italian nationality was emphasized. Nicol's role was fairly small and unchallenging and the alphabetical billing of the cast again meant that he found his name at the bottom of the list. The series was certainly above-average for its type, although something of a historical whitewash, but it is difficult to see what could have appealed to Nicol about the project other than sunshine and a healthy pay check.

In March, Nicol used some of the proceeds from his film work to buy a house – his first permanent residence since his marriage with Jill. The property was a five-storey townhouse overlooking the canal at Singel 56 in central Amsterdam. Nicol had already spent some time living there as a tenant. The owner was the brother of Nicol's former girlfriend, Emma Hamelynck, and Nicol was considered almost part of the family, so he presumably got it for a good price – anyway, it would prove to be a good investment. He installed a grand piano on the second floor and a games room in the basement.

Nicol's house at Singel 56 in central Amsterdam.
(Photograph by author)

Among Nicol's favourite hangouts in Amsterdam were The Princesse Bar (since closed), where he would sometimes drink with Rijk de Gooyer, the Dutch actor who had played his sadistic sidekick in *The Wilby Conspiracy*. One Italian restaurant which Nicol liked was also favoured by Freddy Heineken, the enormously wealthy beer mogul who had been kidnapped in 1983 and released after a ransom had been paid. Heineken was subsequently accompanied everywhere by bodyguards who would try to empty any restaurant their boss wished to eat in. One evening they entered the Italian while Nicol was dining there alone. Characteristically, he refused to leave and ate his meal in an uncomfortable silence with Freddy Heineken and his security team.

For Nicol, 1984 was a year which would prove that his career had become anything but predictable. He recorded his first audio book since *The Hobbit* ten years earlier – a version of *The Hound of the Baskervilles* in which he returned to the role of Sherlock Holmes opposite George Rose as Watson. Rose, 64 at the time, was an eccentric British actor who had made a name for himself in a number of Shakespearean roles before becoming a star in Broadway musicals in later life. A grim fate awaited him – he was beaten to death in the Dominican Republic by his adopted son, the boy's father and two other men in 1988. Rose was a splendid Watson able to deliver wordy dialogue just as fluidly as Nicol. Recorded in New York for Caedmon Audio, a divison of HarperCollins, the adaptation was directed by Ward Botsford, who had helmed many such audiobooks with well-known actors. Several lesser-known (and less able) actors were also featured, alongside a combination of original violin music and extracts from Mussorgsky's *Night on Bald Mountain*. Nicol's Holmes was more traditional and somewhat colder than his previous incarnation, but it was an entertaining and atmospheric three-hour version of an oft-told story.

Nicol next found himself top-billed in a big budget Disney movie, *Return to Oz*, a belated, non-musical sequel to *The Wizard of Oz*. The film marked the directorial debut of Walter Murch, a close associate of George Lucas and Francis Ford Coppola who, through his work on *Apocalypse Now* and other films, had earned a reputation as one of the best and most creative editors and sound designers in the film industry. Murch had originally wanted Leo McKern to play what became Nicol's dual role of Dr Worley and the Nome King. Worley is a quack psychiatrist Dorothy is sent to in order to 'cure' her of the illusion that she had once visited a magical place called Oz. The Nome King is the chief villain of the piece, a rock-like monarch who dwells in a cave. Walter Murch remembered how he came to cast Nicol:

> Leo McKern was a little vague – he implied there were some health issues and I kept trying for Leo because physically he was exactly what I had in mind for the Nome King, and very similar to the drawing in the book. Nicol, who was tall and thin, was not physically what I thought but, as an actor and what he brought to the role, that more than compensated for the fact that I had to readjust what I thought physically the Nome King would look like. I'd seen *Excalibur* and one other film – and I liked what he'd done in both those films.
>
> We talked on the phone and then I sent him the screenplay and he phoned back saying that he was very interested in it but he had a problem coming to terms with one of the scenes in the film. We were getting close to having to make a decision so it made me nervous to hear this. He said it was the scene where the Nome King swallows Jack Pumpkinhead. And I thought, '...okay...' and wondered, 'Why is this a problem?' And, just at that moment – I remember vividly – somebody in the office next door decided to drill through the wall and suddenly there was this noise and there were other crises going on at this time, and so I was torn between [thinking] I *had* to talk to Nicol, we *had* to make a decision and all these other things. Nicol said when he was in grammar school, or when he was 15 or so, he'd had problems with his teeth and he was laughed at by the other kids and so he felt very strange about opening his mouth. This completely floored me and I said, 'Well, you don't have to worry about that because in the film the character is by that time going to be animated and for the other material we will be shooting control footage, but if it really bothers you we can shoot control footage with some other actor opening their mouth.' And I was

desperately trying to think, 'Is there some other agenda going on here that I don't know about? Is this his way of testing me as a director, to find out what my limits are or...?' Anyway, the idea that this scene would be done completely in animation and he wouldn't have to do this on camera, seemed to satisfy him and then we signed the agreement a few days later and everything went very smoothly with Nicol. I mean, the *only* slight disturbance in the forest, so to speak, was this observation about him not wanting to open his mouth on camera.

Actors have to make these terrible, difficult decisions based on screenplays – and I had never directed a film before. They are committing themselves to a project whose outcome – as with everything – is uncertain. And so there are ways, in a sense, of kicking the tyres of the automobile. I don't know what that does, but it's something that people do that tells them about the car! It could have been that or, changing the topic completely, it could have been that he had dentures and was nervous about opening his mouth and people seeing his dentures.

Nicol's sequences were shot at Elstree. The larger and more interesting part was that of the Nome King, and Nicol, having read the *Oz* books as a child, was enthusiastic about Murch's attempt to make a film more faithful to the vision of author L. Frank Baum than the Judy Garland one had been. Walter Murch:

> There was a big gap [between shooting his two parts]. The Dr Worley role was probably in the second week of shooting and the Nome King was probably week 8. I'm guessing Nicol shot for maybe ten days out of eighty, so it was not a long shooting schedule for him and it all went very smoothly and he really got into it.
>
> As Dr Worley, he had the scene with Fairuza Balk in the office. The doctor is, in a sense, *acting* as a doctor to set Aunt Em's mind at ease, so there's a performance within a performance there. He's a person who is acting the role of a doctor, as many doctors do – 'I'm going to be the authority and set your mind at ease.' And that's how he did it, which is exactly the way I wanted it to be.
>
> The Nome King, like many dictators, is somebody who is absolutely sure that he's right and, from a certain point of view, he *is* right! The emeralds are part of this underground world. All of these minerals and

everything were taken away to build the Emerald City and he just wanted them back, so he had his reasons and yet there was this yearning to be human along with that. He didn't want to be just alone with all of his toys, he wanted something else, and by turning human beings into objects, he would somehow acquire some of their humanity – which is also a longing of some dictators! We discussed it in these terms and I left it up to Nicol completely to come up with an interpretation and then, on a shot-by-shot basis, I would nudge that interpretation in one direction or the other, but by very little. I was basically very happy with what he came up with.

The film involved a sequence in which the Nome King transformed from rock into flesh and blood. This was achieved partly through the Claymation of Will Vinton, who had to build a number of miniature replicas of Nicol, and partly through the intricate make-up of Robin Grantham. The transformation involved five stages – the first three utilising Claymation, the latter two featuring Nicol in make-up. Walter Murch:

> As the Nome King and with the make-up that was applied to him – he was very patient with all of the make-up people – which involved three or four different stages of 'rockiness', maximum to minimum and then two in between. When there were any big make-up issues, you had to be very clear on those shooting days what you were going to do and how long it would take just because the preparations were extensive. But he was very good.
>
> I remember I was in the room full of cabinets with the 31 heads and we were looking at something to do with the architecture of that room and suddenly there was this sound of something happening and I turned around and it was Nicol in his full Nome King costume and make-up. He twirled around showing me and was very proud of how it had turned out.
>
> Robin Grantham designed the make-up and then figured out how he was going to do it and what it was going to be made of and he brought drawings to me. I may have made one or two suggestions, but basically I was very happy with what he came up with.

> Their technique at the time – it's all changed now because of computers – was to do face-on and profile shots of Nicol just to give them a sense of his shape and then we would shoot 16mm control footage. We isolated all of his lines of dialogue as the Nome King where he is the animated version rather than the human version and we shot close-up footage of Nicol saying these lines and it went exactly the way it would in any kind of performance. We'd do take one, then I'd make a suggestion and we'd shoot another… So we'd do four or five takes, which was par for how I shot the whole film, and then those 16mm footages were sent to Will and they would simply, in a viewer, look at frame 1, then they would sculpt something that looked like that and take a frame and go to frame 2, change the sculpture…
>
> We did what we called a 'rockisation' [of his voice] to give the idea that his vocal chords were made out of stone. He was already 60% of the way there in his performance – he had a Nome King voice, but we then took those lines of dialogue and generated what's known as a 'square wave', which is like a sine wave – which is undulating – but these are like Lego blocks of sine waves and we used that to control the amplitude of his voice, and we could dial in the rate at which it would do that. And so that chopped up the voice into these very discreet units and we had to find the right sweet spot between having the effect and understanding what it is that he's saying, and that was something that we just tuned in at the final mix.

Murch encountered a great many difficulties in making the film, as he explained:

> There were one or two days of shooting when there was just Nicol and Jean Marsh when it was a huge relief just to be dealing with actors and no puppets and we could rehearse and not have to worry about seeing the cables. They got along great as actors.
>
> We were always behind schedule, sometimes slightly, sometimes a lot… and I'm sure there was a lot of back corridor gossip about that. I was fired from the film after five weeks. Disney came in and said, 'You're too far behind and we don't like how it looks and – goodbye!' Ultimately, I got re-hired four or five days later. So it was full of trauma and none of it was secret, it was all out in the open. Nicol was around I think at that time because he and Robin were working on the make-up

part. He was present on set or at the studio for more days than actual shooting days because of shooting this control footage for Will Vinton and also because of the considerable work that had to be done with the make-up and costume.

The main headline is that there were many problems on the film, both technical and administrative and I had my hands full, especially as it was the first film that I had ever directed and very complicated on many levels and Nicol not only did not add to that complication, he helped tremendously.

Upon hearing that his friend had been removed from the picture, George Lucas decided to intervene. He liaised with producer Richard Berger and convinced him to reinstate Murch and expand the shooting schedule. Francis Ford Coppola, Steven Spielberg and Philip Kaufman – all successful directors and all friends of Murch – also made individual visits to the set to offer advice and encouragement.

Robin Grantham had been a movie make-up artist for a little over ten years when he worked on *Return to Oz*. He had some experience in dealing with temperamental stars, such as Patrick McGoohan, with whom he had worked on *The Man in the Iron Mask*; McGoohan was drinking heavily at the time and apparently had it written into his contract that he was 'not to be touched'. Nicol must have been impressed by Grantham as he referred to him in a subsequent interview as a 'very good make-up artist', although he exaggerated the amount of time it had taken to transform him into the Nome King, claiming it to have been a five hour process. Grantham recalled:

I'd never met him before but I was a bit concerned because he had a reputation for having a short fuse and the make-up took about two hours to apply! I think I first met him at the make-up test, which was me, Nic and Lord Snowdon taking pictures for *The Sunday Times*, which was added pressure! Snowdon didn't impinge at all – you were aware of him in the background snapping away, but that was it.

When we did the life mask, you can see in the photo in his eyes he looks a bit concerned! Having a life mask done is a bit traumatic because you're completely covered. The first layer is alginate, which is what dentists use for taking an impression, so it's made of seaweed and it's sort of gelatinous, it gets in all the cracks and gets all the detail. You back that up with plaster. You have to put that underneath and over the eyes and they have to close their eyes as it sets. With their nose, they have to take a deep breath in, you put it on, then they blow out. If that doesn't work they can suffocate, so it's a bit heavy-duty! So, you can see the apprehension in his eyes. I had mine done once. It's a strange experience – when it comes off it's like being born and it's a relief.

The thing that really convinced me about Nic's acting ability was that he was a big, six foot, butch guy and the Nome King was a big, butch kind of character, but there's a bit in the film where he has the ruby slippers on and Fairuza asks him to return her ruby slippers. He says, 'No – they're my ruby slippers now!' like a little kid, which was a nice subtlety.

Nicol did indeed play the Nome King like a spoilt child – one with a misplaced sense of entitlement whose power has isolated him and made him unable to comprehend the harm he causes to others. It was an impressively nuanced performance despite the fact that the heavy make-up rendered him almost unrecognizable. Unfortunately, the $25 million film failed at the box office, taking only $11 million. However, such an amount would have counted as a decent return on a more modestly budgeted film, so *Return to Oz* was seen by a large number of people. At the time, it was considered by some to be excessively dark and disturbing for a film aimed at a family audience, but it is difficult to imagine this objection being raised today. The film's reputation has, in fact, grown over the years to the point where it has gained something of a cult following. There are many aspects of the film which deserve appreciation, including the 10-year-old Fairuza Balk's astonishingly persuasive lead performance, the memorable villains of Nicol and Jean Marsh, and the constantly clever and inventive design of both sound and visuals throughout. One suspects that *Return to Oz* flopped largely because it failed to satisfy many fans of *The Wizard of Oz* rather than due to any inherent flaws of its own.

At the end of January, Nicol had been offered the title role in *Lord Mountbatten – The Last Viceroy*, a major 6-hour mini-series focusing on Mountbatten's time as Viceroy of India, when he oversaw the British withdrawal and the formation of Pakistan. India had become a popular subject for film and television makers at this time in the wake of Richard Attenborough's *Gandhi*. The production of *Mountbatten* was financed by Brent Walker, the company founded by George Walker, a cockney who had worked as a porter at Billingsgate Fish Market before becoming a boxer and, later, a minor gangster. As a result, he served two and a half years in Wormwood Scrubbs. After his release, he had become an entrepreneur and a series of shrewd business deals had made him a multi-millionaire. Walker attracted investment from Mobil Oil for *Mountbatten* and the budget was set at $12.5 million.

Nicol was attracted to the part not only for the substantial fee but because it was very different from the parts he was usually offered. Mountbatten was something of a hero to many as well as an aristocratic, romantic figure who had enjoyed a glamorous lifestyle. It seems highly unlikely that Nicol could have been the first choice for the part as he was far from an obvious one, but from his point of view it was a welcome challenge which he thought he could meet successfully. His casting also apparently received the approval of Mountbatten's cousin, the Queen, after she had been shown photographs of Nicol in costume dressed in the uniform of a Rear Admiral. His appearance was subtly altered by straightening and darkening his hair. In order to gain insight into Mountbatten's character, Nicol read a number of relevant books and also made use of his recent acquaintanceship with Lord Snowdon, who had taken publicity photos for *Return to Oz*. In a later interview, Nicol recalled,

> I talked to Lord Snowdon, who knew him, and I said, 'Can you help me?' He said, 'He was essentially a very private man and nobody knew much about him, but I can tell you two things.' I said, 'Please, because nobody knows this man and nobody will tell me anything!' He said, 'Well, number one, he had the most real charm of anyone I've ever

met… never mind the common touch, he had the human touch to be able to make anyone that he talked to in the world feel completely at ease. Number two, he said, he had the best manners of anyone that I have ever known. So I thought, 'Well, this should be dreadfully easy!'[76]

Janet Suzman was cast as Lady Mountbatten at the suggestion of Princess Margaret (Snowdon's former wife) and later spoke of having an 'excellent rapport' with Nicol. Somewhat controversially, Ian Richardson was cast as Nehru, the Indian Prime Minister, causing some to object that an Indian actor should have played the role. However, this was balanced somewhat by the fact that Gandhi was played by Sam Dastor, who actually *was* Indian. Nicol managed to wangle a minor role for Andrea Weber as Mountbatten's daughter, and they stayed together throughout the filming. The director was Tom Clegg, whose experience had mainly been in television shows such as *The Sweeney* and *Minder*, although he had made a couple of features, while producer Judith de Paul had mostly worked on television versions of Gilbert and Sullivan operas.

Filming commenced on the 2nd of July 1984 with seven weeks shooting in the UK, mostly at Luton Hoo, a large country estate which had already provided a useful location for a number of British films, including the Peter Sellers *Pink Panther* sequel, *A Shot in the Dark* and the James Bond film *Never Say Never Again*. After a short break, cast and crew flew to Delhi, where they filmed in and around the city for the next two months. This was followed by a short final stint in November in Kandy, a city in the centre of Sri Lanka which had also served as a location for *Indiana Jones and the Temple of Doom*.

While in India, Nicol and the other main actors met Prime Minster Indira Gandhi in her garden just a few weeks before she was assassinated in the same location. Despite the scorching heat, clouds of dust and the crowds of onlookers who gathered to observe the cast and crew at work, the Indian section was completed slightly ahead of schedule on the 30th of October. However, the production was not without its problems and, on one occasion, Nicol lost his temper with explosive results and 'chinned' the Director of

Photography, Peter Jessop. The story first came to the author's attention via Robin Grantham during the conversation about *Return to Oz*. Grantham did not work on *Mountbatten*, but heard about the incident later from a fellow industry professional and provided some background about the film-making process which may be helpful in understanding Nicol's point of view:

> The thing about film crews is that often the individuals are constantly seeking to establish their domain. Actors tend to defer to no one, except the director and the producer. Lighting cameramen or Directors of Photography [DOPs], in general, constantly battle to have director and actors defer to them, on the basis that 'I am the professional that knows about these things.'
>
> The way a shot is constructed is this: the actors are called to the set and together with the director they 'block' the scene. For example, if the scene is: a guy arrives at the café doorway, pauses, looks around, catches the eye of the waitress, grins at her, she smiles back, there is some electricity between them, he sits down, she comes and takes his order, more chemistry, she walks off and he smiles at her retreating bum, she looks back at him over her shoulder and grins at him, etc, the actors will walk it through, with all the crew watching attentively. The guy will open the door and pause in the doorway. The camera focus-puller will mark where the actor's feet are, his first mark. The actress will appear from the kitchen, pause to gather some cutlery, the focus-puller will crouch down and make her first mark and so on until the whole scene has been blocked. Unless the lighting is going to be very quick according to the DOP, the actors will be released and free to return to their dressing room or Winnebago. When the DOP has finished lighting, the actors are called back to the set, for an all too brief 'artistic rehearsal'. This is the only time (unless there have been any pre-shoot rehearsals, probably weeks or even months ago) that the actors and director get to work out the performance, so for actors these brief few minutes are very precious.
>
> The story, as I heard it, is that the shot was a long tracking one. That is, when the camera is mounted on a dolly (a kind of high-tech cart) that runs on rails. What was said to me, quite specifically, was that the scene had been blocked, the actors released, and their stand-ins had replicated their moves as many times as the DOP required. When he announced

the lighting was ready, the actors were called to the set for their brief artistic rehearsal. *If* the version I heard is true and *if* – as is quite commonplace – the DOP in question said, once Nic had arrived on the set and walked the shot through a couple of times, something like 'Hang on a couple of minutes, I need to just tweak the spot for your close up 3/4 of the way along the track,' I think the actor would be quite justified in feeling miffed that the DOP had had his allotted time and was now trying to pull rank and maybe even dismissively nick his few precious minutes of artistic rehearsal. If it happened several times, I can well imagine a head of steam building up in the actor. Even more galling, would be if the DOP was making it up, just to establish his right to do as he pleases, in which case I can well imagine the temptation to chin him, especially in an imposing guy like Nic, who earned his 'difficult' rep from not liking to be treated cavalierly.

A member of the crew later said that Nicol had seemed rather nervous whenever he had a long scene to play and had taken a dislike to Jessop, whose manner he found irritating. In a letter to the author, Jessop himself said that he had been worried that the light was fading in the windows as they were shooting and had inadvertently 'annoyed' Nicol 'by moving an exposure meter about him' with the result that Nicol 'sprang up and aimed a punch.' Fortunately, although Jessop was knocked down, he was not seriously hurt and insisted the incident was forgotten so that shooting could continue. The DOP is generally considered the most important person on a set after the director, so Nicol's action may easily have had serious consequences. The producers managed to keep it out of the press, but further trouble lay ahead.

Mountbatten was to be aired in America as part of the *Masterpiece Theatre* series and would therefore be introduced by series host Alistair Cooke, also known for his long-running *Letter from America* broadcast on BBC radio. At the end of an interview for the *L.A. Times*, Cooke made an offhand remark to the effect that he thought Nicol too much of a 'lug' to play Mountbatten. Cooke was subsequently mortified to see his remark appear in print, while Nicol was, according to Cooke, 'outraged and had every right to be'. Cooke wrote a letter of apology to Nicol and was apparently forgiven, but the incident triggered some debate in the press about Nicol's suitability for the role. In an interview for the *New York Daily News*, Nicol defended his casting, citing Martin Sheen's portrayal of John F. Kennedy in a recent mini-series as a prime example of good acting triumphing over a lack of physical resemblance. Meanwhile, producer Judith de Paul told another newspaper that she felt Nicol deserved an Emmy for his performance and he had been 'a good colleague to his fellow artists'.

Nicol participated in a variety of events set up by the producers to generate publicity and sell Mountbatten to various markets. In the UK, the series was released on rental video cassette prior to being screened on television. Nicol's performance was widely praised and seen as a convincing demonstration of his range and abilities. The series itself was also well-received although, despite the considerable attention which had been paid to historical accuracy, many felt that the portrayal of the British in India was a little too benevolent to ring true.

Nicol returned to New York at the end of January to prepare for the role of Henry in Tom Stoppard's *The Real Thing* at the Plymouth Theatre on Broadway. The play had already won a slew of Tony and Drama Desk awards and been running successfully for a year, initially with Jeremy Irons and later with John Vickery. When Vickery also had to depart due to other commitments, director Mike Nichols contacted Nicol, who accepted quickly despite learning that the box office takings were in decline by this point and being told by friends that it was a 'bad career move'. More important to Nicol was that he admired Stoppard as a playwright and loved the play. The fact that he would only have to commit to a limited run of two months before the play was due to close also appealed to him, as did the opportunity to further broaden his range.

The Real Thing is a clever, thoughtful comedy about the nature of love and literature, in which Stoppard delights in wrong-footing the audience in a number of places. Nicol's role was that of a successful playwright in love with an actress named Annie, who happens to be married to the actor playing the lead in Henry's latest play. Henry has a horror of bad writing and his character at times has a threatening edge, which is perhaps why Nicol seemed a good fit for the part. Annie was played by Nicol's former *Rex* colleague, Glenn Close. Nicol debuted on the 19th of March and enjoyed the run, even accompanying Anne Bobby, the young actress who was playing his daughter, safely to the Port Authority bus terminal every evening after the performance. *The Real Thing* closed on the 12th of May, but Nicol received few reviews as he had not opened the play. It was to be his final collaboration with Mike Nichols.

Shortly after Nicol's play closed, Andrea Weber also appeared alongside Glenn Close in a double bill of two one-act plays by the French author Nathalie Sarraute, *For No Good Reason / Childhood*. The production was staged at New York's Samuel Beckett theatre, opening at the end of May and running for a month. Meanwhile, Nicol set off for Singapore to appear in the TV movie *Passion Flower*. The director was the prolific Joseph Sargent, perhaps best known for his New York subway train hijack thriller, *The Taking of Pelham One Two Three*. Nicol played Albert Coskin, a tycoon with a murky past and fingers in sundry dubious pies including ruby-smuggling and gun-running. Setting his voice to booming-mode, he effortlessly dominated his scenes; unfortunately, however, the film itself was an unconvincing concoction featuring waffling second-rate actors, soft-focus close-ups, cod-Chinese music and women in shoulder pads. Even the supposed hero, portrayed by Bruce Boxleitner, came across as a shallow, wealth-obsessed narcissist. Nicol was impressed with Barbara Hershey, however, and complimented her English accent in an interview, but there was little else in *Passion Flower* to warrant such praise. The film must have seemed highly old-fashioned even in 1986 and is almost entirely forgotten today.

Nicol returned to New York in mid-August and spent time in Los Angeles later in the year, telling the *L.A.Times* that his new agents (the William Morris agency) had been trying to persuade him to move there, but that he was only interested in going to the city to work. In January, Nicol celebrated five years of being together with Andrea Weber. In the spring, he took Luke to Europe for a holiday before returning to the USA in mid-April to appear in a film being shot in Washington under the direction of Bob Rafelson, best known for his collaborations with Jack Nicholson such as *Five Easy Pieces* and *The Postman Always Rings Twice*. *Black Widow* was a restrained, intelligent thriller starring Debra Winger as a federal agent on the trail of serial husband-killer Theresa Russell. Nicol had a fairly small role as William McCrory, a museum curator who becomes one of Russell's victims, but his American accent was convincing and he made the most of his limited screen time to deliver a finely detailed, nuanced portrait of a wealthy, slightly stuffy academic falling in love. Nicol liked Russell very much, but had less time for Winger and found Rafelson 'distant'. Although the film received largely positive reviews and did well at the box office, grossing $25 million, it was really a vehicle for its female stars, so any positive impact it may have had on Nicol's career would have been relatively minor.

In June, shortly after returning to New York, Nicol married Andrea Weber in a private ceremony with only one guest in attendance. The event received no press coverage as Weber had urged Nicol to keep the marriage a secret until later. The couple had their honeymoon at Nicol's house in Amsterdam where, much to Nicol's chagrin, they were soon joined by Weber's brother and his girlfriend. Weber's closeness to her large family would become a major source of irritation to Nicol as he cared little for any of them and felt that he was continually forced to host them at his own expense. Weber returned to the States ahead of Nicol, who stayed on in Amsterdam. He had received an offer to do a theatre evening in Hollywood and began planning a revival of his one-man show. He then made a short trip to London before returning to New York and Andrea Weber in July.

Luke visited his father for a few days in August, after which Nicol flew to the West Coast to prepare for his new show. The venue, the

Hollywood Playhouse, was not very grand – a 240-seat theatre just off Sunset Boulevard on Las Palmas Avenue. Under the title *Nicol Williamson: An Evening with a Man and His Band*, the production was to run for four weeks from the 25th of August. Backed by a five-piece led by Billy Bremner, Nicol performed his usual eclectic mix of songs and poems, but included material by artists such as Lenny Bruce, Johnny Cash, Little Richard and Stevie Wonder for the first time. Also new were standards such as 'Ol' Man River' and 'Granada', Randy Newman's 'Love in Cherokee Country', Roger McGough's 'Separate Ways' and the Walter de la Mare poem 'De Profundis', whose unflinching view of death had frightened Nicol as a child. During an interview with the *L.A. Times*, Nicol made the surprising assertion that 'The supreme irony of my life is that my metier is light comedy,' and went on to explain how the evening was an attempt to recreate the feeling of the past when people would make their own entertainment, speaking nostalgically about Saturday nights with his family when they would gather together to sing songs and tell jokes and stories. The opening night went well and Nicol played to a full house. Weber had flown out to join him and a number of celebrities were in attendance, as well as press photographers and TV crews.

In the *L.A. Times* the following day, theatre critic Dan Sullivan wrote that Nicol's delivery had frequently been impressive, especially in a piece designed to demonstrate his ability with accents, which Sullivan described as 'a survey of British speech from Cork to Perth to London.' However, he also felt that the show was too random in construction and Nicol had not opened himself up enough to the audience. The television reviews were much more positive, but after the first week the audience numbers dropped drastically and it became clear that a four-week run had been over-optimistic. At the beginning of the third week, Nicol – who had been paying for the band himself – was forced to pull the show.

Shortly after his return to New York, Nicol was approached by a writer, Henry F. Mazel, who lived in the same building. Mazel had written a screenplay entitled *Favouring Harry Gold*, which he bravely thrust into Nicol's hand. When he read the script a few days later, Nicol was pleasantly surprised to find it an original, witty New York comedy with elements of fantasy. He met with Mazel to discuss the project on a number of occasions, but it would remain unmade.

Chapter 22 – Things Fall Apart

Nicol and Andrea planned to spend Christmas and New Year at his house in Amsterdam, where they would be joined by both Luke and Hugh, Nicol's father. In order to ensure that Andrea was happy, Nicol suggested that she could bring her family as well – an offer she enthusiastically accepted. Nicol went ahead to Amsterdam to prepare the house before his guests trickled in over the next few days. The festivities proceeded happily enough at first, but when Jeannie Weber arrived on the 30th, the atmosphere became tense. Nicol had always felt that she had tried to poison Andrea against him and was convinced that she was attempting to stir up trouble. On New Year's Eve he finally exploded and told her in no uncertain terms exactly what he thought of her. The result was that Jeannie left the house that night, taking Andrea and the rest of the Webers with her. Nicol returned to New York a couple of days later and met with Andrea, but the two were unable to reconcile.

Nicol had suffered from a dearth of good offers on the acting front for the previous six months, with the result that he had accepted an unchallenging but well-paid role as the heavy in a western TV pilot entitled, appropriately enough, *Desperado*. Brooding about the state of his marriage throughout the flight, he flew to Tucson where the film was to be shot. On his arrival at the airport, he was unimpressed with the attitude of the driver who had been sent to collect him and decided on the spot to do a U-turn. He backed out of the film and returned to New York to commence divorce proceedings. The producers of *Desperado* managed to find a last-minute replacement in Nicol's former colleague, David Warner, but it was to be one of a number of incidents which would damage his film career.

Returning to New York, Nicol managed to persuade his lawyer to arrange a quick divorce and by the end of January he was no longer married. Nicol never fully recovered from the breakdown of his second marriage and the next few years were to prove difficult to say the least. Luke Williamson:

> When his second marriage ended it really put him into a depression that he never recovered from. There were four or five years after that where I honestly didn't know if he was going to make it and during that time my grandfather's life collapsed – he'd never gotten over the death of his wife and he was paralysed after that, he let his brother take over the business, he just took his hands off the wheel, he didn't care. Everything fell apart and, during this time, Dad was also falling apart and he was not present enough. It was one of the greatest and most terrible regrets in his life that he was so clouded by what he was going through that he wasn't aware and he was unable to help Papa. He could have fixed that for him financially but he was just unavailable. He and I didn't see each other very much and when we did it was dark and difficult. Dad suffered with extreme depression. I wouldn't call it manic or bipolar because he didn't really seem to have ups. He was just in this incredible depth of depression and it made him react to things in a dark way. It led almost to a state of paranoia where he just assumed that everybody had it in for him and that he was just getting fucked from every angle and he could see the next knife coming.

Due to a lack of better offers, Nicol recorded an audiobook version of the Jack Higgins thriller *A Prayer for the Dying* while waiting for a more fulfilling role to come along. That finally happened when he was offered the lead in a Stephen King adaptation, *Apt Pupil*. The screenplay, by brothers Jim and Ken Wheat, was strong and the director, Alan Bridges, was one of the most underrated of British filmmakers. Bridges had previously made a number of acclaimed features, such as *The Shooting Party* and *The Hireling*, the latter of which had won the Grand Prix at Cannes. The film's producer, Richard Kobritz, had enjoyed success with two previous Stephen King adaptations, *Salem's Lot* and *Christine*. The story concerned a teenaged boy in a small American town who discovers that the old man living down the road is, in fact, a Nazi war criminal in hiding. However, the boy is more interested in learning about history first-hand than he is in revealing the identity of the fugitive. The role of the Nazi, Kurt

Dussander, had originally been intended for James Mason, who had died, and subsequently for Richard Burton, who had also died. Paul Scofield, Alec Guinness and John Gielgud had all turned it down. Ignoring any feelings of trepidation about a role with such ill-luck attached to it, Nicol accepted the part with some excitement. It was undoubtedly a juicy role unlike anything he had played before and the production promised to be a quality one. Former child star Ricky Schroder, who had played Jon Voight's son in *The Champ*, was to play the title role.

Shooting began on the 13th of July 1987 in Los Angeles. Emma Hamelynck stayed with Nicol at the Franklin Hotel in Hollywood throughout the shoot. During his time with Andrea she had been in a relationship with someone else but had also recently split up, so they tried to console each other as best they could. She remembered Nicol at this time as having suffered a tremendous blow to his pride. He felt that Andrea had betrayed him and was furious about it. The role of Dussander may have provided a welcome distraction for Nicol, but it was to prove short-lived – the shooting of *Apt Pupil* was brought to a halt after five weeks when cheques to the cast and crew began to bounce. There were supposedly just ten days more shooting necessary to complete the film. The financing had collapsed, just as it had on *The Human Factor* eight years previously. Unfortunately, in this case there were no moguls prepared to sell houses and valuable works of art in order to proceed. A restart date was announced for the 9th of September but, when it came around, the required funding had still not been found and any possibility for a restart was delayed indefinitely. Several attempts were made to continue, but by the time it may have been possible, Schroder was year older and his appearance had apparently changed so much that the film could not be completed. Nicol felt he had been giving the performance of his career as Dussander, so the disaster was a tremendous disappointment for him at a time when he was already low after his divorce. Stephen King, a writer not always enthusiastic about adaptations of his books, was later quoted as saying he had seen the footage and it was '*real* good!'

Nicol had another film lined up to begin shooting in October, first in Madrid and then in Berlin. *Berlin Blues*, a $3 million Spanish production to be shot in English, was an update of the German classic *The Blue Angel*, which had made a star out of Marlene Dietrich. The remake was intended as a vehicle for American soprano and actress Julia Migenes. Nicol was cast in the Emil Jannings role as the stuffy professor who becomes obsessed with a nightclub singer. He arrived in Madrid on schedule and completed the first week's shooting, but shortly into the second week he walked off the picture. Julia Migenes remembered that Nicol 'blew up at the director and producer and stormed out of Madrid,' then 'left without telling anybody, with the "do not disturb" sign hanging on the hotel room door.' The reason for Nicol's explosion is unknown,[77] but when the producers replaced him with Keith Baxter, not only did they have to reshoot Nicol's scenes, they also had to rebuild some of the sets they had used and subsequently torn down.

It is difficult to judge the extent to which the *Desperado* and *Berlin Blues* walk-outs may have affected Nicol's career. The first incident received no press, the second only a brief mention in *Variety*. The fact that it had taken place in Spain on a production with a modest budget may account for this, along with the fact that Nicol's fame was by this time on the wane. However, it seems likely that people in the industry would have got wind of such stories and become understandably nervous about employing him. It is certainly the case that the next couple of years would prove to be quiet ones for Nicol, at least on the acting front. In 1988, his name was seen only on an audiobook adaptation of Paul Erdman's financial thriller *The Panic of '89* and as the voiceover narrator of a Channel 4 documentary about Neville Chamberlain's policy of appeasement towards Hitler, entitled *Peace in Our Time?*

Nicol finally returned to acting in the spring of 1989. The television series *Mistress of Suspense* (also known as *Chillers*) was an international co-production based on stories by the American crime writer Patricia Highsmith, best known for *Strangers on a Train* and *The Talented Mr Ripley*. Robert Bierman, who had recently directed the cult classic *Vampire's Kiss* (in which star Nicolas Cage famously ate a live cockroach), was given the opportunity to direct one of the eight 50-minute stand-alone episodes that would comprise Season 1. Bierman opted for a script entitled *A Curious Suicide* and remembered:

> I think that was the best one because the characters were good and they'd actually fitted very well in the Highsmith style of storytelling… it was written by Evan Jones, who'd done a lot of good films before, like *King and Country* and *Modesty Blaise*.

One of the production companies involved in the series was Disney, who presented Bierman with a list of fifty approved actors, one of whom was Nicol. Although it may seem odd for Nicol to have appeared on such a list given the *Berlin Blues* incident, it is perhaps understandable as his only previous association with Disney had been on *Return to Oz*, during the filming of which he had been one of the few elements which had *not* presented a problem.

Bierman had previously worked in film preservation and one of the films he had helped to preserve was *Inadmissible Evidence*. He had been deeply impressed by Nicol's performance so, when he saw his name on the list, he decided that he had found his leading actor. The Disney executives repeatedly asked Bierman if he was sure that he really wanted to cast Nicol Williamson, but did not attempt to dissuade him. For the female lead, Bierman opted for Jane Lapotaire, and remembered,

> I had seen her in the theatre and a few TV things before, but it was because of a movie called *Eureka* by Nic Roeg, where Jane played opposite Mickey Rourke and she was great. The performance stuck in my head and when the part to play Nicol's wife came up I immediately thought of her. I had no idea she had worked together before with Nicol. I just thought they seemed well matched and believable. She was terrific in the part, a wonderful actress to direct and brilliant with Nicol.

Nicol was to play Steven McCullough, an American doctor holidaying in England with his wife. The two are clearly trapped in a loveless marriage. She wants to spend her time shopping and encourages him to visit an old university friend, Roger Fain (played by Barry Foster), who now lives in Wales. He agrees, apparently with reluctance, but in fact he has the perfect murder in mind. McCullough has secretly never forgiven Fain for 'stealing' and subsequently marrying his true love, who has recently died. The one flaw in his plan is that, despite his best efforts, McCullough has never been able to deceive his wife. She knows very well that he has never loved her and is, in fact, still in love with Fain's dead wife.

Nicol liked both the script and the director and agreed to play the part, which would be shot in Cardiff in late April – May 1989. Bierman asked Evan Jones to write a monologue for Nicol which would give his character more of a back story. Thinking that Nicol would be pleased, Bierman was in for a shock:

> He'd been great all the way up to that point. The part had been good and not difficult to do and he'd been working well with Jane and the other actors and he'd been no trouble. But the morning of this big speech, the prop man came to me and said, 'Nicol has been raiding the prop drink – he thinks it's real drink and he's been drinking it.' I said, 'Have you gotten all the real drink away from the location?' He came back and said, 'Nicol's found the real drink…' or he'd found a bottle of something. So Nicol turned up on the set… and he hadn't been drinking at all [until then], but obviously this particularly long speech he had to give had made him quite nervous and he'd turned to the drink. And he was bright red … you know, like a stop light! He was this Scotsman and he had that sort of skin and everybody could see he'd just turned bright red – obviously the drink had flushed him out – and he was swaying a little bit and we thought, 'Oh my god!' We sent him off to make-up to try and powder him down and ply him with coffee and… this went on for hours! And Barry, the other guy who he had this big speech with, was so fabulous and so good with him. We kept bringing Nicol back and he could only do like two lines of this speech and then he'd forget it and then I'd send him back for more coffee and powder, and this went on

nearly all day, and I cursed myself for giving this fabulous speech to him which was obviously exactly what he didn't want. But we were committed to it... so we spent the whole day shooting this one speech in little bits because Nicol just couldn't actually command the whole speech, which was my fault – I should never have given him such a big speech. Anyway, I think it really upset him and he kept apologising and we'd got on very well, and he'd ring me up from then on at two o'clock in the morning in my hotel, apologising, and saying, 'I'm not happy about tomorrow.' He became much more delicate and tricky to work with after this thing, and he'd gone back on the booze.

Nicol had perhaps viewed *A Curious Suicide* as a suitable project for him to test the waters and return to acting without diving straight in at the deep end. The original script was strong and gave him a character of more than one dimension, but at the same time did not demand anything too taxing of him. His confidence was still very low after his disastrous marriage to Andrea Weber, as Jane Lapotaire observed:

> Having been through a divorce myself, it shakes you to the very roots of your being... and you can't be as great an actor as Nicol was without being that sensitive... I think the break-up went a long way to destroying him, because by the time we worked on *A Curious Suicide*, I used to beg my driver to get me back to the hotel in Cardiff before Nicol because the bar was in the entrance of the hotel and if I came in after he'd got back there, I would be nabbed and have to listen, as I did on many occasions, to this musical that he had written about how much he hated his mother-in-law. It was evident to me then that this was a person who'd gone off the rails. He had this big script that he'd written – the songs and the book under his arm – most of the time that we were filming there.
>
> Knowing what I know now and looking back on it, at the time I didn't know how vulnerable a person Nicol was during those *Macbeth / Uncle Vanya* years, but once we got to doing *A Curious Suicide*, I realized he was being eaten up by something very dark. I don't remember him being drunk on stage *ever*. Even when we were doing *Macbeth* at the

BBC, never did I smell alcohol on his breath. I think he was in control of it, but by the time we did *A Curious Suicide* that control had gone.

However, the remainder of the episode was shot without any major problems, although Bierman did experience one more difficult situation at the wrap party:

> We were in Cardiff and we went to a big club with all the crew and the actors. We were having a great time. Nicol managed to down a lot of drinks and started to get into an argument with the bouncer of the club, who was this rather short but stocky black guy who looked very tough. Nicol was very tall and he was looking at this guy and sizing him up. I knew this guy would completely and utterly decimate Nicol if they got into a fight, which was looking quite probable, and then I walked up and I heard Nicol say, 'Okay, let's get our trousers down and see who's got the biggest cock!' and I thought, 'Oh my god!' so I grabbed Nicol, dragged him out of the club before this bouncer smashed him one. It was closing time, so I was dragging him down the street as all the people were coming out onto the street, and Nicol was bumping into them and trying to pick a fight. I stopped him from having at least three or four fights on the streets of Cardiff, and took him back to the hotel. We stayed up all night and he downed a few more drinks and then eventually I put him to bed. Fortunately, we'd finished filming and the next day he'd forgotten all about it. We had our breakfast and he'd given me his next script and he wanted me to direct his next film… we stayed in touch for a bit and then that was the last I saw of him.
>
> He seemed to be a man of two parts – the drinker and the non-drinker. The drink seemed to have a really bad effect on him and… [at this point] it seemed to be very destructive in his memory and his confidence had gone. But when he wasn't drinking he was very confident, he was great to direct, he did anything I wanted and he was a fabulous actor and could be subtle and do all sorts of lovely things. But as soon as he started to get on the drink, which I think came from nerves and lack of confidence… I'd created a rod for my own back by having this long speech written for him thinking it would make him so creatively happy… but it was obviously the worst thing I could have done.

I remember when I was talking to him you could see that there was this…this thing that was like a dual personality, almost schizophrenic. I felt that he was always suppressing something, I think there was an anger and a possible other side to him that he constantly needed to suppress and I think drink brought about the other face of Nicol that probably wasn't the face that he wanted to show, but the face that came out. And it was aggressive and, you know, when he started to take on this bloke in the bar who would have decimated him… he'd started to almost visualise himself as another person, as if he was young or something… this bouncer would have just destroyed him! He'd got this bizarre, quite aggressive courage to take people on, and I don't know if people have reported fights or anything but he looked like he wanted to have one!

In terms of a bloke, I got on *really* well with him and I liked him a great deal. He was very kind and gentle and very good to me and marvellous with the other actors. But I remember we were shooting a scene outside… somebody jumping off a bridge or something… anyway, it was a big scene, and my first assistant wasn't particularly good and Nicol laid into him and gave him a mouthful and destroyed him… and he wasn't wrong, but the guy just wasn't as good as he should have been. So I think the thing I saw with Nicol was that he would judge people and if he didn't think they were up to it he didn't give them much chance. He would find their weaknesses and he'd really let them have it. He didn't suffer fools and he didn't suffer people who couldn't do their job, and he was obviously very good, but it was very interesting – as soon as he got himself into a position of weakness, he was castigating… so it was a strange cycle when I worked with him. He seemed to go in this cycle that came with booze, lack of confidence… but when things were working he was terrific.

I was quite young when I did this and I thought it was great having Nicol and I was really pleased to have him. I thought also he was a Patricia Highsmith-type person – because he was damaged and he was good for the part because of his damaged quality as all her characters carry these kinds of damaged back stories. So, besides the long speech which we eventually cut together, it was okay. I think Nicol was right for the part and I know Disney were absolutely thrilled with him and thought it was the best one they'd done…

In the finished episode, Nicol's complexion does indeed look quite florid in certain scenes, his eyes appear a little bloodshot and his speech, although not slurred, seems slacker than usual. However, although it is clear that he was at his lowest ebb at this time, he still manages to give an eloquent performance and, as Bierman points out, his damaged quality fits the character, who also appears to seek solace in alcohol. In fact, all three leads give well-judged, understated portrayals in which a look often conveys more than the dialogue, and both Evan Jones and Robert Bierman deserve credit for trusting their actors and avoiding any clumsy exposition.

In a bizarre footnote, Bierman also had a problem with another famous actor during the shoot. Anthony Perkins appeared Rod Serling-style at the beginning and end of each episode to introduce the story and provide some pithy comments. Bierman recalled what happened when he arrived in Cardiff to film his part:

> He was staying at the same hotel as me and there was another Anthony Perkins staying there, and before the actor Anthony Perkins arrived, a package had arrived for him and gone to the other Anthony Perkins, who opened it – and it was full of drugs! So the actor Anthony Perkins had sent ahead some drugs for himself and unfortunately for him the other Anthony Perkins who was already there had got it, opened it, the police came, and as soon as the actor Anthony Perkins arrived he was arrested to be put on the next plane home. So the producers begged to have two hours before the plane came in which to shoot him, which is what you see, and then he was sent home never to be able to come into Britain again!

Chapter 23 – Last of the Controlled Madmen

By the end of the '80s, Nicol had become frustrated with having to wait until a decent role happened along. This was no doubt partly due to the fact that his career was not in good shape and the wait was becoming longer and longer. He was also now well into his 50s and mortality was creeping closer – his former agent, Milton Goldman, died in October 1989, and Samuel Beckett followed in December. It was understandable, then, that Nicol wanted to spend his remaining time doing work he believed in. He decided to take matters into his own hands.

Nicol had been greatly impressed by the posthumous autobiography of Sergei Kourdakov, an ardent young communist and naval cadet who had been assigned the task of raiding clandestine religious meetings held by Christians in the USSR. Although the official policy was that citizens had the right to religious freedom, the country's officials considered those who believed in Christ to be a danger to the Communist Party. Kourdakov and his men would receive tip-offs from insiders, then break up their gatherings in the most brutal and violent fashion. However, Kourdakov became interested in a young woman named Natasha, who continued defiantly to attend meetings despite being badly beaten on several occasions. As a result, he began to read parts of the New Testament in order to understand why she refused to abandon her faith. Moved by what he read, he subsequently became a believer himself, defected to Canada and later died in mysterious circumstances, probably assassinated by the KGB.

It seems that Nicol was attracted to the story purely because he felt it would make a strong basis for a film. Certainly, neither of the twin themes of communism and Christianity were especially close to his heart. However, being a classic tale of redemption, it was not unrealistic to believe that it might be possible to attract the interest of studios and investors. Nicol was too old to play Kourdakov, who died at the age of 21, but made sure there would be a good role in it for him – he intended to play the KGB agent, Captain Shaposhnikov, who recruits Kourdakov for his anti-Christian campaign. The character was loosely based on the real-life Ivan Azarov. Nicol developed a screenplay at his house in Amsterdam with writer Alexander Pym, which they titled *The Alpha Man* in reference to Kourdakov's status as the best in his group of cadets. Whether Nicol was dissatisfied with their first attempt or advised by someone else that the project required more work is unclear, but he later hired the English playwright David Pownall to re-work the script. Pownall had had success with his Soviet-themed 1983 play *Master Class*, which it is likely that Nicol had seen when it was staged by the Roundabout Theatre Company in New York in 1986.

Nicol spent some time at Pownall's house in Muswell Hill discussing the project. The title was changed to *Forbidden Belief*. The character of Shaposhnikov, described in the screenplay as 'a tall, well-built, quirky and intense looking middle aged man' was a fanatic reminiscent of Major Horn in *The Wilby Conspiracy*, although this time the character had an addiction to vodka rather than cigarettes.

Maurice Landsberger, who had worked on a number of films as a production accountant, was to co-executive produce together with David Dao, a novice. They managed to attract the interest of Sir Maurice Laing, one of the senior executives of the Laing construction company, who promised to help with part of the finance, and New Moon, a production company based at Pinewood Studios, also became involved. Juliette Caton, a young actress who had appeared as an angel in Martin Scorsese's *The Last Temptation of Christ*, was tentatively cast as Natasha (renamed Tatyana) and the plan was to shoot most of the film in Russia. Pownall remembered Nicol 'going to Hollywood to get studio backing and constantly changing the script himself to fit in with their suggestions.' As a result, he finally washed his hands of the project, but remembered Nicol with great affection as a 'genially demonic force, an intense spirit' who would play piano at the playwright's house with great passion, 'which was his way with everything'.

It seems safe to assume that Nicol's bank balance must have been running low by this point. For Dove Audio, he recorded abridged versions of Mary Stewart's popular Merlin trilogy, *The Crystal Cave*, *The Hollow Hills* and *The Last Enchantment*. Originally published in the 1970s, the novels retold the story of King Arthur from Merlin's point of view.

William Peter Blatty had heard on the grapevine that Nicol's career was not in great shape and felt that he owed him a favour for extricating himself from *The Ninth Configuration* so that he had been able to cast the more suitable Stacy Keach. Blatty was directing his second feature, based on his own novel, *Legion*, a sequel to *The Exorcist* which Twentieth Century Fox had insisted he re-christen *Exorcist III*. After seeing Blatty's first cut, they had then objected that the film did not contain an exorcism, forcing Blatty to come up with a new ending. Blatty created a new character to wage battle with the demon during the climax, a priest called Father Morning, whose previous experience of performing an exorcism had made his hair turn white overnight. Requiring an actor with a commanding presence, he saw a perfect opportunity to help Nicol, who remembered it this way:

> On two occasions [*Exorcist III* and *Spawn*] I have accepted something which was piss-poor to me, but for a bag full of money when I was about to lose my house in Amsterdam… I got on the plane and I threw myself into it [*Exorcist III*]. I made two or three suggestions because unless you play it as Chekhov – or like you feel it is – you're never going to make what *is* there work.
>
> I was very nice to them at the end of that movie. They had me strapped in a frame and flying around and I thought, 'Who needs this?'… They were really fucking everyone about, so I waited until about 11.30 and they said, 'We'll get this – it might be two in the morning, but we'll get it.' I said, 'Not with me you won't.' They said, 'What do you mean?' I said, 'Well, there is in my contract a clause which says that on

the stroke of midnight you have to pay me $55,000 a day.' He ran over to the Second Assistant and there was some conflab and it came back, 'He's right!' That put the bullet right up the anus! Their faces drained and that was it – so, at 11.59, I was released from the thing and they put the stuff in the can. I had already done four extra days at something like $20,000 a day extra. I was saved again at the last minute.[78]

Nicol's sequences were shot at Fox studios in March 1990. Despite his low opinion of the material and the fact that the part of Father Morning offered little challenge, *Exorcist III* was a well-made, often genuinely scary film with a witty, intelligent script full of well-drawn characters portrayed by some of the finest actors in the business, including George C. Scott, Ed Flanders, Brad Dourif, Jason Miller, Scott Wilson and Viveca Lindfors, many of whom had been in *The Ninth Configuration*. Nicol spent some of his surplus *Exorcist III* money on recording a batch of songs produced, oddly, by Midge Ure, but the recordings were never released.

On the 8th of January 1991, Nicol returned to New York on a 6-month working visa and moved into apartment 1-R at 407 West 44th Street. He had accepted a part in a Broadway production of a comedy entitled *I Hate Hamlet*, which would mark his first stage appearance since *The Real Thing* in 1985. Nicol was to play the ghost of the American actor John Barrymore, who had been a star of stage and screen for thirty years before his alcohol-related death at the age of 60 in 1942. The plot, such as it was, concerned a modern-day actor about to play Hamlet who rents Barrymore's old apartment only to find it haunted by the ghost of its famous former tenant. The mischievous spirit then proceeds to interfere with the young actor's life and offer a great deal of unsolicited advice. Paul Rudnick had been inspired to write *I Hate Hamlet* after having rented Barrymore's former apartment himself.

The play was to be staged at the Walter Kerr Theatre on West 48th Street, which had a capacity of 975, making it one of the smaller Broadway theatres. It was the third Broadway production to be directed by Michael Engler, who later moved successfully into television. The cast also featured Alan Arkin's son Adam, Hollywood veteran Celeste Holm, known for her roles in *Gentleman's Agreement* and *All About Eve*, and Evan Handler as the young actor. Handler, a 30-year-old New Yorker, had been acting in film and theatre for ten years.

In a piece published in *The New Yorker* in 2007, Rudnick stated that he had initially felt very lucky indeed to have been able to obtain the services of Nicol, who assured him that he had 'not touched a drop in over a year' despite visible evidence to the contrary. Shortly after the play opened, an interview with Nicol appeared in the *Evening Standard* in which he said he thought that the play was 'silly, but nice silly' and had been hoping that the Barrymore role could be expanded to give it 'a little more juice' but that he had found Rudnick 'a little intransigent'. He also told the *Standard*'s Michael Owen that he thought of himself as 'the last of the controlled madmen' and, significantly, went on to say, 'I'll get ten more years of acting, no, maybe eight. After that you become a side-show and a side-show I will never be.'

The first week's rehearsals went smoothly enough and Nicol appeared to get on well with his colleagues. He invited Rudnick to his apartment one evening and sang him some songs from the musical he had written about Andrea Weber and her family, accompanying himself on a Hohner organ. On another occasion, to prepare for a scene in the play in which Barrymore's ghost is summoned, the cast gathered at Rudnick's and performed a séance. According to Rudnick, the medium they had hired instructed them to focus on a particular door, which supposedly moved of its own volition when Nicol urged Barrymore to manifest himself. Rudnick also stated that Nicol had begun phoning him in the early hours with various suggestions including, on one occasion, that Handler be removed from the play so that Nicol could play his part as well. Rudnick felt that Nicol had been 'sensational' during the early previews, which began on the 18th of March, but soon started to behave unprofessionally in a variety of ways. These included propositioning the stage manager, commenting on other actors' performances during the show, leaving the stage when his character was supposed to be observing the action and even, on one occasion, taking a swing at Rudnick. In a 1994 interview for *The Guardian*, Nicol had a few words to say about Rudnick and his colleagues, whom he saw as a kind of Jewish clique who sat around laughing at their own in-jokes in an irritatingly 'self-congratulatory' fashion. After opening night on the 8th of April, the cast gathered at the Tavern On The Green, where Nicol utilized the house band to accompany him while he performed a number of songs.

Writing for the *New York Times*, David Richards had nothing but praise for Nicol's performance, noting how he was able to switch from extracting every ounce of humour from the dialogue to delivering Hamlet's speech to the players completely straight. Richards also defended the light comedy nature of the play, but had harsh words to say about Evan Handler's performance.

According to one of the show's producers, James B. Freydberg, during the performance of the 2nd of May, Nicol began coaching Handler on stage, telling him to 'put some life into it!' Later, during the swordfight towards the end of the first act, the choreography broke down and Nicol struck Handler rather too enthusiastically on the backside with the flat of his sword. Handler walked out then and there. Nicol turned to the audience and asked, 'Should I sing?' The curtain came down on the first act and the audience, which included Gregory Peck and Elaine Stritch, applauded enthusiastically, perhaps thinking it was all part of the show. However, when the curtain went up on the second act, Handler had been replaced by his understudy, Andrew Mutnick, who took over for the remainder of the run. Handler told the press that he had quit the show because, from the first day of rehearsals, he had 'endured the show's producers condoning Nicol Williamson's consistent abusiveness to other cast members.' Nicol declined to comment. The incident received a considerable amount of press attention, even making the front page of the *New York Post* under the headline 'B' WAY SWORD PLAY:

Hamlet actor storms off stage after co-star whacks him in butt.' The story would become much exaggerated in the years to follow, and it was frequently claimed that Nicol had actually stabbed Handler with his sword. While the publicity did no harm to the box office receipts, the same could not be said for Nicol's already tarnished reputation. The play closed on the 22nd of June after 88 performances and Nicol returned to Amsterdam.

Another quiet period followed for Nicol. He recorded an abridged audiobook of Jude Deveraux's historical romance *The Duchess* for Simon & Schuster and continued his attempts to get *Forbidden Belief* off the ground before finally dropping it the following year. He also began working on another project which he instigated himself – he had become interested in John Barrymore as a result of *I Hate Hamlet* and began researching the actor's life in order to write a one-man play about him. He related to Barrymore on some levels – both actors had given ground-breaking performances as Hamlet, for example – but, more than anything, he admired Barrymore as the only actor to have begun in vaudeville and gone on to become a matinee idol, a great classical actor and a versatile Hollywood star able to alternate between romantic leads, character parts and comic roles. He also respected Barrymore for not complaining when his career declined to the point of self-parody in later years.

In 1992, 48-year-old writer, producer and director Leslie Megahey received an opportunity to make his first feature film. Previously, Megahey had (at separate times) been the editor of both the BBC's major arts documentary strands, *Omnibus* (for which he had won a BAFTA) and *Arena*. The BBC had agreed to co-finance Megahey's film *The Hour of the Pig* alongside Harvey Weinstein's Miramax and a number of other companies. Megahey's script told an original story based around the strange but true medieval practice of putting animals on trial for so-called 'crimes'. He managed to assemble an impressive cast headed by Colin Firth as the defense lawyer who abandons his career in a Paris he sees as cynical and decadent in favour of what he expects to be a more honorable practice in the rural town of Abbeville. The cast also featured Ian Holm as the local priest, Donald Pleasence as the prosecuting attorney and Harriet Walter as an unfortunate peasant woman hanged as a witch. As the director remembered, Nicol was not the first choice to play sinister local nobleman Seigneur Jehan d'Auferre (a role rather similar to the one he had played in *The Monk*, which Megahey had not seen):

> I actually had Max von Sydow for the part and I had a call from his agent saying that he was walking around a lake in Sweden feeling guilty because he'd decided to do a horror film[79] in Hollywood for a huge amount of money instead. I was so proud of getting Max von Sydow to be in my film so it was very disappointing and as we were getting near shooting they'd already started making the costumes. So I went through the usual suspects who could play the heavy – Richard Harris, Oliver Reed and people like that, and they were all occupied doing other films. At one point I offered it to Alan Rickman who quite rightly said, 'No, it's too much like the Sherriff of Nottingham.' As in a villain with a bit of a sense of humour and who's a bit flip. The character's someone who looks like they might be the classical mediaeval heavy but actually turns out to be a rather modern entrepreneurial rationalist. And then – I'm sure this question must have happened so many times in the film business around this period – somebody said, 'Whatever happened to Nicol Williamson?' Well, the first thing I did was I rang Jack Gold and said, 'What's Nicol really like?' And Jack was such a lovely bloke... I was his First Assistant at one stage when I joined the BBC. I worked on his very first drama and my main achievement was to drive Jack's car up onto a Cotswolds ridge and leave it in such a vertiginous position over a river bed that we had to hire a tractor to get it out. It was like the ending of *The Italian Job*, but sideways. I wasn't a very good A.D. Anyway, he said, 'The thing about Nicol is he's got this terrible reputation but when he appears on set, if he feels secure and he feels you know what you're doing and the people around you know what they're doing, he will be absolutely professional. He'll just turn up, he'll do his bit and he'll probably go off and sit in his dressing room until you need him next.' So he was very positive about him.
>
> Nic took a bit of tracking down – which was typical of him – but then they found him in Amsterdam and got the script to him there.

Nicol said yes very quickly – he read it straight away and was over in London as fast as we needed him, which had to be pretty fast as Max von Sydow's departure hadn't left us much time to make the costumes, etc. I remember one particular idea got lost because of this delay – when the Seigneur first appears I had wanted his costume made to look exactly like (i.e. to merge into) the colour and pattern of the tapestry behind him in the hall of the castle, so that he would be invisible when Courtois walked in, then he would turn to speak and it would be a shock. Our costume designer couldn't get it made in time and had to find a similar off the peg one.

Much of the film was shot in Perouges, a medieval town near Lyons which had changed little over the centuries. However, as Nicol's scenes were almost entirely interiors, his parts were shot later at Ealing Studios in November 1992. Leslie Megahey:

His reputation preceded him, so the actors were all going round saying, 'Who's he going to punch first?' I think people were generally pretty nervous, because he wasn't there for the first part of the shoot, so I told them, when he arrived, they had to call me from the studio. And I deliberately went out – which you don't normally do, you normally wait for someone to turn up on set, then you go and greet them and tell them how pleased you are to see them and all that stuff. But I got them to call me. He was in make-up at the time, so I went to the make-up room and just said, 'I'm really pleased you're doing this and I'm looking forward to it.' He seemed slightly surprised, so I assume this wasn't often done to him, so I felt we got off to a good start. Then he came and he did exactly as Jack said.

When he'd settled in a bit, he'd come on and make some baleful jokes, like he'd walk in at 8 o'clock in the morning saying, 'Only twelve hours to go!' but he was really on his best behavior and he was in a very good mood. I think he enjoyed it and he threw no strops at all. The only time I saw him getting slightly rattled was when something had taken much longer than it should have taken and I just went straight up to him and said, 'Don't worry – if we have to, we'll finish it in the morning, so you're not going to be rushed.' And he just completely calmed down. And generally he was terrific.

We didn't socialize after the shoot. In fact, nobody did. When you work at Ealing or one of the big studios, you tend to just go home and put your feet up, so every night he would be off and he would go to wherever he was staying in London and we didn't socialize at all, but by the end of the shoot he got really quite affectionate, and I remember I got in a state which I concealed (or thought I concealed from everybody) because of the BBC suits – the bean counters were all BBC personnel and were rather looked down on by the feature people on it, who were actually much easier to work with than the BBC people were. The actors can just sense what's going on and I was getting quite tense towards the end because I'd always produced my own films in the past, and now I had people telling me I had to go for a meeting and explain how I was going to catch up as I was one scene behind, and all that rubbish that you get when you're doing a feature. And I remember his hand on my shoulder – a great, powerful hand, because he was a huge man and, although he was quite slim, he was very strong – and it sort of gripped my shoulder when somebody was halfway through setting up a shot and he just bent over and he said, 'I can see what's going on and if you need me or any of the other actors – because I know they'll do this – we'll go on working for another two or three days to get this thing done and we'll do it for nothing.' And then he just walked off and I thought, 'This is not the monster I'd been expecting!'

Ian Holm later wrote that he had spent most of the shoot avoiding Nicol as their former friendship had never recovered from Nicol's attempted seduction of Bee Gilbert over two decades earlier. Nicol was visibly healthier than he had been at the time of of *A Curious Suicide* and did not appear to be drinking during the filming. Although the part was not particularly challenging for him, he gave a sly, witty performance which drew good notices from a number of critics, Roger Ebert among them, who praised Nicol for the 'great magisterial vulgarity' he had brought to the role, while Hal Hinson of the *Washington Post* found him 'thin-lipped and viperous, like a cross between George Sanders and the Sheriff of Nottingham.'

Unfortunately, despite a number of favourable reviews, the film was not commercially successful, grossing just $667,078 at the U.S. box office. It had not helped that in America the film had been cut (mainly to reduce the amount of nudity in order to avoid an NC-17 certificate), retitled *The Advocate* and misleadingly promoted as a sexy courtroom thriller in the *Basic Instinct* mode. In reality, *The Hour of the Pig* was too original to be neatly categorised. Although the plot certainly contained an element of mystery, the film was really more of a sophisticated comic drama.

Shortly after *The Hour of the Pig* was completed, Nicol found himself approached by his *Excalibur / Christopher Columbus* co-star, Gabriel Byrne, who wanted him to play police chief Robert Dixon in a film he was producing about Gerry Conlon, one of the 'Guidford Four' who had been wrongly convicted of murder. The film, called *In the Name of the Father*, would go on to be hugely successful. Nicol Williamson:

> It was all these sort of tough Irish guys and this, I thought, rather soft English policeman that gets squelched in the end by Emma Thompson and I just said, 'I'm not wasting my time on that.' I thought, 'There's nothing I can lend to this – you can get anybody to play this. You don't need me and I don't need this.'[80]

The role was eventually played by Corin Redgrave.

Via his then agent Dennis Selinger, Nicol next received an offer from producer Dyson Lovell to play a major role in *Return to Lonesome Dove*, the sequel to the hugely successful TV mini-series *Lonesome Dove*. Concerned about Nicol's reputation, director Mike Robe had telephoned Leslie Megahey beforehand to ask about his recent experience of directing him in *The Hour of the Pig*. Robe had apparently been satisfied with what he had heard. After a couple of telephone conversations with Lovell, Nicol accepted the part of Gregor Dunnigan, an ambitious Scottish cattle baron with a lovely young wife (Reese Witherspoon) who takes the illegitimate son of Captain Call (Jon Voight) under his wing. The son was to be played by Ricky Schroder, Nicol's co-star in the unfinished *Apt Pupil*.

In June 1993 Nicol flew to Butte, Montana, a town of around 30,000 people, to begin filming. According to Lovell, when the driver he had sent to collect Nicol from the airport approached him and asked if he were Nicol Williamson, Nicol denied it, sat on a bench and watched the driver asking other people if they were Nicol Williamson. It is possible that Nicol was enjoying himself at the driver's expense, but it may also have been the case that he had thought the driver to be an autograph hunter as, when approached by stangers, Nicol sometimes chose to deny his own identity in order to get rid of them. When he finally admitted to being himself, he was driven to what Lovell considered to be the 'best hotel in Butte', but Nicol was unimpressed. Nevertheless, he agreed to have dinner with Lovell and Ricky Schroder, whom Lovell had brought along for moral support. However, Nicol apparently drank a lot and ate nothing.

On the following day, Nicol insisted that Lovell come to the hotel and discuss the script with him. When he arrived, Nicol kept him there for the rest of the day making changes which Lovell thought were 'brilliant' and readily agreed to. The next day, after the pages had been retyped and delivered, Nicol again summoned Lovell to the hotel, acted the whole part out for him and then, to Lovell's astonishment, said that now he had played Dunnigan he would be leaving – and proceeded to do just that. The producers contemplated taking legal action against Nicol but eventually decided it would be more trouble than it was worth and simply replaced him with Oliver Reed.

It seems unlikely that such a drastic action on Nicol's part could have been the result of a mere whim, but the reason for it remains unclear. Luke Williamson thought he remembered his father mentioning differences with co-star Jon Voight, while Leslie Megahey recalled him speaking of not being made to feel welcome when he had arrived in Butte. Possibly he may have taken exception to the fact that director Mike Robe had not come to greet him. Robe himself later said that he did not know the reason. Megahey also said that Nicol had been worried for a while afterwards about the possibility of being sued for breach of contract.

Nicol's father, now 80, was ailing at this point, so Nicol spent time with him in Scotland before Hugh passed away on the 6th of October at Stonehouse Hospital. The cause of death was given as 'bronchopneumonia, old age and haematemesis from a duodenal ulcer'. Although Hugh had done impressively well as a self-made man, eventually owning his own steel works, his business had struggled in later years. He had lost most of his money by continuing to employ his workers during a recession and had been living in retirement in a modest house at 4 McLean Gardens in Stonehouse. Nicol was often seen at The Crossford Inn a few miles away around this time. He later told Suzie Mackenzie of the *Evening Standard* that he had asked his father if he wasn't scared of death and oblivion. Hugh's reply had been, 'Nicol, when you go, you go. Life is sweet. And now, if you don't mind, I'd like another cup of tea.' This was not the only death Nicol had to deal with during this period. His old friend Penelope Gilliatt had died in May at the age of 61 as a result of alcoholism. The following February, another of his former agents, Edward Betz, died of AIDS, as Tony Richardson had done in November 1991. Nicol had often predicted he would die young but he was to outlast many of his contemporaries.

Chapter 24 – Too Little, Too Late

On the final day of shooting *The Hour of the Pig*, Nicol had approached Leslie Megahey saying, 'I've got something that I'd like you to read.' He gave him a hand-written script of the play he had written about John Barrymore. After reading it, Megahey telephoned Nicol to say that he thought it could really work and just required a little more structuring. The fact that they agreed to work on it together demonstrates the extent to which Nicol had come to respect Megahey, who had little experience in the theatre, having previously only directed a one-person show at the Old Vic in the '70s.[81] Leslie Megahey:

> All the early script work was done in Nicol's kitchen in Amsterdam or in my kitchen in London. He had read everything he could lay his hands on about Barrymore and the first draft was written entirely by Nicol. I did a lot of restructuring and we then wrote in quite a lot of extra stuff, but I think what lies behind it and lay behind a lot of the *reaction* to it, was the connection between Nicol personally and the Barrymore character. I encouraged him because I thought it was an interesting way to do a one-man show, where you're playing another person but the other person has characteristics and experiences that are so much in common with your own that, in a sense, the character is as much Nic as it is Barrymore. I encouraged him even in things like, at the beginning, when he says, 'I've been accused of punching out fellow actors but I've never punched out a fellow actor in my life!' which is obviously based on the fact that he whacked that guy in *I Hate Hamlet*. I think I gave him the license to make it even closer to him than it had been originally, which offended many people because some people thought you shouldn't do that and that, if you're going to play a character, it should be very strictly that character, but I enjoyed that part of it, and so did Nicol.

The play also contained thinly-veiled digs at both John Gielgud and Kenneth Branagh. Originally entitled *Confessions of an Actor*, it was retitled *Jack – A Night on the Town with John Barrymore.*

A number of people had been trying to entice Nicol back to the London stage for years, although he had apparently himself approached the National Theatre at one point only to find himself rebuffed. He had been absent since the revival of *Inadmissible Evidence* in 1978. Plans began to be hatched for a triumphant comeback. Backing was found courtesy of the 588-seat Criterion Theatre at Piccadilly Circus, which had recently been bought by impresario Sally Greene and her husband Robert Bourne. They had formed their own company, Criterion Productions, with Richard Attenborough as chairman, and *Jack* was to be the first in-house production. It was booked for a run of nine weeks. Nicol made the role of Barrymore an extremely demanding one as he wanted to show everyone what he was capable of. He was attempting something which he felt that no other actor would be able to pull off. For two and a quarter hours a night he would not only play Barrymore, he would play Barrymore playing an array of around seventeen other characters, including Winston Churchill and George Bernard Shaw. He would also play the piano and sing snatches of *The Laughing Policeman* and *Nessun Dorma* to show how Barrymore had trained his voice to achieve an astonishing flexibility, just as Nicol himself had done. Nicol worked hard to get himself in shape, hiring a personal trainer, going for daily runs and sessions at the gym as well as cutting down on alcohol and counting his calories. Leslie Megahey:

> We didn't have the use of a rehearsal room or a theatre until we actually got the thing funded and we got the Criterion. Nicol kept saying, 'You just wait 'til you see me on stage – you don't know what's going to hit you!' And it was absolutely true! When he first got up on stage he just went for it and it was like a tornado – incredible! It was like him in the old days. Hugely energetic, huge booming voice, then the quiet bits, then the funny bits and it was an absolute knockout.

He used to slap his stomach, saying, 'Gotta get rid of this lard!' in that slightly transatlantic accent he had. And in many ways it was almost too energetic a part. I went along with it, occasionally thinking, 'God – am I going to be the cause of Nicol Williamson having a coronary or something?' Because I'd put the thing in about the voice coach teaching Barrymore how to do the speech by running alongside her as she rode her horse and he wanted to wear a running vest – he quite liked wearing scanty clothes! When his physique looked good, he enjoyed showing it off. So he donned this running vest and shorts and I said, 'Well, while you're doing it we might as well put a radio mic on you and you can run out of the wings and round the entire theatre doing 'to be or not to be' and come back in through the front door and down the aisle. He arrived back on stage just as he reached the end of the soliloquy. Of course, that's a hell of a marathon and it's only shortly after that that he gets up and sings *Nessun Dorma*! So it was an enormously physical part – apart from the fact that he's on stage the entire time. He got tired, but for a man of his age it was like doing the Olympics!

Interviews with Nicol appeared in all of the major British newspapers, 'Return of the danger man' being a typical headline. He viewed opening night on the 18th of May as 'judgement day' but was resigned to being unable to control how the play would be received other than by simply giving the best performance he could. On opening night the theatre was full but, according to Lynda Lee-Potter of the *Daily Mail*, the audience was 'extraordinary for its lethargy' and the applause 'perfunctory'. The attitude of many seemed to be not one of celebration at the return of one of the great British actors, but one of challenging him to impress. This may have been an unfortunate result of the pre-publicity strategy – even the posters advertising the play proclaimed at the top 'NICOL WILLIAMSON RETURNS TO THE WEST END.' Nevertheless, an undaunted Nicol invited the audience to stay on after the show and he sang jazz songs with a five-piece band for over an hour.

However, the reviews which appeared the following day were not as positive as had been hoped. Although they were by no means entirely negative, it was a case of being damned with faint praise.

Nicol had perhaps been expecting to blow everyone away and the half-hearted response of the critics may well have given his confidence a knock. Writing for *The Daily Mail*, Jack Tinker felt 'disappointed' that Nicol's power had 'rusted slightly at the joints', whereas Michael Billington in *The Guardian* went further, saying Nicol's old power was 'absent.' Ian Shuttleworth of the *Financial Times* had found Nicol somewhat nervous and restrained at the beginning but felt that he came into his own during the sequence involving Barrymore's voice coach and ended his review by saying that it was 'damned good' to have him back. However, reading between the lines, the main objection seemed to be that the play was not serious enough. If Nicol had come back in a play by Shakespeare or Beckett, he may have received a more enthusiastic response. But not everyone was unimpressed.

Paul Moriarty, Nicol's colleague from his RSC days, attended the first night and remembered, 'we went out drinking afterwards and we were just having a great time because his show had been so wonderful. We were all euphoric, and then – bang! The next day it was all ashes again.' The reason was that, six minutes into the second night's show, Nicol stopped the performance and left the stage. Leslie Megahey:

> It was very near the beginning. There was a sight gag that I'd written in around the point where he said, 'I've never punched a fellow actor in my life! The only time I ever punched somebody was an incompetent spotlight operator who couldn't hit his mark!' and while he said that, he was supposed to walk across the stage and I got the spotlight to stay still so it didn't follow him and then when it got to the line 'he couldn't hit his mark' he glared upwards at the spotlight operator and the spotlight would shoot onto him like it was frightened. And it always got a laugh and then this night he just fluffed the line and stopped and said, 'I never punched anybody really' and then he started walking and the spotlight didn't know what to do and I thought, 'Christ – that's the gag gone down...' and then, to my amazement and everybody else's, he looked at the audience and walked to the front and said, 'I'm sorry, I can't do this anymore. I'm sorry this has cost you money,' and he walked off.

I was in the dress circle and I got down to his dressing room in under a minute. He was already half dressed and ready to go and I said, 'You can't walk out on the audience, you can't walk out on the production crew and you can't walk out on this thing that we've both worked on together.' And he said, 'I'm sorry, I can't do it anymore.' And off he went, into the night. I took it that he meant his career, that's how I read it. But then I knew he'd done things like that before. He was still in make-up but he had all his street clothes on and he absolutely wouldn't continue, there was no way. The poor stage manager had to go on and say, 'Sorry, Mr Williamson's indisposed and we'll give you your money back.'

Luke Williamson was there on the night and Nicol later recalled how Luke had run after him and tried to persuade him to return, arguing that he was playing right into the hands of his critics. They walked around and talked, but Luke had to accept that his father was not going to go back. Meanwhile, word of the incident had rapidly reached the ears of the media, as Leslie Megahey remembered:

Within half an hour of Nicol walking out, the stage door was absolutely blocked with journalists and there were two television news crews outside the front of the theatre. I took the production crew to a pub behind the Criterion.

I think probably just the sheer physical difficulty of the piece might have got to him but it's possible that maybe he'd stayed up too late as well. The weirdest thing of all was that, early the next morning, I met Sally outside Nicol's block of flats – we'd put him in a flat in St. James and I arranged to meet her there at half past eight or nine in the morning. We didn't know if he'd got on a plane and flown home or left the flat, we didn't know where he was. The front door bell was broken, which didn't help. Sally went and sat in a café and I stood by the front door waiting for someone to come out so I could get in and bang on the actual flat door. And Nicol came down the stairs, opened the door, and I said, 'Good morning,' and he said, 'Good morning,' looked in a very good mood, and I said, 'Do you want to take a walk?' and he said, 'Yeah, sure.' We walked around St. James' Park and talked about everything except the show and when Sally couldn't stand it any longer she said,

'Look – are you coming back tonight?' And he said, 'Oh, sure,' as if it was a fait accompli and there was no question about it. He came back and he was fantastic that night. He did the rest of the run without any problem.

Nicol wasn't frightened by things but I think there was a kind of recognition in him if he wasn't going to be able to do something, and he acted on it, in a way, with these walk-outs. But I've begun to wonder whether somehow they re-injected a kind of adrenalin into his work or his performance or his general outlook. Something so dramatic becomes a kind of kick up the backside because it was so noticeable that after that walk-out in London he was so good in the following performances. It is the most extreme thing any actor could possibly do – he's denying his entire profession and craft and disappointing the people who are there to see him, so you wonder if it's like an injection of speed into the veins or something. With Nic or anyone with that kind of self-possession or self-will and lack of regrets about things – because he was one of those real 'never apologise, never explain' school – it's too easy to fall into looking for pseudo-psychiatric motives. Everybody does it with him, everybody tries to find the solution – was he frightened of exposing himself in public? Well, no, really – he lived for it. It was something much more complex than that.

The walk-off received a huge amount of publicity, but unfortunately it was not the kind to boost the box office and the Criterion was inundated with telephone calls from people requesting refunds. When Nicol did return for the third night's performance, it received less press than his dramatic departure had done and those who were aware that he had decided to continue were understandably nervous that he might walk off again. On the third night, a Friday, the theatre was only one third full. However, Nicol received a standing ovation after which he uncharacteristically apologized for walking off, explaining that he had underestimated the amount of energy the show required and said that he would rather refund the audience out of his own pocket than give a substandard performance. The theatre did not hold him to this but at the end of a performance a few weeks later, Nicol offered to buy everyone in the audience a drink if they cared to join him in the bar of the Criterion restaurant next door. Quite a few of them took him up on this and Nicol was as good as his word, also taking the trouble to chat to each of his guests individually. However, he was not always so friendly, as Luke Williamson remembered:

> On the third or fourth night we went out to dinner with Sally Greene and the stage manager and Leslie – I think – and we went to the Ivy. There was another table a couple of tables away that had Mick Jagger, Jerry Hall, Tom Stoppard and one of Tom Stoppard's kids I had actually gone to school with – William, I think. He wasn't in my class, he was a year or two ahead of me, so we didn't really know each other at school but I knew who he was. They were halfway through their meal when we arrived and at one point Dad says, 'Fuck! I hope they don't come over here and say something.' We had just been served our entrées and Dad's fork was halfway to his mouth when Mick Jagger arrives at the table and puts his hand out between Dad's face and the plate and he says, 'Oh, Mr Williamson, I heard you've got a play on – I haven't seen it yet, but I've heard it's great and I just wanted to congratulate you.' Dad just stares at his hand, looks at his plate, looks at his hand, looks at the plate and there's this uncomfortable silence. Jagger says, 'I'm Mick,' and Dad doesn't say anything, so he says, 'I'm Mick Jagger!' And Dad still doesn't say anything, so Jagger pulls his hand back and walks over to the door, at which point Tom Stoppard comes over and says, 'Nicol! It's so great to see you!' Dad's already pissed off at this point. Stoppard says, 'I haven't seen you since we worked together on *The Real Thing*!' Dad says, 'We never worked together.' Stoppard says, 'What do you mean – you were in my play!' Dad says, 'Yeah, I was in your play, but we didn't *work* together – it's not like you were there, you didn't show up every day!' I felt uncomfortable, so I stood up and I said, 'Tom,' – because I'd met him before – 'I'm Nicol's son, Luke, and I went to school with William.' He said, 'Oh, you went to school with William!' William's now standing by the door with Mick Jagger and Jerry Hall waiting to leave, so Tom waves him over and Mick thinks *he's* being called back over. Tom says, 'William, this is Nicol's son, Luke – you guys went to Caldicott together.' I'm sure William wouldn't have remembered me, but I had to lean around Mick Jagger to shake William's hand.

> When I tell people this story, they always cringe, but it's a pretty good indicator of who Dad was and the fact that he didn't back down from how he felt about stuff. He didn't like Mick Jagger much, for a number of reasons – he didn't think he was a good singer, for one thing. In the early '80s in Lindos, we were sitting in Mavrikos. We were the only people apart from Mick Jagger, who was sitting at another table looking at us, and I remember Dad saying, 'Don't look at him, don't make eye contact!'

Writing for the *Independent on Sunday*, Irving Wardle was much more positive than the reviewers writing for the dailies had been and encouraged uncertain theatergoers to give Nicol another chance. The box office gradually began to improve, but it was to be a case of too little too late. Leslie Megahey:

> He made a speech to the audience every single night. There was no stopping him! He took the applause and he'd walk to the front of the stage and have a chat with the audience about something he'd read in the papers or something about the reviews… Jack Tinker wrote a not very nice review, so he had a go at him, and the audience loved it, of course. One day, Sally Green pulled the show and said that we were going to have to close in two weeks. Just coincidentally, on the same day I had a phone call at home from Bernard Levin, the theatre critic of *The Times*. He was ringing me to check a line from the play and I said, 'Are you writing about us *now?!*' Because we'd been on for a number of weeks and we were closing in another two weeks. He said, 'Oh yeah, I can write a review any time. It's going to be a good one!' His review said this was one of the great theatrical experiences of his life.

Indeed, Levin's full-page review could not have been more enthusiastic – he wrote of 'acting not just on the grand scale but acting that breaks the scale to pieces', going on to say that 'a British actor of genius who has been away from Britain for nearly 20 years has come back to us and has done so with a vehicle that allows him to demonstrate that the phrase "actor of genius" is no exaggeration.' Leslie Megahey:

The place was full that night and Nic walked to the front of the stage, looked around, nodded and said, 'Yeah, we all read Bernard Levin, didn't we?'

On the last night, Nic had a go at Sally Green because she'd closed the play. I felt badly for her because she was in the audience, just a few rows ahead of me. She'd taken the thing on in the first place, but he had this go at her and I felt quite uncomfortable about it because she'd been supportive up to then. But Nicol really didn't like entrepreneurs and people who kind of made a lot of money off of the talents of others – he hated studio bosses. He denied this to me at one point, but he told me that while we were shooting *The Hour of the Pig*, Harvey Weinstein had invited him to his office. Weinstein had put some money in to get the American rights to the film, and then he faffed around making unnecessary teeny weeny cuts and redubs, and changed the title, and put a long roller at the beginning with supposed 'historical facts' in a ridiculous Gothic script. I think Harvey had asked to see Nicol because he'd never met him and these studio bosses don't interview your major actors but they like to meet them to, I suppose, look like the overlords. Nicol used to be invited quite often to somebody's office for a meeting and he used to just say to the secretary, 'I don't go to offices, but I'd be glad to meet him for a drink in any bar down the street.' And it didn't go down too well with these movie moguls that he'd have a beer with them instead. So, he had no time for these people and I think it was the same with theatre owners. Sally actually owns the theatre. When I got out of the theatre the night Nic walked off I had to call her. She was at the opera, so they had to page her during the interval. She came back and we sat in her office on our own and she said 'You know, this could be disastrous. We could lose the theatre.' So she had actually been through it a bit.

We're all sort of child-like when it comes to putting something out in front of the public and an actor, of course, is putting his whole self out – his physical appearance, his skills and his voice – everything! So, in a way, we both hoped that it would be 'the conquering hero returns to the stage' and that all the press would talk about it like that. Well, one or two did, Levin in particular, which is quite something for Levin to say it was one of the great experiences of his life in the theatre, but it wasn't enough. You want a Niagara of praise – you don't want the occasional trickle! You want everybody just to tell you you're absolutely wonderful and I think there was a feeling that we would have liked people to have unhitched the horses and pulled us round London in a carriage. So in that sense it wasn't as successful as we'd hoped, but, just speaking as a director, and as somebody watching it, because it was, in a way, Nicol's show and I became a sort of sounding board for him, for what seemed to work and what didn't, I thought it was a brilliant job and he did it fantastically well. I still think of the moment when he did that bit from *Hamlet* when Hamlet's father's ghost appears and we kind of duplicated the way he had done it in Tony Richardson's production with the crosslights and him on his knees and his own voice as the voice of the ghost. That still gives me goosebumps when I think about it. You just saw from things like that and the extracts from *Richard III* – all of which were put in to show not only what a great actor Barrymore had been but to show what a great actor Nicol had been. They were a kind of showcase, almost, for how brilliant he'd been in his lifetime and, I felt, quite right too! I still think they were amazing bits. I was proud to have done it but I know from his point of view just how great it would have been if people had said, 'He's back and he's great as ever' – or 'greater than ever!' You've got to be the toast of the town these days in order for your career to take that sudden upturn after so many years. He knew he was a sitting target and I think that caused a lot of tension inside him in that he *knew* people were as much waiting for him to make a mess of it as to be brilliant in it.

Jack was due to run until the 16th of July but closed two weeks early on the 2nd. It was nominated for an Olivier Award for 'Best Entertainment', but did not win. Leslie Megahey: 'Nic of course refused to go to the ceremony, so I sat there alone with the usual rictus smile of the loser when it was announced.' Nicol subsequently recorded an audio version which was broadcast in December on BBC Radio 4 as part of their *Monday Play* series. Before *Jack* had opened, there had been talk of a three-play season featuring Nicol at the Criterion the following year but, unsurprisingly in the circumstances, it was not to be.

During one performance of *Jack*, a drunken John Osborne had been in the audience. Not long into the show, he stood up, said loudly, 'This man used to have talent before he went to America!' and walked out. Nicol must have noticed but displayed no visible reaction. It was to be the last time he saw Osborne, who died the following Christmas Eve. Nicol once recalled how, when he, Osborne and Samuel Beckett had been at a party around the time of the 1978 revival of *Inadmissible Evidence*, Beckett had again said, 'I love ye, Nic,' and, when Nicol replied, 'I love you too, Sam,' he received 'the most chillingly baleful, hateful glare' from Osborne who, he added, could at other times 'be the nicest, warmest, most engaging man.'[82] However, his opinion of Osborne's talent never wavered and in a later interview he paid tribute to the author of the play which had made his reputation, calling him 'a flawed, but great, man,' and going ont to say that, 'For 12 years anyway he was the greatest living English playwright... the words, the power and the brilliance of Osborne, to me, are the chronicled Shakespeare of his time.' [83]

Chapter 25 – Almost Done

One evening during the run of *Jack*, Nicol had received a visit backstage from Kenith Trodd, the producer of many of Dennis Potter's television dramas. Potter had been the most famous British television writer for years and was known for pushing the boundaries in both form and content, as well as for his trademark use of romantic songs, which were often juxtaposed with scenes of tawdriness and misery. He also exploited his own personal psychological and physical problems quite blatantly in his drama, a propensity which had undoubtedly fed his legend. Potter died of cancer during the run of *Jack* (on the 7th of June) and Trodd's visit took place shortly after. He was there in an attempt to persuade Nicol to play the lead in the twin series which Potter had been racing to finish before he died, *Karaoke* and *Cold Lazarus*. The main character, a television dramatist in poor health named Daniel Feild, was closely based on Potter himself. Over twenty years later, Trodd remembered,

> The person I took with me that evening was Mary Selway, who at the time was one of the most revered film casting directors in the country. *Karaoke* and *Cold Lazarus* were virtually the only television she ever did, and so going in with her showed that we did mean business.

Trodd had in fact attempted to cast Nicol in two previous Dennis Potter dramas, the first of which Nicol seems to have instigated himself at some point in the mid-'70s. Nicol himself later remembered:

> I went to Jack Gold[84] and said, 'I'd like to do a film on Al Bowlly.' I've always been interested in music and singing, and he was supposed to have been the British Bing Crosby. They brought in Dennis Potter, who changed it from the life of a crooner to *Pennies from Heaven*. They brought it to me and said, 'Look – isn't this great!' I looked at it and

thought, 'Where's Al Bowlly gone? I don't want to do it.' It was almost arbitrary, I didn't delve into it deeply enough.[85]

Potter had envisioned *Pennies from Heaven* as the first novel written for TV. Set in the '30s, the lead character was now a travelling sheet music salesman who, frustrated with his dull wife, looks for a more romantic love 'like in the songs.' A wide variety of period songs were featured, but they were to be lip-synched by the characters. The six-part series was eventually produced by Trodd with Nicol's former Dundee Rep colleague Piers Haggard directing and Bob Hoskins in the lead. Hoskins became a star as a result, and the series won a BAFTA for Best Original Programme.

In 1986, Trodd once more attempted to cast Nicol in a Dennis Potter series, *The Singing Detective*, and remembered it this way:

> I was again very much an enthusiastic advocate that we should have Nicol but both the director Jon Amiel and, to a degree, Dennis Potter himself weren't that keen. The reason that there was a feeling that Nicol wasn't right… was a sense that he didn't have the range or he couldn't deal with the inner torment and the variety of that, but all I can say is we'll never know. When Jon Amiel talks about this, he's talking with the comfortable hindsight of a success – it could have even gone wrong with Michael Gambon, who wasn't a particularly celebrated figure at that point.

Nicol later recalled that he had been offered the role while in Singapore making *Passion Flower* and had declined the part. He did not explain his reasons but admitted it was one of the few parts he had turned down which he later felt he should have accepted. Once again, a Potter series made its lead actor a star and Nicol had missed another opportunity to be back on top.

When Trodd offered him *Karaoke* and *Cold Lazarus*, Nicol would undoubtedly have been intrigued at the idea of having a third chance to appear in a major Dennis Potter series. Thinking it would help to persuade him, Trodd also offered the direction of *Cold Lazarus* to Leslie Megahey, who later remembered that, 'When Nicol rang me to ask if I'd read it, I said I didn't understand a word of it. "Neither did I," he said, "let's say no."'

Trodd had no memory of receiving a formal rejection, only that Nicol had 'faded away'. Patrick McGoohan and Malcolm McDowell were also considered for the role, but finally Albert Finney was cast. However, in this case Nicol had far less cause to kick himself. Perhaps because Potter had written the two series while taking a variety of strong painkilling drugs for terminal cancer – an impressive achievement under the circumstances – they were not up to the standard of his earlier successes. *Karaoke* was rather too similar to *The Singing Detective*, only somewhat less subtle, whereas *Cold Lazarus* was an often tedious sci-fi sequel in which the main character was featured mainly in flashbacks from *Karaoke*.

The Dennis Potter series were not the only offers Nicol turned down at this time, an astonishing attitude considering he was by then in no position to be choosy. Luke Williamson:

> He was offered the role of the king in *Braveheart* that Patrick McGoohan took and I remember having an argument with Dad about that and saying, 'Well, why wouldn't you take that part?' And he'd ask what was there about that character that was redeeming. He wasn't going to take a role with a character that didn't have some kind of redeeming quality.
>
> Dad was offered bad guy roles constantly, but he wasn't interested. The characters that he chose generally had to have something redeeming or sensitive or sympathetic about them and he was very, very selective about his roles. There were many roles that he would turn down in what went on to be popular movies but there was something about the character that just didn't sit right with him. I think he felt that he had to find something about the character that was worth living and, if it didn't have that, it didn't matter what the offer was or what the movie was, he just wasn't interested.

During the same period, Nicol even had a meeting with Steven Spielberg, who sent a limousine to pick him him up, although whether he was actually offered a part is unclear. 1995 was to be another quiet year for Nicol, although he was hard at work on his debut novel and recorded an album of William Blake poems for Hodder Headline's *Poets for Pleasure* series. Meanwhile, Terry Jones (of Monty Python fame), was planning a film version of *The Wind in the Willows*. He wanted the actor portraying Badger to be big and Scottish and initially hoped to cast Sean Connery. However, when Connery dropped out, Jones thought of Nicol, cautiously phoning Leslie Megahey first to ask if he was really as difficult as his reputation. Apparently satisfied with what he heard, Jones offered the role to Nicol, who accepted.

Jones himself played Mr Toad with the help of much padding and green make-up, and fellow Pythons Eric Idle, John Cleese and Michael Palin also appeared, while Steve Coogan played Mole. Nicol was not the only heavyweight Shakespearean present, as Anthony Sher played the part of Weasel. Jones added some songs and a subplot involving a dog food factory – both of which were ill-advised – but was otherwise reasonably faithful to Kenneth Grahame's book. Filmed in various locations in the south of England in late 1995, the result was a mostly charming family film with good visual design and amusing characterisations. Nicol's make-up was minimal, consisting largely of long silver hair and black and white striped sideburns. He seemed to enjoy playing the tetchy, belligerent outsize Celtic mammal living a hermit-like existence in the middle of the woods, but it was perhaps not much of a stretch. Leslie Megahey:

> Nic was staying with me for some part of the shooting. I remember him coming back and telling me he'd been trying to tell Steve Coogan or somebody how to do a line and he more or less said, 'These young people don't want to learn!'

Unfortunately, despite mostly warm reviews, the film died a death at the box office thanks to poor distribution. Aiming for the ignoramus market, Disney later changed the title to *Mr Toad's Wild Ride* for home video in the USA.

Nicol spent early 1996 in London. The publication of his novel was imminent and an opportunity had arisen for him to do a twice nightly residency for a week at Pizza On The Park as a singer, so he did a number of interviews to help with publicity. Backed by a quartet led by Cliff Hall, Nicol performed popular pre-war jazz songs such as 'I Can't Give You Anything but Love, Baby', 'My Blue Heaven' and 'Baby Face'. The show was reviewed in *The Independent* but, although critic David Benedict found the band a 'class act' and did not question Nicol's technical ability, he felt that his performance was 'completely anodyne' and that he would do better to stick to acting.

During the run of *Jack*, Nicol had received a fan letter from Paul Sidey, a 50-year-old literary editor with an interest in actors. Sidey had been impressed with Nicol's performance as he had also been when he had seen him years earlier in *Inadmissible Evidence*. As a result of the letter, the two met for lunch a week later. Sidey was working for Hutchinson, a division of the Random House publishing company, and Nicol naturally told him about the novel he had been working on, subsequently inviting him back to his dressing room at the Criterion, where he played a couple of excerpts he had recorded. One of these was an elaborate anecdote about a friend of Nicol's who had suffered a bad case of diarrhoea with hilarious consequences. Sidey was impressed and soon found himself offering Nicol a publishing contract. Nicol submitted his writing either in handwritten form or on audio tapes, so it was a time-consuming process but Sidey found him co-operative throughout. When the book was finally completed, Nicol told Sidey that no-one would buy it because everyone hated him.

Nicol's novel, *Ming's Kingdom*, published in hardback by Hutchinson in February 1996, tells of an actor, 'Rick Neilsen', and the ups and downs of his doomed relationship with 'Adrienne Rader', an aspiring actress half his age. She has a dominating mother, Alice, a would-be actress jealous of Rick's success who attempts to drive a wedge between the couple. Rick dubs her 'Ming' after Ming the

Merciless, the villain from the 1930s serial *Flash Gordon*, hence the title. The book is clearly an account of Nicol's relationship with Andrea Weber written as a form of catharsis. However, it is open to question whether the process really helped Nicol to come to terms with what had happened between them, and the fact that it was published around nine years after their relationship had ended suggests the extent to which he had been affected. The book contains almost nothing about acting, but a great deal of explicit sex as Nicol charts the disintegration of an obsessive love which mostly went unreturned. This is interspersed with humorous anecdotes such as the aforementioned diarrhoea episode. Nicol's writing style is highly individual, jumping back and forth in time and from interior monologue to lengthy dialogue, but he credits the reader with the intelligence to follow him and for the most part it works despite some embarrassing moments when the relationship is going well and the lovers coo over each other with the type of baby talk to make the strongest stomached of readers reach for the sick-bucket. The main problem with the book is that it is so intensely personal that there is very little to appeal for the general reader. Nicol's prediction that nobody would buy it proved all too true and the planned paperback edition was cancelled. John Osborne's fifth and final wife Helen wrote a blistering review for *The Spectator* in which she called the book 'quite dreadful' and said that someone should 'take this man's pen away, please, and give him a decent part.'

Shortly before publication, Nicol had given an interview to Lynda Lee-Potter for the *Daily Mail*. Originally, the two were to have lunch at the Ritz, but Nicol was informed by the waiter that he was 'not suitably attired'. He stalked off angrily, the journalist trailing behind, and they had lunch elsewhere. This incident was typical of Nicol, who detested dress codes and rarely dressed to impress. In the interview, he spoke of how he was attracted to cold, blonde, Germanic types who he felt were usually opportunistic. He went on to say that it had taken him a long time to realise that such women were temperamentally unable to return his love to the same degree through no fault of their own. Nicol was a romantic who believed in love at first sight and rarely pursued one-night stands. In the same interview, he was scathing about the acting abilities of Ian McKellen, Anthony Hopkins, Sean Connery and Michael Caine, while noting that nobody offered him work in London theatre any more. Trying to sound unconcerned, he was beginning to sound bitter. In a later interview, he spoke of how he felt he had been denied a lot of opportunites because his refusal to toady to those with power had made him too many enemies.

Nicol and Leslie Megahey had given a mutual friend of theirs, Freddie Hancock, the go ahead to see if she could find any interest for an American production of *Jack*. Hancock was the second wife of the British comic actor, Tony Hancock. As a result of her efforts, Nicol and Megahey flew to Los Angeles on the first weekend of March to rehearse for a week at the Geffen Playhouse, a 512 capacity theatre where the play would officially open (after a couple of previews) on Wednesday the 13th of March and run for four weeks.

On opening night, there were apparently some technical difficulties with the sound which caused Nicol to stop the show at one point, reprimand the sound engineer and apologise to the audience. According to UCLA's student newspaper, *The Daily Bruin*, Nicol also had some trouble remembering his lines, but writer Jennifer Richmond was still enthusiastic and pointed out that his flubs were 'so natural they seem like they were specifically written for the character.'

Given that the theatre was located close to Beverly Hills, it may be unsurprising that a number of stars came down to see the show, but one visitor in particular remained memorable for Leslie Megahey:

> After one performance, Christopher Walken rather shyly came up to me and said that was the greatest stage acting he'd ever seen and asked if he could possibly meet Mr. Williamson. So I took him to Nic's dressing room and they got on very well and talked for an hour or so.

Nicol became good friends with Walken for a while as a result of this. Luke later remembered his father telling him about an evening in New York when the two actors had a long drinking session together which resulted in Nicol waking up in the street the following morning. Checking his pockets to ensure his wallet had not been stolen, he returned to the bar in which they had done most of their drinking to see if they had news of Walken. He learned that Walken had called in earlier as he had also woken up in the street and had lost his bag, which had his wallet and passport in it. The next time Walken ran into Nicol he was invited for a drink but claimed to be on the wagon and beat a hasty retreat.

Another backstage visitor was Rod Steiger, as Nicol himself later recalled:

> People were always saying he's over-the-top, he's a bully, he's an asshole. I found him a very personable, very straightforward and very charming man and I'm not *easily* fooled on that. He had his wife and a battered old Mercedes outside, like he'd fallen on hard times… Anyway, he looked at me and he said, 'I've just sat all afternoon watching you and listening to see if I could fault your accent. I couldn't find one vowel [wrong] and apart from that I was able to enjoy and admire the performance.' He said, 'Answer me one question.' I said, 'If I can.' He said, 'Why aren't you playing in big movies, leading roles all the time?' I said, 'Because nobody asks me.' His wife turned round, looked at him and said, 'See?' But the 'See?' wasn't about me, I think it was about him, as in, 'See? There's somebody else like you, Rod.'[86]

The L.A. production of *Jack* was also the occasion which reunited Nicol with Jill Townsend. The two had not spoken directly for many years until Nicol, telephoning Luke, was surprised when Jill answered the phone. They began talking to each other again. Jill Townsend:

> When Nicol was in L.A., I was off doing something, and I said to Luke, 'Why don't you have him stay here with you?' so they stayed at my house in the Hollywood Hills. We went out for a meal together and

Nicol said I was a very good mother and he really appreciated how I'd raised Luke.

I'd never wanted to say anything against Nicol because of Luke – every kid should be given the chance to love their dad, and Luke did. So I have a great fondness for Nicol and I certainly didn't mind him having this enormous personality because I was very happy to be the audience, it was not a competition.

After the play closed at the Geffen, star and director flew to New York, where *Jack* had also been booked for the Belasco Theatre – where John Barrymore had given his final Broadway performance – to open on the 24th of April after four previews. Leslie Megahey:

> The Belasco was supposed to have been haunted by the ghost of John Barrymore, which made it rather amusing. It was being produced by John Heyman, and I had a feeling he was putting quite a bit of his own money into it as well. He'd been the agent for Liz Taylor and Richard Burton and people like that. I remember when we were discussing it and he was asking about Nicol's behaviour and the walk-off at the Criterion, he said, 'Do you think he'll behave himself?' And I said, 'The one thing that I will *not* guarantee to you is that I have any influence over Nicol's behaviour at all, or over his late night gigs or his love of having a drink with friends and so on. He is entirely unpredictable from that point of view.' And I remember John Heyman saying, 'Oh, it's alright – I worked with Burton and Taylor. I know what these difficult people are like!' And I said, 'You ain't seen nothin' yet!'

The theatre was twice the size of the Geffen and, unfortunately, this proved to be over-ambitious at this stage in Nicol's career. However, reviews were mostly enthusiastic – *Variety*'s reviewer, Greg Evans, wrote that Nicol had seemed 'never to stop moving, barely pausing for breath as he ransacks the play for more humor and... pathos than any other actor could find...' Meanwhile, Ben Brantley of the *New York Times* found Nicol to be not only on his 'best behaviour' but 'courteous, even, to a fault' and concluded his review by saying it was 'heartening to see this actor in such good shape on a New York stage again.'

Jack provided Nicol with his thirteenth leading role on Broadway – more than any other British actor – but it was also to be his last. It closed early, on the 5th of May, after 'playing to less than a quarter of capacity' according to *Variety*.

During the New York run of *Jack*, Nicol met a young woman with whom he became very close. Valerie Manahan was at the time a 25-year-old American writer and aspiring actress. Manahan remembered:

> I had moved to New York in 1991 and saw *I Hate Hamlet* shortly after. It was one of the best performances I've ever seen anywhere to this day. He had this amazing stage presence and was really, *really* funny. When he came back to Broadway for *Jack*, I went to see it by myself. I was supposed to meet a guy for a date that night but he couldn't get down there, so I did what I'd wanted to do anyway, which was to see Nicol. It was absolutely amazing and I was sitting next to these two guys who said at the end, 'We've got to go to the stage door – come with us!' I had bought the poster and we went to the stage door, they asked for his autograph and I did too, then I headed off to the hotel where I worked. After a little while, I realised that he was walking behind me, also going the same way, and I thought, 'Wow – I'd really like to talk to him!' I thought to myself, 'If he turns uptown, then I'm going to get the courage and tell him how great I thought he was, but if he turns downtown I'm not going to bother him.' He got ahead of me and turned uptown, so I said, 'I'm not following you – I really am going this way!' He said, '*What?*' like he didn't even know what I was trying to say. I was aware that he had this tremendous temper and persona and I was afraid that he was upset, so I said, 'Mr Williamson, I was stood up tonight and so I came to see your show instead and it was just amazing – thank you so much!' He said, 'Well, I'm just going for a drink but you're welcome to join me.' I was shocked! I walked along with him and we went to a restaurant that happened to be right across the street from the hotel where I worked. The people at the restaurant knew him and they also knew me as someone who came after work, so it was a really jarring thing for the regulars to see us together!
>
> We got along extremely well from the very beginning. That night, he asked me what I thought of the recorded music which had been used during the show and I said, 'I love Bing Crosby!' He said, 'That wasn't

Bing Crosby, that was me singing!' I happened to really love the '30s and so did he. Later, we walked through the streets of New York together singing 'Don't Fence Me In', with him singing the Bing Crosby part while I sang the Andrews Sisters part. At the end of the evening he put me in a cab and I said, 'Mr. Williamson, I think you're wonderful.' And he said, 'I know.'

We had a lot in common and he was very lonely, so we started to hang out all the time but... alcohol dominated Nicol, certainly when I knew him. He needed it and, physically – by the time I met him – it had taken a terrible toll, so mostly what we did was go out and he would drink alcohol and I would drink coffee. I was drinking so much coffee in an effort to match his drinking alcohol that my teeth started to turn brown and I was jittery all the time.

He was living in a borrowed apartment on 79th Street and Broadway for the run of *Jack* and a woman called the apartment to talk to the man who lived there. Nicol said, 'I'm terribly sorry – I'm afraid he's died.' Completely untrue! She said, 'Who's this?' He said, 'I'm the coroner,' and he went through this elaborate routine, talking about how the owner had died and said, 'Do you know, he looks very like he did in life!' She called him back later, screaming and infuriated, having found out it was a lie. He would do that kind of thing to keep himself entertained.

He would walk into restaurants and sing opera. People would look up and not know what to do, so they would start to clap and he would take a bow. I've never met anyone else who would do that. It's almost like he was performing every day.

One time we went to an Indian restaurant on Central Park South in a penthouse. It was very fancy and as usual Nicol wasn't wearing very nice clothes because he couldn't be bothered with that stuff. Anyway, we probably didn't appear to be particularly elegant people, and so they were taking a long time to seat us and Nicol got fed up with waiting. He said, 'Come on, let's go,' and we went to take the elevator back down. All these well-heeled people come off the elevator, and we get on. Right before the doors close, Nicol yells out in his big, booming, theatrical voice, 'THIS FOOD IS TERRIBLE. I THINK I'M GOING TO THROW UP!' It reverberated throughout the whole restaurant. I was scandalised, but Nicol looked like the cat that swallowed the canary. It was classic Nicol and one of my cherished memories.

Nicol cannot have made much, if any, money from the American productions of *Jack*, so it was perhaps for that reason that he recorded audio versions of two more Jack Higgins thrillers, *Toll for the Brave* and *Wrath of the Lion*. However, it would not be long before his finances were in much better shape as he had signed on for a big budget Hollywood movie. Luke Williamson:

> When he was out in Los Angeles doing *Jack* at the Geffen he was staying at the Westwood Marquis and I went over to his hotel room. We were watching a basketball game, which he didn't really care for, and there were these *Spawn* comics on the coffee table. I knew Dad wasn't someone to read comic books, so of course I asked him and he said, 'Oh, I've been offered this role but I'm not gonna take it – look at this character!' And he showed me the comic books and, of course, he's talking about Cagliostro, who in the comics is short and fat and has a beard and he's belching and stuff and Dad couldn't really attach to it in anyway. I was never a *Spawn* fan, but I used to read comic books as a kid, so I knew that Todd McFarlane had a huge cult following and I was also aware that it was the first African-American superhero who wasn't a sidekick and I figured that if they did it well it could be hugely popular. So I told him that he should think about it.
>
> Eventually he signed on to do it but they showed up with a costume that he said was like a dime-store wig and beard and he said, 'There's no way I'm wearing that!' The producers were summoned and asked what the issue was and Dad said, 'You can wear that but I'm not going on camera wearing that!' He called me that night – he hadn't even told me, which was the way Dad operated – and he said, 'I'm in L.A. to make this *Spawn* movie, but I think I might be getting on a plane because I don't think it's going to happen.' But as it was they made a costume change and I went down and saw him on set the next day.
>
> The whole thing about Dad was, if you just presented things in the right way there was no problem, it was the way people sometimes presented stuff that he would take umbrage with. They realized pretty quickly on the set that, if they asked me something to ask Dad, everything seemed to go really smoothly. So I hung out with him for the duration of that movie. It was difficult to watch some of it. Guillermo Navarro was the cameraman and he's a terrific director of photography.

He and Dad became good friends and I remember standing on the set with Dad and we're waiting and shit is not happening and finally Dad turns to Guillermo Navarro and goes, 'What the fuck is going on here?' and Guillermo Navarro leans over and says, 'They do not know what the fuck they are doing!' and Dad goes, 'Oh *great*!'

Spawn director Mark Dippé later said on the film's DVD commentary that he had found Nicol extremely difficult on the first day, but that everything had gone smoothly once the costume change had been made. The film was budgeted at $42 million and shot between August and November 1996 at Hollywood Center Studios in L.A.

To see Nicol Williamson in *Spawn* is a disconcerting experience. It was to be his last film, though nobody knew it at the time, and it was the only time he appeared in the type of special effects-laden superhero movie that has come to dominate multiplexes around the world. His character, Cagliostro, has little to do with the historical figure, and becomes an avuncular sort of sidekick to the hero. Martin Sheen was also present as the villain, which may have made Nicol feel a little better as Sheen was an actor he respected. Nicol gave a competent performance but in truth the part was a waste of his talent and he was reduced to delivering lines such as 'Alright, you overgrown gecko – come and get your throat cut!' *Spawn* made a healthy profit, grossing $87 million at the box office, but it was not quite enough to warrant a follow-up. The film had also not been terribly popular with fans of the original comic books. Nicol had signed up for two proposed sequels as well, which would have done wonders for his bank balance, but perhaps less so for his self-respect.

The following year, Nicol wrote a screenplay and accompanying musical score for a film version of his 1967 stage success, *Diary of a Madman*. Feeling that the use of his own name on the screenplay might scare off rather than attract potential backers, he adopted the nom de plume 'Jonathon Maslin'. Another project Nicol attempted to attract interest in was a remake of the Vincent Price vehicle *Theatre of Blood*, in which a Shakespearean ham actor fakes his own death and takes gleeful revenge on the critics he believes tried to destroy his career. Nicol was to play the Price part and had devised his own versions of the various grisly means by which the critics meet their ends.

At around the same time, Nicol became a regular at a bar close to his Amsterdam home called De Beiaard.[87] He took a liking to one of the staff, a Dutchman named Kees Kaandorp, who had no idea who Nicol was but took the time to chat with him when he was not busy serving other customers. One day, Nicol invited Kees to lunch. The lunch was a success and Kees subsequently became Nicol's closest friend.

Kees is a friendly, down-to-earth man, a hard worker who seems to have done an impressive job of educating himself as a result of his own natural curiosity and thoughtfulness. Something of a freethinker, he distrusts politicians and religions and believes people would do better to put their faith in science. However, he does not take life too seriously, enjoys a drink and a smoke and believes in having a good time while you can. After meeting Kees, it is not difficult to understand what Nicol saw in him. He and Kees got on so well that they ended up travelling together on a number of occasions, as Kees recalled:

> The first trip we did was to Vlieland, one of those islands above the Netherlands – the Wadden Islands, we call them. And it was fantastic because it was very impulsive. I'd said to Nicol, 'I'm going to be away for a week. I'm going to Vlieland just to take a break,' and Nicol said, 'Why don't I come along?' which he did and we had a fantastic stay. It was in the month of May, beautiful weather, not crowded at all – which we liked – and we had long walks and long conversations. Nicol was absolutely *great* company – he always had great stories to tell and I loved listening to him. I was his favourite listener, although I wasn't exactly silent myself! He was a very, very interesting, intellectual man. He was 23 years older than me but we never felt that distance, we were just close friends.
>
> Nicol and I also took a trip down to Luxembourg City. We rented a car – a Volvo stationwagon – and I drove us there. Nicol was trying to get into contact with studios down there to find interest for his own

script, *Diary of a Madman*, and we went down to a film studio where he had an appointment with one of the big guys. One person from the studio drove us around in Luxembourg to look at locations. They knew who he was, but not as much as he wanted them to. This studio was interested in making quick series for the masses and I don't think it was the right studio for Nicol to walk into.

Needless to say, the trip to Luxembourg did not result in a deal. Nicol also attempted to interest Leslie Megahey in the project, as Megahey recalled:

He came over from Amsterdam one Christmas and we walked around the West End in the freezing cold and snow. I got a virus and then double pneumonia and it was at that point he brought the script with him and I ended up in Charing Cross Hospital really, really ill. I was on oxygen and being pumped with antibiotics and the phone rang – I was in a private room – and it was Nicol. He asked if I had read the script and I said, 'Nic, I'm actually on oxygen and I've got double pneumonia in both lungs and it's not looking very good at the moment, so no, I haven't – I'll just have to try and get better and get out,' and he just sort of said, 'Oh, ok. Good luck! See you,' and that was it! And then I didn't hear from him for a couple of months.

I wanted to make a one-person film because I'd decided that he wasn't any longer an ensemble actor, that there was something about his temperament and so on that meant it was better to work with him on his own. I'd wanted to do a film based on Albert Camus' *The Fall* with him playing a part that I'd once heard Paul Scofield do on the radio. I think I said to him, 'I'll pursue *Diary of a Madman* if you'll agree I can also pursue *The Fall*, because that would be very easy to make and it's set in Amsterdam.' It was set in all Nicol's favourite places – little bars, smoky restaurants and all that stuff. Well, not smoky restaurants – he hated smoking… and so he said, 'Yeah, alright,' and I gave him *The Fall* to read. He tried to be polite, but he said, 'I dunno… maybe it's not for me,' and it actually would have been more suited to a rather crisp, intellectual voice like Scofield's. I realized much later that Nicol probably thought the character was too intellectual and not passionate or sensual enough and that he didn't really want to do it. And I think for some reason – although I can't really remember it – I didn't really take to the *Diary of a Madman* script, so both those things fell by the wayside.

Nicol accepted a film role in early 1999. *From a View to a Death* was to be a version of Anthony Powell's novel about a mercenary artist hired by a wealthy eccentric to paint a portrait of his attractive daughter. Nicol was to play the wealthy eccentric, Stephen Dillane the artist and Kelly MacDonald the daughter, while Robert Young was to direct, but the film was never made.

Chapter 26 – The Swirling Purple Mantled Elbow

Nicol had first met Terry Hands on the opening night of *Macbeth* in Stratford in 1974. Hands, five years younger than Nicol, was then an Associate Director of plays for the Royal Shakespeare Company and had come backstage to congratulate him on his performance. Hands later became joint Artistic Director of the company in 1978 alongside Trevor Nunn and, in 1986, Chief Executive.

In 1994, Hands attended the last night of *Jack* and was hugely impressed, later saying, 'Nicol was absolutely brilliant, quite superb on every level – it was imaginative, it was quick, it was lithe, it was light, it was funny, it was really a tour-de-force.' He again went to congratulate Nicol in his dressing room, but on this occasion his enthusiasm was such that he suggested they work together and asked for a meeting. Nicol accepted, but when they met they were unable to agree on a project. Hands wanted him to play Antony in *Antony and Cleopatra*, but Nicol was not keen on the play. However, they agreed to remain in contact.

Three years later, Hands became Artistic Director and Chief Executive of Clwyd Theatr Cymru, situated on a hill just outside the small town of Mold, Flintshire, in north-east Wales – an odd location for a theatre, and a difficult one to access without a car. However, the theatre had already managed to survive for over twenty years by this point, although Hands was eager to raise both the creative bar and public awareness. He telephoned Nicol, who was at that point working on his screenplay of *Diary of a Madman*. Again, they discussed possible projects but nothing was agreed. Finally, in August 2000, Nicol – depressed over the lack of interest in *Madman* – telephoned Hands and suggested they do *King Lear* together. Hands immediately agreed and began making arrangements, presumably unaware of quite how impulsive Nicol's call had been, or that Nicol had read only part of the play and never even seen a production. The excitement which Hands felt was not shared by everybody, and he later recalled that, 'when they heard I was doing *King Lear* with Nicol, everybody said, "You're mad!"'

Hands invited Nicol to Mold for preliminary discussions, which began on the 13th of September. A deal had been made whereby Nicol would receive the theatre's top salary of £400 per week, along with accommodation in a hotel and a driver. The play would be staged in the building's Anthony Hopkins Theatre, which had a capacity of 570. By this time, Nicol had read the play in detail and was able to talk about it knowledgably. The initial meetings, over *al fresco* lunches at Nicol's hotel, went smoothly, and both clearly felt they were on the same wavelength. After a couple of days, Nicol left and returned to Lindos, where he was staying at the time.

In mid-December, Hands flew out to join Nicol for a week:

I enjoyed it very much, although it was very strange. Nicol was a very good host and a very generous man in every way and he would do the cooking usually. I ate well, I drank cautiously and we even went swimming together at one point. He was a good swimmer.

I went with all my scripts and things expecting to go through the role line by line. He wasn't the least bit interested in doing that. What he did was, for a week, he simply *was* King Lear. He behaved like him, he was tempestuous; kind and generous one minute, aggressive and violent the next – not with me, but with the odd person in the street, who he would berate, and at the same time he would be very kind, very generous, very thoughtful. He was everything you could imagine a King Lear should be, so it was a fascinating week but I had to work with an actor who simply didn't bother with the text initially.

I don't know [whether he was deliberately behaving in this manner in preparation for the role]. I didn't ask him that – I just watched it happening and unfolding! But in fact the behaviour patterns were very, very similar to King Lear's. We're talking about a man who knew the play. He knew the play very well.

He was known in the town and there was an English woman who had married a Greek and was living in Lindos who he suddenly attacked vocally one night. The following day one of the guys who ran a bar where we went for a lunchtime drink said to him, 'Nicol – cool it!' And he did, straight away. But it was a friendly admonition, it wasn't a chiding.

He had a kind of system [for his drinking]. It was kind of self-preservatory in a way. He would get up about 9 and finish off any bottles that were still unemptied the night before. Then we'd go off for his first pint, then there was lunch, which was a lot of Metaxa and ouzo or whatever they call it and a lot of beer and wine. And then in the afternoon he would have a sleep. He ate very little, but he would sleep in the afternoon and get up in the evening for another pub crawl and a bit of food – not much – he cooked in the evenings – and he was in bed again at about 9, so in a sense it was preservatory because for half of the 24 hours he was asleep and not drinking.

While Hands was in Lindos, Nicol asked him not to hold a performance of *Lear* on the second night. Undoubtedly, he wished to avoid a repetition of what had happened with *Jack*, when he had had a big aftershow party on the first night and then been unable to perform on the second. Nicol does not seem to have considered the option of cancelling the aftershow party instead. Hands, willing to compromise normal practice to get Nicol back on the stage, agreed there would be no second night.

Hands returned to Wales shortly before Christmas. Nicol went out to join the company on the 2nd of January, staying at the Plas Hafod hotel. The following day he was taken to the theatre by the driver whom Hands had arranged for him. Remembering how a read-through had helped him to break the ice when he had joined the Royal Shakespeare Company for *Coriolanus* back in 1973, Nicol had again requested that they begin in this manner. Hands saw little value in read-throughs and did not usually bother, but once again he acquiesced to the wishes of his star. The rest of the company already knew each other well and were mostly Welsh, so Nicol naturally felt uncomfortable as the outsider with a reputation which had no doubt preceded him. Unfortunately, he discovered that what works well once does not always have the same effect a second time, and he attacked the role with great gusto as the rest of the cast looked on in stony silence. Afterwards, the others went to an afternoon workshop while Nicol, well aware of how badly he had begun, went for a drink. Over the next few days, he realised that the best policy was to keep as low a profile as possible in the circumstances and let Hands take control. After the first week around the table they began to rehearse on stage and had four weeks before previews began. The ice gradually thawed and most of the company eventually warmed to Nicol, partly because his performance was moving enough to make a number of them cry in rehearsal. However, Steffan Rhodri, who played Edgar, remained wary:

> I didn't dislike him but he could be difficult to warm to. I can't look back with rose-tinted glasses. I can look back with compassion and think, 'This is a terrified man in the throes of his alcoholism.'
>
> He wouldn't rehearse beyond one o'clock any day. And he would be on form between 10 and 1. He didn't appear drunk at all then, he was fine. But he'd then spend the rest of the afternoon in the pub with the script and was very inflexible about that. He hadn't been on stage for many years, it was a hugely demanding thing to ask of him, not being match-fit in any way, and he was full of fear. I think if you're sat in the pub on your fourth pint trying to learn it, during rehearsals, you don't stand much of a chance.

Nicol later admitted that he had not come as well-prepared as he should have been and that he felt he had slowed down the rehearsal process as a result. However, despite a great deal of time spent on the staging of the first scene, the play gradually came together and Nicol was deeply impressed by the rest of the company, considering them to have been even better than the RSC.

The first two previews were not a resounding success, but the performances unfolded without anything untoward happening. However, it was on the third night that *'it'* happened again. In Nicol's own words:

> We're in previews. Everyone's racing and I'm treading water. Everyone's motoring, I'm standing still. Why is work so hard for me now? Because I feel the child in me is lost? Or dying? Am I the too infrequent Phoenix trying to remake itself in a snap? Sporadic flash of firefly-flicker mocks

the blaze of the old Christmas eyes. These thoughts race through my mind as I wait to go on in the third of the previews.

Here I stand I can do no other. It's not enough. I walk on and it happens. The unpredictable. The unpreventable. I stop. For the fourth time in my life, stage time freezes, the cast turn to stone and I turn to the auditorium. Denouncing my efforts as embarrassing and unacceptable to me I vow the audience its money back and give it the swirling purple mantled elbow.

I change into civvies. Nobody knocks the door. I leave. Past a downcast helpless Terry. Past a staring cast. Out into a freezing winter night with a frozen mind, a frozen soul, a frozen heart. I begin the numbing pub crawl. Not to drink but to run. Three pints, three drinks. The favourite's run off the course and the Jockey Club's gone nuts. I call a cab, grab a bottle at Plas Hafod, lock my door and take no calls. I can't explain the inexorable inevitable. I can't apologise for Kismet. Except to say that on each of these four moments in my life I've always known it is the end. I am beneath the slough of Despond. In the methane pit. Being strangled by The Anaconda. I am mute, wordless, untalkable to, unreachable. In a cell of self-loathing and aware of nothing save my worthlessness. I feel the nearness of death, obliteration.

Steffan Rhodri remembered it this way:

That particular day he'd been out drinking all day. I know he'd been drinking all day because the two actors who went with him could verify that. There was a sort of kerfuffle at the half [hour call] – 'Oh god, how is he?!' and so on. It felt a bit weird and somebody said that he'd been going around saying that he was going to do it in Doric Scots that night! There were all these weird sort of giggling rumours about how he was and things. He'd wait until the last minute to get ready and he'd sit there in his big parka coat until the five [minute call]. And he was sat there in the tea room on his own and I remember making a cup of tea and he said, 'It's gonna be fuckin' real tonight!' I said, 'Oh right, okay...' And he said, 'It's been nowhere near fuckin' real enough yet!' in quite a scary way.

And so we started... there's the bit with Gloucester and Edgar / Edmund and then people are coming on for Cordelia's betrothal and eventually Lear sweeps on and is about to launch into the whole thing, and he only got through about half a page and was already struggling with the words. He'd never really nailed that first scene in terms of the words. Which must have been terrifying, in truth. So he got through the first half page or so and was already stumbling and jumping around and making it up, and he started to launch into what can only really be described as a this-is-the-end-of-my-career speech. I think he'd done it before in his John Barrymore and it was almost like that button was there for him – this is what I'll do when I can't go on. He started to almost try to do it in iambic pentameter at first and sound a bit Shakespearean, but basically what he was saying was, 'I'm no longer able to carry on' and made it quite clear that that's not just for tonight, that that's the end of the road for me. I can remember him saying, 'I was once capable of great things,' and he shouted, '*great* things! But no longer…' There was a real sadness there and bitterness too, but I know it's part of the alcoholism – the melancholy grandiosity. He also said, 'I'm not a wealthy man but I'll personally refund you all for this evening.' And eventually he swept off, anyway, and disappeared quick as a shot from backstage. And I think Terry did the wise thing and nobody chased after him, nobody went to look for him or persuade him or cajole him, they just let him be. And *we* all got very drunk and recriminations started and we were saying, 'What are we going to do? Are we going to have a production anymore?' It was very sad and we thought maybe he was on his way back to Manchester to get a flight back to Rhodes, we just didn't know.

Terry Hands:

It was very theatrical, it was apocalyptic. The actors were all fired up and adrenalin-charged ready for the performance which didn't happen – it was the ultimate coitus interruptus! They went off to the pub. One of them came to the office and offered to play Lear, and I got the odd call from actors saying, 'What's going to happen?' and so on.

The following morning I went up to his hotel and he was just driving away with his driver, so I said to mine, 'Follow that car!' It was like some terrible New York B-movie. He went to one of his favourite pubs and I joined him at the bar. It was round about lunchtime and it was very empty. He didn't say anything, I didn't say anything and then, after about 15 or 20 minutes I asked him, 'Do you want a couple of days before you come back?' And he said, 'No – why? I'll be on tonight.' And he *was* – much to the surprise of the company! And also he *did* personally pay back every seat on the night when he'd gone off.

There is a kind of actors' nightmare. When they're asleep they have a dream where they suddenly find themselves in the middle of a stage not knowing a single line of the play that they're in with a full house in front of them. That's fairly common in the profession. And I think what Nicol did was kind of live out the nightmare and, by living it out, banish it.

The amount of money which Nicol paid back must have amounted to around £4500, perhaps more, and thus he not only failed to make any money at all from playing Lear, he made a loss. However, according to Hands, Nicol was not at all concerned about this.

When Nicol returned to work, the incident was not referred to, his policy being neither to explain nor apologise. Steffan Rhodri recalled that,

> The night after he walked off, the euphoria with which he was glad to be back in the game was tangible. But every night for the rest of the run, nobody knew whether he was going to do it again. He never did, but it had instilled a sense of fear in *us*.
>
> They were too brief for my liking, but there were glimpses of a remarkable actor. Not what I would call a generous actor, but it's a very individual part. But he was brave and daring and there was an excitement on nights when he was on form. There was a danger to him which I like in actors.

Press night was on the 21st of February. Nicol invited Kees Kaandorp over from Amsterdam, Valerie Manahan, Aaron Schechter (his accountant), and Schechter's wife from New York but, curiously, invited neither Leslie Megahey nor Luke Williamson. The Crouch End All-Stars Jazz Band, featuring Nicol's friends Graham Tayar and Ian Christie (also a critic for *The Daily Express*) travelled up from London to accompany Nicol at the aftershow party. A few critics also decided to make the journey – Charles Spenser of *The Daily Telegraph*, Michael Coveney of *The Daily Mail* and Benedict Nightingale of *The*

Times among them. Spenser was scathing, perhaps partly because he was a reformed alcoholic who tended to be harsh on those who still drank. Coveney, on the other hand, was complimentary, while Nightingale was on the fence. Terry Hands remembered:

> The first night Nicol did in Wales was not very good – his better performances were yet to come. And, in my opinion, he was the best Lear after Paul Scofield, but not every night. On his night he was an incredible Lear, but the alcohol meant that those nights cropped up infrequently.

Nicol himself felt that, by the time they were ten days into the run, he had 'got the play by the balls.' When it finished in Mold, the company took it to the New Theatre in Cardiff for a week, where it was well received. There was some talk of a West End production and even a film but, as Hands explained,

> It was successful in regional terms but when I did mention it to the odd producer in London they were all frightened to handle Nicol. I can remember one saying, 'Terry, you won't be there every night.' And I said, 'Well, I'll be back running the theatre in Wales.' He said, 'That's what we're frightened of.' So there was no way, but it didn't matter particularly. He'd burnt an awful lot of bridges in the West End and we were just entering the age of producers and if you upset them or you weren't reliable to their credit balance, then work would be more difficult.
>
> He and I talked about doing some more plays together. The trouble was, the plays he wanted to do I thought had passed their sell-by date – like *Cat on a Hot Tin Roof* or *Inherit the Wind*. I wanted to do *The Father* [by August Strindberg] with him in our small auditorium. We discussed it quite a lot. I felt very often with Nicol that he was stuck in the '50s in a way and it was the great days of Hollywood and the great days of British theatre and George Devine and people like that and it was sort of difficult to move him from that, but I would happily have worked with him again. I think Nicol could be a strain on a company, which did concern me, but on the other hand he loved them and most of them grew to like him. They respected him already, that was not a problem; it was, with Nicol, whether you could live on this tightrope or this edge of

tension. But I remember him very fondly as a very generous man, wonderfully talented and a great loss to the profession when he died. He was very special and he *could* do it. All I can say is I enjoyed working with Nicol and I liked him and we got on. I don't regret one minute of the time we spent together. It was all good.

Chapter 27 – Retreat to Lindos

In 2002, Nicol, beginning to weary of Amsterdam, decided to buy a house in Lindos, where he had been spending an increasing amount of time. Whenever Nicol had been to Lindos before, he had rented a house – usually that of Pink Floyd's David Gilmour or that of Mary Clow, whom he had known since the late '60s when she had worked as Tony Richardson's script assistant on *Laughter in the Dark*. Kees Kaandorp:

> I think it had been part of Nicol's plan to eventually go back to Greece. Mary Clow had a beautiful house, very close to Nicol's place. I stayed at her house with him as well for one holiday. When I first went there with Nicol it was the first time he'd been there in many, many years.
>
> I remember him at Mary Clow's house listening to tapes of Andrea until deep in the night. I think it was a musical Andrea was in – anyway, her voice was on it and he was listening over and over to it. I actually said to Nicol, 'Why do you do that? Why do you hurt yourself?' But you couldn't talk him out of it. I have a feeling that his romantic days were over, in a sense. It has to do with the fact that this Andrea was the love of his life. I'm not aware of any kind of serious relationship after Andrea at all. I tried to hook him up a few times but it didn't work! There was an American lady in Lindos who ran a launderette over there and I said, 'Nicol – nice woman, eh?' He said, 'I'll choose my own old ladies, thank you!'

Valerie Manahan confirmed Kaandorp's impression, saying, 'Nicol would call her [Andrea Weber] "the gymnast" and I believe he was absolutely haunted by that relationship. To me, he seemed never to get over it.'

Another long-term resident of Lindos was Willard Manus, an American writer who was best known for writing a novel called *Mott the Hoople*. Although the book itself had not been a bestseller, it was the origin of the name of the '70s band famous for their hit *All the*

Young Dudes. Manus had also written a book entitled *This Way to Paradise* about Lindos and had known Nicol since the mid-'70s. By this time, he had become tired of the increasingly tourist-oriented focus of the town and had returned to the States. His residence was one of the old 'captain's houses' which were originally built in the 16th and 17th centuries by wealthy seafarers. As Manus had already been absent for a couple of years, the house was not in the best state of repair. The local climate, in particular the strong sunlight, means that the houses in Lindos tend to require regular maintenance, such as an annual coat of whitewash. However, the house remained an attractive proposition with an excellent location – although situated in the centre of town, the high walls offered privacy and it was also far enough away from the noisy nightclubs to provide peace and quiet. Kees Kaandorp:

> When Nicol bought his house there he asked me to go along and help him out doing some repairs because the place was old, it wasn't maintained well. But it was like two guys with a screwdriver trying to rebuild the Titanic! I came there and saw the state of the house and we stood there and Nicol said, 'Well, that looks like quite a lot of work, don't it? Let's go out for a beer first!' I tried to clean the walls and stuff but it was useless in the end and, after a week or so, my frustrations grew because I wanted to do something for Nicol but I wasn't able to do it. I think I had two weeks holiday or whatever. And then I asked Harry, who was quite a character – he had a bar in Pefkos and Nicol had known him since he first came to Rhodes – if he knew a painter and he came up with a few Greek guys that really did the work, which I would never be able to do. Nicol forgave me from day one because he saw that as well. And finally when he finished the place, the move came from the Singel to the island of Rhodes. The movers came and took all the paintings, furniture, whatever, and it went into a sea container and was shipped down to Lindos. The rest went into storage in the Netherlands as Singel 56 was a huge place and all that stuff would never have fit in Lindos.

When it was finished, Nicol's house had become a charming home and remains so at the time of writing. The entrance, off an alley in the centre of town, is through a large wooden door set in an arched doorway which leads into a courtyard with a grapevine hanging down from a trellis above. To the right are some stone steps leading up to the rooftop terrace. The courtyard is home to three or four stray cats that are happy to be fed but hiss at anyone who comes too close. On the left is another set of steps leading up to the master bedroom, where Nicol slept. The floor of the courtyard is pebbled in the traditional Greek style known as *hohlaki*, in which the stones are upturned rather than flat and different colours are often used to create a mosaic – in this case, one of an octopus. Various potted plants including a lemon tree are scattered around in large terracotta pots. On the left hand side, below the master bedroom, is a kitchen, while on the right is a guest bedroom, a bathroom and a study. At the far end of the courtyard is the *sala*, the largest room in the house, with a high ceiling and wooden beams. Nicol filled it with various curios he shipped over from Singel 56, such as a wooden Amerindian brandishing a hatchet and a large carving of an Indian deity.

Once Nicol had settled in the town on a more or less permanent basis, he became a creature of habit. He loved eating out and seldom cooked, so he explored the local restaurants, but if the food or service displeased him he would not return. However, when he found a place that suited him, he stuck to it and often became very friendly with the owners and staff. One such establishment was Giorgio's Bar, which has been run by Tsambikos Myrsirlakis and his wife since 1994. Nicol began frequenting Giorgio's shortly after he moved to Lindos. Although Myrsilakis immediately recognized Nicol the first time he came in, he was sensible enough to give Nicol space and not badger him with questions. Only in his 30s when he first met Nicol, he is clearly proud to have had him as a regular customer and remembered:

I knew who he was from *Excalibur*, which was one of my favourite movies. We started talking and became friends. He came every single day and always sat in the same chair reading the *Daily Mirror*, which he bought from my father-in-law, who had a shop next door.

He was a very nice man but he was trying to hide a little bit from people. I remember a few times people saying to me, 'Is that Nicol Williamson?' Once there was a man sitting outside in the courtyard and when he came in to pay, he turned and saw Nicol and got very excited. The man's wife said to me, 'He's my husband's favourite actor!' Nicol took him and his wife to his house for a drink.

He usually went to bed early but sometimes he'd come here at night when he couldn't sleep and have some Guinness as we stay open late. He had a party at his house once and invited us – it was a very nice night with many friends from Lindos.

One day, Marianne Faithfull turned up at Giorgio's looking for Nicol. Faithfull also knew Mary Clow as a result of Tony Richardson's film of *Hamlet*, so this may explain her presence in Lindos. Anyway, she and Nicol spent a few hours together, but this was a one-off as by this time Nicol was beginning to distance himself from his past career.

Another establishment which met with Nicol's approval was a restaurant named Agostino's. He went there often and became friends with the owner's brother, Philippos Mastrosavvaki, who also worked at the Museum Bar[88] during the day. Nicol began stopping by the Museum Bar for a coffee most days and also became good friends with Mastrosavvaki's English wife, Barbara Chappell, and their daughter, Sophia. When the couple opened their own restaurant, Philosophia, overlooking the sea in nearby Pefkos, Nicol went there regularly for lunch, either taking a cab or accepting a lift from Barbara Chappell, who later remembered:

> Nicol was quite shy, really, and I think it took him a while to get to know people. We had him for Christmas a couple of times. One time the turkey was taking longer to cook than expected and he was getting impatient. Nicol stood up and said dramatically, 'I may or may not

return!' and stormed out, but he did come back – I don't think there was anywhere open!

Our daughter, Sophia, at 4 years old used to sing opera with Nicol at the top of their voices from the Agostino's roof garden and also out of the car window when we were driving out to lunch during the winter! Years later he kindly gave her his piano, telling her that she had to learn at least two tunes by the time he returned or he would take it back... she worked hard and learned the tunes, but sadly never got the chance to play them for Nicol. Every time she plays the piano she thinks of him.

Another favourite spot was the Rendez Vous Café Bar in Massari, a quiet village devoid of tourists, where Nicol liked to sit outside in the shade of an old fig tree and sip retsina. His preferred hangout in the evenings was Sinatra's Bar and Restaurant, run by another Englishwoman, a vivacious blonde called Peggy Arnold. She remembered:

He used to come in every day when he was in Lindos. He'd always be waiting at the door to get in. If we were five minutes late, he'd say, 'Where have you been?!'

He used to come and sit in the courtyard. People would come and look at the menu outside and he'd call out, 'Come in! We're terribly expensive but we're bloody good!' and they'd run a mile. I'd say, 'Nicol, I wish you wouldn't do that – business isn't very good as it is!' He'd say, 'Oh, you don't want that sort of people in here!' and I always had to end up laughing because he was usually right!

He had his favourite chair in the restaurant – and in the bar, because there was a bar downstairs. People all knew that that was his chair because if they were sitting in it he'd go up and stare at them until he made them feel so uncomfortable they'd slink away.

He had a tendency to always eat the same thing for a while. At home he would cook himself corned beef hash or curry all the time. I named a dessert after him called Nick's Lemon Mousse. It was like a tiramisu but with lemon instead of the coffee. He always used to say, 'Get me some of that lemon mush!' in front of everyone. I'd say, 'It's called lemon *mousse*.' He'd say, 'No, that *mush*.' He just liked to embarrass me, but in a funny, cheeky manner. I used to put a little swirl of lemon on top of the mousse. He'd pick it up nonchalantly and suddenly fling it up into the air without pausing in his conversation. It would land on somebody's plate or on the floor and no-one had any idea who'd thrown it.

I should have found him a pain in the bum but I didn't, I really loved him. He would be quite insulting to me at times but you still forgave him for some odd reason. I don't know what it was, but he was never boring and and had such a huge personality that it surpassed anything. He always had stories to tell and invariably they were very funny and, on occasions, rude – normally about bowel movements and things like that. He used to say, 'If anybody over the age of 30 says they haven't shat themselves, they're a liar!' and he would get people divulging all sorts of things to him. He had a way of drawing all your personal details out.

He knew that I was christened 'Peggy', not 'Margaret' – which I didn't like – and he'd say, 'Margaret! I'll have another one of these drinks!' Then the customers started calling me 'Margaret'! He would do things like that all the time, so I was his patsy. If anybody was in the bar who was obnoxious or was boring him, he'd pull faces in the mirror or he'd suddenly shout and make them jump, then look triumphant. He used to do this to me an awful lot, but I got so used to it I didn't flinch. He didn't like that and it put him in a huff – he liked it when he could get a reaction, but if anyone approached him and said, 'You're so-and-so,' he'd say, 'No I'm not!' So it was weird, because he wanted attention but he didn't like to be recognized. He just liked to have a game – he was a real prankster. On occasion, when he was leaving, he'd drop his trousers and show his bum to me. Sometimes, when he got up to leave, he'd shoot up and say, 'You didn't know I could get up that quickly, did you?'

He had a scathing dislike for quite a few people in the village, all of whom didn't understand him, but he also had a very sensitive and generous side. We used to have birds nesting in our courtyard and he was really protective of them. We nicknamed the birds Huey and Dewey. I'd also got two cats that were leaping up trying to get them and Nicol would flail about with his paper trying to keep the cats away from the birds. It was hilarious to watch him. People would be eating and watching him, thinking, 'What is that man *doing*?' He was a big softie, really, although he hid it well – very well!

There was a waitress called Sally who had such a crush on him. She was a lot younger, but she said she found him terribly attractive. I once let it slip to him but he wasn't interested. I don't think he had anybody that he had any designs on after his second wife.

He had this huge presence, partly because he was so tall but also because of the way he carried himself. You couldn't miss him. He'd go into the Chinese here and shout at the top of his voice, 'Do you do anything without MSG?!'

He was very, very good at seeing the truth in things, He knew if you were having troubles or things weren't right and he'd just come straight out with it and you'd think, 'How does he know this?' He was very good at reading people.

He loved my daughter, Kara. He was like part of our family. We felt sorry for him because he was always on his own at Christmas time. So we thought we'd go out with him on Christmas Eve. There wasn't much to pick from in Rhodes town, but we found this Italian and he liked Italian food. We picked him up and took him there, he looked at the menu and said, 'There's no pasta!' The guy said, 'Well, it's a Christmas menu.' Nicol said, 'But you're an Italian restaurant!' and let out such a diatribe to this poor guy and then said, 'I'm not staying here!' On his way out, he picked a wine glass up off a table and shoved it into the soil in one of the plant pots. Then we had to spend the entire Christmas Eve walking round Rhodes looking for somewhere. All booked! We ended up in some fleapit and had the most dire meal!

Peggy Arnold also remembered Nicol wearing a Turkish Galatasaray football shirt around the town because he knew that 'Nobody would dare to challenge him for wearing it and this tickled him.' Luke Williamson added that 'he'd always pretend to be confused when the locals mentioned it and claim it was a Partick Thistle shirt, as they have the same colours.' On another occasion, he abused the customary local method of announcing a death – he rang a bell loudly in his courtyard for the hell of it and then climbed up onto his roof to watch the locals heading up to church because they thought someone had died.

Nicol's old rival Richard Harris passed away in 2002. Harris had played the part of Dumbedore in the first two Harry Potter films and a replacement was needed. Nicol's career had often shadowed that of Harris in the past and continued to do so after Harris's death as the producers approached Nicol about taking over the role. However, giving the ludicrous excuse that they could not have Dumbledore played with an American accent, they subsequently withdrew their offer and cast Michael Gambon instead. A friend of Nicol's later remembered him being approached in a restaurant by a wellwisher who had mistaken him for Michael Gambon – an error which was, needless to say, not well-received.

It seems to have been around this time that Nicol decided he was finished with acting. He made no announcement to this effect and probably did not want to close the door completely just in case an exciting offer were to come his way. Even those closest to him have struggled to provide a simple answer to the question, 'Why did Nicol stop acting?' However, if we consider his career from around 1987 onwards, it might perhaps be better to ask why he would continue. Some thought that the reason for his absence from stage and screen was alcoholism, but only on rare occasions had his drinking interfered with his acting. It could, of course, be pointed out that Nicol's self-control had weakened by the time he did *King Lear*, but while this may have made stage work difficult, it would have been less of a problem for film roles. Both Richard Harris and Peter O'Toole continued to work in films up until their deaths despite alcohol problems at least as damaging as Nicol's.

Others have concluded that Nicol made himself unemployable through his difficult behavior but, again, there were more difficult actors than he who were always able to find work – George C. Scott and Klaus Kinski being a couple of prime examples. Nevertheless, this may seem to be a reasonable conclusion considering the walk-offs both from film sets and stages over the years, and it is a factor which undoubtedly dissuaded some who had considered casting him, but there is evidence that he continued to receive at least a few offers. Luke Williamson:

There was always the option for work. Even when he didn't have an agent for the last four or five years I'd get a certain amount of inquiries every year and sometimes the phone would ring out of the blue and it would be someone who'd gotten the number, so it was always an option for him if he wanted it.

Another rumour that arose regarding Nicol's absence from acting was that he had developed severe stage fright. This initially appears rather ludicrous as Nicol generally gave the impression that he had never had a minute's self-doubt about his acting ability and, he had, of course, made his name in a role so challenging that nobody else wanted to attempt it until many years later. However, it is clear that Nicol suffered something of a loss of confidence in his abilities in later years, although 'stage fright' is too strong a term. Most actors agree that learning lines becomes increasingly difficult with age and, in a profession which produces nothing tangible, do not necessarily feel that just because they have done something successfully before they will be able to repeat it.

Financially, Nicol's needs were few. He was a single man with only one child. Luke had been old enough to fend for himself for some time and, if he did require any monetary help, his mother would have been able to provide it. Singel 56 had been a wise investment on Nicol's part. It was a huge, well-built house in an enviable location, and it would provide him with something of a nest-egg in his later years. At the time of writing, similar properties in Amsterdam are being sold in excess of 2 million Euros.

From the late '80s onwards, Nicol had been unable to get his own projects off the ground and almost everything he had been involved in had not only met with a disappointing response but, in many cases, with reviews which seemed to delight in putting the boot in. Perhaps he brought some of this on himself as he was temperamentally incapable of ingratiating himself with others and could sometimes be rude to people when it was uncalled for. However, the vast majority of those interviewed for this book spoke of Nicol with great warmth and a sense of protectiveness. There is no doubt that he was at heart an extremely sensitive man and that his at times aggressive personality was some form of defense. Given these facts, it is understandable that Nicol did not act for the final ten years of his life. Nobody enjoys the experience of failure, especially in public, and Nicol was no masochist. He withdrew from the world of film and theatre, remaining in contact only with a very few colleagues, such as Jack Gold and Leslie Megahey. He converted the basement of Singel 56 into a separate flat, which he sold off. Around 2004 or 2005, he sold the rest of the house. Luke Williamson:

> We had a few discussions where he said he was sort of tired of living there and he was thinking about selling it. I'd always try to talk him out of it and then one day he told me he'd sold it.
>
> Lindos is an absolutely beautiful place and a lovely place to visit and it's a hard place to live year round. The great thing about Amsterdam is you can walk outside your door, there are any number of restaurants, museums, cafes nearby, or you can get on a tram, you don't have to drive anywhere, everything's really simple. Lindos is a small village and everybody knows everybody and there are a lot of restaurants, but only a certain amount that are good and if you want to go anywhere else you have to get a taxi or drive. It's *not* a stimulating place, and Dad needed a stimulating environment and something with change, so he stopped spending a lot of time there. He would usually stay from September until the end of the year, then go back to Britain somewhere for Christmas, then he'd travel for a bit and come back out to Lindos in May until it got too hot around June, then he would travel, then he would come back in September. That just sort of became his thing, he would go and visit people and places.

On the occasions when Nicol returned to the Netherlands after selling his house, he avoided Amsterdam as much as possible and spent most of his time in Hoorn, a town he had come to like and which was also where Kees Kaandorp lived. Nicol would call ahead and Kees would find him a hotel room and pick him up at the airport. One time at Schiphol, Nicol told Kees to keep an eye on an old-fashioned briefcase he had with him. Kees later discovered it was stuffed full of cash. The two friends also enjoyed a memorable road trip together, as Kees remembered:

> I had holidays and was asked to go along to Rhodes and then suddenly Nicol came up with the idea of going by car. 'I have no car, Nicol,' I said. 'Well, let's buy one!' I think his wife Jill used to own one of those stretch Citroens, the Citroen DS it's called, or the 'Snoek'. He wanted a car like that and I found a place which specialized in them, took him there and he bought one. It couldn't be put in his name, so it was put in my name. He called the car 'Babyface.' Then we took the trip and he turned out to be a wonderful navigator and we meandered through France and Italy. He really enjoyed that and a few years later he did the same trip backwards with Luke. This trip had been in Nicol's mind — he'd always wanted to do it.

Chapter 28 – Seamus the Squamous

Nicol may have stopped acting but he never ceased to be creative and spent a considerable amount of time in his later years writing and recording poetry and songs. He put a small jazz band together with whom he began to record. He recruited Chris Karan, formerly of the Dudley Moore Trio, on drums, Pete Morgan on double bass and Cliff Hall on piano. Hall had been the keyboardist in the latter-day incarnation of The Shadows as well as the bandleader for Nicol's residency at Pizza On The Park eight years previously. On later recordings, Dave Richmond (a founding member of Manfred Mann) took over on double bass and Max Brittain, an accomplished guitarist, joined the band. Digby Fairweather, well-known both as a musician and as a presenter of jazz programmes for BBC radio, provided a cornet solo on one occasion.

Hall suggested Porcupine Studios in Mottingham, south-east London as a suitable place to record. Consisting of what is essentially a large sound-proofed room adjoining a semi-detached house tucked away in a residential suburban neighbourhood, it would be difficult to find a less conspicuous recording studio than Porcupine. Perhaps partly for that reason, it suited Nicol perfectly. It also helped that it had a Steinway grand piano and was a one-man affair run by Nick Taylor, an easy-going individual who was nevertheless very good at his job. Nicol recorded his first session there on the 29th of March 2004. He would go on to record a total of 52 songs, poems and spoken word pieces over the course of around 50 sessions throughout the following seven years. Nicol would usually stay at the Bull's Head in nearby Chislehurst, or occasionally with Nick. He also took a liking to Nick's wife, Margaret, and his mother, Lil, who also lived with them.

The material included a number of songs Nicol had written himself, at least a couple of which were clearly about Andrea Weber. Nicol's own compositions were well-crafted and sat comfortably alongside the standards he also recorded such as 'A Fine Romance' and 'All of Me'. The quality of the work was undeniably high and Taylor remembered Nicol speaking of his intention to send the material to a jazz critic, hoping that it would be released and provide some income via royalty payments to Luke after he was gone. However, Nicol seems to have done little towards achieving this, perhaps because he was worried that the music he had worked so hard on might be received with indifference – by this point the music industry was in decline due to the rise of the mp3 and there was unlikely to have been much excitement about a 70-year-old former actor embarking on a new career singing 1930s-style jazz songs.

In September 2004, a TV producer named David Battcock approached Nicol with a view to making a documentary about him. Apparently, Nicol at first agreed but then later changed his mind, so Battcock cancelled the project. However, Nicol did agree to do a filmed interview for the excellent documentary *John Osborne and the Gift of Friendship*, made by Tony Palmer. He must have forgiven Osborne for his outburst during a performance of *Jack* as he spoke eloquently about the playwright's contribution to British theatre. It was to be his final appearance on film, although in 2005 Leslie Megahey recorded around four hours of interview footage with Nicol on videotape for a proposed TV documentary. Nicol became very enthusiastic about the idea of a programme devoted to him – perhaps too enthusiastic, as Megahey remembered him telephoning to insist that a series of six one hour episodes would be needed in order to do justice to his story. Megahey knew there was no chance of selling the idea of a lengthy series and that they would be fortunate in obtaining an hour of airtime, so he put the project to one side, hoping that Nicol would adjust his expectations to a more realistic view. However, this project too fell by the wayside and the interview remains unbroadcast at the time of writing.[89]

Nicol got into an altercation with a group of half a dozen builders in Lindos during this period. Details are vague as nobody else was present and Nicol would hardly have been keen to broadcast the story. However, it seems that a dispute became heated with the result that Nicol, realising he was outnumbered, picked up some kind of gardening implement and hit the nearest builder with it while the others fled. Unfortunately, it turned out that the one he had hit was an Albanian who had not been involved in the original argument. Nicol discreetly left the country for a while, leaving his lawyer to deal with the situation, and paid the man's hospital fees.

Kees noticed a change for the worse in Nicol around this time:

> When I met Nicol in '98 I thought of him as a very satisfied man. Of course, he drank all his life but he was very in control. When I met him he was about 63, still a very vibrant man and he could handle his drink and all that. Happy might be too big a word, but he seemed satisfied. He loved his lunching and dining and wining and it was nice. But the older he became, I feel the more frustrations came. Many times he said to me – years and years before he got the cancer – 'I think I have cancer!' He became more negative in a sense, as if he felt something horrible was coming towards him. He was a less happy man than he used to be, aging and maybe realizing that his health was going down, as if he *felt* it coming. And that was the last two or three years before the cancer. He seemed more like a disappointed man, in a sense, not the man I met in '98, who was actually enjoying life.

Emma Hamelynck painted a similar picture and remembered how it had been easier for Nicol to keep his drinking under control while he was still acting:

> He was a real alcoholic at certain points. He was already drinking a lot when I got to know him. Before he got sick he would stay in my flat in the Nicolaas Maesstraat in Amsterdam and fly to London now and then to record. In Amsterdam most of us drink a lot too, but this was different – he started having wine in the morning. I found it difficult to see him. During the time we'd been together it wasn't that difficult because he was working a lot, so he looked after himself better. When he worked less and he had a lot of time off, it became worse and I found it very sad. He was depressed, drinking a lot and I used to get angry with him because it was sad to see him. But he was never, ever angry with me

– I think I'm the only one he never shouted at! It was sad to see him just sitting on a sofa and not doing a lot. Maybe he didn't think of his drinking as a problem – he was drinking very good wine!

Luke, worried that his father did not have enough going on in his life, began to spend more time with him and, in 2008, the two embarked on a road trip together. Luke Williamson:

It was a bit of a crazy journey. Dad didn't drive but he had a 1967 Citroen DS that he had bought because it was a beautiful old car and he and Kees had driven it down to Greece. Dad decided that he wanted to drive it back up to England and that I was the man to do that with him. Of course, it had been sitting in the sun for years and it had all kinds of problems. It's a long story but quite funny and we ended up having to abandon the car. It was very stressful for me at the time! We abandoned the car in Belgium, then we got a train, then we flew into London and drove up to Birmingham in a hired car armed with an old A – Z from the mid-'80s and Dad's memory. We went looking for the house that he'd lived in and the schools that he went to, and his Boys' Brigade and so on. The drama school is a listed building which had been gutted and at the time they were redoing it and it was no longer a school. One of the other schools that he went to [Central Grammar] is now an all-Muslim school. We were tackled by security before we got within 30 yards, but once we told them why we were there they were very nice and they showed us around and Dad was able to point out where the bomb shelters had been and stuff like that.

In September 2008, Luke persuaded his father to allow him to set up a website paying tribute to his remarkable career and providing links to recordings of Nicol performing his poems and songs. Luke was keen to remind the public of his father's existence as he had heard about Peter Jackson's plans to film Tolkien's *Lord of the Rings* trilogy and hoped Nicol might be offered a role. This may seem to have been overly optimistic, but Nicol's audiobook version of *The Hobbit* had not been forgotten by Tolkien enthusiasts. Nicol apparently began to consider a return to acting and also to plan an audiobook version of *The Lord of the Rings*. However, Luke seems to have been one of the few people Nicol would take unsolicited advice from, and anyone thinking that these developments were symptomatic of him having mellowed with age was almost certainly mistaken, as this statement published in June 2009 on a website providing information about Lindos shows:

> Should you recognise former actor Nicol Williamson in the village I advise you not to approach him as you are likely to get a rude response. He clearly wants to be left well alone so, please, keep clear of him.[90]

Nicol may have felt no obligation to be polite to strangers, but he was by no means unkind. The following August, he performed a two night benefit concert in Lindos for a local boy who had been paralysed in a motorbike accident. Nicol flew Cliff Hall and the rest of his regular recording band over from England at his own expense. He put two of the musicans up at his house and paid for the other two to stay in a hotel. Luke Williamson later recalled that, 'On the first night, he was starting to not feel well and was having some issues with his throat, so he only did half the show, then let the band play and came home. The second night he felt better and did the whole show.' Peggy Arnold remembered him as being 'quite nervous' as he had not performed in public for a long time, but went on to say that, 'He pulled it off and when he walked through the door afterwards I was bursting with pride as though he were my son and you could see he was really delighted.'

Nicol also had a soft spot for animals, about whom he could be surprisingly sentimental, as Kees Kaandorp recalled:

> In Greece he would feed all the stray cats, although he didn't want them in the house, and I remember once he closed the door and he squashed a cricket. He was *devastated!* He thought it was horrible. Most men would not have cared, but Nicol was touched by it.

Lindos is home to a great many stray cats, and Luke Williamson had a vivid memory revealing the extent of his father's fondness for the creatures:

There was a cat we found that had lost a leg in an accident and we thought it would have to be put down. I said I couldn't do it and he said, 'If we get it back, I'll walk it into the water.' But he was tearing up, getting really emotional at the idea of having to do this.

Leslie Megahey thought of Nicol as someone who loved animals but had no desire to be responsible for any himself:

I remember once he rang me up and asked if he could come and stay. I said, 'We're just going away for a couple of weeks but you can have the entire house if you want and all you have to do is look after the dog.' And he very abruptly said, 'No, don't worry – I'll find a hotel!' And the dog absolutely adored him! When he played our piano and sang his torch songs in the living room, Danny just used to sit and look adoringly at him.

When the dog died some time later, he rang me quite late one night from Amsterdam and sang the whole of 'Danny Boy', then quietly put the phone down.

The throat problems Nicol had experienced during the benefit concert had continued and, early in 2010, Nicol was diagnosed with oesophagal cancer. He dubbed the disease 'Seamus the Squamous.' He continued to record his songs at Porcupine during his illness, but any return to acting was out of the question and the proposed audiobook of *The Lord of the Rings* was abandoned. Luke Williamson:

When he was healthy he was sure that there was something terribly wrong, that he had cancer. I took him in to doctors a couple of times because he was complaining about stuff and he'd go and get scans and everything was fine. Ironically, when he *did* get cancer, he didn't think it was cancer. When he had all the scans after he got it, everything else was fine – his pancreas, his liver, his kidneys, his heart – there was nothing wrong with him except that cancer and the doctor was sure he would have lived into his 90s quite easily. He had the constitution of a horse but he was always sure that there was something wrong. Because of his mother's death, there were two things that he really feared in life, cancer and death – not necessarily dying – but death as the absence of being. The idea of non-existence was quite terrifying to him. The other thing he didn't like was heights. He joined the paras when he had to do his two years because he didn't like heights and he didn't like flying, so he decided to spend those years throwing himself out of perfectly good aeroplanes! That's how he was. If he was frightened of something, he would just get up and face it and not back down. When he got cancer nothing was going to stop him – he didn't want to do anything any differently than he had when he was healthy. Fuck cancer! He was going to beat this, there was no cancer that was gonna kick his ass.

His doctor gave him two weeks and he lasted two years. I've never seen anything like it. When he was diagnosed, the doctor said, 'No alcohol!' I thought, 'Holy shit! How's he gonna deal with this?' And he just stopped drinking. He didn't seem to go through any withdrawals, he never complained about not being able to have a drink. Every once in a while he ordered a glass of rosé. He would maybe have one sip all day and it would just sit there next to him. But otherwise he never drank again. I thought that he would have a terrible time but no – they told him he had to stop and that was it – done! Like it was never a problem – and it was never even mentioned!

He had his cancer treatment in London. I tried to get him to come out to the States and he wasn't interested in that. After the first four months, when it started to get really rough I quit my job and stayed with him for the last 18 months. Even the people he loved and usually wanted to spend time with, he didn't want to see at all. During that period I had to tell a lot of people 'no'. He firmly believed that he was going to beat it – even when he was in the hospice he was talking about beating it and he never gave up. He didn't want people to see him or visit him until he came out of it the other side and he looked like himself again.

Back in Lindos, Sinatra's had been forced to close due to rent issues. In April 2011, Peggy Arnold opened a new restaurant, Bojangles, in nearby Lardos. Nicol went out for the opening to offer his support but felt unable to eat. In June, he was back in England staying with Luke at The Fox and Hounds pub in the Devonshire village of Lydford. Luke was becoming increasingly concerned as he was struggling to get his father to eat anything, so he turned to Peggy for help. Peggy Arnold:

Luke said to me, 'He's going downhill,' and I thought, 'I can't conceive not saying goodbye to him if he doesn't have long', so I flew to England and stayed with them in this pub for three nights. Nicol said, 'You shouldn't have come,' but he did eat. People used to look at us strangely. He said they must be thinking, 'She's too young for him (Nicol) and too old for him (Luke), so where does she fit in? They must think you're a high-class call girl.' I said, 'Thanks very much!'

Luke Williamson:

Towards the end of his treatment, he woke up one morning and he had all this very intense frothy saliva that he had to keep clearing constantly. He couldn't speak in anything other than a whisper. About a week or ten days after that, I actually thought he might have died in the night. He just was not responding to me in the morning and it took a while for him to be able to respond. By this point, I'd had to get a wheelchair for him, but we had a deal that, as long as he was able to get up for one meal a day I wouldn't put him in a hospice but when he couldn't get out of bed any more, then he needed help that I couldn't really give him. He couldn't get out of bed that day or the next day.

One of the things that happens with cancer patients when they're going through the chemotherapy is that they lose not only their appetite but everything sort of tastes like ash. So I spent a lot of time with him talking about what he might want to eat and he'd have a memory or a fantasy of something he'd had somewhere and I'd try to find that and we'd see if maybe that tasted good. I went out at one point and got him caviar and Dom Perignon to see if that was maybe something and, bless him, he did enjoy that.

So it was a time of trying to get him to eat and he was under 50 kilos which, for such a big guy, was very hard to see. The only things that I could really get in him for the last few weeks were Bovril and carrot cake. I had to order a really small amount of food because a large amount would put him off as he knew he couldn't eat it. Anyway, he couldn't get out of bed. I called Kees, and said, 'I think we're approaching it here. I've looked online and there are three hospices in Hoorn. Will you go and look and tell me if any of them are any good?' And, bless him, he called in at work and went out that day, looked at all of them and came back and said, 'There's one that's really good and I think they have room.' So then I talked to Dad and said, 'How do you feel about going to Holland and we'll see Kees and have some fish soup and check out this place and see if you like it...' and he was all for it, so we drove and got the ferry across Belgium and took a couple of days before he went in to try and enjoy Hoorn. I remember we got him in the wheelchair and out of the hotel and he said, 'You have to take me back to bed.' He just couldn't do it any more and when we got him into the hospice he felt such a sense of relief that he could just stay in bed. It was ten days before he died, so we'd kept him out of the hospice for as long as we could.

So unwilling was Nicol to face the inevitable that he had continued to record at Porcupine Studios up until summer 2011. He also avoided making a will, as that would have been an admission of defeat, and was reluctant to discuss with Luke how things should be handled after his death, although he did say that under no circumstances was Luke to dismiss his Greek housekeeper, Tsambika.

Nicol finally passed away on the 16th of December 2011 at the age of 75. Peggy Arnold:

When he died, we knew that it was imminent but I woke up with a start early on the same morning and thought, 'My god – he's gone!' and I found out later it was about that time that he'd died. I'm sure the old devil came to say goodbye. He left a massive hole because there was nobody like him. He was all-consuming – so clever, so talented, so in-your-face and you knew exactly where you stood. There will never be anybody quite like him again.

Before he died, Luke had asked him how he should handle the press, to which Nicol had replied, 'Fuck them – you don't have to tell them anything!' Only a very few close friends and family members were invited to the funeral in Hoorn. Some of those were unable to attend, so there were just six mourners present – Luke, Kees Kaandorp, Nick and Margaret Taylor from Porcupine Studios, and two other friends from Hoorn, Meta and Sandy, who had run De Hoofdtoren, Nicol's favourite restaurant in the town, which was housed in an old defense tower overlooking the port. At Nicol's request, the coffin was left slightly open as he disliked the idea of being enclosed in a dark box. Luke hired a Scottish bagpiper to walk slowly ahead of the car on the way to the crematorium. After the funeral, the guests gathered at De Hoofdtoren.

De Hoofdtoren (photograph by author)

Chapter 29 – Nicol Remembered

Around five weeks after Nicol's death, a journalist got wind of it and managed to obtain Luke Williamson's mobile phone number. Luke spoke to the journalist and soon after found himself inundated with calls and emails enquiring about Nicol or offering condolences. Obituaries were hastily written by journalists on tight deadlines. Under the circumstances, it was understandable that they would not get all of their facts straight. However, aside from the various inaccuracies they contained, the other notable common characteristic of many of the obituaries was a lack of generosity. According to *The Telegraph*, Nicol had 'died in penury' with 'only six mourners' at his funeral. Nicol may not have been a wealthy man when he died, but there was still some inheritance left for Luke as well as the house in Lindos. The news had also deliberately been kept quiet, so the fact that there were only six mourners present could hardly be taken as any indication of unpopularity as *The Telegraph* seemed to imply. In London, Jack Gold and Leslie Megahey organised a memorial lunch in one of Nicol's favourite pubs. Guests included Francesca Annis, Kate Binchy, Edward Fox, Gawn Grainger and Zoe Wanamaker.

It is difficult to escape the conclusion that there was something about Nicol which brought out the worst in many critics and journalists – so what was it? Perhaps the resentment was due to his refusal to play anybody's game but his own. Very few of us manage to live life purely on our own terms and are forced to – or feel we are forced to – compromise. Of course, there had been times when Nicol had taken on a role purely for the money, but in his case he only did so when he genuinely needed to, not because he loved money and luxury. Nicol never kissed anyone's arse and he paid the price for his headstrong attitude but, despite a substantial ego, he appeared to have little need for the adulation of audiences and he was not willing to humble himself or become a public has-been.

As an actor, Nicol is worth remembering and writing about not only for his impressive achievements but for the fact that there was no other actor like him. For me, one of his great qualities was that, despite his considerable versatility, he was by no means a chameleon whose own personality disappeared when he played a character. He was different in every role, but I always felt in his performances he was revealing some very real and personal part of his true self. Not many actors seem to do that. He was also not one of the countless actors who rely on certain expressions, gestures or inflexions which they are aware work well for them and which they exploit to their full advantage. There was no such vanity in Nicol's acting. He demonstrated a willingness to peer into the darkness and show you what he found there without any attempt at sugar-coating. This often made audiences uncomfortable, but it was an essential part of what made him so memorable.

While few would deny Nicol's talent, those who have written about him not just as an actor but as a human being have tended to dwell on incidents such as the slapping of Jim Litten during the curtain call of *Rex* or the walk-off on the second night of *Jack*. Dramatic as these may be, they are isolated events which do not in themselves explain Nicol or what happened to him.

It seems fitting, then, to conclude with some final thoughts from some of the people who knew Nicol best.

Jack Gold:

> When I worked with him, Nicol tended to have entourages, groups of acolytes, who'd trail along in his wake, almost like pilot fish, attaching themselves to him and drifting off. I wasn't one of those, but we used to play football sometimes in Hyde Park on Sunday mornings with a bunch of other actors, crimpers, tailors and waiters. He was a good footballer, a good natural sportsman… he could do a lot of things well. I was a great fan and I always felt that there was a great waste of talent going on in the last years. What a waste that he wasn't king of the RSC or in charge at the National, or playing all the major parts! He was offered quite a lot of big parts and turned them down, so I think if he'd decided to have

become a major theatrical star, he could have gone down that path, but I don't think he wanted to somehow. I think he'd like to have become a film star, but he was never a film *star*. He should have become like Rod Steiger or Gene Hackman in the sense of being the best character actor in the film world, the best number two, the one you would always remember and watch, not necessarily hurry after with your autograph book.

During the later part of his career I saw him in some American films in smaller parts, and I thought there was nothing there for Nicol to explode in or strut his stuff. They were more like cameos. The great cinema actors – like Alec Guinness or Tony Hopkins, for instance, would cut their cloth for the parts and become employable, whereas Nicol I think challenged parts that were offered, or challenged the people he was working with.

He had a lot of money at one time, he was never miserly, he *spent*, and the champagne was non-stop! He was full of hospitality, he'd always be picking up the bill or throwing a party. So he obviously had enough money to buy a little house in Lindos, and he basically became hermity. When he had friends, they were very close friends, they were always very supportive of him, and he built up a group of friends in Holland and in Lindos who were quite close, and he had people round London he would stay with, and everywhere else.

I think producers got wary of him. There were a lot of people he didn't respect. He had a great ego – I think he considered himself to be one of the great actors. And he was formidable. He wasn't always liked, and he wasn't always necessarily as successful on screen as he was in the theatre. He was certainly no-holds-barred in performances. He would *deliver*. And I liked that. Maybe I was good for him in the sense of providing him with an environment in which he felt comfortable… or by staying out of his way, if you like, during the filming! I was very fond of him, and I know he had faults, but I never experienced them myself in any of the productions we did.

Leslie Megahey:

I think Nicol did regret some of the things he turned down. On one occasion he said, 'Sometimes I just reacted against something or it was the wrong moment and once I'd said no, I wouldn't go back on it.' So there was a kind of impulsiveness or impetuousness about his decisions at times. During the period when I knew him and people *knew* I knew him, I used to get quite a few calls from directors trying to get him to do a part he didn't want to do and they were ringing me to see if I could persuade him. I would always say to them, 'If he's decided something, there's nothing I could say.' He used to say if it had no fire in its belly, he didn't want to do it. I guess a lot of things he got offered later on he thought were rather anodyne and straightforward and English.

Jim Sheridan rang me up to try and get him into *In the Name of the Father* and he turned that down. That was the 'no fire in its belly' kind of thing. He wasn't working on anything else and one could well assume he could have done with the money but there was absolutely no thought for that at all. Plus, after years in the wilderness he could have had his name up there next to Daniel Day-Lewis and Emma Thompson, two of the most hip names in the business. But that impressed him not a bit.

I think he needed to be the centre of attention, but not in the sense that he didn't like anyone else to get any attention at all, but that he somehow could only operate under those circumstances. Terry told me he thought Nicol had really liked working with the cast of *Lear* because they were young people and so forth, but all the time I kept thinking it was dangerous to put him in anything with a largish cast because there were too many opportunities for him to suddenly dislike someone or someone's work. I don't mean his dislikes were somehow ill-founded. I think a lot of the time there was quite a good reason for him not liking something or someone. His antennae were pretty bloody good. He was highly intuitive and highly perceptive – he could read what somebody was like. In most situations, and while working, though he appeared very self-contained he was always watching, observing, listening, and when he had reached a conclusion about someone or something he didn't like, his analysis or definition of it usually made complete sense. And this even when you might think the expression of it over the top. I think he took pride in (maybe even enjoyed) keeping his outbursts forensically accurate no matter how angry he felt. So I believed a lot in his instinct, but at the same time I thought that he shouldn't really be working with too large a group of actors – in the theatre, I mean. In film it's different because a film actor is taken away and put in the cupboard again until you need them and all actors know that, but on stage there might have been too many people around or too may irritations.

The end of our relationship was something that I still feel rather sad about because I think it was partly my fault. There was a point at which he'd asked me to go out to Lindos. His idea was to go out on a boat for a week and sail around and I didn't go for various reasons. I think there was something else that happened where he felt I'd let him down and possibly I had. He didn't make these things up. He probably overreacted to many things, but it seemed to me there was always some foundation of reason or truth when he got angry or upset and I think I did upset him over something, and it's something that I'm still sad about.

I didn't even know he was ill as I hadn't seen him for the last three years, but we'd spent quite a lot of time together when he came to London before that. He used to take off, disappear to another country for a while and then there'd be a knock at the door and he'd be standing on the doorstep. His life was in compartments and they didn't often overlap, so I knew he had good friends in Amsterdam, but I didn't know really who they were and I knew he had the occasional girlfriend or whatever but I never knew who she was either. Occasionally he gave people in England my number and I think it was partly to avoid giving them his own number in Amsterdam but sometimes I would get a call from a woman who would want to know if Nicol was around at the moment. He spoke about flings he had with Marianne Faithfull with great relish and great enjoyment, but he would never speak about his present girlfriends if he had them.

Like anyone of that stature or with that talent, he could sometimes be a bit overbearing or go on a bit and you'd think, 'Oh god, I want to go to bed – I don't want to listen to this!' but at the same time I had such fun with him and admired him hugely in many ways. In his own way he showed great affection towards me and towards Jana, my partner, and towards my dog! He did have it in him and I regret this feeling of having just drifted away. Nicol would say, 'Fuck it – don't regret things, it doesn't matter, Leslie. It really doesn't matter!' but actually it *does*.

Kees Kaandorp:

He hated Hollywood and the in-crowds and the fakeness of those people. He just didn't want to be there at all. Acting was his living, his job, and he was very good at it but he was a non-conformist and that makes life difficult if you want to make a living in places like Hollywood. Nicol wasn't exactly a great diplomat – he didn't do that shit! I think it's great if you're like that. It really shows your character but it can also be a nail in your coffin professionally. Nicol refused to sell himself, he was just this is what I am, this is what I can do. He wasn't scared of the devil and he wouldn't trade his soul for a dime.

The biggest enemy Nicol had was the alcohol, at the end of the day. I don't blame him. The book was already written when he was born. Alcoholism is a disease and he was struck by it. He couldn't be helped but it did make him walk the path through life as he did, in a way. And I think that he came quite a long way. It could've been a lot better? It's always like that. Could have been worse, could have been better.

Valerie Manahan:

Nicol had a tremendous amount of mischief and caustic wit. He used to say, 'It's just going *awfully* well, isn't it?' when something catastrophic happened. I had this big picture on the bedroom wall from the movie *Rebecca*, which starred Laurence Olivier, and he said, 'I *cannot* sleep under a picture of Larry!' One time we were walking down 7th Avenue in New York and I said, 'I loved that episode of *Columbo* that you did!' and he said, 'If you mention that again I shall step off this curb and hurl myself into oncoming traffic!' After September 11th I went to visit Nicol in Greece with my boyfriend and we got engaged at his house there. I remember when my boyfriend put his glass down on Nicol's table, Nicol said, 'You need to use a coaster – that's a 400 hundred-year-old table!' Chad quickly picked up the glass and went to get a coaster, then Nicol said to me, 'It's not really!'

He was also an extremely joyful man and very loving, but I don't think people knew that about him. He was very sensitive and generous. One thing I loved about him was that he really couldn't care less about money, although I think that was to his great detriment as an actor, not because he didn't care about his career, but because he didn't value the producer. I think it was a problem because he just looked at the artistry and couldn't see it from a business point of view, so he cost other people a lot of money and that's one reason why nobody wanted to hire him later, although it wasn't just that.

Nicol was never going to be in the position of suffering the indignities of aging and that happens early in the acting profession. When he did *King Lear* he would forget the lines, but he was such an artist that he could ad lib Shakespeare – and that was very stressful for the other people on stage! Perhaps one reason why he didn't do any Beckett plays later on was that Beckett didn't want one line changed ever and his estate wouldn't allow it.

After he died, I had some boxes of his in storage which I sent to Luke, but as I went through them there were so many letters from very well-known people like Mike Nichols and Tom Stoppard saying things like, 'I'm not sure what it was that so-and-so's girlfriend said to you or why her opinion would matter to you, but I hope you can calm down about it...' It's difficult to work with people who make mountains out of molehills all the time.

Once he said, 'I am not an alcoholic, but I am in danger of becoming a heavy drinker!' He went to my GP one time – I can't remember what for – but I talked to my doctor about his drinking later and he said, 'At this point, if Nicol suddenly stopped drinking he would probably get very sick,' and I've heard that alcoholics who suddenly stop can die. Maybe you can dead stop in your 30s, but he was in his 60s at this point. Having said that, he had tremendous physical strength and maybe he could have handled it.

When I visited him in Amsterdam, he would wait until noon, when the bells would chime, and that meant he could get up and go to the bar. He would try to sleep until that moment and would try to manage it, but it was a progressive illness.

I scheduled my wedding for 11 in the morning so that Nicol could potentially be there. He wasn't able to come, but if we'd had the wedding at 4 pm he would have been drinking for too long and you never knew what was going to happen at that point, so you'd have to work around that and be around earlier in the day so that you were actually talking to Nicol rather than later when you weren't really talking to him anymore.

One time, I called him and the answering machine went off and then he picked up the phone and said some insulting things. I completely shrugged it off, because I realised I'd just caught him too late in the day and it wasn't Nicol anymore. The next day, I get a call from Nicol and he's really sheepish and apologetic and at first I didn't understand why, but then I realised that, because the answering machine had gone off, he must have played it back when he was sober and, for maybe the first time, heard how he sounded to other people when he was drunk. I thought no wonder he was so baffled when people were angry with him – he wasn't really there when he was like that and he didn't remember it afterwards. I knew him well enough to just dismiss it when he said these things, but other people didn't.

He was kind of shattered in some ways – as much as Nicol *could* be shattered. He told me that he always felt like the boy looking in a shop window at Christmastime who would never be able to have any of the things inside. But his home in Amsterdam was absolutely gorgeous! He was the strongest person I've ever met in terms of spirit of life. I just don't understand how that strong a spirit could disappear from the Earth. He was filled with life but he had more fear of death than anyone I've ever met. He was absolutely haunted by death and he felt stalked by it.

Samuel Beckett loomed large in his life and they had a bond because they shared the same fear of death. I remember one time coming back into the apartment and he had tears in his eyes. He was sitting on the couch in the dark and I asked him what was wrong. He'd been reading *Damned to Fame*, a biography of Samuel Beckett, in which Beckett is quoted as saying 'there's a touch of genius in that man'. When I asked Nicol why he was crying he said, 'Because I remembered.'

The reason I feel I got on so well with Nicol was because I'm an intellectual – I don't get all emotional, I figure things out, while Nicol was extremely emotional, and I think that was the key to his relationship with Samuel Beckett, because Beckett was an intellectual. I remember Nicol telling me one time he grabbed Samuel Beckett and spun him around the room, dancing with him. But he was the kind of man who *could* grab Samuel Beckett and twirl him around the ballroom – I don't think many people would have been able to!

I think when he visited Beckett in France and had a panic attack, he found that the only thing that calmed him down was having a drink, and I think the fact that drinking would reduce his anxiety may have been the genesis of his alcoholism. I said to him once, 'I think you're having panic attacks on stage and you're suffering from depression. You're saying to people you're having a heart attack, but that's not what's happening – you're having a panic attack.' He was surprised because it had never occurred to him.

I always wanted to know the source of his genius, because there was no question in my mind that he was a genius as an actor. I kind of believed that it was innate, that he was born to it, but he worked really, really hard. I found a script of his and it had all these minute details he'd written in. He was a tremendous fan of Lenny Bruce and he would make notations in his scripts referencing Lenny Bruce and also Tony Hancock, another comedian he really admired. He was bringing in these influences that you would never think would go with Shakespeare.

I also feel like he taught me that genius means life out of balance and I think Nicol's life was out of balance. It wasn't just that he was great on stage – he was that guy offstage too. Everything was quite heightened and I think that was the crux of his problem professionally. He was pure artist – whenever I hear descriptions of Beethoven, I think of Nicol.

Towards the end, he said to me he just wanted to spend his last year with Luke – it was like he had gotten wiser about what mattered. The last time we ever talked, he said, 'Keep the people you love in your life – it is *so* important!' That wasn't usually the way he expressed himself, certainly not until that last year.

Afterword

by Luke Williamson

Helping Martin with this book hasn't been an easy process for me, every page turn a reminder of the huge void in my life these last years.

I had a unique relationship with Dad, and though we had our disagreements over the years, we were very close. He wasn't an easy person, he liked to establish habit and live within it, in many ways he wasn't very flexible, until he surprised you with how completely flexible he was. He was utterly predictable and yet capable of surprising those who knew him best.

He was warm and funny, and as a child I always felt so safe around him, and loved. He wasn't always the most patient man, but he had great patience with me, and delighted in sharing new things, and he relished that delight a parent has watching their child enjoy or discover something for the first time.

He was an incomparable storyteller, he could scare you or make you laugh until you cried, and he had an incredible ability to take something bad that had happened to you and make you laugh over it until it no longer hurt. When you felt his love it was like being loved by the Sun. I wouldn't ask for any other father, I'd gladly live it all over again.

He was a hugely empathetic person, and really lived other peoples experiences as he heard them, reacting as strongly as if it had happened to him. I believe this shaped his life, his defensive mechanisms and his outlook significantly.

Dad was a tremendously honest individual, he absolutely refused to act in life other than how he thought was right, and he's the only person I know that was consistent to his code regardless of his personal outcome. He could have given Hollywood the narrative that they required for his success at any time, but he wasn't interested in that.

In the end, he did most of the things in the acting world that he was interested in doing, and I never heard him express a regret, career-wise.

Many people will be tempted to shrug off Dad's life experience as the results of alcoholism, but in my view the alcohol was the treatment, not the root cause.

Dad experienced everything on a very raw, visceral level, there weren't a lot of softening filters or defences that he could employ against what life seems to be, and the suffering that must be endured before the return to what he believed was the void, the absence of being, the ego death, nothingness.

In the shadow of this terrifying belief he lived, daily. And he would stoke the fires and bank the wood high as he could to live and enjoy as he could. But the shadow is always on the edge of the light, no matter how big the fire, and no flame lasts forever.

Bibliography

The following books were useful in the writing of this one:

Adler, Tim, *The House of Redgrave: The Secret Lives of a Theatrical Dynasty*, Aurum, 2012.
Anderson, Lindsay, *Never Apologise: The Collected Writings*, Plexus, 2004.
Bennett, Alan, *Untold Stories*, Faber and Faber, 2005.
Block, Geoffrey, *Richard Rodgers*, Yale University Press, 2004.
Boorman, John, *Adventures of a Suburban Boy*, Faber and Faber, 2003.
Bowles, Peter, *Ask Me If I'm Happy*, Simon and Schuster, 2010.
Dunn, Kate, *Exit Through the Fireplace: The Great Days of Rep*, John Murray, 1998.
Faithfull, Marianne, *Faithfull*, Penguin, 1995.
Fraser, George MacDonald, *The Light's on at Signpost*, HarperCollins, 2002.
French, John, *Robert Shaw: The Price of Success*, Dean Street Press, 2015.
Fujiwara, Chris, *The World and Its Double: The Life and Work of Otto Preminger*, Faber and Faber, 2008.
Gill, Peter (Introduction) and Haill, Lynn (ed.), *Actors Speaking*, Oberon, 2007.
Hancock, Sheila, *The Two of Us*, Bloomsbury, 2005.
Heilpern, John, *John Osborne: A Patriot for Us*, Vintage, 2007.
Hildred, Stafford and Ewbank, Joe *John Thaw: The Biography*, Andre Deutsch Ltd, 1998.
Holm, Ian, *Acting My Life: The Autobiography*, Corgi, 2006.
Huston, Anjelica, *A Story Lately Told: Coming of Age in London, Ireland and New York*, Simon and Schuster, 2013.
Hyland, William, *Richard Rodgers*, Yale University Press, 2003.
Isherwood, Christopher and Bachardy, Don, *The Animals: Love Letters*, Vintage, 2014.
Knowlson, James, *Damned to Fame: The Life of Samuel Beckett*, Bloomsbury, 1996.
Kretzmer, Herbert, *Snapshots: Encounters with Twentieth Century Legends*, Robson Press, 2014.

Little, Ruth & McLaughlin, Emily, *The Royal Court Theatre Inside Out*, Oberon, 2007.
Manus, Willard, *This Way to Paradise: Dancing on the Tables*, Lycabettus Press, 1998.
Miles, Sarah, *Serves Me Right*, Macmillan, 1994.
Mirren, Helen, *In the Frame*, Atria Books, 2008.
Osborne, John, *Looking Back: Never Explain, Never Apologise*, Faber and Faber, 1999.
Richardson, Tony, *Long Distance Runner: A Memoir*, Faber and Faber, 1993.
Roberts, Philip, *The Royal Court Theatre and the Modern Stage*, Cambridge University Press, 1999.
Rudnick, Paul, *I Shudder*, Harper, 2009.
Sallis, Peter, *Fading into the Limelight*, Orion, 2006.
Secrest, Meryle, *Somewhere for Me: A Biography of Richard Rodgers*, Alfred A. Knopf, 2001.
Sheward, David, *Rage and Glory: The Volatile Life and Career of George C. Scott*, Applause, 2008.
Simon, Neil, *Rewrites*, Simon and Schuster, 1996.
Sinyard, Neil, *Richard Lester*, Manchester University Press, 2010.
Tynan, Kenneth, *The Sound of Two Hands Clapping*, Jonathan Cape Ltd, 1975.
Wardle, Irving, *The Theatres of George Devine*, Jonathan Cape Ltd, 1978.
Whitebrook, Peter, *John Osborne 'Anger is not about...'*, Oberon, 2015.
Williamson, Nicol, *Ming's Kingdom*, Random House, 1996.

Acknowledgements

This book was really a collaboration with a lot of other people. Some helped enormously and made lengthy and generous contributions. Others helped to clarify details, dig obscure documents out of archives, put me in touch with someone I was trying to track down, provide me with free accommodation while I was on a research trip or, in some cases, tried their best to help but ultimately were unable to. Any attempt on my part to make a distinction based on the extent of the help I received seems bound to be unfair, so – in strictly alphabetical order – I would like to thank the following:

David Andrews, Peggy Arnold, Robert Bierman, Kate Binchy, Burt Bluestein, Elaine Bromka, Anita Brown, Barbara Chappell, Robert Clinton, Michelle H. Craig (Special Collections Department, University of Glasgow), Michael Culver, Marcelle d'Argy-Smith, Scott Dennis, Ro Diamond, Kathleen Dickson (BFI), Ray Dooley, Mark Ekman (The Paley Center for Media), Paul Finlay, Penny Fuller, Peter Gale, Rachel Garman (British Library), Tony Garnett, Wendy George (Airborne Assault Limited), Luke Gietzen, Peter Gill, Robin Grantham, Trevor Griffiths, Toby Hadoke, Piers Haggard, Terry Hands, Bernard Hepton, Tamara Hinchco, Judi Hinds, Ian Hogg, Luciano Iogna, Glenda Jackson, Peter Jessop, Kees Kaandorp, Robert Knights, Jane Lapotaire, Lionel Larner, Richard Lester, Peter Dan Levin, Emma Luten, Valerie Manahan, Patricia Marmont, Des McKenna, Leslie Megahey, Jan Merchant (Senior Archivist, University of Dundee), Nicholas Meyer, Julia Migenes, Sarah Miles, Paul Moriarty, Marc Morris, Eamon Morrisey, Walter Murch, Peter Murray, Jim Myers (Actors' Benevolent Fund), Tsambikos Mysirlakis, Colin Nicholson, Ian O'Sullivan and colleagues at the BFI Reuben Library, Kees Van Oostrum, Tony Palmer, Jessie Petheram (Shakespeare Birthplace Trust), David Pownall, John Quested, David Redbranch, Steffan Rhodri, Mike Robe, Sharon Rork (Billy Rose Theatre Division, New York Public Library), Marion Rosenberg,

Tony Rowlands, Rupert Ryle-Hodges, Catherine Simpson (RSC), Neil Sinyard, Ann Skinner, Clive Swift, Edda Tasiemka (The Hans Tasiemka Archive), Nick Taylor, Jill Townsend, Kenith Trodd, John Tydeman, the V & A Theatre and Performance Archive staff, Lillias Walker, David Warner, Zoe Wilcox (British Library), Luke Williamson, Nigel Wooll, Sherman Yellen.

I would also like to thank all of the agents (and their assistants) who put me in touch with their clients and hope they will forgive me for not naming them individually.

Thanks also to those friends who encouraged me along the way – sometimes I needed it. Again, I hope I'll be forgiven for not attempting to name them all in case I inadvertently offend someone by leaving them out.

Three people who were very helpful have since passed away. This book is dedicated to them:

Ann Beach, actress (1938 – 2017)

Jack Gold, director (1930 – 2015)

Norman Twain, producer (1930 – 2016)

Extracts from the unbroadcast 2005 interview recorded by Leslie Megahey are quoted with the permission of Megahey and Luke Williamson.

Cover photo by Graham Attwood (REX/Shutterstock)

Cover design by Luke Gietzen

Notes

[1] *L.A. Times*, 19 August 1986

[2] See Tony Garnett's memoir, *The Day the Music Died* (Constable, 2016)

[3] equivalent to around £8,000 each at the time of writing

[4] A raked stage is sloped, being higher at the back than it is at the front.

[5] Doric is a dialect of northeast Scotland.

[6] Surprisingly, Nicol would never appear in a Pinter play.

[7] clipping held in Glasgow University's Scottish Theatre Archive from unknown newspaper

[8] *Glasgow Herald*, 7 April 1986

[9] Quoted by permission. Shelfmark 1CDR0025479; C1142/28 / http://sounds.bl.uk/Arts-literature-and-performance/Theatre-Archive-Project/024M-1CDR0025479X-ZZZZV0

[10] *The Independent*, 6 June 1993

[11] *Herald Scotland*, 11 June 1994

[12] clipping held in Glasgow University's Scottish Theatre Archive from unknown newspaper

[13] eye-deceiving

[14] clipping held in Glasgow University's Scottish Theatre Archive from unknown newspaper

[15] It still exists but could not be accessed for research.

[16] Equivalent to around £4,000 at the time of writing

[17] When the play transferred to the Royal Court, Anna Gilcrist replaced Hampshire as the latter had a film commitment.

[18] Unbroadcast 2005 interview recorded by Leslie Megahey.

[19] Interview from the film *John Osborne and the Gift of Friendship*. Quoted by permission of Tony Palmer.

[20] Unbroadcast 2005 interview recorded by Leslie Megahey.

[21] Ibid.

[22] Equivalent to around £13,000 at the time of writing

[23] Interview with Coral Atkins found at http://www.theatrevoice.com/audio/look-back-anger-remembered-60-years/

[24] The Globe was later renamed as the Gielgud Theatre in deference to the rebuilt Shakespeare's Globe on the South Bank.

[25] From *The Beckett Piece* by Nicol Williamson. A complete reading by its author can be found on Youtube. Quoted by permission of Luke Williamson.

[26] 136 West 55th Street, now The Blakely

[27] It was previously located on 52nd Street.

[28] *The Corpus Christi Caller-Times*, Sun., Dec. 5, 1965

[29] Footage from the night of Nicol and Jill performing scenes from *Inadmissible Evidence* was used in the film *John Osborne and the Gift of Friendship* and later surfaced on Youtube.

[30] It still exists but is currently only available to view at the Paley Centres in New York and Los Angeles.

[31] Thaw had recently separated from his first wife, Sally Alexander.

[32] Their agency, London International, later merged with Ashley Famous, an agency run by Otis S. Blodget, better known as Dick Blodget, and he became Nicol's agent in the UK.

[33] Unbroadcast 2005 interview recorded by Leslie Megahey.

[34] Ibid.

[35] *The Reckoning* pre-dated *Get Carter* by more than a year in the UK.

[36] see *The Animals: Love Letters between Christopher Isherwood and Don Bachardy* (Vintage)

[37] Unbroadcast 2005 interview recorded by Leslie Megahey.

[38] Ibid.

[39] Nan Martin took over from Constance Cummings. John J.Carney, who had been playing Marcellus, moved up to the larger role of Horatio, replacing Gordon Jackson. Mark Dignam, who had been playing Polonius, now also played the gravedigger, replacing Roger Livesey. Malcolm Terris, who had been playing the captain, now also covered Livesey's other part as the First Player. Peter Gale returned to England, leaving his understudy to take over. Patrick Wymark went to the West Coast, but left before the tour finished to fulfil a film commitment. He was replaced by John Trenaman, who had previously been playing Bernardo.

[40] now The Montalban

[41] Jill Townsend did not attend

[42] Unbroadcast 2005 interview recorded by Leslie Megahey.

[43] a successful musical which debuted off-Broadway in 1969 and featured extensive nudity

[44] equivalent to around £1,800 at the time of writing

[45] Unbroadcast 2005 interview recorded by Leslie Megahey.

[46] Thornton was perhaps best known for his role as Captain Peacock in the long-running British sitcom *Are You Being Served?*

[47] The Dirty Duck is a pub in Stratford-upon-Avon frequented by actors from the Royal Shakespeare Company

[48] On the film *Royal Flash*.

[49] They had also worked together on the film *O Lucky Man!* prior to *Royal Flash*.

[50] Unbroadcast 2005 interview recorded by Leslie Megahey.

[51] *The Authorised Biography of Ronnie Barker* by Bob McCabe (BBC Books, 2004)

[52] Lester preferred the original score by Michael Legrand, which was ditched by the producer.

[53] Nigel Bruce played Watson opposite Basil Rathbone in a series of films produced in the late '30s and '40s.

[54] Anhedonia is the inability to experience pleasure.

[55] Unbroadcast 2005 interview recorded by Leslie Megahey.

[56] *Somewhere For Me: A Biography of Richard Rodgers* by Meryle Secrest (Bloomsbury, 2001)

[57] Better known as a musician, Price was the original keyboard player in The Animals

[58] Moriarty was fired on the first day of shooting.

[59] After Nicol's death, Swift came to his colleague's defence after reading his obituary in *The Independent*, writing in a letter to the newspaper that, 'John Calder's obituary of Nicol Williamson emphasised his aggression. But when reviving *Inadmissible Evidence*…he was… entirely courteous to all his supporting players.'

[60] Castle's age is stated as 62 in the book, but the character is clearly much younger in the film.

[61] Unbroadcast 2005 interview recorded by Leslie Megahey.

[62] Ibid.

[63] The Sheraton Park Tower Hotel

[64] Unbroadcast 2005 interview recorded by Leslie Megahey.

[65] Ibid.

[66] Ibid.

[67] *Excalibur* DVD commentary

[68] Hayden's performance seemed to be an impersonation of *The Asphalt Jungle*'s director, John Huston

[69] Now the SVA Theatre

[70] Unbroadcast 2005 interview recorded by Leslie Megahey.

[71] Ibid.

[72] Ibid.

[73] Unbroadcast 2005 interview recorded by Leslie Megahey.

[74] offal

[75] Gascon was a Canadian actor who was highly respected despite his struggles with alcohol

[76] From *The Museum of Broadcasting Seminar Series: Masterpiece Theatre – 15 Years of Excellence, Seminar No.2: Lord Mountbatten – The Last Viceroy* (held at the Paley Center for Media in New York)

[77] Director Ricardo Franco died in 1998, producer Emiliano Piedra in 1991.

[78] Unbroadcast 2005 interview recorded by Leslie Megahey.

[79] *Needful Things*

[80] Unbroadcast 2005 interview recorded by Leslie Megahey.

[81] *Future Fool*, starring clown / comedienne Nola Rae

[82] Unbroadcast 2005 interview recorded by Leslie Megahey.

[83] From the documentary film *John Osborne and the Gift of Friendship*. Quoted by permission of Tony Palmer.

[84] Kenith Trodd has said that Jack Gold was not involved at any point.

[85] Unbroadcast 2005 interview recorded by Leslie Megahey.

[86] Ibid.

[87] Now known as The Carillon, it is located at Spui 30

[88] now the Moda Lounge Bar

[89] Megahey kindly allowed the author to view it and granted permission (along with Luke Williamson) for a number of quotes to be used.

[90] www.lindoseye.com

ABOUT THE AUTHOR

Martin Dowsing lives in London and (as M.R. Dowsing) is the author of the novel *The Assassination of Adolf Hitler*. He makes music under the name Hungry Dog Brand and has previously written for the music magazines *Bucketfull of Brains* and *R2 (Rock'n'Reel)*.

Thank you for reading.
If you have enjoyed this book, a review on Amazon or similar would be greatly appreciated.

Anyone wishing to contact the author may do so at:
bewareoftheauthor@yandex.com

Printed in Great Britain
by Amazon